INDIANAPOLIS WASHINGTON HIGH SCHOOL
and the WEST SIDE

HISTORY, FACTS, LISTS, BIOGRAPHIES, COMMUNITY STORIES

by Eddie Bopp

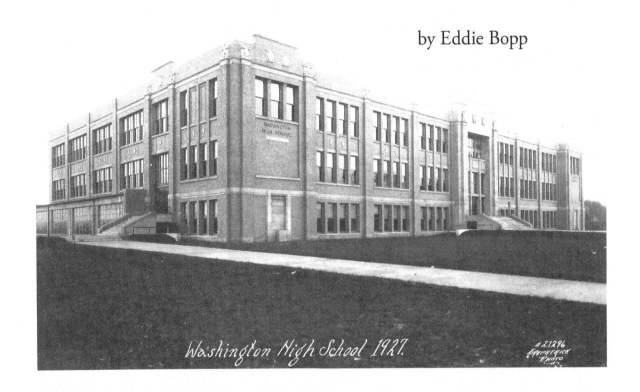

Washington High School 1927.

authorHOUSE®

AuthorHouse™
1663 Liberty Drive
Bloomington, IN 47403
www.authorhouse.com
Phone: 1-800-839-8640

First published by AuthorHouse 11/18/2010

ISBN: 978-1-4520-7226-5 (sc)
ISBN: 978-1-4520-7421-4 (e)

Library of Congress Control Number: 2010912663

Printed in the United States of America

This book is printed on acid-free paper.

DEDICATION

To my late parents, Ed and Thelma.
And to my grandkids, Austin and Audrey Osburn,
may they enjoy their youthful environment in the 21st century
as much as I did mine in the 20th century

**INDIANAPOLIS WASHINGTON &
The WEST SIDE
by Eddie Bopp**

FACTS, HISTORY, LISTS & BIOGRAPHIES

Foreword by Senator Richard G. Lugar

As a freshman quarterback for Shortridge High School, I entered the Washington High School football field in 1946 for the first time, and thus began an introduction to not only George Washington High School, but the Westside of Indianapolis. This discovery, expanded dramatically when I returned in 1960 to Indianapolis from military service in the United States Navy. With my brother, Tom Lugar, I sought to restore the strength of Thomas L. Green and Company, a manufacturing business founded by my grandfather, Thomas L. Green, on the Westside of Indianapolis. We manufactured biscuit and cracker machinery, and we faced a very challenging turn-around situation. My brother, who had returned from service in the United States Army, had a Purdue University engineering degree and I tried to provide overall business management. My wife, Char, and I bought a house on the Westside. Quickly, we established banking relationships for the business and for our families, and learned to appreciate small businesses which were near our factory and our home.

Fortunately, I soon developed a wonderful friendship with Cloyd Julian at Indianapolis Rotary Club meetings. I found that he was the principal at George Washington High School, and through his invitation, I began attending meetings of the Washington High School Businessmen's Club. "Curly" Julian gave me extensive tours of the high school, during which I met talented faculty and students. He encouraged me to provide summer jobs for some of the students and I was eager to do so.

Char and I also became regular attendees at Washington High School football and basketball games. We watched Ed Bopp star in both football and basketball roles, and I asked him to join our factory team during the summer of 1965, prior to his entry into Butler University. During those summer months, the two of us enjoyed workouts on the Washington High School athletic field, which included substantial running, calisthenics, and, at his insistence, various football passing formations.

Eddie was the Trester Award winner on the Indiana State High School Athletic Association Championship Basketball Team in 1965. Char and I, and our four sons, had watched all of the Washington High School tournament games, from the sectional through the final four, and we were wrapped up in enthusiasm for this Westside triumph with remarkable players and an equally remarkable coach, Jerry Oliver. I attended pep rallies in the gym and the final celebration of victory, and I wanted to make certain that Ed Bopp enjoyed a great beginning as a quarterback for Butler University.

Just before the 1964-1965 high school basketball season commenced, a group of Westsiders came to my office at Thomas L. Green and Company and strongly encouraged me to become a candidate for the Indianapolis Board of School Commissioners in the primary election of 1964.

They argued, passionately, that someone needed to stand up for the Westside and provide much more equity for schools, students, teachers, and parents, who were our neighbors.

That School Board election came as Indianapolis was on the cusp of a civil rights revolution, already evident in many other large, northern cities. Nellie Carter, mother of noted Washington High School 1930 alum, Jim Carter, was the major organizer for the Citizen's School Committee ticket on which I ran. A rival slate emerged and individual independent candidates entered the fray. For the first time, the School Board election brought about public debates, and even radio and television coverage. I was elected to the Board in May of 1964 and became much more heavily involved in the day-to-day activities of School Number 30, School Number 50, Washington High School, and the Hawthorne Settlement House, all in the close neighborhood of our factory.

After I was elected Mayor of Indianapolis in November 1967, I found even more opportunities to work with Cloyd Julian and a host of teachers and parents who had important dreams for the Westside.

These experiences flooded my memory as I returned on November 16, 2008, for the 80th Birthday Party of George Washington High School and to celebrate the rebirth of the high school, with remarkable new opportunities for students and the surrounding community. Ed Bopp made a comprehensive presentation, on that day, of the school's athletic history, and shortly thereafter, I learned that he was preparing an even more comprehensive history of Washington High School and the Westside.

This book will be invaluable to all who love Indianapolis and are eager to learn much more about our Hoosier roots on the historical and productive Westside of Indiana's capital city. I was excited to be the receiver for Ed Bopp's football passes in the mid-1960's, and I have been deeply grateful for his loyal friendship ever since.

I am honored to salute his vision and creativity as he provides the text for our salute to George Washington High School and the Westside, a history that we will pass along with enthusiasm and pride to our children and grandchildren.

Introduction

For nearly 60 years I've been intrigued by what I saw as the once unique nature of the near Westside of Indianapolis. And the focal point of that Common Culture was Washington High School. It only lasted for 68 years and its influence may be drifting further away into the past but the foundation from which many lives have evolved seemed a one-of-a-kind phenomena to me.

When Richard Such approached me in 2001 with his request that I write out a history of Washington High for his website, I was emboldened with the knowledge that I had already interviewed two iconic figures in our school's history. I had visited Mr. Julian's Kessler Blvd. home and videotaped about an hour of oral history from his memory bank in 1998. Within a year I visited Harry Cherry's sister's home in Speedway and did the same with him. I already had a leg-up with those two Continental legends. I had first met Harry in 1995 at the school's closing but had known of his reputation since the '50's. I also knew of Mr. Julian's west side pedigree even before I met him as I often watched him on Fridays when he would eat dinner at Huddleston restaurant before home football or basketball games in the late 1950's.

And, in April 2008, Connie Higgins noted to me that Jim Carter was alive and well and living in northern Indianapolis. I was shocked. The first phone number that I called was the correct one and I set up a meeting where I interviewed Mr. Carter for one hour on videotape at his Geist area condo. I had first known of him when I obtained a college football trading card of Purdue All-American Duane Purvis in 1955-56. His three or four sentence biography read something like "Duane was known as a Purdue Touchdown Twin along with Jim Carter." My dad told me that "he's the brother of 'Swivel Hips' Carter," another great player.

A number of personal stories bolster my concept that other Westside and IPS schools had an inferiority complex in their approach to Washington High School educational and athletic opportunities. But after intra-district busing began in 1971 (and then inter-district busing in 1981) realities changed dramatically.

I phone-interviewed Harold Negley, Tony Burchett, John Bradley, and Jerry Lawlis among others. Most of my information I have verified from more than one source.

Special people fed on the key features of our community--other people in a stable school setting. From Gingery to Julian, Bogue to Springer, Barbara Jean to Audie Watkins, Charley Money to John Bradley, Vi Sanders to Nancy Ehret, Leonard to Myron, Hester Baker Bock Erwin and Al Hamilton to Jo Jo and Basil and even Chico. They all added to the mystic, as well as reality, of a once proud school. Without those people and many others there would not have been a Washington High. But no individual made our school; our school helped make them.

I've seen revisionism in too many American History textbooks. Judging events and people in the past based on the standards of the present can be both disingenuous and inaccurate.

I want to set the record straight, albeit with my perceptions, as others may have seen things slightly differently. Facts are facts and opinions are opinions. Too many cannot understand the difference. But obviously one's personal reality comes from how they perceive the world around them. In 2003 I received an e-mail from a former student who had attained a successful professional life in the adult world. He questioned my history of Washington High School on the website we had at the time. "Just because I didn't play sports doesn't mean I wasn't a success then or now," he wrote. I concurred and explained to him that I was only writing about my experiences and my knowledge about certain people who had impressed me in a dramatic way. Extracurricular prominence in high school did not necessarily manifest itself in adult success, I responded. My professional lack of success is a prime example.

So my personal lists are based on my biased opinions but also on my interpretations of the facts of the individual's accomplishments. Actor James Cagney noted that "we all live between our ears." And I believe that everyone's life is a history book. So, to accumulate as much written and verbal information that I have concerning GWHS, I feel a need to share it as History. Misguided "bar-talkers" and wannabes be damned. I have much visual and some audio evidence as well as newspaper copies. The hard work of Ronnie Rogers, class of 1954, along with Gene Robertson when they put the athletic booklet together helped inspired me. And much thanks to John Bradley for all of the football scores. Basil Sfreddo also gave me a ditto with many of the basketball records. Richard Such (class of '63), as earlier stated, established a very good website to which I was the main contributor but a few others also participated with stories like those from the Boyd and Isenhower families along with Larry Glaze's insight on Frank Luzar's mystic.

And the hard work and contact information maintained by 2009 Alumni President Connie Higgins along with fellow 1971 classmate Susan Worland Hartley was important. And they both sincerely avoid the limelight. Also, Al Case (class of '38) offered invaluable stories and insight into the Washington culture as I intruded on numerous conversations between him and Jim Carter, class of 1930, during our monthly lunches. Both have given me newspaper articles and books to bolster my fact base. Jack Hensley and Joe Bridgewater, both class of 1948, are guardians of the Alumni Room located on the top floor of GWCS. Yearbooks and other memorabilia are available the third Wednesday of the month.

My Aunt Anita's annuals from the early 1950's along with my mother's from the late 1930's and my own from the '60's and early '70's were used as cross-references supporting oral history.

Chris Boylan, a positive teacher from new Washington Community School, presented me with the six State Championship team pictures. Tom Schott, from Purdue's Sports Information office, sent me two photos of Jim Carter. Brad Cook, as IU's Curator of Photographs in their Archives division, sent a good Harry Cherry photo from 1936.

My wife's personal photo collection, the military photos (including those shared with me by over 13 different GWHS veterans of World War II who attended my four years of recognition assemblies in the early 21st century), and my buddies who served during the Vietnam era has helped give this book a balanced view of different generations of service men and mid-school-1960's kids who had the common experience of Washington High School.

Mrs. Barbara McGrevy, Jack Woodson, Dennis Ludlow, Terry Sylvester, Cheryl Roberts, Bill Niemann, Dru Miller, Steve Midkiff, Kenny Baldwin, Bernard Garver, Danny Stamatkin, Chuck Dulla, Doris Purichia, Steve Satterfield, Larry Austin, Bob Tillery, Senifta Such, Jerry Sanders, David Beasley and Rick Sylvester all volunteered photos or newspaper articles used in this book.

I have indulged myself a bit including the Marshall All-Time team page and a few other personal acknowledgments. I do feel that I took the "Washington Way" to that far-northeastside school.

Baseball Hall-of-Famer Dizzy Dean once said, "it ain't braggin' if you done it." And I can brag that against top Marion County teams that my teams (including the year that I departed when I continued un-paid workouts with players until I left in June as the principal, one time Washington track coach Tom Haynes, refused to give me a summer job at his school) were unique. Against top programs Cathedral, our Washington, Roncalli and Lawrence North from 1977-1981 Marshall was 13-1. The one loss, ending the 1978 season vs. Roncalli, concluded a week of my inability to quell two dope-smoking star players whose actions destroyed team morale. And Marshall is probably the only IPS school to defeat power-house Chatard in consecutive years since the 1960's, including a 41-6 thumping. Marshall's 27-game regular-season winning streak, I'm sure, is Marion County's all time record. Consecutive 10-0 seasons were not matched until Warren Central teams in '84 & '85. Ben Davis has still not had consecutive 10-0 seasons nor did Washington or Cathedral in the 20th century.

Washington High's personality, which was a compilation of a variety of human and environmental influences, was always my personal inspiration. I have made an intense effort to be accurate, though I'm sure that a mistake or two can be found.

I have only tried to analyze the 68 years of the original school, from 1927 through 1995. The Community High School, which opened in 2001, will write its own history. Hopefully it will be as inspiring to the younger generation as the image and reality of Washington High School was for me and most of my contemporaries.

I.

THE NEAR WESTSIDE

The near Westside of Indianapolis can be described physically by referencing American means of transportation which were built or improved in the 19th & 20th centuries. The National Road (known as Washington Street or Road 40 to westsiders), White River, Eagle Creek, and the railroads (known during most of the 20th century as the B & O, New York Central, and Pennsylvania) helped describe our area.

Street names, community names, and the state government's township system all help define the area name designations. The nine townships in Marion County (one of 92 Indiana counties) can be seen as a tic-tac-toe board. From the northwest (going from left to right) the township names are Pike, Washington, and Lawrence; then Wayne, Center, and Warren; and, completed along the southern border by Decatur, Perry, and Franklin. There are a number of small, incorporated towns with Speedway and Beech Grove as the two largest which have their own school and police systems.

Mayor Dick Lugar's Unigov proposal, which was passed by our state's General Assembly in 1969 and went into effect the first day of 1970, made the nine townships the new Indianapolis in most ways. But the school systems were still basically independent.

As the boundaries of Indianapolis grew in increments via state law, the city's public schools paralleled its growth. Indianapolis had become the state capital in 1825. The Indianapolis Public Schools first emerged in the early 1850's. Reformers of the era both before and immediately after the Civil War saw public education as the great equalizer as well as the view that private, European and slave state type schools helped perpetuate antagonism between the rich and the poor. Indianapolis High School opened in 1863.

Protestant ministers had implemented Sunday schools which taught morals, an idea that was first introduced in England. Public schools were the natural extension with the school year expanding from 110 to 180 days after the war.

An early superintendent noted that children from the "lower walks of life" were most susceptible to the immoral temptations and most in need of academic and moral teachings. His approach was similar to the "Old Deluder Satan Act" of 1639 in colonial Massachusetts which became the first Public School Act 137 years before the Declaration of Independence. "An idle mind is the devil's playground" was a premise that most people accepted as one big reason for public schools; so, public schools were created to exhibit the democracy theory upon which our great nation was founded.

Manual Training High School became the second IPS secondary school in 1888 (moving into a permanent home near Meridian and South Street within the Mile Square area), so Indianapolis High School became Shortridge. Broad Ripple High School emerged circa 1890 but the Broad Ripple community didn't become part of Indianapolis until 1923 so Arsenal Technical became the third high school in 1912 with its campus located on the Civil War arsenal on the eastside.

In 1927 when our school was reluctantly accepted by the school board (West Park minister Rev. Baker personally noted that a near-northside school board member stated that "those kids west of the river won't go to school anyway") the segregated Crispus Attucks school also opened. The tract of land upon which Washington High was built had been the home of two yearly circus visits. Flack's Field, as it was called, was the annual home for two different circuses. Ringling Brothers and, later in the summer, the circus called "The 101 Wild West Show." The disembarking spot at Belmont and the B & O railroad continued into the 1970's.

When John Marshall joined ranks in 1967 at the peak of IPS enrollment there were eleven high schools. Howe (1937), Wood (1953, occupying the old Manual building when a new Manual opened on Madison Avenue), Arlington (1961), and Northwest (1963) were the other IPS schools.

By IPS Central Office statistics there were 62,586 pupils enrolled in IPS in 1939 with seven high schools. The peak total reached 108,703 during the school year of '66-67. In 2005 there were 38,350 K-12th students. Mr. Charles Money, an early history teacher at Washington High, wrote that there were approximately 42,000 residents living west of White River inside the expanded Indianapolis by the early 1920's. And there were only about 670 students attending elementary or high schools with maybe 60 high school graduates per year. A physically closer high school would certainly encourage more attendance and increase the graduation rate, both for the betterment of Westside society.

Center Township is roughly: north—38th St., south—Raymond St., east—Emerson Ave., west—Belmont St.

The George Washington High School attendance district was initially created in 1922 thanks to a state law allowing for the extension of "Indianapolis" across the center township border of Belmont Street into Wayne Township.

Center Township-Indianapolis (before 1970 and Unified Government) grew expediently in relationship to the growing population. Seventeen grade schools plus at least three Catholic schools (Assumption, Holy Trinity, and St. Anthony's) sent kids to our school at 2215 W. Washington.

When the 1950's housing development called Eagledale emerged those kids attended Washington High after 8th grade graduation from either School 61 or 79 along with those from School 90, which was to the northeast of 16th & Tibbs, until 1963 when Northwest H.S. opened. Flackville school, which fluctuated between Ben Davis and GWHS, on Lafayette Road and School 48 (grades 1-6 then on to #46) had some future Continentals. School 5, which once sent students to "old" Manual on Meridian St., was located on California and Washington St. where the IMAX theater is now located. It is currently commemorated with a historical society display titled "Making Americans" and includes two pictures of youngsters with a Continental connection: George Such (circa 1925), who had two children graduate from GWHS, and George McGinnis, our 1969 basketball star. The other grammar schools, which sent students to Continentaland, were: #s 16, 30, 44 (east of the river, north of 16th St.), 46, 47, 49, 50, 52, 63, 67, and 75.

Haughville, the most recognizable community in the Washington High district is often described as the area between 16th St., White River, N. Tibbs, and Michigan St. The area north of Bahr Park (Warman & Vermont) which is south of Michigan St. extending to Tibbs can also be included. And, the Stringtown area can be said to overlap the Haughville area. Stringtown normally is considered west of White River to perhaps Belmont St. But the Indianola area of old

School 30 claims some of Stringtown's homestead projecting south to the old New York Central railroad tracks and as far north as Michigan Street.

The Fairfax area is north of Vermont, west of Tibbs, east of Eagle Creek and up to 16th Street beyond the B & O.

Hawthorne can be said to include the area north of Washington St., south of the B & O railroad, east of Warman, and west of Belmont. Jacktown or Mt. Jackson is bordered by Washington High and the old Link-Belt property on the east, Eagle Creek on the west, Washington St. to the north, and the Pennsylvania Railroad to the south.

West Indianapolis (WI) is best visualized as the area surrounding Rhodius Park. But the boundaries can be said to be: Harding St. (E), Warman Ave. (W), Oliver Ave. (N), and south to Morris St. then to Minnesota St. almost to Raymond.

The Valley was another unique area. With Harding on the western edge and the White River natural boundary to the east, the Valley extended south to north from Morris Street to the Pennsylvania tracks. Oliver Avenue cut a swath down the middle, running east and west.

Other enclaves included Salem Park where a few families lived along, and directly north of, Washington St. between "big" and "little" Eagle Creeks as well as "The Bottoms" which were the few homes between Warman Ave. and Eagle Creek south of the Pennsylvania Railroad to Morris Street.

And the Rollings family, which ran a venetian blinds cleaning business from their home, lived in the last property on S. Tibbs on the east side near the Pennsylvania railroad, a 1½ mile walk to GWHS. They were allowed to attend Wayne Township's Fleming Gardens elementary before heading to, what was considered well into the 1960's, the better educational experience of Washington High School. Their last kids graduated in the 1970's.

In any event, those kids "west of the river" experienced a unique era of social awareness, community growth then decline, intellectual challenges and varied physical activities as they experienced the community focal point called George Washington High School from 1927 through 1995.

Marion County Townships

with adjacent counties

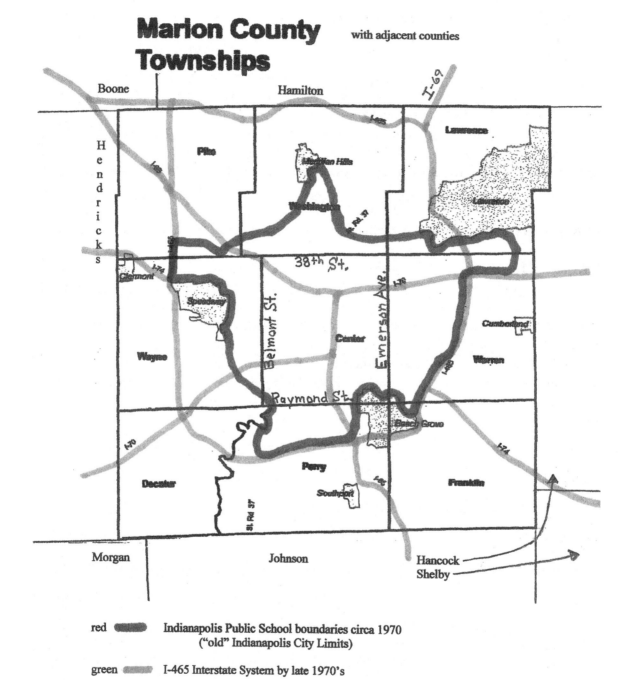

red ⬤ Indianapolis Public School boundaries circa 1970
("old" Indianapolis City Limits)

green ⬤ I-465 Interstate System by late 1970's

4

Westside Map circa 1960 with
18 Elementary "feeder" schools, neighborhood names plus
street and railroad names

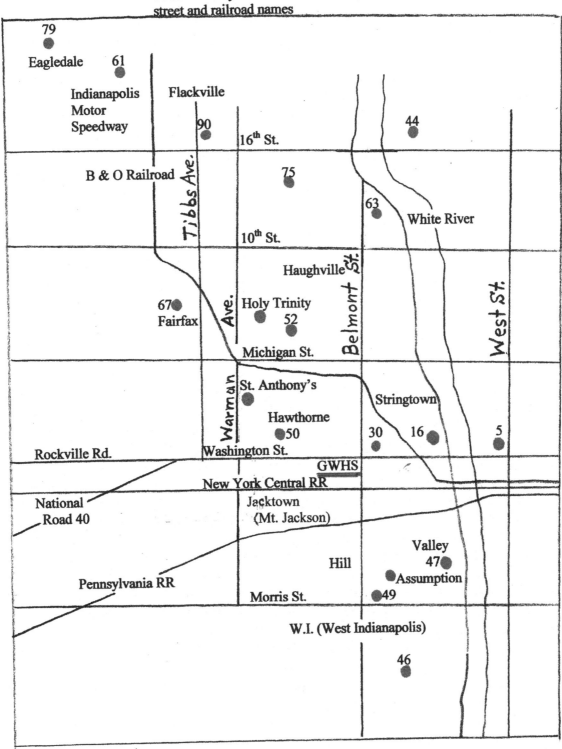

79
Eagledale   61
          Indianapolis   Flackville
          Motor
          Speedway   90   44
                                     16th St.

B & O Railroad   75
                                          63
                                                 White River
                                     10th St.

          Tibbs Ave.

                         Haughville
67 Fairfax   Ave.   Holy Trinity   Belmont St.
                              52   West St.
                         Michigan St.

          Warman St. Anthony's
                                     Stringtown
                         Hawthorne
                              50   30   16   5
Rockville Rd.   Washington St.
                              GWHS
                    New York Central RR

National   Jacktown
Road 40   (Mt. Jackson)
                                          Valley
                              Hill   47
                                     Assumption
Pennsylvania RR   Morris St.   49

          W.I. (West Indianapolis)
                              46

5

II.

SCHOOL HISTORY BY DECADES

A HISTORY OF WASHINGTON HIGH SCHOOL

My first recollections of Washington High are from 1952 when my Aunt Anita Bloomenstock taught me the words to the "Fight Song." Beginning during that period and well into the 1960's my mom and dad related stories to me about coaches and teachers and events from the early years. All stories were positive and optimistic. My mom graduated in 1939. I graduated in 1965. I taught and coached there from '69-'76. I've also interviewed, on camcorder, Washington's first two great athletes (Hoopy Carter and Harry Cherry) as well as "Mr. Washington" Curly Julian. Mr. Julian's 90th birthday party was held December 2000 at the Propylaeum on North Delaware and generated much GWHS history as did his 95th party at his northeastside church, Broadway United Methodist. I have on 16 mm film the first renovation of GWHS in 1937-38. Among those I initially talked with were John Bradley, Jerry Lawlis, Tony Burchett, Bob Tillery, & Harold Negley. My mother was literally shocked when I coached a team that defeated Washington's team in 1977. Washington WAS the community icon that was bigger than anything in our individual lives. My personal attitude has changed but I remember the past and feel that gives me a balanced opinion. Nonetheless, athletics and people are center stage. With a constantly changing legacy it will always be somewhat incomplete.

1920's

In the mid-20's the School Board pondered over two issues. The segregating of "Coloreds" into a high school with what became Attucks High was deceitfully welcomed. But a near-Westside school was reluctantly debated. Rev. Baker from West Park Christian Church and the "founder" of Hawthorne Community Center in 1923 argued the case for westsiders. One near-northside member stated, "those kids west of the river won't go to school anyway." But, grudgingly, construction was approved and George Washington High School opened its doors at 2215 W. Washington St. after Labor Day in 1927. Mr. Gingery welcomed students as the first principal serving until 1951. Only Tech, Manual, Shortridge, and Broad Ripple existed as fellow-IPS schools at that time as Attucks opened its school also in 1927.

Future Mayor of Indianapolis Phil Bayt from Haughville was our first All-City footballer in 1928. As a three year football, basketball, and track man Jim Emerson Carter became our first state champion when he vaulted 12'4.75 in the Championship meet at Tech in 1930. Carter's mother was an original Citizens' School Committee leader by 1932. In 1964 she approached nearby business owner, Dick Lugar, and encouraged him to seek a spot on the IPS School Board thus launching a career in public service which continues in the 21st century.

The first four-year graduating class of 1931 included All-City tackle Ishmael Lawlis (whose son would set a basketball scoring record in '56 at GWHS) and future teacher Frank Luzar (official in '61 NFL Champ game). It was held at Cadle Tabernacle. One of 14 children born in Stringtown, Harry Cherry would graduate in 1934 and receive a full football scholarship to play for Bo McMillan at IU. The Enyert family ran a café which was initially next to the gas-filling station to the east (where most remember the Dairy Queen). Students and all of the team meals were served at the Enyert Café. Later it moved farther east and eventually sold out to what became Princess Tavern. Sixth-grader Georgie Enyert developed a crush on star Cherry. Years later they would marry. Joe Dezelan, Hop Howard, Swede Radcliffe, Lavern Burns, Louie Luzar, Cliff Baumbach (a Christian Scientist who died as a Purdue student after refusing medication for blood poisoning) and Dave Hine were just a few who helped run Bogue's Box Offense and Pony Backfield. Baumbach (as is noted in Purdue University's 100-year anniversary athletic booklet) was a starter as a sophomore at Purdue in football, basketball and baseball before his untimely death. And Henry Bogue was the legendary coach who was innovative but controversial. Curly Julian laughed that "if he didn't like your tie he was compelled to tell you." When he retired as Head Coach after the 1950 season (he retired in June of 1958 as a teacher) he noted to IHSAA Commissioner L.V. Phillips that Phillips needed to improve his speaking skills if he intended to be a good leader. Bogue came from William Penn College in Oskaloosa, Iowa. His Quaker background made him tough but fair. Yet his rule that a freshmen had to weigh 125-lbs. to get a uniform was waived for 123-lb. Harry Cherry. Harry won the Pole Vault spring meet at Butler with a bamboo pole into a sand pit at 11' 6" in 1934. He ran the 100-yd. dash at 10.2 as did two others on the 880-relay team.

Baumbach was clearly one of our early greats. He was a big All-City tackle in football (along with Joe Dezelan), the leading scorer one year in basketball, and a strong 1st baseman for the diamondmen. But baseball would be dropped for four years as a cost cutting measure during the Great Depression and was reinstated in 1938 with Frank Luzar as head man. It was dropped again during WW II but then resurfaced in 1947.

Future basketball Hall-of-Famer Bob Dietz (long-time Hinkle assistant at Butler) class of '35 would star playing on the stage with a "center jump" after each score. Lafe Hooser, who lived on the north side of Washington Street near Warman Avenue and was a classmate-friend of future Eli Lilly Vice President Fred VanAbeele, was the top scorer.

After four years at Wabash, top athlete Frank Luzar returned to teach and coach at his alma mater in the fall of 1935. Jim Otto began his long teaching career then also.

Curly Julian arrived at Washington High in the fall of 1937. He had graduated from Austin H.S. in 1928 in a class of ten. He was most proud of winning the Madison Basketball Sectionals. He attended Depauw University on a Rector Scholarship where he met his wife of 62 years, Betty Brooks. At the National Championship Track Meet at Chicago's Soldiers' Field in 1932 he ran the 2-mile run in 9 minutes 32 seconds which qualified him to try for the Los Angeles Olympics. Instead he returned as one of six teachers at his old high school as baseball and basketball coach. When a new trustee fired all six teachers, Curly became a newlywed and sales representative for an Ice Cream Company in Iowa. When Mr. Gingery wrote to Depauw asking for a track coach who could teach history, Curly had met his fate.

Barbara Jean Sullivan (later Hine) had arrived at GWHS as a 20-yr. old straight from Butler in 1936 to teach English. Vice Principal E.B. Hargrave struck fear in young Miss Sullivan as well as the students (according to Mrs. Hine in 2001). Students nick-named him "Pinky" for his flushed face when angry. Mr. Hargrave had been one of her teachers when she attended Tech. Mrs. Hine retired after 44 years at Continentaland in 1980. The long-term stability of the instructional and support staff was part of the foundation upon which the Westside depended for 68 years. Staff members who served over 30 years "on the job" included the likes of Bogue, Julian, Luzar, Otto, Bob Springer, Audie Watkins, Hester Baker Bock Erwin, Samuella Shearer Sands, Mary Laatz, Margaret McWilliams (she began as a Vice Principal), Johnny Williams (first Indiana All-Star basketball team in '39 from Southport), Lloyd Mann (freshman at Depauw with Mr. Julian), Orrell Negus, Robert Weaver, Mabel Loehr, Paul Carmichael, Anne Burge, Leo Rosasco, Vivian Ely, Rowland Jones, Justin Marshall (served as Vice Principal under four principals), Elizabeth Hatfield, Charlie Brown, Alan Hamilton, Basil Sfreddo and Bob Badgley among others. "Sweet Barbara Jean's" service of over 40 years tops the list. Mary Kay Mitchell, Florina Hendricks, and Grace Arvin were long-time secretaries who all the kids and teachers knew and respected. Margaret Hanna may have served the longest ('27 to '70) but Vi Bazis Sanders, who continued living in her childhood home in the first block of South Belmont as an adult, graduated from GWHS in 1937. She had a mutual love for GWHS of over 50 years. She retired in '87 and died in Jan. of 2004. Hollywood character actor Strother Martin, of "Cool Hand Luke" fame, sat in the back row of Vi's senior English class in '36-37. And her first School #30 boyfriend was Red Carter who starred at Purdue before being killed in a plane crash during WWII. Mrs. Hine died in March 2007. Mr. Julian celebrated his 99th birthday on November 30, 2009.

Coach Luzar retired in 1974 after 38 years on the job plus four years as a student, Mr. Otto unexpectedly died in the fall of '73 during his 38th year, Mr. Julian served 39 years counting his downtown service. Coach Luzar died in the mid-1990's, age 84. Henry Bogue, who was born in 1892, died in February of 1985.

Oddly enough, Ben Davis High School, which had been founded in the 1890's, did not have a gymnasium. They won the 1936 Indianapolis Sectionals while playing and practicing on our old stage-basketball floor or at Hawthorne Community Center before their gym was built the same year as our new gym, which opened in 1938.

Mr. Julian called the class of '38 one of the best. Future community leaders and World War II era heroes like Marion Carter, Mary Jane Howell & Ray Funk, Gladys Huddleston (Radcliffe), and Virginia Garrabrant (Russell) were just a few who stabilized the foundation upon which the greatness of GWHS was built. Virginia's father was Jacktown's last blacksmith into the 1950's with his shop on the Bertha St. alley between Warman and Harris streets (Longfellow wrote, "Under a spreading chestnut tree The village smithy stands; The smith a mighty man is he, With large and sinewy hands...")

Another strange incident to ponder as we see the changing culture of IHSAA rules was the reality of Park Tudor school recruiting two of our top 1930's athletes, Red Carter and 1936 QB Jim Boswell. Boswell, the brother of future Mayor Charlie, convinced his Cathedral buddy Sal Iozzo to go with him and Carter to play football as fifth year seniors since Park Tudor desperately desired to win against a rival private school.

The first renovation of our school was completed by the summer of 1938. The new gymnasium, toward the southeast part of the property near the football field, along with the shop class area and ROTC facilities enhanced a more practical education. The attic area in the southwest top corner included a "live ammunition" shooting range that was used legally and safely into the 1980's. The "Center Jump" after every score was last used during the '36-'37 season. The first year in the new gym was the '38-'39 basketball season. Before that spectators had watched the games from seats in the auditorium as they played on the stage. Now Continentals had a "huge" fieldhouse, seating 1400. It wasn't until the first State Championship season, when only one home game was played due to the lack of seating, that the "new" gym became obsolete. Bob McCalip was among the best athletes in the late '30's as a three-year starting back in the single-wing who led the Continentals to a 17-6-1 record and one City Championship through the '38 season along with Swivel Hips Carter and Bob Kersey.

Al Case, class of 1938 and long time honored employee at the Speedway (1946 and counting), felt that his School 50 buddy Kersey along with Carter were the top stars while continuing to note his Purdue hero to still be Red's older brother Jim. According to Casey, Oren's Drugstore at the corner of Belmont and Washington Streets was the after game meeting place. Once as a youngster, Casey waited patiently to catch a glimpse of his all-time hero, Emerson Carter. He didn't emerged. Casey never saw the elder Carter close-up in-person until April 1, 2009. I arranged lunch for the three of us at Mug 'n Bun drive-in. They both acknowledged another social reality, Harry Marcum's Belmont Theater. It was the second building east of Belmont and survived until almost 1980.

Three sport athlete and future State Superintendent of Public Instruction (1973-1985) Harold Negley described his most memorable play to me from '37. "Bob Kersey played tackle, center, and fullback. Blocking Back Marshall Reed caught the snap and tossed a lateral to Kersey, who had lined up at tackle, for a reverse. As he ran down the field Red Carter blocked out the safety to enable him to complete a 50-yd. touchdown." Kersey and Carter both were future starters in Purdue's backfield. Future Wayne Township School Board President John Sipe also excelled as a football lineman at GWHS, class of '38, along with captain Ralph Chambers who continues to attend alumni activities into 2010. And Thelma Bloomenstock garnered second-place in the city-wide Hayward-Barcus essay contest in 1939. Mr. Watkins was her favorite teacher.

Courtney Garrish was unbeatable in the 880 and, according to Negley, was Washington's best late-'30's basketball player. Yet, in 1995, STAR sportswriter Bob Collins wrote that Kersey was, in his opinion, the best basketball man from Washington in the 1930's. And, Louis Leerkamp (class of '38) starred in basketball and went on to set a Franklin College scoring record before becoming a coach. He was named to the Basketball Hall of Fame Silver Anniversary team in 1963. The first Continental so named. The first full decade for our school, the 1930's, was clearly a golden age in all areas of endeavor.

And into the second decade of the 21ˢᵗ century a number of 1930's graduates continue to attend Washington High alumni activities. Among those resolute individuals are Jeannette Arnold ('30), Edith Herriman-Lewis ('31), Lavern Conway-Crafton ('32), George Heaney ('32) as well as Mr. Chambers, Mr. Case, and Mr. Carter.

1940's

Little did Mr. Gingery know as the '40's began that he would petition the wood shop class to built a most impressive wooden memorial to recognize those who served in another World War (and then the Korean War boys who were later added) which would include 95 "Gold Star" Washington High boys. The memorial is still there.

Class of '40 football stars included Billy Howard and Boris Babe Dimancheff. Babe would later transfer from Butler to become a Purdue All-American and captain in 1944 as well as starting halfback on Purdue's only undefeated-untied team in 1943. (Our Jim Carter starred on the 1932 once-tied Purdue team.) Star columnist Bob Collins would write that Babe scored in the Chicago Cardinals 28-21 Championship win over the Philadelphia Eagles in 1947 in the Card's franchise very last NFL title through 2010. Collins also wrote in his book "Boilermakers: A History of Purdue Football" that Babe, during his 1944 All-American year, would score four touchdowns (65, 50, 32 and 15 yards) while rushing for 265 yards in a 35-0 win against a favored Wisconsin eleven. Babe's older sister was the mother of 1946 graduate and footballer Steve Stephanoff Sr.

Coach Bogue introduced the T-formation to Indianapolis football in 1940. It was said that he studied the Chicago Bears (the Bears defeated the Redskins 73-0 in the NFL Championship game that year). And Rowland Jones would lead the Continentals to their fourth Basketball City Championship in 1942. But the early '40's was dominated by the ominous event we now call World War II. Lloyd Posey ('42) from 501 S. Warman was wounded as an Army Ranger on D-Day, recovered in Scotland, and was later killed in February 1945. A track captain for Coach Julian he's shown often on TV documentaries with a captured Nazi flag (he's on the far right in the picture that is shown on HBO's "Band of Brothers" documentary). Harry Brown from Stringtown had been fullback on the football team and was killed on D-Day. Everitt Tackitt was with the 82nd Airborne on that June 6th (he died Dec. 2001). Harry Northern who parachuted into St. Mere Eglise with the 82nd and was seriously wounded lives in Danville. His wife, Betty, died in early 2009. His younger brother Virgil Northern was killed on Saipan. And Harry's future wife Betty's brother, Bob Cooke, was killed in France in late 1944. Eugene Heicken, who lived at 435 South Harris St., was killed during the war. Charles Bradshaw who grew up in the 400 block of South Holmes was killed and buried on Okinawa until his mother moved his body in 1949 to Floral Park in Indianapolis. Corporal Bradshaw had many commendations as a sniper-scout. And the death of top student-athlete Marion Carter ('38), who played halfback at Purdue University before joining the fight for freedom, was another example of the many sacrifices during that era. My dad called him "Swivel-hips" Carter. His older brother, Jim, had become known as one of the "Purdue Touchdown Twins" for the 1932-1934 teams. Into the 1950's the "Red Carter Award" was coveted by senior Continental student-athletes.

George Avery would become a medical doctor after his GWHS years and often bragged that he was the delivery doctor for classmate-parents at the birth of future IU star Randy Wittman. Wayne Whiffing who lived on South Harris St. would become President of the Indianapolis Chamber of Commerce in the mid-60's. Charlie Leamon, the future Northwest AD, would eventually marry 1940 classmate Elizabeth Alban.

The 1943 class officers, as WW II raged in the world, would all become successful adults. President Walter O'Brien and his twin, Waller, who was vice-President would become basketball starters at Butler University. Secretary Florence Newlin, Treasurer Max Hutton, and Sgt.- at-Arms Carl Roberts all made their marks in the adult world and military service.

Buckshot O'Brien ('46), who broke all of Butler's scoring records later, was Washington's first college super-star two-handed basketball shooter. He is the only Butler basketball player to have played in the NBA by 2010. ('83 grad Darren Fitzgerald would, temporarily, become Butler's single season record holder 37 years later) Bill Deem, who led Bogue's '44 City Champs along with All-City players Jimmy Clevenger and Guy Fish, may have been the best '40's quarterback although Bob Wolfla ('47) starred as QB and All-City catcher in baseball.

Eulah Nelson ('42) placed second in the prestigious, city-wide Hayward-Barcus essay contest.

When track coach Curly Julian left for the military, football coach Bogue took the helm in 1943 and presented Washington High with an individual-track State win. The 440-yd. relay team of Roy Jacobs, Frank Hines, Norman Dunn and Johnny Jacobs became our second champs. Ray Allen ran one of the 110-yd. legs in the City Meet win.

In the spring of 1944 Carter Byfield won the City Pole Vault championship at 11'1½" then Ed "Bud" Jones (Rowland's son) won the State High Jump at 6'0" while Byfield was State Runner-up along with 100-yd. dash man Johnny Jacobs who ran a blistering 10-flat leading the Continentals to a second-place finish at Tech for Coach Bogue's six man team. And, even though Frank Hines never lost in the 440-yd. run in three years of dual competition, he failed to win State. Bogue was Head Coach for only two years. Curly Julian became Head Man in 1940 but left for the service after the 1942 season. He returned and remained Head Coach from 1945 through the 1952 season.

Although the 1945 football team only won two games, they pulled off a big upset of powerhouse Tech 25-18. Coach Bogue had studied the Chicago Cardinals, as he earlier had the Bears, in pre-season. An innovative "wide trips" with QB Wolfla alongside end John Schussler and blocker Bill Hamilton (later of Hamilton well-drilling) performing double passes and hitch screens confused Tech. Second string QB Wesley Jones would initially take the center snap and tossed it to the perimeter.

And the size of the '47 backfield seemed unusual. Single-wing tailback Dick Lipscombe was 6'3" 230, fullback Lowell Lentz was 6'1" 220, wing-back Dennis Jent was 5"11" 170 and blocking-back Bob Reuter was 5'11" 175. And they could run. Reuter was on the 880-relay in the spring along with Bill Niemann, Charley Trotter and Don Carlyle (later a State Policeman). Jent was drafted by the New York Yankees. Lentz was a basketballer and top student. And the towering Lipscombe, whose dad Buck was a professional wrestler in Indianapolis, was our first regular place kicker (with Bob Tillery snapping and sophomore Don Leppert holding).

Spring football practice was in full swing during the '40's before IHSAA rules prohibited such action. Linemen like Bob Trinkle, Bernard Brown, Jack Hart, Frank Kish, Lasalle Flemings, Carl Ebert (track shot putter), and Eddie Kikendall all prospered.

The 1948 Sectional Championship was the first for GWHS. The area's first jump-shooter and track man Niemann (Washington's first Indiana All-Star) led the Continentals along with Don Masterson, Maurice Wilhoite, the Theofanis brothers, and Ralph Lollar. They lost to Anderson in the Regionals. In the fall of '47 C-Lber Tillery was named MVP and sophomore Mike Purichia would begin an 18-year Purichia-legacy with #66 at QB. The Cheerleading crew included the first girls-only squad. Mildred Sue Wilson (her daughter Connie Higgins would be a sophomore Cheerleader for the great McGinnis-Downing Champs of 1969), Betty Voegel and Patty Whitmore were the three in '47-48. The Yankees signed left-handed pitcher Jent in June 1948.

Mr. Gingery had collaborated on the "Washington Hymn" with Ross Campbell. "Where passed the sturdy pioneer with face set to the West, there stands a school to us most dear with many virtues blest...." did not stand the test of time but was heart-felt.

With the retirement of Principal Gingery at the completion of 1951, Washington entered a new era. He had arrived in Indianapolis as Math Head at Shortridge in 1917 and was our first Principal. Mr. Wilbur Barnhart took his position. Future Printing teacher Mike Barrett (responsible for the publication of the school newspaper and yearbook from the mid-50's to the '80's), top athlete Billy Cook, Mary Alice Gill (of the Workingman's Friend), Arlan Lickliter (late North Central coach, his son was Iowa's Head Basketball coach into 2010), Carroll Rance, Phil Riffey (his son was QB in '71), John Owensby, Sid Tillery (dentist Mike Tillery's dad), and future teacher Steve Yerich were a few from the Class of '51 that I would come to know in my Westside life. They won the baseball city championship playing at old Victory Field on West 16th St. even though our greatest baseball player ever had graduated the year before. Don Leppert ('50) hit three major league home runs in one game for the Washington Senators against the Yankees in '63. And long time Brickyard Crossing golf pro, Rollie Schroeder, would be football captain before his graduation in 1950.

During the national debate on school integration, which was highlighted by the 1954 Brown vs. Topeka case, the first two Black graduates from Washington High were Claudia Brunt and Ozetta Troutman in 1953. Both had younger siblings who also graduated from Continentaland. The first Negro students entered in the fall of 1950. There were three sophomores and at least 18 freshmen including the female Burnett twins. Bryan Hudson (class of '54) was a two-year player in basketball for Dave Hine along with early '50's stars Phil Peterson (also, football All-City at end), Carl Meador, Tom Dobbs, and Bill Springer (inducted into the Basketball Hall of Fame in 2001). Hudson along with Collis Blane paved the way for Blacks in basketball as did the first Black All-City football player from our school, Carl Ragland in 1955. The first game under lights was in 1953 with a 33-6 win over Manual. Washington's first wrestling team in '53-'54 was coached by Johnny Williams and included future Head Coach Joe Shires ('55). Frank Opp in '58 became our first wrestling State Champ. He of the First Family of Washington High Wrestling along with his brothers Carl, Reggie, and Gary.

Sue Kepner, class of 1953 from School 50, would marry Ben Davis' Bob Faris of Faris Mailing. In 2010 their granddaughter, Kelly Faris, is the first sub on the great UConn National Championship basketball team. Kelly had led Heritage Christian High School to four consecutive State Championships and had received the second highest number of votes for Miss Basketball in 2009 in Indiana. Sue's father was the highly respected custodian at School 50 who was in charge of discipline in the 30's and 40's and her mother was a teacher at both School 5 and School 67.

Future Wayne Township School Board member Stan Ellis, who was a 30-year teacher before his tenure on the local board, would graduate from GWHS in 1955.

Don Ross tied for the "City" in the High Jump at 6'0" with Attucks' Oscar Robertson in 1956. Hank Easter ('57) would be a three-sport star for three years and his future brother-in-law Elmo Carver ('55) would become Franklin Township Schools' Superintendent in the '90's. Sandy Spuzich ('55) would become a pro golfer winning the 1966 U.S. Ladies' Open with two other firsts through 1969. And the third of six Purichia QBs, Carol, barked signals for the Continentals in '55 & '56. Older brother Bill had died of a cerebral hemorrhage at Chattanooga College in spring football practice in 1956. The next Purichia, Nick, only played for one season (1958) but continued a life-long love for football until his untimely death at halftime of a Chatard football game in August 1979.

Eugene Gallagher ('52), who walked to GWHS from his home near the Taystee Bakery on New York St., would become Chief of Police in the late '70's. The O'Brien family lived next door on Hiawatha Street where today's IUPUI track is located. Gallagher was present as police chief at the strange stand-off with Ben Davis' Tony Kiritsis during the nationally televised confrontation in February 1977.

Football coach Joe Tofil once told me that the best football player during his eleven years ('51-'61) as Head Coach was Dave Porten ('54) from WI (that's West Indianapolis for those who don't know). Tough Dave Sanders ('58) was my favorite (his younger brother, Jerry '63 class, was rough too). Slavie Lalioff ('56) was an outstanding player and City Champ wrestler with a great football name. The two best basketball players during the '50's were Jerry Lawlis and Eddie Williams. Lawlis set a Marion County single game scoring record with 48 points against Speedway in early 1956 only to be upstaged when Oscar Robertson's Attucks teammates fed him the ball and he busted Lawlis' record with 56 points against Sacred Heart a few days later. And Williams, a friend of Oscar's, became Washington High's second Indiana All-Star in 1959.

Cynthia Fendley, class of '57, by the 21st century would have the unique distinction of having two sons as Head Coaches in the NBA, the Van Gundy brothers.

Mr. Julian had left our school in 1952 to become IPS' director of junior high athletics. But with Mr. Walter as the third principal in 1956 Mr. Julian, who had been promised the next Vice Principal's job in IPS, ironically returned to GWHS.

Some people look to the Baltimore Colts of '58 or the Packers of '62 or the Jets of '68 but I've always seen the Continentals of 1957 as my all-time favorite team. With Holmes Avenue's Bill Green and Belleview Place's John Arvin at ends, Harris Street's Bubby Stockhoff and big Howard Earls at tackles as well as sub Petey Saunders, wild Frank Opp and Leon Griffith at guards, likeable Wendell Brown at center, lefty Chuck Hedges at QB, Bill Jones & Dave Sanders at halfbacks, and Bernie Keller at fullback the Connies were hard to beat. The "Drop-Kick" is still legal as a field goal or extra point but the last time I've known it to be used (until Doug Flutie's swan song kick with the Patriots in January 2006) was when I saw Griffith score point number 53 in the 53-14 drubbing of Ben Davis at old BD.

The 1959 football team became Washington's second undefeated team led by touchdown twins Bob Leeper #72 & #64 Ken Corey as well as QB Charlie Prince, Bernie Wainscott, Weldon Beliles, Bill Snowberger, Larry Glaze, Larry Compton, Jim Dill and Tex Boarman. Compton and Boarman were college starters at Louisville and Leeper played basketball at Purdue.* Jim Leeper, Bob's dad, had graduated from GWHS in 1933 a year before his future wife, Mary Liebenderfer. Bob's sister Jane graduated in 1964. Chet's and The Pole continued as after-game meeting places on the active social scene.

A new Science wing was under construction by the late '50's to bolster Mr. Otto's long-time Science department. His "Modern Biology" textbook made up 2/3rds of all U.S. high school usage in the '50's & '60's. And with the introduction of Tether, Julian (as in Curly), & Otto's "Modern Health" textbook (which was the nation's leading high school textbook from 1955 until the early 1990's) Julian and Otto became prosperous educators. Mr. Julian, not coincidently, moved into his Kessler Blvd. East Drive home that same year where he lived until late 2002 when he moved to Marquette Manor. In early 2010 Curly still received residual payments from his published works.

---

* Leeper and Corey graduated at #4 and #8 in the class of 1961 as true student-athletes.

Into the 21ˢᵗ century retired fireman Jerry Gearries and long-time Eagle Creek golf pro Jerry Haslett along with Larry Meador and his wife of almost-50-years Linda Mohr, all from the class of 1960, continue to keep alive the aura of the 1950's.

<u>1960's</u>

Principal Walter had empowered VP Julian as the leader of athletics. So when he made the decision to replace his friend Dave Hine with assistant Jerry Oliver in the late fall of 1960, Mr. Julian began a series of significant changes for the Westside. Mr. Walter left in January '61 to begin the organization of a new high school called Arlington, which opened that fall. (Unfortunately, Mr. Walter died of cancer as the northeast side school got started.) New principal Curly Julian gave his first speech to the fall freshmen in 1961 with his characteristic philosophical personality, "Continentals have a back-bone, not a wish-bone." And, "nothing succeeds like success." That fall the freshmen teams were city champs in football (and later basketball) yet the varsity floundered with what seemed to be much size, speed, and talent. Specifically, the lack of production from three-sport athlete Billy Hattiex was seen as a coaching negative. So, again, Mr. Julian had to approach another friend, Joe Tofil, and ask him to step aside for 28-year-old parochial school coach Bob Springer to begin the 1962 football season.

Oliver and Springer would lead a charge unmatched in IPS athletic history. Starting in 1962 and ending in 1965 the basketball team won three straight City Championships. Oliver would register 102 wins his first five years as Head Coach. His first team had pulled off a big upset in a Sectional game at Butler led by leading scorers Joe Purichia, Jim Rhodes, and Louie Craig. Only our school won three consecutive "Citys" over a sixty year period against a 17 team challenge (even Attucks only won two with Oscar) and Ralph Taylor was the only three year starter (Billy Keller's knee operation sidelined him in '63). Of course, the 1965 State Championship leaves Washington as the first integrated team from Marion County to win. And again in 1969 with the undefeated McGinnis-Downing juggernaut the Continentals remain the only naturally integrated-neighborhood teams to win from IPS (Ripple's '80 team had at least one star from the Manual area). Keller and George McGinnis were both Mr. Basketball. Until Haughville resident Damon Frierson won that title in '95 for Ben Davis, George was the last from Marion County. And after I won the Trester Award in '65 another Marion County athlete was not chosen until class-basketball emerged in the late '90's. The so-called "West Side Mafia" made up of graduates from the '40's & '50's were welcomed by all Continental athletes as they rallied in the east football end zone or at one end of the basketball floor (notably at Southport). Peterson, Rance, Smotherman, Dietz, Hogue, Clevenger, Eddie & Dave Porten, Tooter Rice, Tom Johnston, as well as Russell and Chet Posey were just a few of the loyal Continentals into the late 1960's.

The largest freshmen class in Continental history in '61 had given a preview of things to come athletically. The football team, with Teddy Williams and Mitchell Blane, defeated Cathedral 18-0 for Coach Williams' first ever win over the Irish and a City Championship. Line coach Frank Munshower, a Cathedral grad, had grown up a block away from GWHS on Pershing St. He landed in the showers for the celebration. The Cathedral vs. Washington friendly rivalry would continue with a Cathedral grad (Springer after '62) and a Washington grad (Dezelan through '69) meeting each other the tenth game on the schedule (1960-70). And the frosh basketball team, led by Keller and Taylor, beat Shortridge and one day later Attucks for the Daily Double Frosh City Championship to give Russell McConnell his first Champs. And at 135 lbs. Gary

Sylvester ('64) was a varsity football, basketball, & baseball player for three years. Steve Midkiff and Mike Furimsky (also both '64) would be three-year starters and All-ICC in football at Ball State. Dannie Johnson's 14 tackles in the 1963 Homecoming was quite a feat the night his grade school girlfriend, the Opp brothers' little sister Clancie, was chosen Homecoming Queen.

During the 45-year Cold War most historians feel that the Cuban Missile Crisis in late October 1962 was the scariest nuclear showdown. Respected history teacher Carl Zenor, who soon became the long-time department head, was called to active duty as an officer in the Air Force. But school continued and many were more focused on the Tech football game that Wednesday. Afterall, Tech had an alleged "race riot" in their cafeteria that week which made their team morale vulnerable to defeat. Something like that could never happen at our school, most students felt. We lost a close game, 20-12.

Unsung stars like Hattiex, Jim Knobel (the basketball playing golfer), Bob Murff, Louie Craig, Bobby Komlanc, Calvin Schaffer, Clark Dickerson, Billy Apple, Harry & Mike Tibbetts, William Rogers, Mark Gladson, Sam Kitchens, Mike Parker, "Ducky" Lloyd, Mike Highbaugh, Tim McGrevy, Tommy Gregg, Kenny Strong, Harvey Holmes and "Fancy Steppin'" John Dowdell would all help set the foundation upon which the well-documented State Championship era would stand. Between 1965-1974 we would win two football and two basketball State Championships. In the '60's and '70's no other school in the entire county would win even one at the top level of those two high profile sports. Our school's enrollment and facilities were similar to the other ten IPS schools and less than most of the county schools. Yet, we clearly had more statewide success. Contrast that with an area school that entered a new era with the largest enrollment in the state along with excessive facilities and money by 1978. It took their new inexperienced regime six years to win their own basketball sectionals. And another eleven years to finally stumble into their first State Championship, albeit with Washington High as the main roadblock as well as Haughville athletes as stars thanks to forced busing.

Clovis Stinson ('63), who would later become Head Basketball Coach at Chatard, was a teaching buddy of the last original Purichia, Steve ('65), at that northside school. Steve won more City Championships than any other Head Coach in football at Chatard and was probably the best Marion County football coach throughout the '70's. And Landy Lewis ('63), who had played on Coach Springer's first team at GWHS, was the son of 1931 graduate Edith Herriman. She continues an active life into 2010.

Harris Street's Butch Lomen would headline a Surveyor track meet story once reading "Lomen 15, Ben Davis 14." His three Blue Ribbons in the high jump, broad jump and high hurdles would singularly outscore our BD opponents in 1962.

Denny Troth and Sally Reddick were among the last Johnnie & Connie Continentals. Girls and boys clubs continued to thrive only through the mid-60's. The Counts, Jax, K-T-Dids, DDs, Delts, Barons and others would soon see their Tuesday night social meetings diminished. School plays like "Oklahoma," "Our Town," and "The King & I" were successfully presented. The Continental Capers would have its last hurrah in the spring of 1970 as the major school fund-raiser. The Junior Vaudeville, Talent Show, and Poetry Reading Contest were still popular in the '60's.

The "Whites Only" sign at Riverside Amusement Park would come down in 1962 and racial diversity would become the norm. Although "Chet's" closed in late 1963 the Big Boy at 16th St. and Pershing would be the major after-game hangout by the mid-60's.

Miss Rose King became our first African-American teacher in 1955 soon followed by Mrs. Laura Lyons. Mr. Wally Webb became the first male-teacher role-model for young Blacks in the fall of 1964 as a science teacher. Wrestler Tim Giles, class of 1962, became a GWHS teacher in 1966.

Popular 1965 May Queen Karen McDonald lived just a few yards from her beloved Washington (on South Tremont not far from her best friend Cheryl Roberts) and would later marry her high school sweetheart, pole-vaulter Rick Blake. Rick was a member of the '65 Champs who attended Butler & IU Dental School. Cheryl's mom and dad had both graduated from GWHS in the early '40's as had Blake's parents.

Coach Springer's legacy from '62-'93 led to his 1991 Hall of Fame induction. His first team knocked Cathedral out of the city championship the last game of the year. Lomen, Malcolm Marlowe, George Sipe, Larry Austin, Jim Arvin, Jimmie Highbaugh, Randy Payne, Steve Shouse and captain Jerry Sanders led the emotional Continentals. A 75-yd. audible ("purple 85") 500-right TD pass from this author to the eldest Highbaugh would establish the mood for the 1962 Homecoming win over Ben Davis, 35-0. Sipe fell one-yard short of a 4th TD pass in that game on a "check-5" 24-yd. gain. We were the first central Indiana team to call audibles on every down in the early '60's under the innovative Springer. And, we emulated 49ers coach Red Hickey's Shotgun offense during the Ben Davis drubbing. But the talented 1966 Mythical State Champions (led by Bobby Canady, Charlie Walton, Jeff Neely, Ricky Sylvester, John Hill, Rick Thompson and Larry Highbaugh) set a higher standard that was followed by the 1974 Tourney Champs and the 1983 Runners-up to Penn. Punter Mike King, class of 1964 and the son of a city fireman at Station 18, would become a respected obstetrician by the 1970's.

Ironically, Dave Hine would coach the first team State Champs (Golf in 1961). And Randy White won another wrestling State Championship in 1961.

National Merit Scholarship winners and future Ph'Ds Gary Gunther and Ray Knight also displayed the versatility of the liberal educational opportunities found at GWHS in the sixties. Dr. Gunther graduated from Wabash, Rockefeller University, and Yale with degrees including Cell Biology and Immunology. He worked at St. Jude Children's Research Hospital in Memphis in cancer research. Dr. Knight today is on the teaching staff at Louisville's hospital while maintaining a General Practice in Jeffersonville, Indiana. Corporate lawyer and Columbia graduate Fred Hulser was Senior Class President in '65. He practiced in San Juan, Puerto Rico at the turn of the 21st century. The first Black Valedictorian Frank Starkey ('62) exhibited the racial tolerance that seemed to be so common under Mr. Julian's leadership as Barbara Brunt became the first African-American Cheerleader in 1964. And Linda Jeter (Edwards), class of '63, would become Human Relations chief for Wayne Township Schools in the 1990's.

Ronald Weaver, class of 1963, would be proclaimed as the State Champion weight lifter the summer following graduation. With a combined weight of 997-lbs. in the clean 'n jerk, military press, and dead lift. He weighed about 190 at the time.

As mentioned, the '61 freshmen counted 1,000 strong (with over 3,000 in four grades) and most students shared lockers. But when Northwest H.S. opened its doors in 1963 about half of the frosh and sophomores migrated to the new Eagledale high school.

Always humble Charlie Leamon, class of 1940, was named the first Northwest Athletic Director. His future wife, Elizabeth Alban, also graduated in '40 from Washington. They lived on the corner of Jackson and Mount Streets as he began his new job.

President Johnson traveled down the National Road in October 1964 from Weir Cook Airport toward a downtown speech. Mr. Julian had been ordered by the downtown office NOT to allow students to congregate in front of the building. But, quite coincidently, a fire drill (with a "mock" rear of school fire so that all students had to exit the front) was called as the motorcade approached. Everyone will recall that it had been less than a year since the assassination of JFK and we did not have a Vice President under the Constitution at that time. So, when LBJ ordered his driver to stop in front of our school for a short speech in support of Gubernatorial candidate Branigan, there were some concerned Secret Service agents. One student was temporarily restrained as he displayed a "Goldwater" sticker on his notebook and allegedly had a starter's pistol in his locker. That "protest" is pictured in the 1965 yearbook. It was interesting when, in the fall of 1969, new President Nixon was to arrive traveling down the same National Road and Mr. Julian used his same "fire-drill" strategy. But his motorcade barely slowed.

By the mid-60's a place called Vietnam (that most had learned about in geography as French Indochina) became a prominent issue. The first peacetime draft in the history of the U.S., which began in early 1941 and ended in 1973, called for boys at the age of 18 to sign up. Many registered in Mr. Hunt's northeast corner office (Mrs. Nellie LaMar, his secretary, signed me up). At the time (May '65) when Ivan Smith was killed in Vietnam the newspaper called him the first Indianapolis boy and first Indiana Marine killed there. Bill Young ('64), the ROTC Drill Team Commander who grew up in Eagledale, lost both legs to a land mine in that controversial Southeast Asian war.

Indiana All-Star Marvin Winkler ('66) had busted Oscar's single season scoring record of 541 points from 1956 with his one season total of 590 points and then he "broke the color barrier" at Southwest Louisiana. In 1971 he was on the Milwaukee Bucks World Champs with Oscar. And briefly he was on the Pacers roster. Actually in the mid-70's, within a little over a year, the Pacers had six GWHS guys under contract. Wayne Pack, Steve Downing, George McGinnis, Billy Keller, Assistant Coach Jerry Oliver, and Winkler. Oliver, who replaced an ill Lou Watson mid-season '69-'70 was briefly IU's Head Coach. In '70-71 along with his buddy Downing, McGinnis was his old high school coach's top player as the Big Ten's leading scorer and rebounder in only his sophomore year.

Bob Jones, from South Harris St., would start three years in football and two in basketball in the late '60's. His final game in 1967 was as quarterback. Jones ran for two TDs and threw for two, one to junior McGinnis and the other to Cannon, in our school's drubbing of Cathedral 40-6. Then Bill Green took over for IU-bound Jerry Oliver in '68 and his first year with McGinnis and Downing ended 31-0. McGinnis' 53 points and 31 rebounds in one All-Star game is seen as maybe the greatest feat in Indiana high school history. Then Coach Green left after only three years (two as Head) and an 8-14 season.

Dennis Grider won the Cross Country State Championship twice, in '62 & '63, with John Bradley's guidance. And State records were shattered in Track by Washington under Harold Orman's leadership. Mike Cummins was State Broad Jump champ at 23'2 1/2" in 1966. Larry Highbaugh won State in the 100-yd. and 220-yd. dashes in 1967. As a freshman in the summer of '64 he had broken Jesse Owens' 1930's Mansfield, Ohio Relays 100-yd.dash record at 9.2 (wind-assisted). Don Phillips won the Shot Put title in both '68 & '69 the last year setting a record at 64'3 1/2", which would endure for almost 20 years. Shot Put expert Gerald England later coached at Indiana Central.

Linda Howard, class of '63, was the daughter of early 1930's star Hop as well as the future mother of ESPN race reporter Vince Welch. Linda's older brother, who attended Ben Davis, would become curator of the Indiana Baseball Hall of Fame after his induction in 1990 as Jasper's coach.

The "Teen Star" was anxiously awaited every Saturday. It celebrated its 10th anniversary in the mid-1960's. A new Speech class under the direction of Mrs. Allie Dragoo, the school plays under Miss Colleen Stanley, Mr. Charles Hamilton and Mr. Tom McCormick's singers, Mr. Ray Funk's (class of '38) Marching Continentals, and Mrs. Anita Morris' school paper-yearbook work were all going strong in the mid-60's.

Mrs. Morris was only a teacher at GWHS for four years but remains my all-time favorite teacher with her optimistic and energetic personality. When she left with her husband to Texas, Mr. David Knott took the helm of the school publications. His 1967 40th Anniversary yearbook was superior to most college annuals.

The Junior and Senior Proms continued to be held in the school's gymnasium. Most underclassmen still walked to school. And grade schools #5, 75, 67, 50, 49, 46, 47, 63, 52, 16, 30, and sometimes even 44 continued to bolster Continentaland.

The "Shortridge Plan" initiated by School Board member Richard Lugar became effective in 1966 two years before Judge Dillon's first busing order was introduced. Under that IPS plan students had to pass an entrance exam in order to attend Shortridge. Consequently, those who did not qualify for Shortridge were allowed to attend any other IPS school. A number of East 38th St. area students reluctantly traveled by city transit to GWHS. And the alleged discriminating nature of separate Academic, Fine & Practical Arts, and General diplomas were discontinued.

David Garver (class of 1963) and his wife Bobbi Davis (class of 1965) along with Tommy Gregg ('65) continue into the 21st century as the main alumnus who continue to preserve the legacy of the school's glory years. Tom's Rhodius Park wife Nola Havens, who traveled south to attend Sacred Heart, is an honorary grad and solid supporter.

1970's

Unrest and disorder, which had infected our nation in the late 1960's, created tension at Washington High. In 1970 we were assigned our first Security Guard, the last IPS school to have one. The Continental Capers ceased existence after May of '70 when a series of fights and lack of parent workers created apathy. A nationwide protest against the Vietnam War orchestrated partly by Jane Fonda saw a number of Continental students vacate the building in October of 1970. Many teachers went on strike in the fall of '72 creating picket lines and some distrust among colleagues. Mr. Julian challenged students who refused to stand for the National Anthem or be attentive to "leave if you don't want to be here" at the '71 Easter Convocation. The "Wild Bunch" walked out. The 1971 choice of Senior Athlete Eddie Boswell was seemingly obvious but was unpopular for a small number of students and a series of fights occurred. Never again would class Athletes-of-the-Year awards be announced at the May Day celebration. And, after a fight at a junior high game between schools #52 & #67 in 1972, never again would junior high students participate in football or basketball league games at Washington. On a positive note, Tom Keating of the STAR would name Vi Sanders' daughter Nikki as the first singular All-County Student in his popular newspaper column in 1971.

For the first time in school history girls were allowed to wear slacks in the fall of 1970. Through the spring of '70 girls were required to wear a dress or skirt to school. Blue jeans were now allowed yet "Senior Cords" faded from the social scene.

Phillip "Quake" Leslie became our third wrestling State Champ in 1970 and the only one in the heavyweight division from Continentaland. He was four points behind with 26 seconds left but pinned his opponent at Southport. Coach Joe Shires ('55) gave assistant Ralph Poehls credit for being "Quake's" year-long practice opponent. Coach Poehls had been football tackle at IU in the early '60's and became Dean of Boys in '73 when Shires became A.D. replacing Russell McConnell, former frosh basketball coach.

Eddie Love ('71) played a tough defensive end in tandem with his brother Arnold. Eddie by 1977 would be named "Mr. USA" body-builder from Hofmeister's Gym.

Eddie's son would start as a football center for Ben Davis in the late '90's. Arnold and sister Dorothy would both become State Police Officers.

The initial implementation of Judge Dillon's busing order began in 1970 with the creation of an Attucks freshmen class at the Cold Springs Rd. Campus. In 1971 intra-IPS busing went into effect. Dozens of families began to move fearing a lack of neighbor-hood stability. Within ten years Grade Schools #5, 75, 63, 16, 30, & 52 would be closed. By late 1973 The Pole, Westlake, and Riverside Amusement Park were all closed.

The 1971 quartet of Wayne Grace, Ruben Timmons, George Russell, and Steve Officer would set a State Championship record in the 880 Relay at 1:27.55.

Ruth Baird would become Washington's first African-American May Queen in 1971. And girls' sports would take a big step forward from the CGAA blue bloomers to Washington's sixth and final State Championship team in 1975 in Track. Debbie Quarles had won the 1974 80-yd. Hurdles and repeated her win in '75 when she also was named Washington's second Mental Attitude Award winner in the Finals. Donna Pope won the Long Jump and Kathy Gaddie joined them on the Relay team along with anchor Joetta Bailey.

Ronnie Hayes would win a football scholarship to Cincinnati after three great years at Washington. Yet frosh coach Williams once stated that "pound for pound Ronnie Dillon was the toughest I've ever coached." Dillon and Hayes were the starting halfbacks for two years and their buddy Don Mallory was our first Black QB in 1972.

Rocky Deakin in the fall of 1973 became one of the few running backs to reach the 1,000 yard career rushing threshold. Both of his parents had attended Washington High as had his older brothers, Bobby ('66) who played baseball and Darrell ('69) who wrestled and was on the '66 football State Champions, as well as older sister Phyllis ('68). Younger sister Candy ('76) was a Continental cheerleader.

In 1974 Coach Springer's 13th Washington squad would win State in only the second year of the play-offs. Under the original play-off system, which lasted for ten years, we would be the only Marion County State Champs in the top division, and the only IPS school to even qualify, other than Marshall High School. Earl Branson and Kevin Weatherby were three-year starters and Danny Butler would lead the Continentals along with Armond White, Doug Beets, and Ron Heinrich. Heinrich, who wrestling coach Poehls would persuade to play football his junior year, won a full scholarship to Louisville. On Christmas Day 1978 Ron was captain for the Blue-Gray game. In 2010 he runs the Budweiser distributorship for the state of Florida.

Arlene Coleman ('72) would become Vice Principal by 2000 at Warren Central H. S. under Principal Tony Burchett ('71) who was a two-year quarterback as well as a baseball star during his Continental years. Tony would become a teacher at his alma mater in 1977 but was forced to leave by the inter-district busing order in 1981.

The late '70's would see another building renovation. An Olympic-sized pool and separate diving facility at the east end and a new gym plus weight-room at the west end were added along with air conditioning.

Jerry and Larry Lish were not star athletes but they were loyal Continentals. Their parents, from near 10th & Tibbs, had both graduated from GWHS and continued as perhaps the last consistent non-school-personnel adults who seemed to attend all football and basketball contests. Their presence was a steady and prideful loyalty.

Washington's fifth basketball coach Basil Sfreddo ('70-'89) would lead the Continentals to five Sectional Championships (more than the previous coaches combined); three of them in the '70's. The White brothers, Armond and Doug, along with Anthony Pippen, Chester Washington, and Ricky Smith would give him his first in '75 and Donnie McCoy, George Harris, Kerry Noble, and Leonard Sullivan would deliver two others in '77 & '79. Harris' kid brother (Corey) would star for the World Champion Baltimore Ravens in 2001. Sullivan's dad, Leonard Sr. ('56), held the school record for the Mile Run for six years. Noble was named City Athlete of the Year as had Highbaugh ('67) and McGinnis ('69). Sfreddo retired with more wins than any other basketball coach. He also won the City once in '78 and two more Sectionals in the '80's.

Kathy Gaddie, class of 1976, was one of our all-time most accomplished students. She was Homecoming Queen, a three year varsity cheerleader as well as volleyball and basketball player, the DAR Good Citizen award winner, a hurdler and relay runner on the 1975 State Champions, and the class Valedictorian. She had two older sisters who were her positive role-models in Terri ('72) and Debbie ('75).

Another Debbie, friend Debbie Quarles, was a great student-athlete. She was a three year varsity cheerleader, volleyball, and basketball player as the star of the track team. Quarles inspired her five younger siblings as Jamboree Queen and two-time State Champ in the hurdles while graduating #4 in the class of 1975.

Mr. Julian would retire after the 1977 school year and was replaced by long-time Industrial Arts teacher then Vice Principal Leon Hunt (I first remember him as the official scorer in basketball). When Mr. Hunt retired in '79 he relinquished his duties to his friend Tom Rosenberger. Coach Rosenberger had been Shortridge's football coach in the early '60's and had come to Washington in 1965 (when Joe Tofil went there as A.D.).

Rick Hightower ('77), who has long been a local TV newsman, was a member of the '77 Sectional Champs; he graduated from Brigham Young University. Teammate Willie Carter, who went on to a record setting college career, was the top scorer for two years in spite of an unfortunate "wrong goal" basket in the '78 Sectionals vs. Northwest. That shot prevented a re-match against a Ben Davis team we had defeated earlier in the year.

Junior Vicki Lynch, who lived yards away from GWHS with her grandmother, would leave school in 1978. She would be named Miss Nude Ohio in 1983, as Hyapatia Lee, before her successful career in Adult Movies as an actress and producer.

And, Kenneth Gilbert became Washington's seventh individual track State Champ when he ran the last 880-yard run at 1:54.8 in 1979. Unfortunately another teachers' strike in the fall of 1979 created added discord.

The Federal Court Ordered Busing in 1981 was probably the beginning of the end for neighborhood schools inside the old city limits. In the late '90's a news story stated that $10.3 million had been paid to Wayne Township in the form of tuition and bus expenses (a November 2002 Wayne Township newsletter stated that $6,200 is paid in tuition form for each of the IPS students and that 17% of over 12,000 Wayne students are from IPS which computes to over $12.6 million yearly. "We hope to delay the process.." of reversing busing, the note emphasized). Desegregation began to be "phased out" in 2000 starting in grade one but, over 22 years, we not only lost money and many prized student-athletes but also teachers like Tony Burchett who presided over the four consecutive football State Championships as Warren Central's principal in the 21st century. It was not a coincidence that he had carried Mr. Julian's "Washington Way" to Warren Township. In 2008 Tony became an Assistant Superintendent there.

In the early '80's a stabbing in an English classroom and the shooting of a student by an irate husband were two indicators that our school was no longer immune from sub-cultural influences. Still, the 1983 football team would continue some tradition before being defeated in the State Championship in a close game. Jim Overstreet and his protective tackles Danny Stamatkin and Jerry Cunningham would anchor a strong interior line along with Baber, Seargent and All-City guard Calvin Fitzgerald. But little Rhyman Rhodes epitomized the heart of Continental football at its best. Against North Central and their future pro Lars Tate, Rhodes at about 5'5" (the bottom part of his #2 was tucked unseen into his pants) hit Tate on the third play of the game and Tate limped off of the field. Our team drubbed them 30-3 and thumped both Bloomington South 22-0 and Lawrence North 32-9 on their drive to the Championship game. Halfback Glenn Carpenter set a single season scoring record with 174 points in a backfield which included two other strong runners and blockers named Luter and Weeden. The 1983 defense gave up only 30 points in the first ten games before the play-offs.

Tom Lyles, who starred as center on the basketball team in the early '80's, became the father of 2010 8th grader Trey. Trey, as a 6'7" 14-year-old, was already being sought out as a college player by both Purdue and IU even before his probable attendance in Tech H.S. where his dad is assistant coach.

Lamont Williams could be said to have accomplished one of the greatest one-day athletic performances in Washington High School history. He won the heat races as well as the finals in both the 800-meters and 400-meters at the 1980 State Championship meet within minutes of each event on North Central's track. Lamont's school records remain at 1:52.8 for the 800 and 48.0 for the 400.

Curtis Kimbrough ('82 City Athlete) and Kenneth Walker the '83 State Champion in the Discus were two top early '80's athletes. And Indiana's Miss Basketball for 1981 Cheryl Cook, who won the first 100-meter Hurdles State Championship in '81, was another unique Washington athlete. The '84 football team lost to Jeff George's State Champs 20-18 in the play-offs when they were unable to score any extra points. An all-weather track, an underground football sprinkler system, new bleachers, and a renovated auditorium with a balcony were all completed in the 1980's. But, unfortunately, vandals permanently destroyed the wooden floor in the "old" (1938) gym the 4th of July weekend of 1988 when they ran fire hose water on the floor for three days. Principal Tom Rosenberger retired in 1989 and was followed by two non-Westsiders.

And, 1983 graduate Darren Fitzgerald would set the NCAA single season record for 3-point shots as a senior at Butler in 1986-87 for Coach Joe Sexson. His record would stand until the 2008 National Tournament when Davidson University's leading scorer, Stephen Curry, would set the new standard in his expanded season.

1990's

Monterio Holder led the transition into the '90's when he set a school record in the High Jump in a U.S.-Canada Duel Meet of 7'2 ¼" in the summer of '89. He followed that with the 1990 State Championship clearing 6'10". Track Coach Walt Stahlhut, so strongly assisted by John Bradley who retired in '89 and football great Leonard Cannon ('68), had many outstanding teams. And Al Hamilton after 35 years as Science teacher, equipment man, official scorer, and statistician left the friendly confines of 2215 W. Washington the year it closed. Future Heavyweight Boxing Champion Lamon Brewster was one of Coach Springer's football stars as the decade began.

Washington's last football game was a play-off loss to East Central in '94. First year Coach Myron Newland had replaced Coach Springer. Newland had arrived as assistant coach in 1976 but had earlier starred on the 9-1 '68 team with Louie Day, Reggie Williams, and Big George. Newland was Head Coach at Northwest through the 2002 season.

Ibn Rasheed would achieve a school record in two field events in 1995. His 64'5" shot put outdistanced Super Don Phillips' 1969 record and his 193'4" discus throw would be over 30' longer than Kenneth Walker's 1983 mark. Phillips and Walker were both State Champs as would be Ibn in the Discus even as the school was officially closed.

But the most shocking loss was our last basketball game in the Regionals of '95. Jack Owens, All-State in football and basketball, had sunk two free throws with five seconds left for a one point lead. In an unrehearsed floor length dribble Ben Davis' Ahmed Bellamy, who had recently been reinstated on the team, hit a three-point fade-away for a win at the buzzer. Ben Davis went on to win their first State with the help of their MVP who had played at Pike the year before, a three-year starter who lived in the Northwest H.S. district, and their Mr. Basketball from Haughville. Neighborhood schools just weren't what they used to be. But Owens, who is a Purdue basketball assistant coach in 2010, and R.J. Williams displayed Continental greatness for one last time under fifth-year Coach Joe Pearson. Pearson attended GWHS as a freshman before going to brand new Northwest in 1963. And Gene Robertson, from the class of '54 who had come home again in '81 after stints at Shortridge and Wood as football coach and A.D., would close Washington sports as our last Athletic Director.

Long time secretary and late-50's graduate Nancy Fletcher Ehret would organize the closing ceremonies along with the Shires & Robertson families. And Ernest "Chico" Smith closed out his loyal years at GWHS from the '60's through the '90's.

Unfortunately the January 1995 murder of Washington sophomore Derrick Hale was the darkest chapter. He was "stomped" to death in the parking lot of the Village Pantry at Belmont and Washington Streets while walking home from school on a Friday by two or three students. The main attackers were a GWHS freshman and a BD student. On Channel 6 on Monday another student shrugged his shoulders on camera and bragged (?), "we're basically immune to violence." Does anyone remember when a normal fist-fight, no kicking allowed, was usually the end of any male disagreement? Bogue, Luzar, and Johnny Williams into the '60s would allow boys to don boxing gloves and settle their argument, one-on-one. The world has changed and so has the Westside.

From Yavonovich, Lovisek, and Ivancic…to Jacques, Lickliter, and Komlanc… to O'Brien, Nash, and Green…to Blake, Hayes, and Branson…to Smith, Cook and Jones plus hundreds of others, the Continental legacy remains alive in many hearts and minds.

The re-opening of Washington as a Community School in the fall of 2000 and the first freshmen class in the fall of 2001 did keep some hopes alive. The first Community School graduation took place in 2005. Their history remains to be written. But the $27 million renovation completed in 2008 gives renewed hope to a struggling community.

III.

BIOGRAPHIES

JAMES EMERSON CARTER (1930)

Touchdown Carter and his teammates were taught to ignore the generic-sounding, non-referee whistle of the other three officials so it was surprising when he pulled up short of his second first half touchdown. Only the referee's whistle stopped play. And, when Fordham's Les Borden smacked him to the ground in the Polo Grounds, he suffered a season ending shoulder separation with only the Old Oaken Bucket game remaining. Purdue won 7-0 behind Carter's TD but, the following week against IU, would lose only their fourth game in the three-year careers of their famous Touchdown Twins and All-Americans, Jim Carter and Duane Purvis. That season ending loss cost Purdue their second Big Ten title in three years.

Emerson Carter, as he was called until his frosh year at Purdue, was born on the west side of South Elder on November 12, 1911. Then, when he was three years old, his railroader dad built a new family residence which still stands today at 101 S. Elder St. in Indianapolis just two streets east of Belmont St. Older brother, Dick (b. 1907), and their younger sister, Nadine (b. 1913), moved with their mom and dad into the house just off of the National Road in early 1915 during the war in Europe two years before the U.S. joined the fight. And, just a day short of Emerson's seventh birthday, it seemed that the entire city traveled to Monument Circle in celebration of Armistice Day. His family never owned a car and Emerson never had a driver's license until college graduation. Transportation consisted of either the city street-cars or the interurban railroad system. The New York Central Railroad, just two blocks south from their home, saw Daddy Carter as an employee for over 47 years. First as brakeman and eventually as conductor, Mr. Carter usually traveled the overnight trip from Indianapolis to Peoria, Illinois for the P & E Division of the Big Four. He retired soon after WW II and died in 1952, age 72.

Nellie, the matriarch, was born in Elwood but raised in Portland, Indiana. As a traditional housewife, she was anything but traditional when she helped organize the first Indianapolis Citizens School Committee in 1932. She continued her community activism into the 1960's. She approached local factory owner Dick Lugar to persuade him to run for IPS School Board in 1964. Mrs. Carter could be credited with helping launch his long public career. She died in 1975 at age 96.

And, Jim's first conscious memory was traveling to Broad Ripple Skating Rink where he was deposited into a group bed-playpen with other youngsters as his parents and brother roller-skated.

School #30 only served grades one through three with a single outside pit-toilet so Emerson walked east the seven or eight blocks to School #16 near White River from 4th to 8th grade. Often the girl across the alley from Neal Street would walk with him. Little Georgia Carmichael had a brother who people would know as Hoagy. "Georgia on My Mind" was dedicated to Hoagy's sister when it was written in 1930. Hoagy had ordered lyricist Stuart Gorrell to insert his little sister's name in the title. And it became the official state song of Georgia in 1979 as the Ray Charles version continued its popularity after his most well-known recording in 1960. (Beatle John Lennon once noted that his favorite American composer was Hoagy Carmichael.) Another Carmichael girl, Martha, was mentored by Hawthorne Community Center icon Mrs. Alma Lemen in her Girl Scout troop.

Lauter's Boys Club which was on White River Parkway near today's Indianapolis Zoo offered mostly boxing, wrestling, and tumbling. Although they had a nice gym, basketball was not yet the Indiana staple (at least not on the west side of Indianapolis) in the mid-1920's.

In August of 1926 Emerson attended the first football "call-out" at Tech High School. Over 200 boys attended try-outs for the largest school in the state that had over 7,000 students at the time. With one coach, one football, and three hours of sitting time while all 200+ boys gave their names Emerson decided that he was wasting his time. But 1927 and brand new George Washington High School at 2215 W. Washington St. would provide a completely different set of opportunities for the 15-year-old.

Shorty Morrison, the first GWHS athletic director who had taught at Manual High School the year before, would be the coach for game number one. Then a coach would arrive who wouldn't leave his leadership position for the next 24 years, Henry Bogue. Emerson had never played on an organized team until his sophomore year at the new school. He claims that the best junior high athlete that he ever saw was future Washington star Harry Cherry's older sister, Gertrude. She was certainly a forerunner for girls' sports although she had zero athletic opportunities in high school. But, Emerson's first football leader was junior Phil Bayt who would become Indianapolis' Mayor in the mid-1950's.

The young Continentals had only a tie with Carmel their first year. But they won six in '28 then eight by Emerson's senior year. Frank Luzar, Ishmael Lawlis, Gerald Shirkey, Marion Milam, Norman Long, Chuck Dulla and Orion Gabert were among his buddies and fellow footballers. In 1928 they lost to Cathedral as the first IPS school to play the Catholic team from North Meridian St. and then defeated them 39-0 the last game in 1929. Haughville boys played on both teams. Old Washington Park, where the team played all of their home games until 1930, was located where today's Indianapolis Zoo is found and was also home for the Indianapolis Indians until the 1930's brought the 16th St. stadium.

As a basketball player young Emerson, along with their star back guard Bayt, lost the initial game played on the stage in late 1927 to an Archie Chadd led Bainbridge team, 80-12. But things would get better under another Manual transfer, Coach Rowland Jones. When they won their first game at Warren Central just east of Post Road on 10th Street, the street-car ride home was one of elation after they mobbed each other on the basketball floor.

When he met his girlfriend, Catherine Murphy class of '32, at Oren's drugstore after the game he was chaperoned by his teammate Earl Murphy, her brother. Eventually, Emerson would "pin" Catherine. After high school Catherine would marry another classmate, Jerry Brothers. In later years the Brothers family would normally celebrate New Years' Eve with the Carter family.

Emerson was the first three-sport star in the school's history and became the first individual state champ. He won the IHSAA Pole Vault State Championship in 1930 at Butler University after a 5th place his sophomore year and a 2nd in the spring of 1929 at Tech. Using a bamboo pole he vaulted 12' 4 ¾" into a sand pit. It was the spring of 1961 when Jim's GWHS record was broken by Ken Corey's 12' 6 ½" vault. Jim wrote Ken a congratulatory note which Corey's still has in 2010.

When he graduated from GWHS his first grade teacher from School 30, Matilda Morgan who lived in the first house south of Washington Street on the east side of Belmont, presented him with a fancy pocket watch. Her 4'10" 100 lb. stature belied the respect she demanded from her Westside students.

Emerson's participation in the 1930 summer National Track Meet in Chicago would not have been possible without his dad's railroad pass which he borrowed. His 14' long bamboo pole traveled in the baggage car. Disembarking at the 63rd St. station, he stayed overnight at a U. of Chicago fraternity house. He failed to place in the national meet. But West Lafayette awaited him.

The Indianapolis Purdue Alumni Association would pay the $100 tuition for aspiring football players with the boys working as bus boys or kitchen clean-up to pay for their own room-and-board.

Freshmen could not play varsity in any sport. In practice as a basketball freshman he was normally assigned to guard junior John Wooden from Martinsville. Then, when Jim (the Purdue powers-that-be told Emerson that he would now be known as Jim) suffered a serious thigh infection after a hard hit by a fraternity friend in the pre-season his sophomore year, his football career almost never began. He left school after ineffective therapy but returned in 1932 and still maintained status as a sophomore. Head Coach Noble Kizer from Plymouth, who had been guard and one of the "Seven Mules" with the Four Horsemen Notre Dame team of 1924, didn't name his starting team until they were posted minutes before the game. When the two sophomores, #99 Jim and #88 Duane Purvis, saw their names on the Yankee Stadium wall before the New York University game neither realized that they would become legendary in Purdue annals. Jim was penciled-in ahead of All Big Ten back Fred Hecker. Purvis would become the NCAA javelin champ in the spring of 1933. Both were named All-Stars in 1935.

Coach Kizer's Notre Dame single-wing shift with a balanced line in 1932 allowed Jim to score his first varsity TD against Kansas State, a 35-yd. jaunt. The Twins also accounted for most of the 304 rushing yards against Northwestern in Evanston.

During the 1933 season Jim would score six TDs while Purvis scored three. Against Ohio U. he had a 53-yarder. Versus Chicago, Wisconsin, Carnegie Tech (an eastern powerhouse at the time), and IU he had TD sprints of 52, 40, 85, and 17 respectively with another short TD against Tech in Purdue's 17-7 victory. Purdue, with Jim handling the chore at times, became known as a team that would pass on 1st and 2nd down much like the Rockne-led Notre Dame teams of the 1920's.

The Twins senior year of 1934 saw the graduation of most of Purdue's outstanding linemen. But the first two losses were out of conference to Rice and Notre Dame and the final game IU loss was precipitated perhaps by Jim not playing due to an injury. Earlier Jim had a TD pass vs. Iowa in the 13-6 win as well as a 64-yd. rushing TD against Wisconsin. But the Chicago University Big Ten showdown at midseason with 32,000 fans may have been Jim's showcase game. Chicago's junior star, Jay Berwanger who would win the very first Heisman Trophy in

1935, was outplayed by our Washington High great. Jim rushed for two TDs, one for 60 yards, and passed for another in Purdue's 26-20 win.

The Touchdown Twins, with Jim at left halfback and safety along with Duane at right halfback and DB in their 6-2-2-1 defense, would only lose four games in three years while winning the Big Ten title in 1932. Their loss to Iowa in 1933 and to IU in 1934 cost them a share of the trophy each time. And they also lost only to Notre Dame and Rice outside of the Big Ten. (note: in 1898 there were only eight teams in the league with IU joining in 1899. But not until Ohio State joined in the 1920's did the Western Athletic Conference officially become the Big Ten.)

Things were different in those years. There was no "home and home" scheduling. And Purdue did not have a very large stadium or following. Potential gate receipts always predicated where the game was to be played. All three of Jim's games against Minnesota were played at Minnesota. In 1932 Purdue beat ND 17-7 but the score was turned around in 1934 with both games in South Bend. And Purdue always played Chicago in Chicago. They had few home games. Over three years the Purdue record would read 7-0-1 (Purdue's first undefeated team), 6-1-1 and 5-3 with one co-Big Ten title. They only lost two Big Ten games.

The 1934 IU loss, in which Jim didn't play, was especially hard to take. Their star QB, Don Veller from Sullivan, had been Jim's QB and friend at Purdue when both were freshmen in 1930. Veller would become Head Football Coach at Florida State in 1948 and posted a 31-12-1 record over five years.

Over a three-year career Jim remains in Purdue's record book in average rushing yards per carry at 5.37 yards behind only Leroy Keyes and Purvis. And he had 6.02 yards per run in 1934. Into 2010 Jim is 19th in career rushing yards at 1,547 while #6 in career rushing average.

Both "Twins" would be selected among the 44 college players to play the Bears at Chicago's Soldiers' Field in August 1935. That was only the second year for the annual pre-season contest which endured until 1976 when it was disbanded by NFL Commissioner Pete Rozelle after concerns for injuries to high priced pros as well as the missed practice time the potential first year players lost with their respective teams. But one of Jim's teammates in that game was a Michigan center named Gerald Ford, the future President of the United States. And the coaches challenged a sprint at practice one day. They pitted the Touchdown Twins against USC's Cotton Warburton, Alabama's Don Hutson and Buzz Borries of Navy in a 100-yd. dash. Jim was leading at the 50-yd. mark but finished last in the friendly sprint.

The night before the big game Jim went "nightclubbing" with Fordham's Borden, the same Borden who had injured him the next to last game, along with Stan Kostka (another famous Minnesota fullback) and big tackle Phil Bengtson, future Green Bay coach, also from the Golden Gophers. They set out to see blonde bombshell Kitty Davis and her fan dance similar to the famous Sally Rand flutter a couple of years earlier.

In a driving rainstorm under the lights the Bears won 5-0 behind their star fullback Pug Manders. Like Bronko Nagurski before him he had been a star at the University of Minnesota.

All eight NFL teams contacted him. The best offer was $300 per game but with no insurance or any guarantees. College football was still a bigger draw at the time and if one was injured then that was their tough luck. Only 11 of the 44 All-Stars entered the NFL. But Jim still had to get his very first driver's license and auto. He had worn his first pair of long-pants as a Purdue student. He had always worn knickers as a Continental lad.

So Jim accepted a coaching-teaching job at Lowell High School in Lake County during the height of the Depression. He left after only one year to replace Tech's Emmett Lowery (class of

1929 winning the state tournament sportsmanship award in basketball) at Mankato State in Minnesota as head football coach.

Ironically, Manual High School and Butler University's Walt Floyd would replace Jim. Then Jim was contacted by his college coach, Noble Kizer, and was criticized for not recommending a Purdue guy to take his place. But Floyd had lived on North Sheffield Ave. near what would become Washington High. He was a Manual star in the early-1920's. And Floyd's dad had been the neighborhood barber just west of Belmont St. on the south side of the National Road charging 25-cents per haircut. Floyd would have great success at Lowell, according to Jim, but would eventually return to Indianapolis and Manual High School. Floyd would enter the football, basketball and baseball Indiana Halls of Fame in his later years.

At Lowell in the 1930's the high school had a two hour activities-lunch period at mid-day (11 to 1) and that's when it was mandatory to hold football practice. One of his players became Purdue team doctor. Dr. Bill Combs continued as team physician until the late 1960's.

Coaching only 90 miles south of Minneapolis at Mankato State was not the biggest benefit that Jim garnered. A young beauty shop operator, Florence Morrow, would become his sweetheart and then wife by 1937. They would marry and have three children and three grandkids before her death in 1994. Sharon (1941), Jim (1944), and Jill (1955) are their kids. Jim currently has six grandkids and great-grandkids. One has a classic first name, Carter.

By 1939 Jim was offered an assistant coaching job in football at the University of Dayton in Ohio. The only stipulation was that he had to take the Head Basketball position there, too. The AD noted to Jim that since he was from Indiana he must "know" basketball. Basketball was not a priority in most Ohio colleges, or in many colleges, in those days. One game, a year or two after World War II and just before Jackie Robinson's courageous 1947, pitted his team against Kentucky coached by Adolph Rupp. Dayton received an official note declaring that if they arrived with their one "colored" player that the game would be canceled. Rupp later apologized but segregation was an unfortunate reality at the time.

In 1938 another Carter, Marion known as "Red" (b. 1920), would graduate from Washington High and head toward Purdue. Red also was a starter at Purdue. Curly Julian once noted that he was greatly impressed by the brains, brawn, and good looks of Red. Curly had gone to GWHS in the fall of 1937 for the first time. Mrs. Viola Sanders also told me that her first boyfriend at School #30 was that young red-head who lived a couple of streets east of her. After Red's junior year at Purdue, he was drafted into the military. He joined the Army Air Corps hoping to become a pilot. But, according to Jim, his eyes were not up to pilot status and he was assigned as a bombardier. In a training exercise over the desert in Roswell, New Mexico in 1943 Red's plane had a mid-air collision with another plane. All five on Red's aircraft were killed. The other plane's entire crew survived.

Ironically, famous author John Steinbeck followed Red's crew when they initially trained in Texas. A subsequent patriotic book titled "Bombs Away" would emerge which included pictures of Red whose pseudonym was Alan in the Steinbeck book.

I had seen Red's big smile senior picture in my mother's junior yearbook. But when I saw the larger version in Jim's bedroom in April of 2008 that was signed, "To a Swell Brother, from Red," I barely held my composure. Red was one of 95 Washington boys killed during the four years of WW II.

In 1943 Jim's older brother offered him a job with the Dupont Company. He would be Recreational Director for 65,000 employees in Pasko, Washington. Jim would serve a three plant wide community of workers until the completion of the secret project. Later, they found out they were producing materials for what history knows as the Manhatten Project, components of the atomic bomb being assembled in Oak Ridge, Tennessee.

He returned to Dayton after the war but headed for Terre Haute Wiley in 1949 as football coach. In 1951 he would land in Anderson, Indiana as a teacher-coach. He was football coach for 15 years and retired as a history teacher in 1977 after 26 years. Another prolific Continental athlete and pole-vaulter, Carter Byfield class of '44, would be one of his assistant coaches for five years before heading to Decatur Central as head coach.

And another irony in his life: his future son-in-law, Bill Jones, would win the State Championship in Pole Vault for Anderson H.S. in 1954, twenty-four years after Jim's then-state record vault. Then his grandson, Brad Jones, would win the State Championship in the 1600-meter run in 1980 for Anderson H.S., exactly fifty years after Jim's amazing 12' 4 ¾" feat with a bamboo pole into a sand pit. Both Jones boys went to Purdue and graduated as engineers.

Among Emerson's favorite Washington teachers were principal Mr. Gingery, Football Coach Bogue, Track Coach Cleon Davies, Basketball Coach Rowland Jones, Spanish teacher Mr. Bock and his Shop teacher Mr. Harold Harding who taught him both at School 16 and GWHS. Once history teacher Charley Money inspired him. Mr. Money's reputation was such that it was said that the longer the report the better the grade. So Emerson wrote a long report imbedded with the acclamation that "if you read this I will buy you a coke." Maybe Mr. Money didn't really read the entire essay was Emerson's cynical thought. When he was called to stay after class one day he thought he was in some sort of trouble. But, to his amusement, Mr. Money challenged him to live up to his offer and buy him a coke at Oren's Drugstore on the corner of Belmont & Washington Streets.

When he hitchhiked, along with 20 buddies from Washington and Cathedral, to the Minnesota vs. Notre Dame game in the fall of 1929 Emerson laughed as he told how they all waited at the main gate while the Notre Dame team was admitted into the stadium. As the gates swung open they all charged through with the ND team and most safely "crashed" the football party in South Bend.

Ironically enough, after Jim's frosh season (probably in December of 1930) the featured speaker for the football banquet was Purdue's coach Noble Kizer's college coach. None other than Knute Rockne who would be killed within a few weeks in the infamous plane crash early in 1931.

Mr. Carter would be the featured speaker at Washington High's rededication on November 16, 2008 along with Senator Lugar and Curly Julian. With his granddaughter present Jim noted that he had not set foot inside Washington's building since his 1930 graduation. He also wistfully noted that his greatest wish was for the presence of brother Red with him. Some felt his presence as well as the spirits of so many other Continentals.

Everyone's life is a history book. But, it seems to me, Mr. Carter's history is both unique and inspiring. His independent lifestyle at age 98 attest to his optimistic and positive attitude. He is a living tribute to the possibilities that were offered for over 68 years at beloved George Washington High School.

And his legacy will live on for many more years. In 2009 he presented his great-grandson, Billy Jones (Lapel High School class of 2017), with his white sweater given to all August 1935 All-Stars which reads "All American 1934."

HARRY CHERRY, class of 1934

Two years after the famous White River flood which led to the concrete levee system on the west bank and two years before America's entrance into the Great War, the Cherry family of 114 N. Mickner (now Reisner) welcomed the 12th of 14 kids. Harry Clarence Cherry was born May 21, 1915 in the house on the southwest corner of Ohio & Mickner in Stringtown. In 2010 Harry and his wife of 64 years, the former Georgie Enyert (class of '38), still spend five months of the year at Sun City, Florida away from their Seymour, Indiana home. Only Harry and one of his four sisters survive, Mrs. Mary Harrington. Mary was #13. The youngest, a girl, died at age 8 in the 1920's. Mary and her late husband, Creighton, had two daughters Sherry (Washington class of '61) and Mary Jane (Northwest class of '66) who lived on Jackson Street between Belleview & Addison until moving to Eagledale in the early 1960's. Both attended School #50.

Lauter Boys' Club was Harry's first and probably most significant life changing experience. The Club had initially been built by the owners of the Lauter Furniture factory as a recreational

HARRY CHERRY
Indiana University

facility for their employees. One of Harry's brothers actually survived the 1913 flood crouching in the attic of the Lauter building. In the 21st century the Lauter family still maintains a viable furniture business at Harding and Washington St. In 1913 the Lauters donated the building to Boys' Clubs, Inc. which continued its service to the youth of the area as a community center until closing in 1969. Today the building is used by the Indianapolis Zoo as a storage facility.

E. B. Kelley, the long-time director, became Harry's first impressionable role-model. In 2002 White River Parkway from the National Road to New York Street and the New York Street bridge were officially dedicated as the "E.B. Kelley Parkway and Bridge."

Harry's mom Minnie Bosell Cherry was from Ohio and his dad Edward was born in Virginia. All of their kids attended School 16 on the Parkway but only Harry and sister Mary stayed in high school after the age of 16. His athletic success was undoubtedly the main reason he was able to convince his dad that he didn't have to get a job except the part-time job at Lauter's where he began working in 1927. And Mr. Kelley's advice and encouragement were invaluable to the pre-teen.

Football coach Henry Bogue had a rule that a boy had to weigh 125-lbs. or more in order to play, even as a freshman. Harry weighed only 123-lbs. So he had to plead for his athletic life but his foot speed helped, too. So, Bogue made a reserve give up his football pants. During his junior year the Continentals set a school record, which still stands, by defeating Carmel 104-0. Harry scored six touchdowns in the first half and the reserves played the entire second half. By season's end Harry repeated his All-City status for the second time in 1932 (and a third time his senior year). Joining him on the honor team were tackles Joe Dezelan and Cliff Baumbach along with center Louie Luzar from their 7-1-1 team losing only to the Libby team from Toledo, Ohio and tying Marion. Dezelan was Cathedral High's famous football coach from 1944 through 1969, Baumbach went to Purdue on a football scholarship but died of blood poisoning after his religious beliefs denied him medical attention, and Luzar's older brother was Frank. Frank was the later long-time GWHS teacher-coach (1935-1974) and NFL official.

Other prominent footballers were quarterback (& future grandfather of ESPN personality Vince Welch) Hop Howard, future long-time Bloomington coach Lavern Burns, future Huddleston Restaurant owner Swede Radcliffe, Alex Yavonovich, and future Continental coach Dave Hine. Coach Bogue's "Pony Backfield" was his tactic of sending an entire four man backfield (two platoon) into the game at once to run his "Box Offense." That offensive strategy was slightly different from the Single-wing in that a direct center snap could be sent to any one of the four backs.

Harry was a two-year All-State football player but he also excelled in basketball and track. With Coach Davies in track Harry won the indoor state in the new Butler Fieldhouse in the spring of 1934 clearing 11'6". His best ever of 12'3" did not surpass Washington's first ever 1930 State Champ Emerson "Jim" Carter's almost 12'5" but it was remarkable with a bamboo pole into a sand pit. His best Broad Jump was 22'3" and he ran the 100-yard dash at 10.2 on the cinder track along with Hop Howard and Lavern Burns on the 880 Relay team. Harry was the star of our very first Track Sectional Champs in 1933. Washington dropped baseball after Harry's freshman year during the money crunch of the Depression.

But football was still where he made his mark and met his destiny. After the 21-0 victory over Kirkland his junior year the team had a post game dinner at Enyert's Washington Café then located directly east of the school (Sablosky's was there in the 1960's). Cute little 7th-grader Georgie delivered the bread for her family's restaurant and she developed a "crush" on star player Cherry. They would marry 14 years later. The Enyerts lived at 132 South Belmont.

During Harry's sophomore year he had to don a leather-covered, steel face-mask for his helmet. The neighborhood shoe-maker did the honors. Most players in American football didn't use face masks until about 30 years later (and mouth-pieces were not mandated until the early '60's) but Harry had lost three teeth during their 9-1 season (the team scored 304 points and gave up only 54). The teeth were knocked loose in one of the first two games of the 1931 season and became abscessed. When the dentist, Dr. Hoffer, put him on the floor and, with the dentist's doctor-son holding Harry down, he bound the mouth wounds with 17 clamps. He was then sent downtown for a tetanus shot. That was at noon. At 3 PM he played a varsity game. For a water break Harry had to lie on his back and have it poured into his mouth avoiding the face-mask.

Football admission cost was 25-cents but the 1932 City Championship game at the Butler Bowl cost spectators $1. Tech led the Continentals at halftime in the snow 0-7. But the second half was all Washington. Harry returned an intercepted pass 104-yards for the momentum changing TD and our school won 27-7. His senior football season in 1933 was not as productive without his three All-City linemen and QB Howard who was disqualified from playing either because he had received some cash for playing summer baseball or because he had played community basketball at Hawthorne Center (Hop was reinstated for track season). But Harry at 5'10" 153-lbs. running behind Coach Bogue's unbalanced line still won a full football scholarship to Indiana University.

Harry also found time to socialize even after athletics and the 3-mile round trip walk to school each day ("uphill both ways"). His prom date was Jane Fleetmeyer of 69 North Tremont. They danced the afternoon away on the gym floor with the other Continentals. The gym is today the back part of the stage in the auditorium. He recalls that there were usually only two student automobiles in the parking lot. And, he still possesses scrapbooks that Miss Fleetmeyer accumulated for him.

Washington had only been in existence for three years when Harry entered as a freshman. Mr. "Pinky" Hargraves was the strong disciplinarian as Vice Principal and Harry fondly brags on Coach Bogue as "before his time and….the smartest coach ever." Assistant football coach Dave Easton was also a favorite along with track coach Cleon Davies. And, of course, principal Walter Gingery was the standard-bearer from 1927 until his retirement in 1951. Ironically Mr. Gingery's son was Harry and Georgie's minister in Sun City, Florida until his 1997 retirement at the age of 75. And his favorite all-time teacher was Miss Hester who taught Biology.

When Harry went to IU his "full ride" included room, board, tuition, books and $50 a month; not bad for 1934-1938 during the height of the Depression. He was the starting halfback for three years under Head Coach Bo McMillan. The three assistants were Coach Graham (an All-American from Kansas), Billy Thom (who was the famous wrestling coach at IU), and Clyde Smith (who would later become head at IU then at Arizona before becoming AD for the Wildcats). Harry was also one of the safeties on defense during the one-platoon days in college. His most memorable games were against Michigan, Ohio State, Minnesota, Purdue, and Nebraska. The Hoosiers won the Old Oaken Bucket games vs. Purdue in 1935 and 1937. But Harry says that the 1936 Bucket game which ended in a 20-20 tie was the most exciting game in which he played.

After working at Armour Meat Packing in Indianapolis Harry joined the Army before Pearl Harbor. During his 5 ½ years in the military most of his time was spent at bases in Florida but he did spend most of a year on Tinian Island in the Pacific (where the atomic bomb planes departed). He was assigned to a B-29 outfit as the Physical Director and Special Service Officer.

In 1946 Harry joined his old mentor Mr. Kelley as a Boys' Club Director. He was assigned to the English Avenue branch. His most prolific boy was none other than future Tech Mr. Basketball, Purdue baseball-basketball star then baseball coach, and Butler basketball coach Joe Sexson. Joe is always considered one of the greatest athletes ever from Marion County. As a nine and ten-year old, Sexson dominated boys two and three years older than he was, according to Harry. After twelve years the Cherry family moved to Seymour, Indiana when Harry was named Executive Director of their Boys' Club. He retired in 1980. His son-in-law took his place. Harry and Georgie's son and daughter were grown and they were ready to play golf year-round spending winters in Florida.

Son Stephen is 60 in 2010 and daughter Melinda Stanfield is 54 with a grandson age 30 and granddaughter age 26 for Georgie and Harry.

"Twinkle-toes" Cherry, as Georgie still calls him (based on his running style), turns 95-years-young May 2010 but he can still remember his first hero. Silent movie cowboy star Tom Mix who visited the Dusenberg automobile plant on the southwest corner of Harding and Washington Streets when Harry was about ten. His shining spurs and large white hat sparkled in the eyes of the young boy from Mickner Street as Mix tooled his Dusey around the oval test track in the mid-1920's. Perhaps a symbol of a bright, glistening future for one of Washington High's most talented athletes and citizens.

Harry says that E.B. Kelley was a father-figure to every boy who entered Lauter Boys' Club. Mr. Kelley arrived at the Club in 1926 as a 21-year-old. He had graduated from Tech High School. He left 43 years later in 1969 when it closed. His stepson, Bobby Joe Kelley, was killed in World War II. White River Parkway between the National Road and New York Street as well as the New York Street Bridge was named and dedicated to Mr. Kelley in 2002.

On Saturday, October 6, 2007 before the 4th quarter of the IU vs. Minnesota football game in Bloomington, Harry walked onto the turf. Along with his wife and daughter, Harry was announced to the crowd as "Mr. IU football." To the growing applause of the crowd, as they realized what was being stated, Harry was proclaimed as IU's oldest living football player at age 92. He also was noted as a 60-year season ticket holder. Harry wore a modern #11 while a picture of him from the mid-1930's showed him in jersey #11 on the electronic jumbotron.

Lessons Learned from Legendary Luzar

(Larry Glaze graduated in 1960. He offered this portrayal of Coach Luzar.)

Any male Continental who was a PE student during Frank Luzar's tenure at GWHS has at least one story concerning this dynamic force in the history of GWHS. His military training came into play on a daily basis while Coach Luzar directed physical education classes and coached the baseball team. He had been an All-City fullback graduating from our school in 1931 before attending Wabash College. He served at Great Lakes Naval Station during World War II where he learned many of his physical education tests and scoring practices. Frank had returned to his high school in 1935 and was an assistant football coach into the 1950's. He also coached golf his last few years as a teacher, retiring in 1974. He died in 1997.

To this day in 2010, after I shower, I wipe all excess water off before toweling. Anyone who had Frank as a gym teacher probably has continued the same routine. He was a stickler for discipline and cleanliness. The towels provided by GWHS were thin by today's standards and the personal "squeegee" procedure made the drying process bearable. As you threw the towel in the hamper on the way out of the shower, he would conduct a spot check to see if your towel was damp. If you had skipped the shower (so you wouldn't be set when you walked your girl to class), he would wait until you were almost dressed and request you get back in and soap up. Now you were on the verge of being tardy to Mrs. Lyon's English class—not a good idea!

Every Friday, Frank was at the door as you exited checking to make sure you took your gym clothes home. Frank had a specific way you rolled and folded in the shirt outside your trunks, socks, and that other item every young man was required to sport. Every Monday, Frank would line us up and seek out anyone who attempted to slide by without having our gym clothes laundered over the weekend. Heaven forbid if your wrinkled, grimy t-shirt gave you away and death to you if you forgot your gym suit at home. Your punishment would be to sit out gym class in your street clothes, be "debited" points on your grade and generally be in the Luzar doghouse, which was not a good place to be in, for a period of time.

His main penalty for various and sundry violations of his "code of conduct" in gym class was laps. Laps around the gym, laps around the track, anywhere a lap could be run. He came from the school of thought that laps were good for the body, mind, and soul.

The baseball team was another avenue for Frank to institute his form of discipline. The baseball dressing room was no place for horseplay, at least while Coach was around. Of course, our group of Westside diamondmen were challenged by this and pulling a stunt or two without getting caught in the act was the name of the game.

One of the most memorable happened during the 1959 season. Senior pitcher Jeff James, drafted by the Phillies after graduation, gave that day's starting pitcher a certain purgative disguised as a chocolate bar, better known as Exlax. This act of kindness took place at lunch. The result was that crafty lefthander Horace Mitchell spent the afternoon sitting behind a green metal door in the locker room pondering his fate. Of course, the afternoon's activity sapped every bit of Mitchell's energy.

We all kept the strictest code of secrecy concerning who the jokester might be. Coach Luzar, who appeared to know nothing about why Mitchell was in such bad shape, wryly wrote James' name onto the lineup card as the starting pitcher. James, with only a day's rest from his last start, knew he had been discovered. I don't recall Jeff's performance that day, but I do recall him complaining of sore legs and a sore elbow the next day. Coach Luzar's remedy for a sore arm—you got it—laps! "Gets the blood moving." Hence, no player ever spoke publicly about any soreness, no matter how much pain you may be enduring.

Horace Mitchell, who had a round house curveball that dropped batters to their knees, did not return from the Vietnam War....I think of him often.

Somewhere in Coach Luzar's "medical training," he acquired an all encompassing method to assist in the healing of all types of injuries. He had a plastic squeeze bottle full of merthiolate that was used for all kinds of ailments. Although we were issued a primitive set of sliding pads, most of us were still susceptible to abrasions on the hip from improper sliding techniques. At the end of practice or a game, you could always spot the players who had burns. They would be in and out of the shower as quickly as possible trying to avoid Coach walking around the room taking target practice with his stinging spray.

Since GWHS was nestled into a neighborhood, we practiced and played our home games at Rhodius Park. What seemed like a ten-mile hike was only a few blocks. Coach would drive his car to practice. He would never take the same route or leave school at the same time. Therefore, nobody knew where he might be lurking. If he caught you walking to Rhodius: laps. If he caught you fraternizing with a coed along the way: laps. Have you ever run on pavement with baseball cleats?

Finally, we never questioned Frank Luzar's authority. He was always in great shape. His finger-tip push-ups were a distinctive Luzar-exercise. He did not initiate fear, yet the respect we had for him caused us to stay in line. He kept his distance. Yet, we knew he cared about us. Always calling us by our last name, Coach had a way of getting our attention.

He was always in excellent physical condition. His body fat must have been no more than 5%. His square jaw, muscular frame and no-nonsense attitude gave him the look and presence of a man made of steel. I recall seeing Frank on television refereeing a New York NFL football game on Sunday afternoon. Hall of Fame Giants linebacker Sam Huff challenged Frank on a call. Guess who backed down?

I taught and coached for four years out of college and I instituted many of his disciplinary rules and regulations. You always hear "you coach (and teach) as you were coached." I can say that I copied one of the most decent persons I was privileged to know. I'm sure that Frank Luzar kept many a young man on a straight path that later made a difference in their life.

CLOYD "CURLY" JULIAN
GWHS 1937-1977

Washington High School's principal, Mr. Walter, was named as the first principal of brand new Arlington High on Indianapolis' northeast side for the grand opening in the fall of 1961. So, 50-year-old Vice Principal and long-time Continental, Curly Julian was cast into a much-deserved position as the school's fourth leader. He took the helm in January 1961.

Curly was born November 30, 1910 in southern Indiana's Scott County on a farm near the small town of Austin. He was one of seven boys born to a musically-inclined mother who, according to Curly, longed for a girl who would aspire to a career in music. But all the boys were athletes much to their mother's dismay, Mr. Julian laughed.

In Curly's senior year of 1928 with a 9th through 12th grade student roster numbering only 46, and with ten in the graduating class, Mr. Julian reminisced that perhaps his happiest moment in his athletically motivated life was the basketball championship at the Madison Sectionals. It was the very first thing that he noted to me. And it was the year that a Johnny Wooden led Martinsville team lost to Muncie Central in the title game by a score of 13-12. So much for the older generation's thoughts on class basketball.

Then he traveled about 90 miles to the northwest to Depauw University. His voyage started north on Highway 31, then west to Bloomington, then on to Spencer where #231 carried him into Greencastle. Receiving a Rector Scholarship included an obligation to "wait tables." One of Curly's assignments in the fall of 1931 was at a sorority where Rockford College transfer Betty Brooks resided as a junior year student. One of her sorority sisters set up Betty on a "blind date" with Curly for a campus dance. It was "love at first sight" according to the erstwhile busboy.

But the 1932 National Collegiate Track Championship at Soldiers' Field in Chicago may have been Curly's greatest sporting achievement. His two-mile time of 9:32 qualified him for the Olympic tryouts for the Los Angeles Olympics in the brand new Coliseum. He missed the cut but continued to hold the Depauw two mile and cross country record into the 1960's.

With the depression affecting the entire country Curly returned to Austin where he was teacher for two years as well as the baseball and basketball coach. But then a new town trustee was elected and he decided to fire all six teachers. So Mr. Julian was faced with the decision to leave home to take a job with Swift Co. in Grenville, Iowa as manager of their ice cream plant. But not before he asked Betty to travel with him both to Iowa and for the rest of her life as his bride in 1934. She came to little Austin from her home in Chicago. Their marriage lasted over 62 years until her death in the early spring of 1997.

Unbeknownst to Curly as he took graduate classes at the University of Iowa, Indianapolis Washington's principal Mr. Gingery called Depauw requesting a track coach who could teach history. Little did Mr. Gingery realize that his choice of 26-year old Cloyd Julian would obviously be the best decision of his 24 years as principal. Curly gave up vanilla-chocolate-strawberry for Continental purple with Julian topping.

The first class at GWHS that saw Curly Julian was the senior class of 1938. Continental icons Mary Jane Howell, Ray Funk, Gladys Huddleston, Bob Kersey, Virginia Garrabrandt, Marshall Reed, and Marion "Red" Carter were all noted by Mr. Julian to me at the turn of the 21st century as a "great class."

The Julians first home was on Riverside Drive across from South Grove golf course next door to Washington's Spanish teacher Mr. Bock and his wife Mrs. Hester Baker Bock Erwin (as she often described herself) who continued teaching Spanish and Latin at Continentaland into the 1970's. Her dad was Mr. Baker the founder of Christamore and Hawthorne House as well as preacher at West Park Christian Church. Mr. Bock died of a heart attack while washing his car in the 1950's. Mr. Julian's son Bill and daughter JoAnne were born while they lived on Riverside Drive. Bill would graduate in 1957 from GWHS but JoAnne graduated from North Central in 1965 after their residence move.

In 1943 Mr. Julian saw the head of his draft board downtown who alerted Curly that he would soon be drafted since so many colored men had already been drafted from his area. Some racial sensitivity was present even then, believe it or not. So Curly decided to enlist in the V-5 program. That decision allowed for civilian coaches to teach at a pre-flight school. His second assignment was to Chapel Hill at the University of North Carolina. The one-month intensive training course challenged many of the men physically. But not "in-shape" Curly Julian, according to him. Up at 5 with day-long strenuous physical activity and straight to bed at 9:30 PM. IU basketball coach Branch McCracken from Monrovia, Indiana was in Curly's platoon. Soon Mr. Julian was promoted to Lt. Commander and coached basketball with future Minneapolis Lakers coach and Purdue administrator Fred Shaus. Their teams won 42 of 45 games from their base in Memphis.

After the war it was back to the westside of Indianapolis and a renewed collaboration with Jim Otto who had also come to our school in the mid-1930's. Eventually the "Otto, Julian, Tether" health textbooks would dominate the market throughout the U.S. And the Biology textbooks by those same three accounted for 2/3rds of all high school American texts. Both sales would allow the two Continental teachers to financially enhance their lifestyles. It was not a coincidence that the adoption of their textbooks in 1955 would coincide with the Julian family's move to the Kessler residence where Curly would stay until 2002 when he moved to Marquette Manor on the northside.

But in 1952 Mr. Julian left Washington for the friendly, but somewhat non-fulfilling, confides of the downtown administrative offices. He became a central office consultant for IPS athletics and helped set the foundation for the solid athletic programs that reached a crescendo in the 1960's throughout the Indianapolis Public Schools. But he longed for a "hands on" personal relationship again and was given a promise of the next vice principalship in IPS. Ironically, with the retirement of principal Barnhart in 1956 from Washington High, Curly returned home.

Mr. Walter, who was disinterested in athletics according to Mr. Julian, allowed Curly to direct the sports programs at Washington High as one of his main responsibilities. Soon he would have to make two difficult decisions. In the summer of 1960 Vice Principal Julian asked long-time friend Dave Hine to step aside for young Jerry Oliver as basketball head coach. Coach Oliver had come to Continentaland from Ball State and Rochester, Indiana in 1955. Mush Hine had graduated from Washington High in 1936 and was an outstanding athlete at Hanover College. Then his choice of parochial school coach Bob Springer in 1962, at the behest of Frank Luzar, to replace Joe Tofil was another hard process to effect. Coach Springer, who played at Purdue, had been a star Cathedral athlete for Washington High grad Joe Dezelan but Coach Tofil had been a top IU football player from the football state of Ohio. But great athletic and social results followed.

When Mr. Walter left to prep the new Arlington High, Mr. Julian grabbed the reigns of power and would preside over an unprecedented period in our high school's history in sports and academics. And it is not by coincidence that all six of our school's top-level State Championships were during Mr. Julian's leadership. During the 1960's and 1970's, at the top level, only our school won any state championship in football or basketball among all of Marion County's schools. We won two of each.

His first fall convocation for the incoming freshmen class of 1,000 in 1961 was highlighted with his classic affirmations of "nothing succeeds like success" and "Continentals have a backbone not a wishbone." When he retired in 1977 at the age of 66 his legacy was unmatched. His contemporaries were both his subordinates and his friends. Sweet Barbara Jean, Bogue, Johnny Williams, Luzar, Florina, Mrs. Hanna, Mrs. Hatfield, the Fight Song, Mr. Watkins, John Bradley, Al Hamilton, Basil Sfreddo, Charlie Brown, Vi Sanders and many others. All can attest to the great atmosphere at GWHS under the astute leadership of one special man. Now hear this: It's the ultimate job well done by Mr. Washington High, Curly Julian.

VIOLA BAZIS SANDERS
Class of 1937

Mrs. Viola Sanders died in late January 2004. She was the mother of two daughters who also graduated from Washington High, Debbie ('64) and Nikki ('71). Debbie married 1965 State Championship manager and Marion County Deputy Sheriff John Wesseler. But more importantly Mrs. Sanders was the unofficial queen of Continentaland. She lived in the same house in the first block of South Belmont in which she was born in 1920. And, she continued to try to revive the west side spirit by continuing her support of Washington Community School, which welcomed high school students for the first time by 2001. If there is ever a Washington High School Hall of Fame, Mrs. Sanders has to be the first inductee.

The following lead article was printed in the "Staff Update" for Warren Central High School by principal Tony Burchett who graduated from Washington in 1971 and was a teacher-coach at our school from 1977 until his forced busing "pink slip" in 1981.

Tony wrote: In this town of ours and in our profession, we have many, many individuals who are truly difference makers in the lives of young adults. Where does our influence begin and end with the students of Warren Central is very difficult to determine. Earlier this week, Dr. Hinckley (the Superintendent) made a reference to a remark by her first grade teacher and how that remark had a profound impact on her life.

On Wednesday of this week, Viola Sanders, age 83, was called by God. Mrs. Sanders was a pillar to those students and staff members who knew her at Indianapolis Washington High School (my alma mater). Her entire life from birth to death and including marriage was spent in one house on Belmont Avenue. She had no "fluffy titles" of importance nor was she "trained" in dealing with adolescents; yet her many roles as a support staff person allowed her to influence so many students.

Her showing Wednesday was filled with an overflow crowd of admirers who had come from all parts of the country to pay respects to the "attendance lady," "the athletic secretary," and simply the "First Lady of Washington High." When those in attendance were offered the opportunity to speak about Mrs. Sanders, Ralph Taylor, a black man, said that he puts Mrs. Sanders, a white woman, on the same pedestal as his mother. Ralph's words properly framed the impact of this "difference maker." Mrs. Sanders was laid to rest in a Northwestern purple turtleneck and a sweatshirt that read "Washington Continental, Class of 1937." Few "average" people realize the influences they can have over others. But, of course, Mrs. Sanders was far from average.

STROTHER MARTIN, class of 1937

Strother Martin was born in Kokomo, Indiana on March 26, 1919 and died of a heart attack in Thousand Oaks, California on the first day of August in 1980. The intervening 61 years completed another chapter in the Continental history book.

Mrs. Viola Bazis Sanders, class of '37, once told me that Strother sat in the back row of her senior English class. She also noted that she saw him strolling down Washington Street in 1977 during their 40th reunion activities.

While a young student at Washington he participated as a diver at the old Rhodius Park pool and became the National Junior Springboard Diving Champion in the 1930's. When he traveled to California after high school he became a swim instructor for the children of Hollywood stars Marion Davies and Charlie Chaplin.

During World War II he joined the Navy and was assigned as a swim instructor. After the war he attempted to make the U.S. Olympic diving team in 1948. But he fell short as a 29 year old when he placed 3rd in the try-outs.

But his Hollywood connections would come in handy and he appeared in his first movie as a character actor in "Storm Over Tibet" in 1952. He later won parts in the Disney feature "The Shaggy Dog" and then "The Wild & the Innocent" both in 1959.

Strother also appeared in a classic Rod Serling "Twilight Zone" episode in 1961 with Lee Marvin, Lee Van Cleef, and James Best where he dominated the first half of the 30 minute episode with dialogue framing the tone as well as plot to the story titled "The Grave." In it he rendered a not-quite-classic line "I recon' we can't spend the rest of our days being afraid of a dead man." In the credits he was placed above Van Cleef.

Then he became a Paul Newman favorite and was a scene-stealer in 1967's "Cool Hand Luke" when he rendered an all-time famous line as the chain boss-antagonist with "what we've got here is failure to communicate. Some men you just can't reach. So, you get what we had here last week. Which is the way he wants it. Well, he gets it." And Newman requested him for his "Butch Cassidy and the Sundance Kid" movie in 1969 as well as "Harper" earlier in 1966.

Other movies that he appeared in included "Shenandoah" with Jimmy Stewart in 1965, "Pocket Money" (1972), "Up in Smoke" (1978), "The Villain" (1979), "Hotwire" (1980), and Newman's hockey flick "Slap Shot" in 1977. Strother actually had the star role as Dr. Carl Stoner in the '73 cult classic "SSSSSSS" and suffered a serious snake-bite in the Bernard Kowalski film.

He was another unique and successful Continental.

AL CASE, class of 1938

Watching the coal smoke billowing from the New York Central train less than 30 feet yet ten feet higher than his backyard, young Alvin dreamed about graduating from School 50 to attend Washington High School. It was slightly less than one mile straight down the railroad tracks heading east from his Hancock Street family home to GWHS.

When he was born April 21, 1920 he was the seventh of eight kids. Oscar, Forrest, Barbara, Chet (long time west side lawyer who graduated from Manual H.S. while living in the first block south of Washington Street on Hancock, 3000 west), Orie, Nickie (mother of 1964 top student Janet Blake), and younger brother Norval (who would die in infancy) were his beloved siblings. In 2010 only Al and Nickie survive.

Casey, as he is affectionately known by Tom Carnegie and others, seems to be able to relate almost all things in his active life with his family and one of three things: Washington High School, Purdue University or the Indianapolis Motor Speedway.

School 50 principal Miss McCardle, all 100 pounds of her, seemed to represent what was both good and proper about society to young Al. And Mr. Kepner, the school custodian who was in charge of discipline and seemingly respected by every kid year after year, reflected the stability of the Mt. Jackson-Hawthorne neighborhood. To understand that the paddling board was wielded by the school custodian seems unrealistic in the 21st century but was normally accepted in the 1920's, '30's, and '40's. Mr. Kepner's great-granddaughter, Kelly Faris, became a star basketball player at Heritage Christian and is UConn's #6 player as a freshman on their nationally prominent team in 2010.

Purdue football was nationally prominent during most of the 20th century. The Western Conference (as it was called before becoming the Big Ten) by Al's 10th birthday was the top athletic conference in America. Once, when he listened to a Purdue loss, he cried over the radio broadcast. And when his childhood hero, Washington High's Emerson Carter, headed to Purdue to play football Al was transfixed. More than once he had lingered outside Oren's Drugstore at Belmont and Washington Street hoping to catch a close-up greeting from Emerson after games in the fall of 1929. Finally the meeting happened April 1, 2009 when he met his all-time hero at Mug 'n Bun on 10th St.

But as a grade school student he admired fellow classmate Bob Kersey from 249 North Pershing Street. Al noted that he always admired Bob's steady confidence as well as his academic and athletic abilities as a single-wing quarterback. So when Kersey traveled to Purdue along with Continental teammate Marion "Red" Carter, Emerson's younger brother, Casey cemented a life-long love for Purdue even though he never attended college. Al reminisced that Kersey became one of the group called the Flying Boilermakers during World War II. He thinks that Kersey was among an initial naval fighter jet escort for the Doolittle Raiders in April 1942. Kersey would eventually marry the widow of a fallen pilot buddy.

Al was sports editor for the Washington High newspaper in 1937-38 where he first began to share his love for sports. About age 13 he had watched as future Purdue three-sport starter, Cliff Baumbach, pulled a long home run over the National Road in 1933. Home plate was located where the 1937 gym's entrance would be built.

Al's mom and dad had come to Indianapolis from Kentucky during the first decade of the 20th century. Older brother Chet, the future Westside lawyer, once was "whipped" by tomboy Georgia Carmichael while walking to Hawthorne School 50 in the early 1920's. The Carmichael family had moved to 27 North Warman after Georgia's older brother, Hoagy of musical fame, graduated from Indiana University. Soon the Carmichaels moved to 130 South Neal where Georgia would then walk east down the National Road to School 16 with none other than a young Jim Emerson Carter.

Sitting next to School 30's Marion Carter in Miss Amy Keen's Home Room in Continentaland gave Al a chance to debate a comparison between his School 50 buddy, Kersey, and the younger brother of his childhood hero, Red Carter. At different times in American athletic Common Culture the debate was Mays vs. Mantle, Chamberlain vs. Russell, Unitas vs. Starr, Louis vs. Marchiano, and even Manning vs. Brady. But for young Alvin it was a win-win argument. Both Kersey and Carter would star as athletes and students through Washington, Purdue and as World War II heroes.

Classmate Marjorie Ryan attended Butler University and married Jim Hauss. Hauss played football for a young Tony Hinkle and would become line coach for Hink through his last team in 1969. And neighbor Carolyn Kord, class of '32, would marry Cathedral's Jack O'Neal, the brother of future Marion County Sheriff Bob.

After graduation Al took a job at Link-Belt on Addison Street and the New York Central RR. Among his many friends at work he was especially happy for the proud mother of 1981 Miss Basketball Cheryl Cook from Washington High. Years earlier he had befriended young Karen Armstrong during the war years. Miss Armstrong had traveled from Mankato, Minnesota seeking a job as the Great Depression was ending. Her connection to Indy was her brother-in-law, Jim Carter. She actually lived with Jim's parents at 101 S. Elder and walked the three blocks to her new job. Eventually Miss Armstrong would marry Don Cox. Don later became the long-time spotter for NASCAR driver Jeff Gordon.

But Al's May-job at the Motor Speedway began in 1946 and continues through 2010 and has allowed Casey to attain a level of popularity best expressed in the following press release in May, 2009:

Indianapolis Motor Speedway Centennial Era—Fact of the Day:

Alvin Case, 89, is working his 64th Indianapolis 500 this May and is one of the longest-serving employees at the track. Case runs the fire department office located in the infield near Turn 1. He worked for Link-Belt, a chain manufacturing company, from 1939-84, starting in the mail room and retiring as a process engineer. A conversation with Case reveals four loves: the Indianapolis Motor Speedway, Purdue University, baseball and his grandkids.

(About his start at the Indianapolis Motor Speedway): "The first two years I worked at the gates and took tickets at Gate 3. I remember the first year, 1946, the race was half over and we were still taking tickets. The cars were overheated and everything. It was a mess. The next year we took tickets again and, just as the bomb sounded, we heard a horrible noise and just about every motorcycle in Indiana jumped ahead of the crowd. Some of them had tickets and some of them did not. I thought, 'this isn't for me.' Clarence Cagle moved next to me in my apartment complex and we became good friends and he put me on the fire department. I've been there ever since. That was in '48. For maybe 12 years I worked on the track. At that time we had what we called the crash truck and it operated out of the pits. Whenever there was a wreck they'd sound the bell and we jumped on and went around the track. It was not like it is today. It was a little Studebaker that they put fire equipment on. We had a regular fireman that drove it. One time, I think it was 1950, a car caught on fire as it came out of the fourth turn and ended up on the straightaway right before the pits. It was the Brown Motor Car Special. By the time we got all around, the thing had burned up. The owner, he was mad. He said he had spent $19,000 while we were riding around the track. That little old Studebaker wasn't very fast. From then on, they put out much better trucks. Today, they've got them all over the place."

(About his office role after 1960): "At that time I took attendance because back then we didn't have these swipe cards. I issued equipment, always kept a count of all of our extinguishers…just ran the office…(now) we've got over 1,000 extinguishers…What I liked (was that) our fire office was under the stands right going into the first turn and victory circle, at the time, was right in front of the fire station office. We were practically on the track. All these interesting people would come in. I remember Red Adair, the guy who puts out all these oil fires, he came in. Nicest guy in the world. The favorite was Jim Garner. Joe Garagiola came down here one time and he was really nice. Even when the race would start, before all these new buildings were built, Mari and Tony and young Tony George would come in and stay for a few laps."

(About growing up on the west side of Indianapolis): "I lived in Speedway, so you had to love racing. I grew up on the west side….and lived in Speedway since 1948. I'm the only one on the fire department from Speedway. Before the war, we came out and watched. If you lived on the west side…..we came out and watched (driver) Billy Arnold and all the big names. My first memory was 1928 or '29 and Billy Arnold, he was my hero, he won the 1930 race. I met George Souders. He won the race in 1927. I came out to qualifications and practice. It was something."

(About his love for Purdue): "But I'm a Boilermaker fan number one. I went to Purdue extension, just couldn't afford to go (to Lafayette). It was the height of the Depression. When I was about 10 years old, Washington High School was brand new then, and (one of our first) graduates went to Purdue. He was a great ballplayer—Jim Carter. He was one of the 'Touchdown Twins.' He still holds one record up there. They're putting a book out on him now. I guess my highlight was when Coach Keady came in and saw us (last year). He came in here and took pictures with us and then sent us a bunch of hats."

(About his love of baseball and the Dodgers): "Why was I a Dodger fan? I don't know. I was born and raised right here in Indianapolis. I finally went out to Brooklyn to see them play. And then they moved to LA and they've been there for 50 years. For some reason, Duke Snider was always my favorite player, number 4. Every time I'd go gambling or at horse races, I'd bet on No. 4. I kept a record. That sucker has cost me about $1,500 over the years. He's the only person I've ever asked for an autograph for myself. He was so nice. When he went up (to the majors) in '47, the same time Jackie Robinson did, they both went up for $5,000 a year and they both made the Hall of Fame."

(About family): "I've got two grandchildren and a son and a daughter. In fact, my son-in-law worked 25 years out here. He worked the crash truck out of the fourth turn until three years ago when he thought he should spend more time with his kids. They're girls who play softball over here in Speedway. Believe it or not, they don't like it. They like sports but, for some reason, they don't care for the track. And they live a mile from here. Isn't that something? But their father sure did. My daughter isn't interested either."

(About other highlights at the track): "I got to be honorary starter last year. That was fun. I was scared to death; thought I would fall down between the (pit wall). That was awful nice of them."

By the 21st century Al has become a "500" icon and was honored in 2006 in celebration of 60 years at the track with a memento including signatures from many national personalities, including broadcaster Brent Musburger.

From Harris Street friend Harry Sullivan (who became Marshall High School's first AD in 1967 and had been a POW of the Nazi's in World War II) to the "protector" of Washington High's Johnny Williams during his many years at IMS, Casey has had a productive and happy life. He's clearly another Continental success story.

GEORGE THEOFANIS
LIFE'S GAME IN TRANSITION

George was inducted into the Indiana Basketball Hall of Fame in 2000. He had graduated from Washington High in 1949, won a basketball scholarship to play for Tony Hinkle at Butler, and actually replaced him as Butler's coach in 1970 after successful tenures at Avon and Shortridge High Schools. The following is an excerpt from the article that he wrote for the Hall of Fame magazine at his induction.

Life is a game of transition….Every person faces daily changes in life….My own childhood, too, was full of adjustments. My family lived on West New York Street across from Military Park…. The new Indiana University Law School is being built where our brick house stood. My older brothers, Jimmie and Chris and I played with kids from different ethnic backgrounds: Jews, Macedonians, Bulgarians, African-Americans, Slovenians, Romanians, Serbs, and Greeks— truly a melting pot.

Lacking finances, we had to improvise. When we played baseball, Chris was a left-handed first baseman. I played second and Jimmie played shortstop. We cut one of Mom's broomsticks to use as a bat. A delivery man gave us some hard rubber balls. When we marked off a diamond we used trees in left field and right field as foul lines.

Later, Chris and I played baseball at Washington High School. When basketball arrived, we improvised again. We'd roll Mom's old rags into a "ball" and tape it. Then we nailed a peach basket to the garage. Naturally, we couldn't dribble that rag "ball." It was always pass, cut, pick and screen. We were building a foundation of sound basketball—and didn't know it. This foundation helped our teammates win Washington's first sectional championship in 1948, Chris' senior year. As a senior in 1949, my last game in Butler Fieldhouse was frustrating. Tourney favorite Tech nipped us by one point.

But all was not lost. On the next Monday, first year Head Coach Dave Hine told me that Tony Hinkle was interested in me. Me? A Westside kid of modest means. I had planned to work in our family restaurant! When I met Coach Hinkle, he asked, "Would you like to play for me at Butler?" Nervously, I said, "yes sir, but I don't have money for college." Then he said, "I'll provide your tuition and books." My Dad was ecstatic! "Take it," he exclaimed, "get an education," even though my Dad never saw me play.

Chris earned a scholarship to Butler as Washington's 1948 class valedictorian. After four decades as Butler's Public and Community Relations Director, he was named to Butler's Athletic Hall of Fame. Chris died in 1999.

Brother Jimmie was born in Greece. He was nine when he arrived with Mom to join Dad in New York City during the 1930's Depression and none could speak English. Chris and I were born in New York City. Jimmie dropped out of school and hitch-hiked to California to try-out for professional baseball. He learned to speak accent-less English and became owner of 17 restaurant franchises, many in New York state.

Jimmie went from our basketball "rags" to his restaurant riches! But making money wasn't my first love. I had to make Butler's varsity. After two years of play I was drafted into the Air Force during the Korean War. Stationed at Chanute Field near the University of Illinois, I managed some 3-on-3 basketball at Huff Gym. But what I learned in the Air Force scarcely prepared me to coach; I became a weather instructor.

I was happiest when I married my fiancée, Colleen Junker of Indianapolis and, after more than three years in the service, I returned to Butler for my senior year. It was a season of Hinkle's wisdom spiced with "Hinkleisms." He blurted, "Hey kid, don't throw that ball away, it cost me $29.95!"

Finally, graduation! Should I coach, sell insurance, or work in our family restaurant? How could I not coach? Coach Hinkle was such a great teacher; he kept everything simple! He stressed the basics—passing, shooting, dribbling, picking, screening—and moving without the ball.

Still, I needed a job but lacked experience. I became frustrated and talked with Coach Hinkle again. "Hey kid," he'd say, "keep going, they can't say 'no' forever."

Within one week, small school Avon High said, "Yes!" I never forgot what Coach Hinkle stressed: "Keep it simple! Don't try to show kids how much you know, you'll confuse them. Kids will better execute simple things that they understand."

I learned that a man's coaching methods should reflect his personality and philosophy of life. I was an aggressive, positive holler-guy. When I went to Shortridge in the early 1960's as an assistant, the athletes there fit my style perfectly. We'd pick up from baseline to baseline and press all the way, changing presses from man-to-man to zone. That's the way I had played. Go after them! Conditioning? Of course. When I played at Washington, Coach Hine had us running cross country to build stamina. That paid off. I was scrawny at 5'11" 140 lbs. and not much bigger at Butler.

In 1968 as Head Coach at Shortridge with our aggressiveness we were very fortunate to upset favored Washington in the Regionals with their superstars McGinnis and Downing. But we met our match in the State Championship game against Gary Roosevelt. We had defeated Marion in the afternoon game but Roosevelt brought in a 6'7" 220 lb. sub who scored eight points and we lost 68-60 with our tongues hanging out.

In 1969 we again faced the Continental super-super stars. For two weeks before the Regionals we practiced ball-control and we almost lost our Sectional. We even practiced against six offensive players to compensate for their talent. When we met in the Regional finals, McGinnis went without a first half field goal. But we deviated from our plan and superior Washington won, 46-39. They were one of Indiana's all-time great teams as they became the undefeated State Champs.

In 1970 came another shocker. Coach Hinkle was retiring at Butler. Not many coaches wanted to follow a legend especially with a low budget against high-level competition. I wasn't sure I could get the job. But I remembered what Lenny Wilkens once said. "If a person can get along with people," Wilkens surmised, "and has had good success coaching at any level, he should be able to coach at a different level."

I was still surprised when Butler University President Alexander Jones called me at Shortridge and offered me the job as Head Coach. Months later UCLA legend Johnny Wooden told me in Indianapolis, "You have one of the toughest jobs in the country. You are following a legend. Be yourself. Don't try to be Tony Hinkle. You will be criticized and second-guessed. Just work hard and be a gentleman, win or lose. Keep your head up and be proud knowing that you gave your best effort."

Bobby Knight's college coach at Ohio State gave me my first lesson in recruiting. Butler was to play Ohio State on Saturday yet when I attended 6'8" Joe Maloney's high school game on Friday night (he played for Brownsburg); Coach Taylor was there too. I eventually convinced Maloney to attend Butler and we beat Ohio State that Saturday.

Flying to Miami/Dade Junior College on a low budget to see a little-known Barry Collier wasn't possible at the time. A friend of mine talked to him and he decided to come to Butler. Barry quickly became an intelligent, 6'7" forward who made All-Conference on our Championship team in his second year. Later he too would become Butler's Head Coach and lead them to three NCAA and two NIT appearances.

In the mid-1970's we played #1 ranked Marquette coached by Al McGuire. We lost by one point to them in the Fieldhouse in 1974. Coach Wooden's advice to keep giving one's best effort resonated. But sometimes a coach's best effort fails because an athlete faces great transitions in his life.

During Shortridge's drive to the 1968 final game our wiry 5'10" guard Jerry Willis flunked out of school after our Regional victory over Washington. He was a top defensive player because of hallmark aggressiveness. Willis lived with his sister because his parents had died. I visited his home to convince him to re-enroll. He later got his diploma and received a scholarship to Wyoming Junior College. Then he played two years at the University of Wisconsin. Today he works as a Milwaukee fireman.

As a junior, George Pillow didn't have Willis' opportunity to play at Shortridge. He had been cut the year before I became Head Coach. As a senior, Pillow showed his tenacity with his powerful body and superior athleticism. In one year he made the Indiana All-Star team and won a scholarship to Indiana State University. And, in 1999, he was named to Indiana State's All-Time team along with a fellow named Larry Bird. Today, George is a successful businessman and proud family man.

As I reflect on the past, I know that man had a hand in the many changes that occurred in my life. While man played a major roll, I have always believed that God is in control of everything. He guided and directed me throughout my life. From a Military Park kid to a basketball Hall of Famer, I give Him all the glory!

William "Bill" Mattox, class of 1953

(from Kim L. Hooper obituary Nov. 11, 2005)

Even though his family lived in the Ben Davis schools attendance district, Bill wanted to attend Washington High. His mother, Bernice, recalled that Bill desired a metalwork vocational education as well as his belief that he would experience a much better athletic experience in the city at the time.

Bill played football, basketball, and baseball at GWHS as he excelled for Frank Luzar's baseball team. Then at Butler University legendary coach Tony Hinkle encouraged him to sign a professional contract with the Cleveland Indians in 1956 when the Indianapolis Indians were their AAA team. But he suffered a career ending injury while playing for the Daytona Beach Islanders.

He earned his pilot's license and would go on to become a successful businessman when he helped to start Taurus Foods, an Indianapolis meatpacking company, in 1974.

Bill had three passions in life after his baseball career ended. "He would not have been happy without his plane, a bowling ball or a golf club," noted his son Bill Jr.

He died in Port Orange, Florida on October 14, 2005. His wife and mother of his five children, Jeanne, remembered that "he used to drive me to the (Weir Cook) airport to watch the airplanes. He thought that was the greatest entertainment for the children."

Life seemed more simple in the recent past.

BRYAN HUDSON, class of 1954

Bryan was the "Jackie Robinson" of Washington High. He was the first black athlete winning two basketball letters under one of his favorite teachers, Coach Dave Hine. And 1954 was the year of the famous Supreme Court decision finally overruling the 1896 segregationist supporting affirmation.

Bryan laughingly downplayed his abilities noting that "don't describe me as a star, I wasn't." He had transferred into Continentaland as a junior from Attucks although he had lived in the 900 block of North Sheffield since his family had arrived in Indianapolis in 1948 from Tennessee. Although Ozetta Troutman and Claudia Brunt were the first two African-Americans to graduate from GWHS, in 1953, Bryan notes that Sherman Marlin was the first Black student to attend Washington High. He lived on Traub north of 10th Street. All attended School #63 located near Belmont Park.

Horace, his real first name, remembers Mr. Bock and Mr. Mann as his favorite teachers. Mr. Barnhart was principal. Bryan had met his future wife while a student at Attucks and when she graduated in 1956 they married. He claims that his hero in the 1950's was a two year younger Oscar Robertson, the great Attucks basketball player.

Bryan had been a substitute forward on Dave Hine's teams along with up-and-coming sophomore Collis Blane. Collis, who would have two younger brothers star at Washington High in football (Mitchell on the 1961 frosh team and Matthew who made the 1973 summer All-Star team), also played football.

Bryan was married in 1956 and they had a son in November of 1957, Brian, who currently is featured often in the Sunday Star as a contributing editorial writer and is the pastor of an Indianapolis church. After high school Bryan worked in different gas stations before attending Lincoln Tech and becoming an auto technician from which he retired in 2002. His wife died in 2003 but he continues to live in the home they purchased in 1967 on the north side.

JERRY LAWLIS, class of 1956

(On Saturday, January 28, 1956 in the Washington High School gymnasium, Jerry Lawlis scored 48 points in an overtime victory against Speedway, 87-85. Until the greatest basketball player of all time, Oscar Robertson, established a new record within the next week, Lawlis' feat was briefly an all-time city record. Ralph Taylor sent nine pages of information from newspaper articles from 1956 relating to Jerry Lawlis and his shining night of glory. The following is a paraphrasing of Jimmie Angelopolous' Indianapolis Times article on Monday, January 30. Lawlis was inducted into the Indiana Basketball Hall of Fame in 2003.)

GARAGE OR NOT, JERRY CAN PARK 'EM

Ishmael Lawlis started to build a garage at his home, 525 N. Centennial three years ago. He laid the concrete floor but decided not to build that garage. What do you do in Indiana when you don't build a garage? You build a basketball court, natch.

So son Jerry Lawlis and his Washington buddies always played basketball. Even in the summer time. Any basketball kid in town will tell you Jerry Lawlis has the most wicked lefthand you ever saw. In fact, most of 'em wished Ishmael Lawlis would have asked for helpers to build that garage and forget about that basketball court.

Today Indianapolis has one less garage on the West Side but who cares about building garages when you can build basketball players like Jerry Lawlis. Now Jerry's the greatest scorer in Indianapolis history with that 48-point splurge.....Jerry didn't know it but his teammates decided at the half they would begin feeding him to break Oscar Robertson's all-time city record of 45 points that was only two weeks old. Jerry had 27 points in the first half. He popped 17 field goals in 32 attempts and swished 14 of 17 free throws.

Jerry is probably the best high school baseball pitcher in town and has been for two years. He'll probably be more famous someday for throwing a baseball than flipping a basketball.......Jerry is a little out of the ordinary. He's quite well liked, very conscientious and he's a scholar.....ranking seventh in his senior class, his coach Dave Hine says because, "he works at his studies just like he does anything else."

When he was a sophomore he was named to the Times All-Sectional team. But he developed a calcification on his thigh and missed his entire junior year of basketball. His teammates could have used him in the 1955 Butler Sectional because they had Tech down some 12 points but couldn't keep the lead.

Jerry's okay now. His father, Ishmael, built a pretty fair reputation as a football player under Washington Coach Henry Bogue in the early '30's. But Ishmael's a punk garage builder.

Long-time sportswriter Jimmie Angelopolous, a School #5 and Manual High School graduate, was always a friend to Washington High School. An excerpt from the Sunday morning story concerning the "Lawlis game" and a copy of the box score is shown below:

---

* The 16 team Butler All-Sectional team in 1956 was Jerry Lawlis, Bill Brown (Attucks), Carl Short (Manual), Herschel Turner (Shortridge), and Oscar Robertson (Attucks). Lawlis attended Purdue University on a basketball scholarship. He became an Indianapolis lawyer and long-time member of the Hawthorne Community Center Board of Directors.)

* Ishmael Lawlis, Jerry's dad, graduated from Washington High in the first four-year class in 1931. He was the All-City right tackle on Washington's first City Championship football team in 1930.)

"With 26 seconds to go in regulation playing time, Don Martin converted two free throws to send it into the overtime tied at 79-79. Collis Blane's bucket with four seconds to go in the extra period netted Washington its two-point decision...Speedway, paced by Joe Cork's 25 points, caught up in a 26-point fourth quarter spree. Both teams now have 10-5 records."

Washington (87)	FG	FT	PF		Speedway (85)	FG	FT	PF
Don Ross	4	1	5		Wood	6	0	2
Jerry Lawlis	17	14	1		Healey	5	3	0
Collis Blane	2	1	4		Smith	6	4	3
Carl Peterson	0	0	2		Stout	5	5	5
Don Pope	1	0	1		Cork	9	7	5
Don Martin	3	6	2		Hunt	2	0	0
Tom Springer	5	1	1		Scott	0	0	0
Dave McAtee	0	0	1					
	32	23	17			33	19	15

	1st	2nd	3rd	4th	OT	Final Score
Washington	18	24	20	17	8	87
Speedway	15	14	24	26	6	85

HENRY "HANK" EASTER
GWHS, class of 1957

Hank Easter was inducted into the University of Indianapolis Athletic Hall of Fame in early 2008. He won 12 varsity letters in football, wrestling, baseball and golf before his graduation in 1961.

As an All Conference lineman at then Indiana Central he was a teammate of fellow Continentals Carol Purichia and Chuck Hedges as well as outstanding footballers Willie Martin, Jim Nyers and Jim Ware. But Red Faught, the Franklin College coach, is the man who nominated Hank for the honor team. ICC won the 1960 football conference championship as well as baseball titles in 1958, '59 and '61. Henry struck out nine batters in a row vs. Wabash his junior year in a big win and, after strutting around for some female admirers, Coach Bill Bright challenged Hank to be more attentive to the on-field activities. Hank noted that maybe he would just stick to golf to which Coach Bright responded, "if you decide to quit baseball you'll never play here again." He also challenged that he should be playing more since "I'm the best hitter you've got." And, when he read a comic book while sitting the bench, his time on the team was over for the year. Thus Hank didn't letter in baseball his junior year. But during his senior year the coach requested that Hank give baseball another try. Hank shared with me that he would have had more respect for the coach if he would have stuck to his 'word' from the previous year. But then he did lead the Greyhounds to the Conference Championship with a 6-1 pitching record including a no-hitter vs. Franklin. Hank was, and is, his own man.

Henry was co-captain of the wrestling squad that won the Little State title in 1960 while lettering twice. Hank also lettered on the links three times as a true man-for-all-seasons.

After graduation he took a teaching job at new Avon High School in Hendricks County. Hank was the first official football coach at Avon in 1961 and also initiated both the wrestling and golf programs. Playing already established programs like Danville, Plainfield and Brownsburg the young Orioles did not have a lot of statistical success with only about 35 players since only two had any football experience. But, Hank noted, the loyalty and intensity of his early charges was never in question. Those boys from the early '60's continue today to take pride in their early quest as the inaugural gridiron heroes from eastern Hendricks County. Former Hendricks County Sheriff Jim Querry was one of about a dozen former Avon athletes and their wives who attended Hank's induction ceremony into the Hall of Fame.

Nonetheless, his $3,000 teaching pay plus $500 to coach three sports was not much of an incentive. And he was soon to marry cute, little Marge Miller. Hank had met her when he took his parents' dog, Missy, to the Lafayette Road Animal Hospital in 1961. Marge was the receptionist. It was love at first sight. They had two boys, Gary and Jon. In a strange twist of fate, the Easters attended the Washington vs. Columbus football game on Sept. 4, 1964 and little Gary fell through the bleachers on the northwest corner but escaped serious injury in a dramatic, scary moment. Jon in the 21st century is the teacher in charge of the Ben Davis High School radio station and communications.

So in the early '60's, when a newly elected School Board (Hank had been hired under the old trustee system) demanded that the athletic director send back the delivered football field lights, Hank took a teaching job at School 75 in Haughville for $5,900. Avon basketball coach George Theofanis, another Washington High icon, left the Hendricks County school at the same time heading to Shortridge as an assistant coach. Mark Twain is said to have once stated that "God first created idiots. But that was for practice. Then he created School Boards."

Henry spent five years at School 75 mentoring future Continental stars Ronnie Hayes, Bruce Brentz, and Bruce Smith among others. Then he went into a two-year counseling program between Schools #67, 61, 52 and 79 before spending three years at Harry E. Wood High School in Career Education. Howe High School was Hank's next stop in 1972. He left there after seven years to become Vice Principal at Broad Ripple until his retirement in 1997. They had moved from their North Eleanor residence in Farley off of 10th Street in 1996 after living there a quarter century.

Henry Easter graduated from School #67 and began his Continental career in football in 1953. Henry Bogue and Johnny Williams were the frosh coaches. Their unique coaching styles are well known to most Washington watchers. It was the first organized football that Hank had experienced. He then was cut from the basketball team, although he considered himself to be good enough, so he then headed to the first year of the Washington High wrestling program under Johnny Williams. But baseball was his main indulgence. Hank made the All-Star teams in D-league and C-league before high school but he and Coach Frank Luzar didn't always see "eye-to-eye." (Hank's mom, Twila, laughed to me once that "I don't know how he ever could play for any coach. He always thought that he knew more than any of his coaches.")

Hank claims that football inside the old city limits was second to none in the state. Tech, Broad Ripple, Howe, Cathedral, Sacred Heart, Shortridge and, of course, the Continentals all touted top notch talent. Tech, playing in the old North Central Conference, was normally considered the benchmark team. So, when Slavie Lalioff smacked a Tech runner on the opening kickoff and Hank picked up the ball and rumbled for a 40-yd. TD it looked as if the Continentals could win in 1955. But they missed the extra point and eventually Tech won 7-6. Still the biggest disappointment was against Broad Ripple on the northside. (I witnessed that game in 1956.) With Washington leading 13-0 at halftime, Broad Ripple with QB Chuck Holle and halfback Byron Broome, scored late in the game after a negative-yardage punt by our boys to win 14-13. Two big lost fumbles also hurt.

Henry says that Jerry Lawlis was the best athlete he saw in action during his four years at Washington High. He proclaimed him to not only be an excellent left-handed jump shooter in basketball but also a great southpaw pitcher in baseball. But the only high schooler that he saw hit a home run at old Victory Field on 16th Street was his future brother-in-law Elmo Carver, the future Superintendent of Schools in Franklin Township. Elmo married Hank's attractive sister, Sherry. They had both graduated from Washington in 1955. Hank graduated in 1957.

Into early 2009, Hank and his wife of 46 years Marge live near St. Petersburg, Florida. He no longer plays golf, the game he mastered and loved, but he does like his poker games with his buddies in the sunshine south.

(Hank died in early 2009 soon after this story was written.)

LARRY GLAZE

Larry lived on Wilcox Street near Belmont and Michigan Streets while he attended School #30 and Washington High, graduating in 1960. Like others at School #30 he walked two or three times a week to take Shop class at nearby School #50.

At Washington High Larry played football, basketball and baseball his first three years. Then he voluntarily approached basketball coach Dave Hine before his senior year, when he realized that maybe he would not be an important cog in the Continental machine, and decided that he would not try out. Larry noted that it was a strange experience when he did not have to practice a sport after school for the first time in his high school years.

Like many Continentals who experienced Johnny Williams and/or Henry Bogue, Larry was introduced to a unique style of coaching. Coach Bogue was frosh coach in the fall of 1956. He had been the varsity coach from 1927 through the 1950 season. Coach Williams coached at GWHS from 1944 until his 1974 retirement and was well know as a high school official in both football and basketball. John officiated the afternoon State Finals in 1967 when he called the fifth foul on Ft. Wayne Southside star Willie Long. And, he served at least two stints as President of the central Indiana Officials' Association.

Thus Larry was introduced to a typical Bogue-Williams first practice. Most feeder schools did not have football and, besides, junior high prominence meant little to the high school coaches in those days. The Bogue rule was, according to Larry, that after a line-up from shortest to tallest that the fastest runner of the frosh sprint-off was to be the running back while the second fastest runner was assigned as center. Bill Snowberger was fastest. Consequently, Larry spent his freshman and sophomore-reserve years as center on the team.

By his junior year young line coach Jerry Oliver recognized his foot speed and moved him to end. He consequently became an All City blocker and receiver for the undefeated 1959 team.

Larry also was selected as the class athlete of the year for his first three years but lost out his senior year to a cross country-track athlete.

But baseball was his forte. He was one of Frank Luzar's best. Yet his brother Ralph, known as Iron Arm Glaze who graduated in 1954, may have been better. Catcher Bill Cole tried to negotiate a spot on the bench when it was Iron Arm's turn to pitch in the rotation, according to Larry. Nonetheless, Larry's reputation began strong when he was assigned as the starting right fielder his sophomore year. It seemed to Larry that only junior Petey Saunders supported Coach Luzar's decision to replace a senior with a second year baseball man. Larry eventually became the strong-fielding, strong-hitting center fielder for the Continentals.

Larry raised his family in Carmel in Hamilton County. His two sons played on successful Greyhound football and baseball teams before attending Rose-Hulman.

WILMER ISENHOWER
(Sharon Trisler, class of 1973, writes about her brother.)

My brother Wilmer Isenhower who was also known as Buddie, Bird and Bill served in Vietnam from 1970 into 1971. He had graduated from GWHS in 1968. He was fortunate enough to come home from Vietnam. Many of his fellow soldiers were not as lucky. A number of his friends in the service were killed in a blast when my brother was home on leave six months into his year long tour.

Bird was very private about his tour in Vietnam. He only shared the most vivid and horrific stories with my husband, Jeff. Unfortunately, we lost Bird in November of 1999 at the age of 49. He had a major stroke when he was only 41 and never fully recovered. Doctors found a brain tumor in September of '99 and that is what took his life. I miss him a lot and I'll always wonder what effect the defoliants used in Vietnam had on his health.

Buddie's mother, Betty Brant Isenhower, was a 1947 graduate from GWHS. His brother Dean got his diploma in 1970 and another brother, Mike, graduated in 1971. I graduated in 1973. Our sister, Beverly, didn't attend Washington High. She spent her high school years with our grandmother and graduated from Cloverdale H.S. in 1975.

The PURICHIA Family

As a small kid my dad often repeated stories of Washington High athletes. In our middle-class to poor, west-side neighborhood with many multi-children families, I heard about the Carter, Howard, or Luzar brothers of the 1930's or super-star Harry Cherry. Ironically enough I experienced in first person much of the most prolific brother acts in Washington history---the Purichias. There were others before (the Deem, Theofanis & Tillery brothers), some after or near the end of the Purichia dynasty (the Branson, Highbaugh, Sylvester, White, Tibbetts & Boswell brothers) and many contemporary to them (the Keller, Arvin, Sanders, Porten, Blane & Opp brothers). But only the Purichias can claim a sibling in either School 50 or GWHS continuously from Catherine's 1934 Kindergarten appearance to Steve's 1965 IPS graduation. That's 31 consecutive years.

The nine original Purichias and each of their graduating classes: Catherine ('47), Spiro ('48), Mike ('50), Nula ('52), Bill ('55), Carol ('57), Nick ('59), Joe ('62) and Steve ('65). Only P.A. (Spiro) didn't graduate having left school to join the Army. In June of 1950 he was headed home from Okinawa when the Korean War began.

Of course it all began with Pop Angelo Purichia who arrived in the United States in 1913 as an 18-year-old from his native Romania. While helping construct parts of Indiana's railroads he sometimes stayed in the Lombardi rooming tenements at Senate & Ohio Streets (where the State Library now stands). Once he met young Josephine Lombardi and the rest is west-side history. They first lived on South Holmes then moved to the famous 515 South Harris in 1941. Daddy Purichia worked as a molder at Link-Belt for 33 years walking the five or six blocks to work each day. He retired in 1961 at the age of 65. Mrs. Purichia began working in the high school cafeteria in the mid-1960's, usually in charge of the cold lunch line, and retired in the early '80's. Before that she had been active in the P.T.A. and usually worked in the old concession stand at the northeast corner of the football field. She preferred selling hot dogs and popcorn rather than watching her sons under football pile-ups on the field, Nula said. Angelo had become a

Naturalized U.S. citizen thanks to his attendance twice a week at School 5 classes. He worked his 8-hour shift then took a street-car downtown for citizenship class. When Lee Iacocca renovated Ellis Island, the immigrant entering center in New York City, the Purichia family had their father's name inscribed there.

The brothers' act could not have been possible without the two girls. Catherine was like a second mother with her selfless sacrifices and protective nature. While still maintaining her good student status she worked many hours at Irrgang's market at Ida & Warman Ave. (where Jimmy White's market later prospered) to help feed the fast growing family. Thelma Posey and Marie Gilbrech were two of her good friends whenever she was able to find any personal time. As an adult she would marry Al Dugar from Haughville and their two girls (Mary & Christie) would become Ritter High School volleyball and softball players. And Nula, who would become the first college graduate in the family after leaving Washington in 1952 as a National Honor Society student, would become a Speedway school teacher of 4th and 6th graders. Her principal John Bainbridge, who later became Speedway High's principal (in 2004 he was a Unigov councilman), called her "the best teacher that I think I ever had under my charge." Nula married Joe Harmon from Cathedral High and Notre Dame University. Their kids, three boys and one girl, attended Chatard High as well as Notre Dame and St. Mary's College, both in South Bend. All participated in sports at Chatard. Joe, Jr. is a medical doctor, Julie an art major, Nick was a varsity boxer at N.D., and Mike pitched at N.D. and is currently the baseball coach at Chatard after a stint as football coach at Brebeuf.

Catherine and Nula's bedroom needed a reservation book for phone usage since that's where the only phone was located. The "Melrose 6-0642" moniker was dialed by many among family and friends. And it seemed one rarely saw Nula without one or another of her neighborhood girlfriends Shirley Barker, Janet Savage, future sister-in-law Doris Neff or the girl-across-the-alley Anita Bloomenstock for whom she waited until 1953 so they could attend Indiana State Teachers' College together as 1957 graduates.

Oldest boy P.A. married Millie Lambert after his military service in the early '50's. They had five kids (Terry, Trina, Catherine, Joe, & David) who played football, baseball, and golf at Decatur High School in the '60's & '70's. P.A.'s Joe helped coach football at Ritter in the 21st century before his death in early 2010.

Big Mike entered high school in 1946 and his quarterbacking abilities soon were recognized by Coach Bogue. Nula tells the story that years later Coach Bogue revealed that he took out a life insurance policy on Mike before the South Bend Central game "because he was not real sturdy built" (Nula says) and Bogue was concerned about a possible family hardship because he knew that with "lots of children" an injury could devastate family finances. In any event, Mike became a star by the '49 season throwing passes to favorite target Bill Cook. And his other buddies were Russell Posey, Tooter Rice, Bud Gott, and Charlie Garver. After he married the girl-next-door Doris "Duke" Neff they had five kids including two boys who played football, wrestling, and baseball at Ritter High School; Little Mike in the late '60's and Vince in the mid-'80's. Their three daughters Becky, Nula, & Theresa attended Ritter and/or Ben Davis. And their grandson was a freshmen quarterback on the 2003 State Championship team and star of the 2006 State Runners-up for Ritter.

Brother Bill is the one of unfulfilled promise. He died on the spring practice football field in 1956 during his freshmen year at Chattanooga University of a cerebral hemorrhage. He had been an All-City quarterback and a favorite of sportswriter brothers Angelo and Jimmie Angelopolous.

He was elected as Vice-President of the Senior Class at Washington High and he also was in the Madrigal Singers, who were the best singers from the Colonial Chorus, as well as a basketball and baseball Continental. He was Henry Bogue's first freshmen quarterback in 1951 when Joe Tofil became varsity coach. Bill's buddy, Tom Johnston, was his center and another good friend, Ronnie Abner, was fullback.

Carol filled Bill's quarterback shoes admirably in 1955 and then again in 1956. He continued the tradition of wearing #66 for the Purichias. Carol was also a starter on the basketball and baseball teams. He and Bernie Keller were both power forwards for Coach Dave Hine while Ernie Slinker and Joe Morgan handled the backcourt. Carol was probably the most versatile of the boys in sports. And Ed Porten, along with Chuck Hedges, were two of his closest friends. Then Carol traveled a few miles southeast to Indiana Central College with Hank Easter to play football. At one time he led the nation for small colleges in passing during his junior year. Carol volunteered as a coach at his high school alma mater then became assistant to Washington grad Joe Dezelan at Cathedral before his five-year stint as Chatard's Head Coach. He finished his high school coaching career in 1968 with an undefeated team. Carol then became an assistant at Indiana State, Western Illinois, and again at ISU before entering private business in the late 1970's. Daughter Toni ventured into the entertainment industry after attending Brebeuf and Angela graduated from the Air Force Academy (her mother Donna's brother Tony Marietta graduated there after playing for Carol at Chatard) after volleyball at Chatard. She served her country as an aviator before becoming a commercial pilot.

Dr. Nick Purichia, class of '59, reached the highest academic prominence when he received his Ph D from the University of Cincinnati. In high school he excelled in Cross Country his first three years then opted not to "defend his letter" and tried out for the fitting #66 in football becoming the starter in 1958. Nick was always creating new activities for the neighborhood kids. During the summers of '57 & '58 he had the "Purichia Invitational" track meet up and down the Harris Street alley. The cross country run headed south down the alley then west along the railroad tracks to Eagle Creek then back east on the north side of the foundry on Victoria Street. Butch Lomen was his marquee trackster as he would be later at Washington High. Bubby Stockoff, Bernie Stinnett, and Billy Homan were Nick's best grade school and high school buddies. Bub traveled to Indiana State Teachers' College with him where they graduated in 1963. Nick was head of the Biology department at Marian College from 1972 until his untimely death in August of 1979 while attending brother Steve's Chatard game. Tragically his wife, Elaine Romer, had died in the fall of 1973. Their son Mark lost both of his parents within six years of his young life yet followed his dad's footsteps as an honor student at Marian College. Nick started the Nursing program at Marian. And a scholarship for the top biology student is named for Nick & Elaine.

Joe was the third Purichia elected Senior class President in six years. The elite singing group was now called the Continentalaires and Joe was one of the leaders. His non-sports buddies were Tommy West, Jim Wilham, and Butch Waltz. But his forte, too, was football and basketball. He was probably the best Purichia basketball player. In Jerry Oliver's first year as Head Coach, Joe scored 32 points at Butler Fieldhouse in a Sectional game upset of North Central as a junior. But he won a scholarship to play football at Butler University for Tony Hinkle, thanks partially to Mrs. Hine at Washington High who was the only Guidance person at the time. Joe's last game at Butler was against Western Kentucky. At one time the Bulldogs trailed 20-0 but Joe threw into the end zone with 59 seconds left to win the game. Soon after college Joe married his Washington sweetheart, Janet Mitchell. He first coached at Scecina in 1966 along with his friend Ken Leffler in football and soon became the Head Basketball coach for four years until 1972 when he left to become a football assistant at Brownsburg. In 1973 the Bulldogs were undefeated in the regular season but didn't qualify for the tournament under the rules of that era. Joe left Brownsburg to become Head Football Coach at Vincennes in 1976. In 14 seasons with the Alices, they were 75-63 while winning nine games three times and were Conference Champs three times. In 1990 he became Washington, Indiana's high school coach delivering their first winning season since 1974 in 1992. He ended his Head Coaching career with 99 total wins at coaching retirement in 1996. Like his favorite high school teacher, Barbara Jean Hine, in 2004 he was Director of Counseling at Washington High. His son Jeff, who was a quarterback for his dad then was student manager at IU for Bill Mallory then coached at Noblesville before becoming Head Coach at Charlestown High School. And their daughter, Heather, became a Ph'D in Educational Psychology at Southern Illinois. Joe, like his younger brother Steve, was President of the State Football Coaches Association. And in 1978 both brothers led teams to Semi-State Championship games in different divisions.

The youngest of the original Purichias entered Washington High as a mid-term January 1961 freshman. He played football, basketball, and baseball his freshmen year but then concentrated on football his last three years. In 1963 he had the longest run from scrimmage for the ten game season at 24-yards vs. Shortridge even though he was not the fastest runner on the team. His future coaching abilities were probably enhanced by having played all four positions in the offensive backfield, both ends on offense, both outside linebackers and both halfbacks on defense. Steve was a sports writer for "The Surveyor" weekly school paper and was a Senior class officer. His best high school friends were Mike Parker, Dannie Johnson, and Kenny Strong. Like Nula and Nick before him, he attended Indiana State University. After graduation in 1969 he returned to coach for Carol's successor at Chatard, Dick Dullaghan. In 1972 he traveled to the University of Cincinnati as a graduate assistant in football then returned as Head Coach at Chatard for the 1973 season. During his ten years at Chatard they won five City Championships and qualified three times for the play-offs (which was no easy task under the original play-off system). Steve then became Head Coach for four seasons at Perry Meridian leading them to their best seasons ever. In '87-88 he sold insurance but then returned to coaching again under Dullaghan at Ben Davis in 1988 when they won their second State Championship. Steve coached the line, special teams and was assistant head coach for five more State Championship teams. He was probably the most successful Purichia coach. Steve had married Sylvia in November 1977. Their daughter, Susan, played volleyball and softball at Chatard. She attended Purdue University.

There are currently over 40 great-grandkids and counting.

Like many others I'm reminded of the Purichia legacy because of dozens of experiences over the years. When I hear of Bobby Plump I think of Joe and me in my basement shooting at the makeshift goal on our basement steps in '54 & '55. I remember Mrs. Werthman, long-time Washington English teacher, sending her impressionable son to spend summer days with rough, but morally sound, inner-city kids with Nick as his mentor in '57 & '58. Then there were the times Nula traveled to Brown County and to Merritt's Park (just west of 200 N and Rd. #267) with our family and Aunt Anita where they waded in the creek and had to have leeches burned off their feet. Or when Nula was sitting behind me in our 1950 Studebaker at Westlake Drive-in and she bit down on an apple and my smart-alec response was "Hungry, Nula!?!?"

My dad took Nick and Steve with me to the 1960 Washington vs. Noblesville up north and had taken Joe and Nick with me to the 1956 Shortridge game near Butler where we saw our first racial confrontation after Carol's game. Carol also tells the story about Coach Johnny Williams (GWHS 1944-1974) dispensing the gray Washington t-shirts with blue lettering to the frosh team. As he ran out of one size John recommended "boy, if you want another size you could go down to the Purichia house, they've got any size you want!" Once Steve enticed me into the 1950 Ford sitting in front of 515 as Joe came running out of the house. We locked the doors as Steve shifted through the gears. When I refused to unlock my side door, Joe dented my bike fender then hung it on the foundry fence. I still ride my '57 Schwinn Corvette bike. The dent's still there.

Big Mike many times would play street football with a cigar hanging from his mouth. Mike was always a First Round Draft pick as was Tooter Rice and Butch Lomen. And, when Carol picked me & Steve to challenge Bub, Joe, & Nick once, we impressed him with a victory highlighted by the "man in motion" and the "Shuffle Pass" in the mid-50's before Lee Grosscup at Utah supposedly made the "Shovel Pass" famous. The Purichia-street games were legendary in the 1950's. In the mid-80's when the Colts were struggling under Frank Kush, Catherine was serious when she suggested, "what the Colts need are Carol, Joe and Steve as their coaches if they want to win."

In May of 1956 when Steve and I entered the Belmont Theater one Friday night we sat in the middle section on the right side aisle and cried together about Bill's recent death. We were still young kids and death did strange things to the pit of one's stomach as it had when neighborhood 12-year-old Carl Morrow had died in a cave-in near Eagle Creek in August of 1954. And every time I travel on Highway #67 (a couple of counties south) past the Centerbrook Drive-in, I think of the only time my family went there in our '55 DeSoto and Joe went with us. I wonder if Joe ever went by there on his way from Vincennes and remembered the name of the movie? Joe and I were transported to the Indiana Theater by my dad for my first "without parents" foray downtown. I do remember that we saw "I Was A Teenage Werewolf" starring Michael Landon after we had gone through the old Em-Roe store and visited Joe Kelly. Joe and Steve accompanied my family to pitch and hit baseball at Riverside Park in the mid-50's, which seemed like a long trip then. Joe moved back to southern Indianapolis in 2008. Joe and I work at Lucas Oil Stadium during Colts games as retiree ushers into 2010.

And I'll never figure out how Nula, 'Nita, and Shirley ever fitted into Anita's single bed for a sleepover in 1953, but they did. 'Nita and Nula also had a big party in our basement probably in 1955. Nick and I really got an eyeful of teenage stuff especially watching Slinker in a corner of our basement smooching a girl. Gene Gallagher (the future police chief) and Harley Starks, among other Washington boys, were always polite and respectful. And then there were the consistent poker games that we had in the early 1970's. The only three regulars were Big Mike, Daddy Purichia, and me. Others like John Wirtz, Tom Stevason, Ernie Slinker, Joe Shires, Mike McKee, Billy Apple, Mike Tibbetts, "Butts," Joe Gorham, Art Neff, and sometimes Steve had to be coaxed to donate their money. The Purichia family will always be synonymous with a large part of my concept of the real Westside neighborhood and our successful and safe public school culture.

The Wrestling OPP Family

When little sister Clancie was crowned Homecoming Queen at halftime of the Broad Ripple football game in October of 1963 it seemed to be a fitting tribute to the first family of wrestling during the 32 years of Continental grapplers. As a sixth grader at School 50, Clancie was in awe of her brother Frank's football buddies. Chuck Hedges, Bill Green, Leon Griffith and Bill Nave were just a few of the 1957 players who attended a half dozen or more post-game parties at the Opp house near the corner of Turner at 350 N. Belleview. But she made her own "name" as a popular student and majorette for Ray Funk's Marching Continentals. Still it was too bad girls couldn't wrestle.

Patriarch Franklin, Sr. grew up in Findley, Ohio. At age 18, he headed to Franklin, Indiana where he acquired a job at the Franklin Ketchup Factory. But when he attended the Johnson County Fair in 1937 the sister of young Letecia Jiggs introduced him to the 17-year-old who would become his wife and spiritual mate for over 40 years until his death in 1979. The two sisters had bicycled to the Fair. The Franklin Pentecostal Community Church became their social meeting place and they were soon married. Frank Sr. took the nickname "Jiggs" and they moved to the capital city where he worked for Indianapolis Power & Light while Mrs. Opp worked at Central Coil making radio parts in the later 1950's.

Frank and Letecia's first child, Janetta, was selected as one of the cheerleaders in the early 1950's. But not at Washington High. The Opps lived in Flackville in the Ben Davis school district at the time. So, when they moved to 337 North Addison for what then was considered a better school district, Janetta balked at the move. She walked in the front door and out the back in protest. But their sons leaped at the opportunity. Young Frank would play on Guy Fish's first football team at School 50. Mr. Fish had been All-City right tackle in 1945 at GWHS before becoming captain and All-ICC for Tony Hinkle at Butler University. Then Frank would walk two blocks farther to Washington High where he would graduate in 1958 as an outstanding football guard and as our first wrestling State Champ at 154. Coach Johnny Williams called Frank "Crazy Opp" because of his perpetual aggressiveness. He was never warned for stalling. Frank was one of 33 IPS boys to become wrestling State Champion during the decade of the 1950's in the 12 weight classes of that era. During the 1960's IPS claimed 21 individual champions, in the '70's there were seven, and in the '80's only three. The last IPS State Champ was in 1991, the only one in the last decade of the 20th century. In 2009, for the first time in IHSAA history there was not a single State Champion from Marion County.

With a wrestling scholarship to IU, Frank traveled to Bloomington. But college life was not his "cup of tea." He joined the Marine Corps and was ordered to Camp Pendleton, California. There he met his future wife, Jerri. Eventually they had three kids in the Golden State. By the 21st century Frank was retired while still holding ownership of his own Real Estate company.

The third child, Carl, graduated in 1959. He finished 3rd in the State as a 133-lber in the Opp-selected sport of wrestling. Along with Mr. Fish's cadet teacher, Bob Milatovich who wrestled at 175 and whose father owned a South Belmont Street bar, Carl was the driving force behind an after-school, unofficial wrestling camp for School 50 boys in '59-'60 with younger brother Reggie making guest appearances to teach the basics of the referee's position and other matmen fundamentals. Carl was only 11 months younger than Frank. But soon after high school he would join the U.S. Air Force.

His wife, Carol Keene, also graduated from Washington High. They had two kids, Robin and Karla. Living on Ohio Street just west of High School Road until his death in 2003, Carl and Carol owned a family upholstery business. But they were most proud of their affiliation with the West Side Gospel Tabernacle and eventually Lakeview Temple. As a deacon in their faith he held weekly prayer meetings at their home. Their son Robin wrestled for Ben Davis High School.

The third wrestling Opp, Garland known as Reggie, would win the City Championship as had his two older brothers and was 2nd in the State Finals at 138. He made it three consecutive Opp graduation years when he received his diploma in 1960.

His daughter lives in California but Reggie has lunch with sister Clancie on a weekly basis. He currently lives near Morris and High School Roads.

Gary, class of 1963, made it four City Championships for the Opps when he won at 138. But when he finished 2nd in the Sectionals it was unluckily the first year that only the winner was allowed to advance. Nonetheless a post-graduation Gary became prosperous in the construction business also in California. He married fellow '63 graduate Catherine Woodall but they eventually separated. Their four sons live in Indianapolis but he lives in the beautiful mountains in the far west.

And the aforementioned Clancie, class of '64, in 2010 lives on the eastside of Indianapolis. Her many teenage friends included Vicki Hampton, Mabel Garrison, Cindy Showalter, Paulette Frye and Becky Mraz. One of usually six or so kids plus two parents who circled the dinner table while pre-meal prayers were being said, Clancie claims that each kid was always awarded only one pork chop. So the Opp family affirmed their faith but always with one eye opened to try to spot the biggest chop for the quickest forking.

In the summer of 1965 while parked at the famous Pole drive-in crammed into a small Corvair with her friend Mabel, two eastside boys in a big car stopped nearby. Mabel had dated one of the boys and was asked to accompany them to the Tee Pee drive-in. She refused to go without another female. Clancie was hesitant but was pushed by Mabel out of the backseat into the front seat of a "442." A push of fate.

But Clancie was confused by the "442" designation. What's that? The large Olds engine was in sharp contrast to the four-cylinder Corvair. But she did give the other boy, Doug Reno who graduated in the first Arlington H.S. class in 1964, her phone number. He called the next day. It was love at second sight. They were married April 2, 1966. Eventually they would welcome three children, Debbie and Darren and Brian. Naturally the two boys would wrestle. At Warren Township's Creston Jr. Hi. Darren was undefeated one year at 95-lbs. and at Warren Central Brian lost the Sectional Championship match at 155-lbs.

The most unfortunate incident in the Opp family story occurred just three months after Clancie left home to marry. Cute little Larita, who was scheduled for her senior picture the next day, was tragically struck by a semi-truck on Sunday, July 24, 1966. Beginning in the summer of 1963 when the southern rim of I-465 was not yet opened, Washington kids would travel down Harding St. parking immediately south of I-465 just west of Harding. After crossing the concrete pavement teenagers would swim in the Power & Light gravel pit, which remains there to this day. So, even after the opening of what then was a moderately traveled highway, kids continued to be drawn to the swimming hole. Rita was a victim of being unable to judge an unusually high speed. Life would never be the same, especially for Mrs. Opp after her baby died.

Reggie laughingly told a family story from better times. Oldest sister Janetta had a pet raccoon, which she kept in a basement cage; a situation which distressed her dad. One Thanksgiving in the mid-'50's Jan commented favorably on the gamey taste of one of the three meat dishes. Daddy Opp stated that it was rabbit from a recent hunting trip. During after dinner relaxation Daddy Opp corrected himself by suggesting that Janetta give water to her pet in the basement. It was much to the delight of the boys and the chagrin of the girls when it was discovered that Ricky Raccoon had been one of the main courses. One has to understand the testosterone rush of a true wrestling family of boys to appreciate the humor. But the family did experience an economical dish.

And more than once, according to Reggie, two or more of the Opp brothers would attend a movie at the Belmont Theater then walk home cutting through Hawthorne Park. If they saw an unfortunate in the park or near their house just yards from the B & O Railroad tracks, they would invite him to their home for a bed-then-breakfast stay. Mom Opp was never made aware of that unusual invitation, even during the '50's when many in the "old" neighborhood left their doors unlock on a regular basis. Her reaction to the "bums" or "hobos" in her home, even years later, cannot be repeated. But the social awareness of such an attitude was indicative of the Opp family religious foundation.

Yet, it was surprising when Mrs. Opp arrived home unexpectedly from a trip to California the summer of 1961. The senior Opps along with their two daughters, Clancie and Larita, traveled to the west coast to visit older daughter, Janetta. Reggie had decided to host a musical jam session overnight. Clancie's freshman boyfriend, Richard Such who was a drummer at GWHS as well in a band called "Kings Men" in 1960-61, was found sleeping in mom and pop Opp's bed with empty White Castle containers littering the floor throughout the house. Good thing that the girls had made the western trip. Still, Richard didn't stick around for breakfast at the Opp homestead that morning.

Mr. and Mrs. Opp moved to the first block of North Pershing in 1965. Mrs. Opp died in 2006, age 86, surviving 14 years after a stroke. She had outlived her oldest and youngest daughters as well as Carl.

But the Opp family will permanently be celebrated in the Indiana Wrestling Hall of Fame on South Emerson Ave. where they were enshrined in the late 1980's. And it all started because two people of faith attended the Johnson County Fair.

Fred Van Abeele
class of 1935

For the 13th and final year the traditional season ending game between Washington High and Cathedral saw a 20-14 Irish victory in 1972. The game had been postponed for two days because of weather and it would be the final football game in Indiana before the beginning of the state tournament in 1973. But it seemed that the real loss was to be the loss of Cathedral High School to the whims of a tightening economy.

But Fred Van Abeele, Bob Welch and others financially rescued the North Meridian school. Thus another connection between the two friendly rivalry schools which also included the irony that Fred's son-in-law, Ralph Poehls, was the Continental line coach.

Dr. Fredrick R. Van Abeele was born in Chicago, the youngest of three children. Due to family problems, he spent his early years at Catholic Children's Home in Vincennes, Indiana. After his graduation from 8th grade, he moved to Indianapolis where he attended Washington High School.

Fred met classmate Jeanne Nealy who lived in the first block of North Warman and attended School 50 before GWHS. Her family had lived in Cleveland, Ohio but her dad acquired a job in Columbus, Indiana at the Cummins factory. He traveled the 100-mile round-trip daily south on Highway 31 to support his family. Jeanne graduated in three years by 1934 before attending Business College in Indianapolis. They would eventually marry in 1940. In high school their mutual friendship with the future Betty and Lafe Hooser, the basketball star, would stand the test of time.

But in 1935 Fred wanted more in life so he enrolled at Purdue University. With empty pockets he paid for his tuition holding miscellaneous jobs in West Lafayette and in his new home town. He established a major course of study directed toward a chemical engineering degree. But he switched to chemistry since it was less expensive.

Upon graduation he worked briefly at U.S. Royal but then went to Eli Lilly & Co. in Indianapolis. At Lilly Fred began as a bench chemist in the lab. Then he took an educational leave to complete his doctorate in Biochemistry at the University of Illinois.

When he returned to Eli Lilly he was placed into the Research and Development Department. Eventually he was given responsibilities in senior management in penicillin research. He soon became President of Elanco Products Division and then Vice President of Pharmaceutical Research and Development for Lilly.

After he retired in 1972, Fred served as a consultant to the research department at St. Vincent's Hospital and as a consultant at University Heights Hospital. Then he became President of the Board of Directors at University Heights and was instrumental in the development of the new hospital on the south side of Indianapolis.

After Fred and Jeanne were married they were blessed with five children. Andra, Richard, John, Thomas and Peter attended Sacred Heart, Cathedral and Martinsville High Schools. Along with his love of family, Fred was deeply involved in later years with his hospital work. And gardening was his favorite hobby.

Unfortunately Jeanne died in 1978. Later Fred married Phyllis Pickering. When he died in 1985 of prostate cancer he left a legacy of eight grandchildren.

Fred's "Red Gates" estate just off of Highway 37 along with their cottage on Sweetwater Lake and other farmland properties reflected the success of a highly intelligent and motivated kid from the Depression era and Washington High.

The BOYD Family

Raleigh Boyd died in 1929 leaving his widow, Georgia Hybarger Boyd, the task of raising and educating seven boys and one girl. The family lived on Morgan Street in West Indianapolis at the beginning of the Depression.

Mrs. Boyd faced the tremendous burden of feeding, clothing and educating her children. She had only finished the fifth grade before going to work in a factory. So Georgia was determined that her children would not face the same fate. She realized the importance of receiving an education. All of her children eventually graduated from P.S. #46 as well as George Washington High School. There was at least one of her children who was enrolled in Washington High from when it opened in 1927 until the youngest child graduated in 1945.

Lynn Boyd graduated in 1931. He worked for the next forty years as a Linotype operator on newspapers in Indianapolis, Marion and Bedford all in Indiana as well as in Tacoma, Washington.

Robert received his diploma in 1933. Ten years later the Indianapolis Star carried the following article titled "Local Fighter Kills 83 Japs in Solo Machine Gun Charge"

"Guadalcanal, Tarawa, Saipan. All have taken their toll on Indianapolis young fighting men. But one Indianapolis marine, Gunnery Sgt. Robert G. Boyd, probably has killed a Jap for every local man who has died there.

It was on Saipan that he really scored against the Japs. His company was pressing up the northeast coast and had killed Japs by the hundreds when, before they fully realized it, their rank's flank was snowed under. Three machine guns were put out of commission by enemy grenades.

Then Sgt. Boyd went into action. He seized one of the heavy, water cooled machine guns in his hands and made a 150-yard dash under enemy mortar and machine gun fire. Three times he fell to his knees as he stumbled in the darkness, but he made it to the extreme right flank, dropped the gun into place and started firing away.

The next morning the company commander counted 83 dead Japs in the arc before Sgt. Boyd's weapon. Some of them were only three feet away from the gun's snout. Nobody knows how many Japs he killed on Tarawa. But it's a safe bet the Japs suffered under his fire there for Sgt. Boyd had a score to settle with them for Guadalcanal

It was on Guadalcanal a Jap bullet hit his chin, the rifle ball coming out of his neck just below his left ear. The force of the bullet knocked him down but, according to a report by one of his buddies, 'the sergeant came up fighting, blood streaming from him fore and aft. He routed those Japs until he was so faint from lack of blood they had to cart him away on a stretcher. But you could hear him cussing and calling the Japs everything under the sun for yards around.'

And then on Saipan July 2, Sgt. Boyd made another dash under Jap machine gun fire. But this time not to kill Japs but to rescue a fallen marine. He saw the man go down after being hit in the head by a Jap bullet and lost no time dragging him from under enemy fire. When he reached safety with his burden and turned him over he discovered he had rescued his best friend, Sgt. William W. Rogal, Lehighton, Pa.

Through all of this bitter struggle, Sgt. Boyd was fighting with his brother, Platoon Sgt. Paul T. Boyd, who has made a record of his own. Paul had been wounded twice, once while fighting on Saipan within a few yards of his brother, who received his second wound there, and again on Tarawa. He had been forced to take command of his rifle platoon three times on Saipan and Tinian, after his leaders were killed, and the third time earlier on Guadalcanal, replacing his leader who had been stricken ill. Both men wear the Presidential unit citation and have been awarded the Purple Heart with stars for their second wounds."

One of Robert's sons, Robert Lewis Boyd, played on the Washington High School football teams in the 1950's. Another son, Larry, graduated from GWHS in 1965 and served his country as a Marine in the Vietnam conflict.

Hazel Boyd, the lone girl, graduated in 1936. During World War II her husband, Thomas Crosley, who is listed on the school's memorial display along with 94 others, lost his life in Cherbough, France on June 22, 1944.

Paul graduated in 1937. He had enlisted in the United States Marine Corp Reserves on May 3, 1937. He went to summer camp at Great Lakes Naval Training Station. On February 11, 1938 he reached the rank of PFC. He was assigned to active duty November 8, 1940 heading to Camp Elliott, California with the 1st Defense Battalion and was honorably discharged on May 19, 1941.

He then re-enlisted December 16, 1941 and was assigned to A Company, 1st Battalion, 2nd Regiment, 2nd Marine Division. He saw action against the Japanese on the islands of Florida (in the Pacific), Tulagi, Guadalcanal, Tarawa, Saipan and Tinian. Paul's son, Jeff, was also a Marine during the 1960's in Vietnam.

Another Boyd, Charles, graduated in 1940. He was drafted into the Army. The following is an excerpt from the book "Report From The Pacific" by Leo Litz published by the Indianapolis News in 1946:

"They told me that he was a Hoosier, was nicknamed 'Bombsight' and had a pet monkey that answered to the name of 'Bombsight Jr.' So I dropped around to the military police unit of the 24th Army Corps to call on T-5 Charles D. Boyd, 24, who lived on Reisner Street in Indianapolis to see what it was all about.

'Everyone has a nickname in the Army,' he told me. 'I got mine on Attu. One of the company clerks in the 7th Division was looking over my service record and noticed I was employed at the Lukas-Harold bombsight plant in Indianapolis before I joined the Army. This nickname has stuck. Scarcely anyone knows my right name.'

Now I'll tell you about Bombsight Jr. who was strictly a prohibitionist, very fond of grasshoppers, but had a definite dislike for K-rations. Charles told me he had always liked animals, had a dog, coon, pigeons and even a crow for pets at home. He had a big monkey in Leyte, thought it unwise to bring him to Okinawa and sold him to a sailor for $25. Bombsight Jr. was something of a doorstep pet. Charles saw him in the area one afternoon and knew he might be shot by guards if he remained there during the night. Apparently brought from Leyte by another service man, the monkey eluded all efforts at capture. Charles climbed three trees to no avail, but he finally coaxed the monkey to him with a wild sweet potato. Bombsight Jr. soon became the company pet.

Drafted in December, 1942 he had not been home since he had been in service. After twelve weeks of basic training at Camp Wheeler, GA., he was hustled to the west coast and sailed for Attu only two weeks later. At Okinawa he was in charge of supplies and rations for the military police and kept jeep radios repaired as a sideline….."

Phillip graduated in 1940. He was in the Navy Sea Bees and was in Tokyo Harbor, Japan at the close of the war. John graduated in 1943. He served in the U.S. Army during the Korean conflict 1950-1953.

Needless to say, there were many brothers who served during the World War between 1941-1945 with the Fighting Sullivans being immortalized in a sentimental and inspiring Hollywood movie. But the Boyds can obviously lay claim to being a very selfless family perhaps typical of the Depression era families in the United States.

The youngest Boyd, Joseph whose dad died when he was only two, graduated from Washington in 1945. He received a B.S. from Indiana University in 1949 and a M.S. from Butler in 1953. He did his student teaching at his old high school in 1949. He retired from teaching in the late 1980's.

Georgia Boyd died in 1977 at the age of 91. She died a proud woman. Despite enormous handicaps, she had graduated all eight of her children from high school. She was also proud of the fact that five of her sons had served in the military defending our country.

JOHN BRADLEY

Understated but not under-appreciated, at least by those in "the know" at our school. John Bradley arrived on the steps of Washington High in September of 1961. He had transferred from Ben Davis High School at 6200 W. Morris Street where he had mentored their State Championship Cross Country team members to be. Back-to-back undefeated freshmen cross country teams in 1958 and 1959 led to their championship squad that fall. One young runner was so impressed with Coach Bradley's relaxed style and sensitive leadership that he would name his first born in 1965 after his favorite coach. Bob Dickison would name his first born, Brad.

John Bradley's parents were both born in Iowa. His dad, an iron-worker, followed a job to Indianapolis. When he was born in 1929, his sister was eight and his brother was seven in the close-knit Catholic family. Johnny would enter Tech High School during the middle of World War II in 1943. Since Tech was the largest populated school in the state of Indiana at the time, it was extremely competitive to even win a spot on any team. Young John became a varsity runner in the quarter mile as well on Tech's mile relay team. Two of his fellow relay members would become well-known Indiana names. Future Superintendent of Public Instruction, H. Dean Evans, and the son of the founder of Safeway Markets, Julius Defabis, were friends and competitive teammates through the 1947 track season. Then John would head to Butler University to run for Galvin Walker's team.

Walker encouraged Johnny B. to run fall cross country as well as spring track. But after two years, when the Korean War began, he enlisted in the U.S. Navy in August of 1950 to serve his country. With ports of call in the Phillippines, Hong Kong, Japan and then in South Korea, Mr. Bradley's horizons were broadened. Russian MIG fighter planes, manned by Soviet pilots, probably only buzzed within 30 miles of his ship in Korean ports but service in that fluctuating war-zone was no picnic.

In 1952 Johnny B. became a member of the Naval Olympic Track team in Long Beach, California. The Armed Services Olympic Trials were one week before the U.S. Olympic Trials. Ohio State's Mal Whitfield, the 1948 Olympic champ, was in the Air Force at the time and John was hard pressed to challenge him in the 800-meters. Whitfield won at Long Beach and eventually repeated at the Helsinki Olympics in 1952. A bonus for our future Continental was that John watched Eddie Matthews play baseball for the Navy baseball team while on the west coast. John was always an enthusiastic baseball fan. Of course, Matthews would soon bat behind Home Run King Hank Aaron for the Boston then Milwaukee Braves for the next 15 years before he also entered the Hall of Fame.

When he was honorably discharged in 1954 as 3rd-class Yeoman, John had served on two attack transport vessels, the U.S.S. Okinogon and U.S.S. Montross.

On November 23, 1955 John would marry Patty at St. John's Episcopal Church in Greencastle and take on the immense responsibilities of fathering her two girls, Karen and Kathy. Both would graduate from Howe High on the eastside. In 1956 he was working at Continental Baking (a hint at his professional destiny) when he decided to finish his education at Indiana Central.

And he continued his track career as IC's Angus Nicosin paid his tuition to be the school's Cross Country coach while he benefited from the GI Bill of Rights to finish his education. In 1958, with diploma in hand and a resume which included both military and coaching experience, he was hired as an assistant coach at Ben Davis H.S.

Track coach Tom Haynes would leave Washington High after the spring of 1961 to become Vice Principal at new Arlington High, so John acquired a better paying job in IPS as Head Coach in Cross Country and frosh coach in spring Track. Over 1,000 freshmen entered Continentaland that fall including frosh cross country man Bill Keller.

But sophomore Dennis Grider was Coach Bradley's #1 man. He finished second in the competitive city meet and 14th in the State Meet at South Grove Golf Course. He set a school record of 10 minutes-16 seconds for the two-mile jaunt.

Grider would become the back-to-back State Champion in Cross Country in 1962 and 1963 establishing a new state record each year. He was primed in practice to smash his own state record from the previous year with a predicted time of 9:26. But it snowed and, with wrestling tights and stocking cap firmly pulled over his ears, Dennis set a new state record but at a disappointing 9:44. Dennis received a full scholarship to the Univ. of Kansas, a powerhouse at the time. But he returned to the Valley, homesick, after a year. Grider had also been a top wrestler. He finished 2nd in the City in 1963 at 103-lbs.

When Grider's younger brother Ralph invited his African-American teammates to shoot pool on their billiards table in the dining room, it was probably the first time the segregated Valley neighborhood had experienced such a social event. Kenny Brunt, Cliff Cook (who became a Vietnam War veteran), Perry Officer and his brother Jerry all were witness to a significant example of camaraderie in the Grider household. Coach Bradley along with Kenny Morrow and future career Army man John Willoughby also played.

Yet Mr. Bradley's selfless loyalty to Washington High had only just begun. He had started as a Social Studies teacher. And he immediately joined the ranks of Springer-loyalists as his Continental career commenced in 1962. Coach Bradley became the statistician in 1971 and continued in that unofficial capacity through 1994, even though he had retired as a teacher-counselor in 1989. By the late '60's he had joined Springer as a member of the Guidance Department.

In the fall of 1971 he had been enlisted to join Johnny Williams as a freshmen football coach. A cross country man coaching football was unusual. They welcomed the future State Champs nucleus of Butler, Branson, Weatherby and White. The two Johns melded well as a coaching team. Johnny B. noted that Johnny W., once each season, would sincerely lament to the team about when he had not given his best effort and had cost his team a victory as a Southport athlete. And Williams would also state "Johnny B., I'm goin' to the end zone...they're all yours....I'm done" as he would stride away only to return within minutes of his motivational tactic. It also seemed predictable that Williams would toss a frosh player off of the bus when that kid seemed unconcerned after a loss, usually about a mile from the school. Needless to say after that noted practice, frosh players acted as was expected of them after a loss, which usually was followed by a win the next game. Continentals were always taught to be dissatisfied with a team loss.

And, in 1974, he welcomed a new man to Washington High. Walt Stahlhut would replace Coach Williams, as frosh football coach, as well as Frank Luzar, as head of Phys. Ed., after those two long-time coaches retired in June. Stahlhut also became a close friend to John. Their friendship endured 35 years until Walt's death in late 2009.

Johnny B. was assistant to Coach Orman, as was Amos Slaton and Jerry England, on the State Track Runners-up in 1967 at Tech. He was also assistant with Leonard Cannon to Coach Stahlhut for the State Runners-up in 1980 at North Central.

Into the 21st century, Johnny B. continues friendships with ex-Continental teachers Charlie Brown, Al Hamilton, and Mike Barrett as well as continuing volunteer work for Warren Township schools with the encouragement of Assistant Superintendent Tony Burchett. Wife Patty and husband John both sit on the Warren Arts Education Foundation Board. They continue their community involvement, which began in 1990.

COACH BOB SPRINGER

Little Bobby came into this world in 1934 on the living room couch at 1226 Finley Avenue just east of Garfield Park not far from Fountain Square. He was the baby of the seven children of Frank and Gladys Springer. His academic-athletic abilities began to display themselves early under the tutelage of Father Higgins at St. Catherine's Elementary School and Parish on Shelby Street just south of Raymond.

His older brother Joe, better known as Chonky, was a star football player at Tech High School and began a stellar college career first at Danville's Canterberry College until it closed around 1950. Chonky then attended Hanover College on the Ohio River before his invitation to the New York Giants football camp as a 320-pound lineman. By the early 1960's Chonky would be the Head Football Coach at Goshen High School in northern Indiana. His three assistant coaches were Bill Doba, Kenny Mirer, and Joe Shires (Washington '55). Doba would become Head Coach at Mishawaka High School (Washington's 1974 State Championship game opponent) then an assistant at Indiana University. In 2006 Coach Doba was Head Coach at Washington State University. Mirer would follow Chonky as Head Coach at Goshen and his son would become quarterback at Notre Dame before his selection as the #2 draft pick in the NFL. And, JoJo Shires in 1965 would become an assistant football coach under Coach Bob Springer at Washington High through the 1972 season before becoming Athletic Director.

So, Bob had at least one set of big shoes to fill. He chose Cathedral High with Washington grad Joe Dezelan as Head Coach in football. His basketball coaches ranged from Jimmy Doyle to Cleon Reynolds to Pete Weingard. As captain with QB John White his senior season in 1951 they nearly ended undefeated season losing only to Hammond High in a 9-1 season. Growing up not far from Washington High near Addison & Ohio Streets in the Hawthorne area while attending Cathedral, STAR sports writer Bob Collins in 1952 named Bob an all-time great Indianapolis basketball player along with Joe Sexson, Willie Gardner, Dick Nyers and Bailey Robertson.

Bob had to choose between IU, with Bernie Crimmins as Head Coach, and Purdue, with Stu Holcomb as head man. He liked both but chose Purdue. By his senior year Jack Mollenkopf was Head Coach and junior Lennie Dawson was quarterback. The future college and pro Hall of Fame QB threw his first college touchdown pass to Bob "Choo Choo" Springer in the 1955 game against Missouri. And Dawson's first Big Ten TD pass at Ohio State was also to our future great coach. The "Choo Choo" nickname came from his intensely motivated breathing as he ran a pass pattern. And his habit of allowing his tongue to dangle toward the corner of his mouth cost him 23 stitches before the mandate of mouthpieces in the early '60's. Face-masks were not required until 1959.

After college graduation Bob became Head basketball coach and assistant football coach at little Sacred Heart High School in southern Indianapolis in 1956. Coach Springer was called to active duty with Indiana's National Guard by the summer of 1957 and he didn't return to Sacred Heart until December. His basketball team's loss to Deaf School in the Butler Sectional in 1958 influenced him to pursue his first love, football. But his inaugural game in 1958 was against one of the all time great area teams, Manual. Little Sacred Heart lost 61-6. But by putting the only small blemish on Washington High's undefeated 1959 season with a 7-7 tie, then with their dramatic 0-0 tie versus powerhouse Cathedral in 1960 and a share of the City Championship, young Bob established a four year reputation of hard-nosed yet intelligent leadership by the end of the 1961 season.

Curly Julian was not the first to call Coach Springer but he was the most persuasive. So, 28-year old Bobby Springer became Washington's third coach in 1962. The season ending tradition against Cathedral ended at 13-13 (it was 13-6 late in the game, Washington leading, when the extra point was fumbled under rules before two-point conversions were possible) costing the Irish the City Championship on a dramatic rainy Friday in November. In 1963 he moved to the Guidance Office. That gave him the freedom to fully develop the potential of the Continental football player. And, with his dominating personality, he would discourage "skirt chasers" although he would eventually note that his "male only" education at Cathedral was probably not the way that schools should operate. Cathedral became coed at their new campus by 1976.

In Coach Springer's fifth year the Continentals would claim Marion County's first and only mythical State Championship in football led by Bobby Canady, Larry Highbaugh and Rick Sylvester. Sophomore George McGinnis was on the second string that year, behind John Hill and Benny Wooten, but by his senior year McGinnis would become a High School All-American in both football and basketball. Coach Springer gets much of the credit from George for motivating him down the proper attitude path.

The summer before Coach Springer's 1966 champs he would marry Carol Holmes, one time Washington Physical Education teacher and North Central grad. Her dad had coached at Bedford High School and her mother taught for years at IPS School #69 on North Emerson. Their two children (Mike, born in the spring of 1969, and Mary, in the fall of 1970) would enhance an already active life. Mike is currently a Vice Principal at Monrovia High School. And Mary works in corporate America. Both are married.

As the second President of the Indiana Football Coaches Association, Coach Springer would be instrumental in the development of the football play-offs by 1973. And, in the second year, Washington would become the only Marion County school to win State at the top level in the ten-year run of the original system.

The 1983 team came within a touchdown and field goal of winning another championship in game #14 and gave up only 30 points with six shut-outs in their first ten games. With his retirement after the 1993 season Coach Springer would end his 36 years as Head Football Coach with a 253-109-8 record (he was Head Coach at Washington for 32 years). His election to Indiana's Hall of Fame in 1991 was a crowning glory for one of Washington's most prolific and success figures in the school's 68-year history.

Mr. JULIAN'S "MY STORY"

In November of 2002, Mr. Cloyd Julian published a series of essays in the form of "Letters to Erin." Erin is Mr. Julian's granddaughter. The following excerpt is from the chapter titled "Unique Happenings at GWHS." Mr. Julian was principal, 1961-1977.

MEETING WITH PARENTS—Audie Watkins, Dean of Boys, brought a dear elderly black lady to my office and said that he wanted her to tell me what she had just told him. She said, "I told Mr. Watkins that I wanted him to do anything to Jermane that would make a white boy out of him." Jermane had been cutting school. That was the reason she had been called by the Dean. Well, maybe we succeeded. A few years later I got a call from Jermane who was changing planes at the airport. He wanted to know how Bill, my son, was. He and Bill were friends. Jermane reported that he was teaching English in a junior college in California. He was doing well; white boy he didn't need to be.

CURIOUS HAPPENING WITH A TEACHER—We had a new young music teacher that I thought would be a valuable addition to our music department. But one morning when I arrived at my office, three boys who were leaders in our school were waiting for me. I am pleased that most students were proud of their school and wanted to protect its reputation. They said, "Mr. Julian, you need to do something before we all get into trouble. Boys are lining up outside of the new teacher's apartment." I immediately sent for her and repeated what I had heard. She said, "I made a mistake. The first two that I took home I thought were college students." I couldn't believe what I just heard. My answer: "You can go to the personnel office NOW and resign or I'll make a federal case out of this." I don't know what I meant by a federal case but she went directly to the central office and not back to class.

ENCOUNTER WITH A PARENT—Two boys were suspended for three days for fighting. This was standard procedure at our school. This fight happened to be between a black boy and a white boy. However, the fight had nothing to do with race, just an altercation between two students. Our rule was NO fighting. The father of the white boy demanded to see the principal. He ranted and raved and called me a "nigger lover" not once but several times as I quietly listened. Finally, when I thought that he was exhausted, I said "Did your son tell you that?" "No," he replied, "you have him brain-washed. He says that you treat everybody the same." My response: "If your son felt like you I would be concerned and upset. I can't help what you think and I know that I can't change you. So I can't worry about what you think. Your son will serve his suspension like any other student. I am sorry that you feel the way you do."

DEALING WITH PEOPLE, A SINCERE COMPLIMENT—Gladys Huddleston Radcliffe was Parent Teacher's Association President, and a good one. We got along well and she made an important contribution to the school. But one day she came in with a big idea that I didn't want to undertake. I don't recall what it was and maybe she was right. I'm sure that she has forgotten the request. I have. But after we had discussed the idea and I had turned it down, she got to the door to leave then turned around and said, "Curly, you can tell people to go to hell the nicest of anyone I know."

ANOTHER COMPLIMENT, I THINK—A new journalism teacher joined us, fresh out of college with a lot of new ideas. She had been taught that the school paper could publish anything that a student wrote. I thought that the school paper was a "House organ" that should be controlled by the school. And that the journalism teacher should exercise control over what was printed in the paper. She wanted to publish anything that her students wrote. I did not want to critique the paper but thought that it was her job. We had several arguments. Her husband was transferred to Texas and she went with him. In a few years she came back to visit our school. To me she said, "Mr. Julian, when I worked for you I said some awful things about you. I'm sorry. I have a principal now who is stupid." I think that she meant to compliment me, but you can never be sure.

TEACHER RUTH—Good teachers are creative, and I liked that type. A case in point: a beginning music teacher who was a hard worker but immature. I got calls from parents that she was keeping instrumental music students until 9 PM. When I confronted her that this was unreasonable, she said that I was complaining because she was working hard. She had a violin player who was a star pole-vaulter. The track coach complained that she wouldn't let him come to track practice but kept him playing the violin. When I called both to the office, she said: "I'll share. He can have him on Fridays and I'll keep him the rest of the week." Sometimes when she didn't get her way, she would come to the office crying. Finally, when she came in crying I said (I don't know why), "If you come in here crying one more time I will give you something to cry about." Well, she came in on a real crying jag. I got up and started toward her (I wouldn't have hit her) but she backed away saying, "You wouldn't hit me?!" I kept coming and she said, "You would!!" She quit crying. Finally, she married a shop teacher and gave up teaching. They have a fine family and live in a beautiful home in north Indianapolis. Her name is in the paper, now and then. She is an avid advocate for affairs in her community. I think that she is usually right but she sure makes lots of noise and usually gets results. Yes, she was an excellent teacher but a real pain for the principal.

Mr. Julian signed at the end of the chapter, "Your loving Grandpa J."

RALPH TAYLOR

The following is an excerpt from Ralph Taylor's personal acknowledgement for his induction into the Indiana Basketball Hall of Fame in 2001. It was printed in the "Indiana Basketball History" magazine and was titled "1965: The Year of the Continentals." Ralph, in 2010, is the Chief Program Officer with the Central Indiana Community Foundation (CICF) while serving as President of the Indiana Basketball Hall of Fame since 2009 as well as President of the Indianapolis Downtown Rotary Club. He is the fourth leading scorer in school history behind George McGinnis, John Sherman Williams, and Marvin Winkler. Ralph is also third on the all-time rebounding list behind only McGinnis and Steve Downing with 1005 boards over three years. Here, in his own words, are Ralph's memories of a glorious season:

In the fall of 1961, a significant event occurred at George Washington High School that would eventually change the basketball power structure in Indianapolis. This occurrence would culminate with Washington High becoming only the second school and the very first racially integrated school in Marion County to win the coveted IHSAA Basketball State Championship. Entering the high school as freshmen were Eddie Bopp, Billy Keller, and me. In our freshmen year, we won the freshmen City Championship and finished the season with a 14-3 record. It was a sign of things to come. In our three years of varsity competition, we amassed a 72-8 record and became the first basketball team in the highly competitive city to win three consecutive City Tourney Championships since Tech in the early 1930's when only five teams competed. By the '60's there were ten IPS teams (11 by 1967 with Marshall) plus five parochial schools and the School for the Deaf competing for the City Championship. It's significant to note that none of the powerful Attucks, Shortridge, or Tech teams of the 1950's were able to accomplish the feat.

During my three years as starting center we never had a player taller than 6'3". But what we lacked in height was more than compensated for with quickness, sound fundamentals, intelligence, hustle, a zone press, excellent coaching, and the belief that we could not be beaten. In three years we were never out-rebounded. Our style of play was exciting and this generated a tremendous fan following not only from Washington students and alumni but also from fans outside of the "Washington family." Our popularity and huge following led to our playing only three home games our junior year and just one in our home gym in '64-65. In February 1964 (at 20-0) we played our City Championship opponent (Tech at 19-1) before a crowd of almost 12,000 at historic Butler Fieldhouse in a single regular season game with our reserves playing the preliminary.

Our 1965 success only came after two straight varsity seasons coming to an end with disappointing losses at the Southport Sectional, which had replaced the Butler Sectional as the toughest in central Indiana. In our sophomore year, we lost to Southport High on a jump shot by the legendary Louie Dampier in the final seconds. In our junior year we suffered a devastating loss to Howe when a knee injury prevented me from playing. We had defeated them by 26 points in their gym the first game of the season and had been ranked in the top ten of the state the entire year. That third consecutive loss for the Continentals in the Sectional Championship game ended a 23-1 season (Southport had defeated the 1962 team my frosh year). Personally, I always felt that the 1963-64 team was the most talented of the three teams and we could have challenged for the state title that year with Bob Komlanc, Calvin Schaffer, John Dowdell, and Sam Kitchens.

After the two sectional losses that I was involved in an eerie thing would occur on the ride back to the school. I would have my transistor radio playing and the same song, "Our Day Will Come" by Ruby and the Romantics, would be playing on one of the local radio stations. Talk about omens—that song was released in 1962.

The 1964-65 season began with some doubt about how we would fare in our final season. Billy Keller, Eddie Bopp, and I were the only returning lettermen. Marvin Winkler moved into the starting unit and Harvey Holmes, Mark Gladson or Bill Rogers alternated as the fifth starter. Despite the uncertainty, local newspapers viewed Washington, Broad Ripple, Wood, and Crispus Attucks as the strongest teams entering the season. There was one team overlooked that would prove to be our biggest hurdle in getting to the state—Manual High.

Our final season began with a victory over Howe at our adopted home court at second year Northwest High School thus avenging our Sectional loss. We finished the regular season with a 20-2 record and were ranked 3rd and 4th in the AP and UPI ratings respectfully. We lost to Manual on January 2 and Ben Davis on February 6 with both games played at the Indiana Central gym as our home games with SRO crowds of more than 4,500 fans. On the eve of the most power packed Southport Sectional in history, we were picked as favorites once again to win our first Sectional since 1948 (which was Washington's first). Billy, Eddie, and I knew that this was our last "hurrah" and we were determined that we were going all out for this elusive title. After drubbing Chartrand (the predecessor of Roncalli), we played our old nemesis Howe High. We defeated them before an SRO crowd of more than 7,200 fans to move into the title game against Manual. They had defeated Wood whom we had defeated twice in close games that season. Wood had been our City Championship game opponent. They had a front line of 6'6", 6'7", and 6'9" as well as a guard once touted as the next Oscar Robertson. They were coached by 1946 Mr. Basketball, Johnny Wilson.

Manual was ranked in the Top Ten in the state and was lead by 6'5" Mike Hargraves. Because of a severe snowstorm, the game was postponed from Saturday to the following Monday. Despite the weather conditions another SRO crowd came to Southport and witnessed a classic battle that was reminiscent of the 1950's Butler Sectional battles between Crispus Attucks and Shortridge. We defeated them 67-61 thus ending our school's string of three disappointing final game losses and, in the process, I felt that we were destined to win State.

Our Regional opening game opponent was the Butler Sectional Champs Ben Davis. As noted they had defeated us during the season. We were determined to avenge the defeat but our third leading scorer, Marvin Winkler, had severely sprained his ankle during our Wednesday night practice at the Fieldhouse and was forced to sit the bench. Prior to the game our locker room was quiet except for the singing and laughing just feet away where the Ben Davis team was dressing. We avenged our only other loss 81-66 behind Keller's career high 31 points before over 14,000 fans to advance to the title game against favored Anderson. We wanted to advance to the first Sweet Sixteen in our school's history. But their 6'5" center (who later played for IU in basketball and then the Cincinnati Bengals football team) presented quite a challenge. We won 75-71 and I was lucky enough to score 24 points with 15 rebounds against big Ken Johnson.

By now our bandwagon was packed but still growing. We were drawing SRO crowds and our fan base of students, faculty, and alumni was tremendous. Our fan support was unbelievable for all three years of my varsity competition. However, the tournament run generated an unprecedented following that left me completely amazed.

We were favored to win the Semi-State round. By now we were being viewed as Indianapolis' brightest state title contenders since Manual High with the VanArsdale twins in 1961. Playing before another packed Butler Fieldhouse (capacity 14,943) we defeated a tough Brookville team in the afternoon Channel-6 televised game and then came from nine points behind at halftime against Muncie South to win 69-52 to advance to the Final Four. Although Keller, Winkler, and I had been the scoring leaders, Bopp was our unsung hero that night by scoring 16 points in the second half to validate his importance to our overall success. By now it seemed that the whole community of Greater Indianapolis was joining the Continental bandwagon. It was great.

Princeton along with Ft. Wayne North and the favorite to capture the 55th State title, Gary Roosevelt, joined us in the Final Four. From a size perspective we matched up well with our opening opponent, Princeton. However, we were aware that both Ft. Wayne North and Gary Roosevelt were much bigger than us. After beating Princeton in the opener, we were all set to play Roosevelt that night. But it was not to be as the Ft. Wayne team upset the team from Gary.

In the State Championship game both teams were tight and the poor shooting reflected that as we shot only .315 and North only .375. Moreover, I had one of my worst games as I was surrounded by a zone defense that was anchored by their 6'8" center. But we prevailed 64-57 coming from behind again trailing by seven points at halftime.

We became, at the time, only the second school in Marion County history to win the State Championship. Although we were one of the shortest teams to win in recent years we never once viewed our lack of physical size as a detriment in my three years of varsity competition. In reality I think that our lack of size was our secret weapon. Other teams would look at us and think that there was no way they could lose to us. As the starting 6'2" center for all three varsity seasons, I was usually shorter than my opponent. However, I always felt that I could out jump anyone regardless of their size because of my quick leaping ability that was combined with solid fundamentals of the game.

We closed out our most memorable season at 29-2 having avenged both of our losses while defeating three teams in the state's top ten during the tournament. On the way back to West Washington Street, I had my transistor radio playing and the song "Our Day Will Come" was played. Indicative of our fan support, more than 4,000 fans waited over 90 minutes in 20-degree weather for us in the stands of our football field in order to celebrate a great victory.

Throughout my career at Washington, I was fortunate to have played with many outstanding players but none were finer than Billy Keller and Eddie Bopp. We had helped to start a powerful basketball dynasty that would have a legacy all of its own. Billy and I were selected to the Indiana All-Star Basketball team. Billy was Mr. Basketball and we both accepted basketball scholarships to Purdue University where we would play in the National Championship game four years later against UCLA. Eddie received a football scholarship to Butler University.

The school loyalty and faculty support over three years was fantastic. During the early 1960's most students attended games and there was always a Student Cheer Block. But with the unusually strong support of the faculty I knew that I was in a special environment that epitomized the spirit of Washington High School. Under our principal, Cloyd J. Julian, sports and other extra curriculars had a special place in the school but he made sure that academics was first. To this day I still encounter people from around the state who share with me what a pleasure it was to watch our '65 team perform. Our three year run was the genesis for the athletic dynasty that our school maintained above all other area schools through the early 1980's in both basketball and football. Of course in 1969 two "small fellows" named George McGinnis and Steve Downing led the school to its second state title going undefeated.

I would be remiss if I did not mention the fine coaching staff at the school that began with our freshmen coach, the late Russell McConnell, and the varsity coaches Jerry Oliver and Richard Harmening plus Howard Leedy who was a volunteer coach and statistician my senior year. A special acknowledgment to my grade school coach at IPS #5: Mr. Clifford Robinson took the time to teach me the game and turn me into a good player with a sound fundamental background in all aspects of basketball. He was also the individual who taught basketball to Winkler and McGinnis at School 5. Mr. Robinson had graduated from Crispus Attucks High School in the early 1950's and was a member of their basketball team under Ray Crowe.

(note: The Boys Basketball Tourney was "the only game in town" starting in 1911 until baseball in 1967 and then football in 1973 followed by Girls Basketball in 1976 added team tournaments. Team Champions in track, wrestling, and other sports emphasized individual winners. In that sense, the basketball spotlight was both elitist and more pressure packed. The television coverage was not only statewide but was received live by at least one former Hoosier family, actually 1935 player Lafe Hooser's, in Maryland. Only boys' basketball was awarded championship rings. There was only one statewide top athlete named each year (Mr. Basketball) and only one sportsmanship award each year (Trester Award). Taylor was the leading scorer for two years and leading rebounder all three years. Keller outscored him slightly their senior year. The 1963-64 team averaged 75 points per game while allowing 56 per game. The 1964-65 team averaged 78 points, allowing 60. And that was before the 3-point line with two of the greatest-ever Indianapolis outside-shooters on the team. Keller eventually set the Pacers career 3-point standard by 1976 that Reggie Miller busted in the 1990's and Winkler would break Oscar Robertson's single season scoring record in 1966. And our own Ralph Taylor would be named as one of the "most popular" Purdue players of the 20th century by Boilermaker basketball fans.)

GARY GUNTHER, class of 1965

In 1987 when four year younger brother Greg arrived in Indianapolis he was faced with a life altering, life threatening situation. Older brother Gary had come home to Indiana's capital in 1984 with the kidney disease that had taken the life of their father in 1957 when Gary was 8-years-old and Greg was only 4. Polycystic Kidney Disease (PKD) was inherited by Gary and he had undergone dialysis since 1984 when he also was put on a transplant waiting list. Their father had no such choice. Transplants were not an option and, ironically, dialysis first became an accepted procedure in America during the late 1950's. So Gary was, in one sense, lucky. Lucky modern science had evolved. And lucky he had a loving brother. Greg was only 35.

Gary Richard Gunther was born March 30, 1948 in Methodist Hospital. His mom was a nurse there. She had grown up a couple of blocks directly southwest of today's Lucas Oil Stadium on Chadwick Street where I-70 now runs. She was one of eight siblings. Gary's dad lived his teenage years near Tech High School with five others including his older sister who was boss while their dad was gone most of the year working in the gas fields of western Pennsylvania. Gary's dad eventually achieved an Electrical Engineering degree from Purdue University by the time he was married. But he wanted more. He entered what today is IUPUI law school in the 1950's. And even had his 7-year-old son campaign with him in the neighborhood when he unsuccessfully ran for City Council as a Republican. But his life was cut short by the unforgiving PDK.

The young Gunther family had moved into the very last house near Lafayette Road on a short stretch of 22nd Street between Cold Springs Road (Coffin Golf Course) and Highway 52. From there Gary would walk the four or five blocks south across Lafayette Rd. and 16th Street to School 75 in Haughville. His high IQ and academic ability was evident at an early age. He also excelled musically. One of his best friends at the academically accelerated School 75 was Bob Evans. Young Bob chose to attend Shortridge High. But Gary headed to the National Road school along with other good buddies Rusty Redenbarger, Jerry Shepard, Vicki Benson and Greg Shelton.

Entering Washington High School in the fall of 1961 in the largest class in Continental history he was one of about 25 (of almost 1,000) assigned to a special advanced Biology class taught by Donald Kramer who soon became an academic doctor. (Dr. Kramer eventually married fellow teacher Mary Melick when he headed to brand new Northwest High School in 1963)

At Washington Gary played trumpet for Mr. Funk's band and Pep Band while singing in Mr. Thatcher's Continentalaires. He also was in the Junto Club (history) with Mr. Thomas. But his intensity and personal experiences seemed to direct him toward a love of science. He and good friend Ray Knight were two of a very few in the state of Indiana who became National Merit Finalists. Both would head toward Wabash College in Crawfordsville after high school graduation. Eventually Ray would graduate from Wabash in 1969 and matriculate to John Hopkins to study bio-chemistry. In 2009 Ray has a family medical practice in Jeffersonville and is a teaching doctor at the University of Louisville. One of his antique British roadsters is unique worldwide.

Gary's journey was a little different. He too graduated from Wabash in '69 with a major in Chemistry and a minor in Biology. By 1975 he achieved a doctorate in Immunology from Rockefeller University. And then he did post-doctoral work at Yale in cell biology. He was awarded a degree there in 1978.

Between 1978 and 1984 he was employed at St. Jude's Children's Research Hospital in Memphis, Tennessee. PKD was something he seemed to research often. But, unfortunately, his disease forced him to head to Indianapolis. He also worked in Chicago but after his transplant operation he took a job at the Indianapolis Medical Center doing research in physiology, pulmonary hematology, leukemia and oncology. In 1992 he began a study of microparticles in relationship to diagnostic blood tests.

In 2000 he was hired by Roche Diagnostics. Today he develops theraputic blood tests for Thermo-Fisher Scientific near 79th & Georgetown Road. But he may be headed to southern California if that company moves there. Luckily his cousin, Marvin Winzenread, lives there. Mr. Winzenread was a math teacher at Washington High in the early 1960's and teaches Computer Science part-time at Hayword College in retirement.

Gary has been married twice. He met his first wife, Donna Cunningham from North Central High School, while working at Eli Lilly shortly before he went to Memphis. They had a daughter, Sarah, who was born December 5, 1980. She lives in Hancock County today. His second wife, Cheri, was a Ben Davis graduate.

And his life saving brother, Greg, in 2009 is the boss at the Botanical Gardens in Memphis, Tennessee.

When Gary and good friend Vic Reardon began a senior prank on June 4, 1965 they couldn't avoid respected Latin teacher Miss Thelma Parks' prying eyes. But, unlike some school authorities both then and now, Mr. Julian and Mr. Watkins both understood the inappropriateness of severe punishment. A good laugh in 2009 is possible thanks to the common sense and good will of what most continue to see as the Washington Way of confronting things both good and bad. And Gary is one of the all time good and accomplished Continentals.

BILLY KELLER

In his rookie season as the Indiana Pacers long-range bomber at the old Coliseum, Billy tallied a career high 44 points in late 1969. After seven seasons and three American Basketball Association Championships, he retired with a per-game average of almost 12 points as well as the highest free throw and 3-point percentage in Pacer history at the time. His 506 three-pointers remained a Pacer career record until a guy named Reggie Miller broke it 15 years later on his way to 2,560 3-pointers in 18 years. Keller remains number two on the Pacer list into 2010.

Bill was born the third of three Keller kids to Roscoe and Margie. All three opened their eyes to this world in Bloomington. Billy's dad had met young Margie Curry at the skating rink near the Bloomington airport in the late 1930's. He was a short order cook. She was a resident of Ellettsville about halfway toward Spencer on Highway 46 just northwest of Bloomington. Roscoe was from Lyons in Greene County just west of Monroe County, a small town that in 2000 still only registered 748 residents. They were married in Gosport. In 1942, the year their second child was born, Roscoe obtained a job at Allison's on west 10th Street in Indianapolis. For the next six years he made the daily trip from Bloomington of over 50 miles. He would retire in 1975. Margie worked years at the Indiana State Board of Health, also retiring in the '70's.

The two eldest Kellers, Bernie (class of '58), and Barbara (class of '60) were ages seven and five when the baby arrived. William Curry Keller was born in August of 1947. In March of 1948 the family moved to 1416 N. Livingston in the state capital, just yards from 16th Street and the Indianapolis Motor Speedway. Roscoe left the home in 2009. His wife of 68 years had died July 25, 2008.

Billy's older siblings set a positive example for him athletically as competitive swimmers for Rhodius Park's Indianapolis Times City Parks Swim Meets in the 1950's. Little Billy excelled as a diver from the springboard as well as the high dive. But he seemed to always be dribbling a basketball. First in his own driveway, then south to 10th Street on east to Tibbs Avenue arriving at the Sellers family backyard basketball court. Meadowood Park and Speedway courts were among his favorites into high school.

Mr. Vernon McCarty, who would later teach and coach at Northwest High School, was Billy's junior high coach. Along with his year-older buddy, Steve Midkiff from Rochester St., Keller dominated as quarterback on the football and basketball teams. Most of their football games were played on Washington's field but their basketball league games were at School 90.

At Washington High, where his brother had been fullback on the football team and a power-forward on the basketball team while his sister had been a popular cheerleader, Billy decided to concentrate on basketball and baseball. He had been known as "King Kong Keller" in the baseball leagues in nearby Speedway. His skills as catcher and #3 hitter could have served him well in a college, maybe pro, baseball career. But his amazing quickness and shooting eye were soon the envy of every central Indiana basketball coach, especially Jerry Oliver. And his intensity also served him well on John Bradley's cross-country team in the fall.

The Continental frosh ended the season at 14-3 but swept through the City Championship defeating tradition-rich Crispus Attucks in the final game in our gym, 28-27. Keller normally was a starting guard along with Glenn Teddy Williams, the brother of 1959 Indiana All-Star Eddie. Ralph Taylor was the rebounding center while the forward spots usually saw Charlie Rowland and Steve Warren in supporting rolls on Russell McConnell's team. Williams, Taylor, Rowland and Warren had all gone to School 5. Sometimes Billy's School 67 running mate, Bill

Hedges, would start at times as did two boys from Eagledale's School 79, Steve Woolsey and Mike Morris.

An unfortunate accident in cross country practice in the fall of 1962 at Rhodius Park when he stepped in a rut in the ground led to a knee operation and kept Bill on the sidelines in basketball until January. So it wasn't until his junior year in the City Championship game against Tech at Tech in January 1964 that he displayed his first defining moment. With the defending City Champ Continentals down by ten points with just over two minutes left in the game, Bill took charge and scored five consecutive jump shots to tie the game. They all may have been 3-point bombs but the 3-point phenomena was still almost four years in the future with ABA basketball. The final score, 73-71, was the second of three consecutive City Championships. Ranked as the #4 team in the state, Washington stood at 20-0 facing a re-match with Tech scheduled for Butler Fieldhouse. We lost 69-71 but still arrived at the Southport Sectionals final game as the favorite against a Howe team that we defeated our first game at Howe, 85-59.

But the Continentals were denied in the final game for the third year in a row. The 1964 team ended at 23-2 averaging 75 points per game while allowing only 56 on defense. Better luck seemed to be in the future. And the '65 team became the first Marion County racially integrated team to win the State in the 55th year of the tourney while averaging over 78 points per game.

Bill was named as our school's first Mr. Basketball in the annual All-Star game against Kentucky. He averaged almost 19 points per game on his senior year 29-2 team. He tallied a total of 47 points in the two State Finals games. Against Ben Davis in the Regionals afternoon game he scored a career-high high school total of 31 points.

But bigger things were yet to come. Purdue University assistant coach Bob King had been shadowing Keller for much of two years. His personable style won our westsider over to the Boilermakers even though his relatives had hoped that he would return to Bloomington as an IU player. Western Kentucky was Billy's second choice.

On the freshmen team with future professional star Herm Gilliam, Billy thrived. But it wasn't until his junior year when a spanking new Mackey Arena premiered in October 1967 against the defending national champs UCLA led by former Purdue star Coach John Wooden. Bill was now the ball-handling guard along with 1966 Mr. Basketball Rick Mount from Lebanon. The Boilers lost 71-73 under third year Head Coach George King. They ended the season at 15-9 and 9-5 in the Big Ten.

Once, in the summer of 1966, Billy had arrived at his high school stomping grounds known as Meadowood Park. Gilliam, his roommate Ralph Taylor, and Purdue's football tight end were with him. Gilliam wowed the pick-up-players, which I think included a young George McGinnis, when he dunked two basketballs at the same time.

Keller and Gilliam were co-captains for two years in an unusual display of respect for their leadership. The Boilers ended the 1969 season at 23-5 and National Runners-up to a third consecutive UCLA Championship led by Lew Alcindor. Purdue defeated North Carolina in their first Final Four game, 92-65, at Louisville. But they lost to the Bruins 72-92 without Purdue's 7' center Chuck Bavis. Still, Billy scored 20 points.

Co-Captain Keller's Purdue team won the Big Ten Championship with a 13-1 record losing only to Ohio State in Columbus. The Boilermakers defeated IU twice. The score was 96-95 at Bloomington but 120-76 in West Lafayette. And Bill was named as the inaugural Naismith Award winner as America's best college player under 6'.

In the summer All-Star game at Hinkle Fieldhouse in 1969 Keller bombed in 39 points. His long-range shooting skills continued to attract the professional scouts.

Billy was drafted in the 8th round of the ABA draft by the hometown Pacers. He was also drafted by the NBA's Milwaukee Bucks. The Pacers offered him a $25,000 one-year contract with incentives (he collected just over $33,000 that season). He grabbed it and became part of Pacer immortality. Keller was a mainstay on all three Pacer ABA Championships in 1970, '72 and '73. He set another Pacer record for 3-pointers in a play-off game against San Antonio when he tallied 39 points including 9 of 13 3-pointers.

Known by many as the "Milkman" when he was hired by the American Dairy Association as a pitch-man, Billy also was the recipient of a popular song in his honor titled "The Ballad of Billy Keller." The lyrics included, "He stands 5-foot-5 when he starts to drive, but when he fakes it in he's like 6-foot-5, that's Keller, Bill Keller, home-grown Hoosier with the red-hot hand."

He had begun his summer camps in 1974 so, when he was released by the Pacers in the fall of 1976, he continued his love of basketball. Bill's video "The Lost Art of Shooting" continues to inspire many young basketball players.

Bill was an assistant to Purdue coach Lee Rose during his final season when the Boilers lost in the Final Four to UCLA in 1980 at Market Square Arena. Eventually he coached the girls' team at Brebeuf before a seven-year stint at Indiana Central with 1962 Mr. Basketball Larry Humes as an assistant. Humes noted to this writer that Keller was highly respected by players and coaches alike. Ironically, Billy was replaced by Bill Green who had first gained prominence while coaching at GWHS.

Bill married Joyce Thompson in 1979. They have one daughter and two grandchildren in 2010. As he continued his year-round shooting camps, Billy was approached by Pacer President Larry Bird in late 2008. Bird asked Bill to see if he could improve the free throw shooting skills of young center Roy Hibbert. After a few practices, which included more and more Pacers in attendance, Keller was unsure about his status or responsibilities. But Bird approached him with an offer he couldn't refuse. Bill became the Pacer shooting coach in January of 2009.

Popular Pacer Coach Bobby Leonard recently noted on a radio talk show that he first remembered uttering his signature line "Boom Baby" while coaching when "McGinnis dribbled to the baseline, then passed it to Billy and 'Boom Baby' it was a 3-pointer." No one can deny that Billy Keller will always be recognized as one of the top five most popular players in the history of the Pacer franchise. And at Washington, too.

TONY BURCHETT

Part of all I've known—Fred Hofmeister, Bill Welcher, Mr. Counts, Gary Baker, Mr. Bradley, Ruben Timmons, Mr. Coverstone, Chuck Dulla, Miss Dragoo. Just a few of those hearty personalities that have had a significant influence on WI's Tony Burchett.

Burchett's family history began in the Dale Hallow area of eastern Tennessee. His mom's family owned farmland that was displaced by the Tennessee Valley Authority which began in 1933 as part of President Roosevelt's New Deal to help the poor in America. The TVA was to give electricity, fresh water, and recreational stimulus to the destitute areas of the Deep South. Tony's grandfather was a respected "moonshiner" who supplied his neighbors with special libations. One friend was the grandpa of current University of Texas football coach Mack Brown. His mother, Edna Adelaide Melton, would become the rock in his life. She married another descendent of southern roots with sympathy for the Lost Cause but with an attitude of much empathy for the downtrodden. James Odell Burchett was a Staff Sgt. in the U.S. Army during the Korean War. After Tony was born the Burchetts moved north to become migrant workers. While picking tomatoes for 15-cents a hamper alongside Hispanics from the southwest, Tony's mom and dad enrolled him in Hopewell Elementary in Franklin, Indiana in 1958. Education was the "way out" for the motivated and idealistic among those in the USA then, and now. Then they moved to the Valley, east of Harding Street, and he enrolled in Indianapolis Public School Thomas Edison #47.

When the Burchetts moved to Belleview Street just south of Oliver Avenue, the transfer to William Penn School #49 continued his grandiose dream. Teachers like Mr. Fuqua, Mr. Black, and Mr. Coverstone all greatly impressed the young Tony. But the father of Harvey and Tommy Holmes would help set in motion the dream of becoming a sports star. When Mr. Holmes taught Tony the skills of being a baseball catcher on the Carnine field just north of his new home, he reviled in some self-confidence and a new feeling of high self-esteem. He wanted to be Mickey Mantle, albeit with the "tools of ignorance" behind the plate.

His enduring friendships with Chuck Dulla and Jim Clevenger, who were year-older idols, as well as Jay Clevenger would help steer his positive attitude toward becoming a student-athlete at Washington High. Clevenger's father had been captain and star of the 1945 team. Dulla's dad had been a starter on the very first teams circa 1930. When Tony first saw "hunky bread" (brown hard-crust bread) at the Dulla household, he thought he was in a higher-classed society. In reality, he was experiencing the "melting pot" existence on the Westside in the home of a Romanian descendent.

And Tony was introduced to football at School 49. To "Dream the Impossible Dream," which was the 8th grade theme, was becoming a self-fulfilling prophesy.

Nothing Secedes Like Success—Tony entered Washington High School in September of 1967. But he had already become the starting quarterback on the freshmen football team after the August 15 practices began. He would "start" for 38 consecutive games at QB, first on the frosh team then the reserve team and then two years at the varsity helm.

His dad had left home two years earlier but Tony's mom never waivered in her strong belief that education came first. Tony's reputation as a serious student never faltered. Washington High teachers Al Hamilton, John Bradley, Don Counts, and Frank Luzar were teachers that Tony highly respected. And this author was lucky enough to watch Tony's "edge of his seat" concentration in U.S. History class. But Miss Allie Dragoo's new "Speech" class was Tony's most memorable academic experience. As a sophomore, he was in the same class as senior George McGinnis. Miss Dragoo, an eastern Kentucky lady, was a no-nonsense teacher with strict rules and a firm grasp of the difference between right and wrong. She reminded Tony of his mom. And McGinnis has publically commented on Miss Dragoo's importance to his future public speaking presentations on television and radio. Tony benefited, too.

Although Tony was a very intense baseball catcher, thanks to Carnine's Mr. Holmes, his emotional forte was football. He thrived under the tutelage of coaches Johnny Williams, Vasco Walton, Ralph Poehls, Eddie Bopp, Tom Rosenberger, Jerry England, and the always-impressive Joe Shires. But Head Coach Bob Springer was "the greatest influence on me," noted Tony in 2010. During the 1969 season the fourth game saw the Continentals confronting arch-rival Southport on the southside. At halftime the score read 6-22 in the Cardinals favor. Tony often carried a copy of the 23rd Psalm in his sock. He asked Coach Springer if he could read it to the team. Coach concurred. The final score read: 28-22 with Washington High as victors. Tony was 9-12 passing for 141 yards with two touchdown passes, including one to George Russell. George was a close friend who often visited Tony's home, regardless of the fact that he was an African-America. Russell, in the spring of 1971, would be on the 880-relay State Champions that would set a State Record. Also on that record-setting team was Tony's close friend and one who would make a strong impression that would greatly influence Mr. Burchett in future years. His name was Ruben Timmons. The diminutive Timmons didn't look like a football player, especially when standing beside stars Eddie Boswell and Steve Stanfield. But he was quick and energetic. Ruben was of Hispanic descent and was adopted by a couple living near Rhodius Park. But the summer before his senior year, Ruben was sent back to the Orphans' Home in Lafayette, Indiana.

John Sims, Tony's only rival at quarterback and a strong wrestler, would convince his parents to offer Ruben their home as refuge for his senior year in high school. Ruben agreed and was the speedster for the Springer-Burchett "South Carolina Crossbuck 45."

Ruben would become Dr. Timmons as an anesthesiologist. In 2010, Ruben is considering an offer from his blood-cousin, who is the leader of the nation of Panama, to become the Health Minister of that Central American country.

Along with John Bopp, Tony would be Sports Editor of the Surveyor headed by Mr. David Knott. He would also win the Kiwanis Academic Award as Washington's top football-student. In baseball he would be named MVP and All-City catcher. His brother, Jeff, followed in his big brother's footsteps and was an outstanding baseball player too.

Yet Tony's experiences as a high school student didn't just come in the classroom and on the athletic fields. Indiana All-Star Gary Baker seemed to constantly prod Tony into more repetitions when running the Rhodius Park hill or in Fred Hofmeister's gym on the bench press. Hofmeister, the legendary proprietor of Indianapolis' only known weight training gym from the 1930's into the 1970's, would be another motivator for young Burchett at his 3rd floor facility in the first block of West Ohio Street. But Baker's way of personalizing his encouragement seemed to greatly motivate Tony. "I bet the Ben Davis quarterback is running two more sprints today.....I bet you Sims has done another set on the bench today....you wanna be a winner or just another player?" Gary would say.

Tony would also try to emulate Packers great Bart Starr but his summer routine of dropping to pass by back-peddling didn't always met with approval from Coach Springer. Nonetheless, requesting jersey #15 was a choice well thought out.

Jim Byers, John Moses, and Nick Voris—Tony was determined to continue his football career. The University of Evansville was his target. As a walk-on, Tony felt that maybe he was too short and too slow to continue as a college QB. Luckily, quarterbacks during Coach Springer's regime were consistently required to block and tackle in drills as well as "hitting" the sled. Linebacker seemed a natural for ex-QB Burchett.

Coach Voris was Tony's "position coach" at linebacker. Under Head Coach Byers and Offensive Coach Moses, Tony prospered. Tony was a three-year letter-winner and was named defensive captain while playing on one Indiana Collegiate Conference Champion as well as a Division-3 NCAA semi-finalist. His bachelor's degree in education was the cherry on top of the sundae. And sealed his fate.

Although high school teammate Bill Welcher didn't finish his college career at Evansville along with Tony, Welcher first became an Evansville policeman before a distinguished career with the United States Marine Corps, retiring as a Lt. Colonel. Bill was another of Tony's positive influences and a continuing friend.

In 1975 Coach Burchett joined the football coaching staff at Richmond High School in eastern Indiana. Hub Etchison was the respected Head Coach. Tony taught English at Pleasant View Junior High School. But Tony returned to his teenage roots in 1977 when his resume was accepted by Principal Curly Julian at 2215 W. Washington St. Mr. Julian's remonstrative "nothing secedes like success" would be modeled by Tony.

RIF and Warren Central—Coach Burchett's four years at Washington High continued his journey to educational greatness. Working for Coach Springer along with fellow Continental alums Myron Newland and Leonard Cannon, Tony gained an increased knowledge of football as the coach responsible for accumulating scouting information. When he would physically lead the Demo Team, Coach Burchett's experiences as a quarterback would bode him well. Running the Scout Team (called Demo Team for both Demonstration and Demolition, a reality for the quarterback) was no easy task at Washington High since full contact was the order of the day most of the time. Full speed and hard-hitting replication of that week's opponent was one of the reasons for much of the success, especially defensively, that is so well documented by low defensive numbers over the Springer years.

Tony's greatest benefit during his Continental coaching years occurred after a scouting trip. His old friend Dulla introduced him to a childhood friend of his wife. Southport High School and Ball State University graduate Pam Turner would become Tony's wife in 1978. They lived in Speedway's Westchester Apartments before buying a house north of 30th Street east of Kessler Blvd. The young Mrs. Burchett, who had graduated from Ball State, acquired a job at Central State Hospital as the Psychiatric Social Worker and continues working in the same capacity at the School for the Deaf. But in the spring of 1981, the Indianapolis Public Schools finally succumbed to the forced busing order that had been hovering over the city schools since the 1960's. RIF or Reduction In Force sent Coach Burchett packing. He was one of 532 lost by IPS. But Warren Central High School called.

Coach Burchett was an assistant to Jerry Stauffer for Warren Central's 1984 and 1985 State Championship teams led by the great quarterback Jeff George. In the classroom he was an English teacher until he was recruited as an assistant principal in 1994. Then, in the spring of 1996, Tony was approached by members of the School Board and given a choice. He could become Head Football Coach or Principal. It was an offer he couldn't refuse. But he pondered which position was most appropriate for a 44-year-old and his family? When he chose the top administrative position at Warren Central High School he vowed to himself that he would balance academic achievement with extra-curricular participation, much like he experienced as a student-athlete, with strong leadership from the principal's office. He would hire three football coaches during his ten-year tenure. All three would lead the Warriors to State Championships at the top division. One coach was from Sheridan, another from Decatur Central, and the latest from Tony's old stomping grounds, Evansville. Presiding over four consecutive State Championships in football at the highest level in the state was quite an accomplishment. In 2010, Mr. Burchett continues as Assistant Superintendent for Warren Township Schools.

Scotch-Irish—In Tony's own words: "Being Scotch-Irish is to recognize that once or twice or several times in your life defeat will seem certain, but never to give up when faced with this moment. Instead, persevere, to advance…being Scotch-Irish is to recognize that only you, the solitary individual, will make your own way in the world. Loneliness can be full of existential angst, but it can also provide room to rest."

But Tony wasn't lonely in his household with two active daughters. Courtney, the oldest, attended North Central High School where she lost the Senior Class Presidency by one vote before her graduation with honors. Then she matriculated to Wittenberg College where she played soccer. Currently she is Assistant Sports Information Director at Appalachian State. When her daddy called in 2007 requesting tickets to the Michigan football game, she didn't realize that she would afford her dad bragging rights from witnessing perhaps the biggest upset in the history of the Big House in Ann Arbor. Younger daughter Cora graduated from Warren Central and is now playing soccer for Butler University. She is chasing a degree in education, no less.

Mr. Burchett often maintains his life is blessed with mom and wife and daughters at the forefront followed by friends and colleagues. Lou Gehrig notwithstanding, Tony's "I'm the luckiest man alive" admonition has become his new self-fulfilling dream.

GEORGE McGINNIS

Big Mac is usually considered the greatest athlete in the 68-year history of Washington High School. He was a high school All-American in both football and basketball. The 1968 football season ended on a disappointing note with an unfortunate loss to rival Cathedral, finding George on the sidelines. Earlier in the game he had snared a pass from quarterback Billy Beard putting the Continentals ahead. But a confrontation with an Irish linebacker, who many suspect was staged, effectively ended our season at 9-1. But George continued to support his teammates from the sidelines with his helmet firmly on his head. And the 1969 basketball season was one of legendary repute.

As a youngster George lived on New York Street between Blackford and Blake. He walked the four or five blocks south to School #5 at California and Washington Streets. Jumpin' Johnny Wilson, Mr. Basketball 1946 from Anderson, was the school's coach during George's early years in elementary grades. Mr. Cliff Robinson replaced him by his junior high years. But living on New York Street afforded George a more significant effect on his life. Just around the corner lived "the prettiest girl in school." Her name was Linda Dotson, but she was a couple of years ahead of George in school. At age seven, when George first developed a crush on her, she seemed unattainable. When they were married in 1975, it cemented a life-partnership that had begun in 1957.

George commenced his days as an athlete playing basketball in nearby Military Park as well as on the Riverside Park courts. Once, when the older kids wouldn't let him play in a pick-up basketball game, he chucked rocks at them as they kicked up dust near Lockfield Gardens. Calvin Schaffer, an unquestioned leader on Washington's first two City Championship teams in 1963 and 1964, noted with a smile that George was destined to be an intense competitor.

School 5, with Mr. Robinson as coach, mentored many of the top competitors that spearheaded the charge by Washington High to the top of Indiana athletics in the 1960's. George was obviously one.

The McGinnis family moved to Haughville after George graduated from School 5 in 1965. The family home in the 1400 block of North King was modest but practical for the family of four. Sister, Bonnie, had recently graduated from Attucks. When George entered Continentaland in September 1965 he joined January 1965 mid-termers Steve Downing and Wayne Pack. Downing measured about 5'6" at the time as did Pack. All three would eventually sign professional contracts and were on the Pacer roster in 1975.

Bob Springer's fifth football team in 1966 saw sophomore McGinnis as a substitute end behind senior John Hill and junior Bennie Wooten. But the team almost didn't see him at all. Teammate tackle Danny Derringer convinced George to return to the practice field after one brutal practice. Those who remember the Dog Days of August on the Continental practice field, without the benefit of a water break, know what one means when discussing the conventional attitude in "old school" coaching. Gatorade was first introduced in central Indiana during the 1966 football season and things did become less harsh. No longer were salt tablets mandatory and Coach Springer began to moderate his practice customs, as did others. The '66 season ended at 10-0 and with the mythical State Championship. In a year and a half the Continentals had won State in basketball and football. No other Marion County team would win even one at the top level in over 20 years during the 1960's and 1970's. George was well aware of the strong tradition.

Starting in tandem with Wooten in 1967, McGinnis was one of a pair of powerhouse defensive ends as well as a main target for quarterback Bob Jones.

The '67-68 basketball team, Coach Jerry Oliver's eighth and last, would win the Butler Sectionals for the first time since 1948. But the loss to Coliseum Sectional Champs Shortridge coached by George Theofanis, GWHS class of 1949, left a bad taste in the mouth of Continentaland. Things would change in 1969.

During a game against Cathedral in George's senior year, his confidence if not earned-cockiness displayed itself. Cathedral star Jay Gorman, who would play at Oklahoma, had scored a basket followed by a long-range corner shot by Big George. Then George looked at Gorman and acknowledged, "you're good...I'm great."

The Final Four field in March of 1969 saw all four teams undefeated against other Indiana teams. Gary Tolleston had lost one game to a Chicago team but southern Indiana's Vincennes was unscathed as were the first game opponents, Indianapolis Washington and Marion. A foul whistled on 6'9" Steve Downing in the 4th quarter scared our sidelines. We feared that it was his fifth. But an earlier foul had been tallied against Big George. So, with the Continentals down by ten points and just over two minutes left in the game, Downing tipped in a two-pointer from a jump ball. The westsiders rallied to win by a score of 61-60. Both big men ended the game with four fouls. George tallied 27 points followed by Jim Arnold's 12 and Pack's 11. Big Steve only scored three baskets but his defensive presence, as always, was intimidating. Football great Louie Day was the point guard for the 1969 champs.

The final game seemed anti-climatic. But Tolleston rallied late and made the score closer than it seemed with Washington winning only 79-76. George's 35 points along with Downing's 20 and Pack's 13 led our team to our second State in five years. And our school ended the season at 31-0 becoming only the second team in the 59-year history of the State Championship tournament to end the season undefeated at the time.

George set the all-time Sweet Sixteen scoring record with 148 points over four games, which included Semi-State wins against Silver Creek and Jac-Cen-Del. McGinnis would credit first year coach and future legend, Bill Green, with allowing him to "bring the ball up the court" as a 6'7" big man. It was unconventional at the time for a forward to be a ball-handler. But it helped him enhance his already amazing skills.

McGinnis was the unanimous choice as Indiana's Mr. Basketball for the annual classic dual games against Kentucky's high school stars. After winning the first game in Hinkle Fieldhouse, but with an average McGinnis game, Kentucky's Joe Vosquel was quoted that "McGinnis is overrated." The following Saturday at Lexington, George responded with a legendary performance of 53 points and 31 rebounds in a 40 minute game. Unfortunately, that would be the last game George's dad would see him play. On his job at Eli Lilly he would fall from the third floor when a gust of wind caught a plywood piece that he was transporting and hurled him to his death.

A phone call from Vosquel in 2009 served as an unsolicited apology as well as an opportunity for a friendly laugh. George has never been underestimated by westsiders.

Indiana University loomed on the horizon for the Big Two from Washington High. Freshmen could not compete on the varsity level at that time so the 1970-71 sophomore year for both George and Steve was their first serious season since the 1969 championship. Under Coach Lou Watson and assistant Jerry Oliver, Big George would become a one-year All-American and Big Ten MVP. He averaged 29.9 points scoring 719 in 24 games along with a 15 rebounds per game average for IU's 17-7 team. He scored 45 points in one game for his college career high.

With the arrival of first year coach Bob Knight from the Military Academy, George signed with the Indiana Pacers. He initially played four years for his hometown team before signing to play with the Philadelphia 76ers alongside Julius Ervin. After three years there he signed with the Denver Nuggets for two years and then finished his career with the Pacers for two years through the 1982 season.

George had been named ABA Rookie of the Year in 1972. He was a young leader on the ABA Champions in 1972 and 1973. The Pacers were incorporated into the NBA in 1976 so George was an All-Star in either the ABA or NBA over ten seasons. He was named co-MVP in the ABA along with future teammate Dr. J in 1975. His Pacer career average was 25 points per game, which included a record 58 points in one game in 1972. George also snagged 35 rebounds in one Pacer game for another record.

His solid marriage to Washington High graduate Linda Dotson and his successful business, GM Supply Company, both exemplify George's drive and commitment to excellence that first emerged on the sandlots near School 5.

ANTHONY ALLEN-COOKSEY, class of 1974

After Christmas vacation when Indianapolis Public School students returned to the classroom in January of 2005, a sparkling new multi-million dollar School #44 opened its doors for the first time. Thirty-five years earlier, "old" School 44 (which still stands adjacent to the new building at 2033 Sugar Grove Avenue near old Victory Field) graduated one of the most unique individuals who ever attended Washington High and who would later become a world record holder in track & field.

Anthony Louis Allen and his close friends Herman Humbles, Alvin Strong, Cynthia Curry, and Judy Squires among others were assigned to our Westside school. The fall of 1970 was the first year of intra-IPS court-ordered busing and, although many previous School 44 graduates had attended Washington High since the 1940's, within the next four years their students would be assigned to Manual, Northwest and Shortridge as well as Attucks in consecutive years. Luckily, Tony would welcome his Continental fate and become a true "renaissance man" while excelling in many extra curricular activities.

Anthony's mother, Bobbie, had married James Cooksey when Anthony was just four years old. Almost twenty years later, Tony Allen would add Cooksey to his name as an honor to the man he always knew as his "daddy" even after Tony had moved to southern California to train for the Decathlon.

But growing up at 1525 W. 25th Street, less than a block from Riverside Park, Tony did not think of himself as an "athlete" while in elementary or high school. Athletics was just one of the varied activities in which he participated with equal intensity. In the spring of his freshman year his gym teacher, Rudy Dotlich who had been a State Champion wrestler at Ben Davis in 1963 as well as a pole vaulter, encouraged him to try to pole vault in Phys. Ed. class. Tony vaulted eight feet with an old, orange, rigid, aluminum pole. But he was better than any one in class. So Mr. Dotlich, who was only a teacher at Washington for two years, encouraged him to try out for the track team. Fate had reared its head and Tony jumped at the chance.

But it wasn't until his senior year that, in his own words, "I figured out what being an athlete meant." A childhood friend two classes and one year younger than him named Kenny Thompson was, by the spring of 1974, a track star at Northwest High School. Tony had always been dominant over Kenny in younger years being older and bigger. But now it seemed that Kenny was "the man" as a sprinter. Tony had won the pole vault City Championship as a junior but participated on the relay team as a runner only half-heartedly. Tony's family had moved to 327 W. 31st St. before his junior year so his sisters, Pat and Sandy, could attend Shortridge. So he had not seen Kenny in a few years. And his sprinting ability made a big impression on Tony.

As the call came for the long jump, Kenny removed his sweat clothes and his bulging muscles seemed to intimidate his competitors. Tony had "tried" the long jump at Coach Jerry Arvin's request only recently but wanted to challenge himself against his old neighborhood buddy. In Tony's words, "I went to the beginning of the runway. I couldn't see anything else on the track, no people, no trees, no athletes, just the runways and the sand in the landing pit. When I ran down the runway, I didn't feel tight; I didn't feel scared. I remember being determined, bordering on being obsessed with that one jump.....All I knew was that I didn't want to be beaten by Kenny Thompson." He wasn't. Tony leaped a foot and a half farther than he had ever jumped. It resulted in the longest jump in the state that year until the Regionals when Tony set a new record of 22'9 ¾" at North Central. But it was the "Kenny-factor" that was the impetus for lighting the competitive fire that began to burn inside Tony.

During Tony's four years at GWHS his favorite teachers were Colleen Stanley, Anderson Dailey, Dorothy Lunsford and Carole Fisher. Miss Stanley was his freshmen English teacher who encouraged his speech and thespian skills. But she transferred to Marshall High in 1972 and was replaced as drama director by Mrs. Lunsford. Tony was involved in three plays and three musicals over his four years and had the lead as the French plantation owner in "South Pacific." During his senior year Mrs. Lunsford persuaded him to enter the poetry reading contest. He won the first place plaque reciting "Casey at the Bat."

Mr. Dailey was the musical director of the Continentalaires singing group where Tony also excelled while savoring each and every practice and performance, he says. But Carole Fisher was his self-proclaimed most influential teacher. Miss Fisher was his speech and debate coach. Tony notes that Miss Fisher "opened me to a world of promise and potential which lead me to having confidence in every aspect of my life." According to Tony, Miss Fisher "showed a tremendous amount of enthusiasm, respect and care for all of her students....I will always be indebted to her."

Track and cross country coach Jerry Arvin showed "as much commitment to me as any teacher." Mr. Arvin eventually moved to San Diego in 1985 with his family in part to help Tony train for the 1988 Olympic try-outs. Mr. Arvin also became Head Men and Women's Track and Field and Cross Country coach at Point Loma Nazarene University in San Diego.

Tony never had "sports idols." But he was inspired by one-time Washington track coach Harold Orman's "Records Board." Thus he targeted Pole Vault record holder Danny Diehl (who Tony has never met), Long Jump State Champ Mike Cummins and sprinter Billy Wayne Grace. Tony finally bested Diehl's indoor record but he didn't tie Cummins' record 23'5" long jump until his first college competitive jump. And Tony says that "I've competed in Europe, Canada, Russia and many parts of the United States and I have yet to see a sprinter who ran as relaxed as Wayne Grace."

In any event, Tony eventually outperformed every Washington High track record holder's best, except for Larry Highbaugh's 100-yd. and 220-yd. dash records, during his competitive years in the decathlon and pentathlon in college or as a pro.

Tony decided to try wrestling for the first time as a senior in '73-74. And, in his only season as a grappler, he actually had a 8-5 winning season for Coach Poehls.

After graduating 4th in a class of over 300, Tony matriculated to Rose-Hulman Institute of Technology near Terre Haute, Indiana. By his graduation in 1978 he had been a four time NCAA Division III All-American in Track and Field. He was selected three times as team captain, held nine individual school records and three relay team records, was a 21 time conference champion, and won the prestigious Ruel Fox Burns Most Outstanding Rose-Hulman athlete award . Little wonder he was inducted into the Rose-Hulman Athletic Hall of Fame as an inaugural inductee in 1993. Tony also participated in the Christian Fellowship Group as well as Drama Club at Rose.

But February 21, 1981 was Tony's defining moment. On that day in Amarillo, Texas at the West Texas State Activities Center 25-year-old Anthony Allen-Cooksey, from Indianapolis Washington High School and Riverside School #44 via Rose-Hulman, would set a World Record score in the Pentathlon and established himself as one of our all-time greatest student-athletes. Entering the last event, the 600-yard run, Tony needed to run 1:14.3 or better. Robert Baker, one of Tony's Santa Barbara teammates and the world decathlon 1,500-meter record holder, helped pace him and zipped by him in the final yards to post a winning 1:12.1. But Tony's 1:12.6 gave him 4,322 points and the World's Record. His other four scores were: Long Jump—24'11 ¼"; Shot Put—46'5 ½"; High Hurdles—7.4 sec.; and High Jump—6'8 ¼"

Eight months earlier on June 19, 1980 at the Olympic Trials at Eugene, Oregon Tony had challenged himself in the Decathlon. He had gone from the Terre Haute Track Club to the highly regarded Athletics West of Santa Barbara coached by Sam Adams. He didn't qualify for the grueling Decathlon, which first became famous in America thanks to Jim Thorpe at the 1912 Stockholm Olympics, but the ten event test did fit his personality. As he stated in a newspaper article, "It expresses in athletics what I feel about life—being a total person."

Indianapolis Star writer and former UPI scribe Kurt Freudenthal wrote about Tony's 1984 Olympic decathlon tryout in a May 13, 1984 article. Tony had placed fifth in the 1980 trials after only a year of training but the U.S. boycotted them anyway. So, the 1984 Olympics became his goal. He fell short but, as he expressed earlier in his career concerning his pursuit of a seemingly financially depressing "track" vocation, "To me, I would've failed if I didn't try. When I'm 45, am I going to be glad I made a lot of money when I was 25?.....I want to do the best I can, whether I make the Olympic team or not. That sounds romantic, but it's the way I feel."

It was in 1979 when Tony had left a management job with Proctor & Gamble in Green Bay, Wisconsin and set out for Santa Barbara to seek his goal of becoming a world-class track & field athlete. Today he lives in San Diego. He has never been married and has no children but is still seeking "the woman of my dreams."

As he reflects back on his life at Washington High he always thinks of his close friends Herman Humbles (a one-time top official in the Marion County Sheriff's Department), Alvin Strong, Cynthia Curry and Judy Squires from School #44 as well as Cheryl Wilkins and Patty Tucker from School #75. Stepbrother James Michael Cooksey, class of '75, was another close companion who ran track and also played football at Washington High from Kenwood Avenue.

And if Tony were to take the same route from his childhood neighborhood to travel to today's Washington Community School, he would pass through the confluence of Lafayette Rd.-16th Street-Pershing Street and see a sign in front of an "old school" gathering place called The Pole that reads: Haughville, USA. He's traveled a long way from Riverside and Haughville and Washington High to world-class athlete. And he did it his way.

Some career highlights:

High School

Long Jump	23'	1974
Pole Vault	13'	1974
Triple Jump	44'6"	1974

City Champion in Track---Long Jump 1974; Pole Vault 1973 & 1974
North Central Regional record holder---Long Jump 1974
3rd place in State Championship Meet---Long Jump 1974
Tri-State Champion (Indiana, Michigan, Ohio)---Long Jump summer 1974

College

    4-time NCAA Div. III All-American

    National Championship Meet---2nd Long Jump (1975), 4th Triple Jump (1976),
                                2nd Triple Jump (1977), 5th Decathlon (1978)

    Long Jump---23' 6 ½"

    Triple Jump---49' 4"

    50-yd. dash---5.5

    60-yd. dash---7.5

    400 meters---49.64

    110-meters High Hurdles---14.6

    Decathlon--------------------6759 points

Post College

    U.S.A. & World Record Holder---Indoor Pentathlon   4322 points in 1981

    Runner-up National Decathlon in 1981

    Long Jump---25' 7" (1981)

    Triple Jump---52' 2"

    2-time National Champion Indoor Pentathlon (1986 & 1987)

    World & American Pentathlon Long Jump record---24' 11 ¼"

    Silver Medalist in Decathlon at U.S. National Championship 1981

    5th in Decathlon in Olympic Trials in 1980

    Captain of U.S.A. National Decathlon Team 1986

I'M LAMON BREWSTER

When Pamela Hardy, with her stylish and perfectly cut Afro, walked to Washington High School south on Belmont Street in the early 1970's she could never have imagined that more than 30 years later she would be walking into a boxing ring to hug her son as a Heavyweight Boxing Champion.

Lamon Brewster was born June 5, 1973 in Indianapolis. A few years later he too would walk the walk from Haughville to Washington High where he would graduate in 1991. His mom had married Melvin Blakey and Lamon began to box at Riverside Community Center in 1980 at age seven.

Christamore House on West Michigan Street with 80-year-old Bill Brown and his assistant John Deardorf saw a unique personality in young Lamon. Brown had "rubbed elbows" with Jack Dempsey in the 1920's and considered him a friend. And Lamon's dismantling of one-time top contender Andrew Golota on Saturday, May 21, 2005 was reminiscent of a Dempsey mauling from any many of his fights.

Lamon is the oldest of Pamela's four sons. He has become an internationally famous and respected boxer in the new century. His 53 second, first round victory over Golota in defense of the World Boxing Organization Heavyweight Championship which included three knock downs was both methodical and inspiring. His post-fight interview may have been more impressive.

Lamon's first comment to long-time boxing analyst Larry Merchant was to offer his condolences to Merchant concerning the recent death of the announcer's mother-in-law. Although Lamon pounced on Golota at the opening bell, it was Golota who seemed anxious as he moved to the middle of the ring before the bell as Lamon stood stoically in his corner. His relaxed self-control was soon replaced with an aggressive pummeling of his opponent. The second knock-down was an "out of the ring" experience again reminiscent of Dempsey's fight against Louie Firpo in 1923.

A more recent comparison with a young Mike Tyson, who seemed to be at his best during the first round, would belie Lamon's quiet self-control. But the Golota fight was his 13th first round knock-out. In mid-2005 his record stood at 32-2 professionally with 27 KOs.

But his first nationally televised fight on April 10, 2004 against highly favored Wladimir Klitschko was inspiring for all Americans. Klitschko won the first four rounds before being dispatched by a series of head and body shots at the end of Round 5 on HBO's Saturday night boxing. Lamon was WBO World Champion.

So he gave his friend and one-time sparring partner Kali Meehan, the Australian Heavyweight Champion, a big payday in September of the same year. In a lackluster and disappointing fight, many observers acknowledged, Lamon was awarded a controversial split decision win. Then he treated Meehan and his family to a pizza dinner. Later, Lamon admitted that he couldn't stop thinking about Meehan's children and the financial hard-luck that family had suffered. One critic called Lamon's sensitivity a "career-threatening disposition." He answered his critics noting, "I never saw in the Bible a man serving God by being mean."

Before the Golota fight his new manager Sam Simon prophesised, "this is a fighter who's all heart against a bully and a quitter. You know who wins that one every time." Simon, who is an executive producer of the television series "The Simpsons," also proclaimed that "the thing that has always amazed me about Lamon is how gentle and thoughtful and lighthearted he is outside the ring and what a deadly killer he is inside." He seemed to be describing a 1990's George Foreman in a much younger body.

By mid-2009 Lamon's record stands at 35-4 with 30 KOs. He lost his title on April 1, 2006 to Sergei Liakhovich of Belarus when he suffered a detached retina.

His July 7, 2007 rematch with Klitschko in Cologne, Germany was for both the IBO and IBF Heavyweight titles. Lamon's trainer, Buddy McGirt stopped the fight at the end of the 6th round. Lamon's most recent fights have been a 5th round knock-out of Danny Batchelder and a unanimous decision victory over Michael Sprott.

Lamon remembers listening to Indiana Pacer John Long suggest to youngsters at Riverside Community Center that they should focus on one thing to become great. Still he played football at Washington High during the Springer-Newland-Cannon-Shires era with the same quiet toughness that he now displays on the international stage.

He had begun Golden Gloves boxing under Bill Brown at the age of 15. But after his high school graduation he moved to Los Angeles to train under the late Bill Slayton. Lamon became the California Golden Gloves Champ in both 1992 and 1993. And he still considers Slayton his personal hero. In 1995 he became the national champion then proceeded to win a Silver Medal at the Pan American Games.

With hobbies like fencing, yoga and chess one can sense a cerebral restraint as he is introduced as "Relentless Lamon Brewster." He even thanked ring announcer Michael Buffer with a hug after his Golota KO. And Riddick Bowe entered the ring to congratulate him. Bowe and Golota had two very controversial bouts.

Lamon had a part in the movie "Daredevil" as well as appearing on TV shows "Martin" and "Ally McBeal." Yet this "gentle giant" is best self-defined on his website acknowledging that he has "faith in God along with the will, determination and ability to prevail." His wife Juana along with four kids, family, friends and God come first in his composed life. He's also cousin to former Heavyweight Champ Chris Byrd.

At the conclusion of the Golota fight when he climbed the ring ropes to declare "I'm Lamon Brewster" the boxing world took notice. His earlier visitation in the week to an inner city Chicago school also revealed a Spartacus temperament. Lamon told the children that "I am you. You are me. I'm the guy growing up across the street from all of you guys. The greatest part of being Heavyweight Champ is not getting in the ring. It's not being able to knock guys out. It's getting to speak to you."

In his own words he had "put myself on the radar screen" with the victory over Klitschko. He has had some good paydays since. He's earned it. And so has Pamela Hardy.

HIGHBAUGH family

James Highbaugh, Sr. was born in Indianapolis and graduated from Crispus Attucks High School before enlisting in the U.S. Navy during World War II. While stationed at Norfolk, Virginia he married Ida Mae who was born in the Virgin Islands. In November 1945 the young family of three returned to Indianapolis after Mr. Highbaugh was honorably discharged from the service. They bought a house at 940 North Belmont Street in Haughville. Their kids attended IPS #63. Mr. Highbaugh would also continue to serve his country through volunteer work in the Westside community with the Civil Defense Service well into the 1960's including a consistent responsibility of directing and policing the parking lot during Washington High activities for over ten years.

Their oldest child, Jimmie, was born August 1, 1945 in Norfolk while his dad was still serving his country. They had six other children including their youngest three---Kathy, Mark and Linda. Those three graduated from North Central High School in the 1970's. Mark was a star on both the football and track teams at North Central, which was to be expected. Middle sister, Sandra known as Sissy, would graduate from Washington High in 1968. But the three oldest boys would make an indelible mark on the athletic and social history of our school that remains to this day.

Jimmie, who would graduate in 1963, set a standard of conduct for his younger siblings as a serious, intense student-athlete for four years. As a senior he caught a 75-yard touchdown pass against Ben Davis that established the tone for the Continentals' ninth consecutive football victory over the Giants. But he also participated in Miss Thelma Park's Latin Club. He was a reserve basketball player but began to emphasize football and track by his junior year. Jimmie's track specialty was the 440-yard run along with leading the 880-yard relay team. Shirley Hunt was his high school girlfriend.

But as a young adult, Jimmie seemed to have found his fate as an Indianapolis police officer. He had first obtained a job at Eli Lilly on Morris Street. But his 14 years as a city cop marked him as a highly efficient, yet sometimes controversial, officer. His effectiveness as a patrolman, then in vice (temporarily with Jack Cottey) and finally as a top homicide investigator was indicative of his hard-nosed attitude. When he died of a heart attack on September 8, 1982 at the age of 37 he was in charge of security at Wishard Memorial Hospital. He had been tossing a football with a neighborhood kid.

In 1974 he had married Eugenia Porter. They had one son, Darren.

Michael, class of 1964, was another Continental who was a distinctive individual. He was an active and serious member of the school's ROTC. But he also was an outstanding football player. On Coach Springer's first team in 1962, when his brother was a star running back, he played tackle. But during his senior year he moved to right end and caught four touchdown passes while he maintained the reputation as a strong blocker. Michael claims that "Coach Springer was #1... he changed my whole life....I doubt I would have played football after 1961....he taught me a 'no quit' attitude....even on the department (police), I would think about Springer." Ironically enough, Michael noted that a teacher from Wood, who taught summers at our school, named Stahlhut was another "favorite." Walt Stahlhut would not officially become a Washington teacher until 1974. And his other top teacher was none other that Johnny Williams who taught Michael in drivers' education, phys. ed., and was freshman football coach. Michael continues to respect Johnny's physical discipline including when he told a student to "get your dad to come in here,

I'll whip him too." As a city policeman he was called to School 67 once by a timid principal in the 1970's. A student could not be convinced to remove his coat. When Officer Highbaugh picked him up by his shoulders, the boy cried but removed his coat. Michael remanded the principal not to call him again over such a trivial matter. Days later, at the Kroger on Michigan & Holmes, Michael was in uniform when he was approached by a lady from Haughville. "Did you grabbed my son at School 67 the other day?" she voiced. Michael was waiting for a harsh reaction to his "yes." Instead, he was commended by the single mother for his astute discipline.

Michael joined IPD in September 1967 but was sworn in during January 1968. He retired in February of 2000. The intervening 32 years saw him for five years as a K-9 officer as well as almost two years on the vice squad. Once, when he took his personal dog to work security during an Attucks vs. Washington football game, young mayor Dick Lugar and his family approached him and his family pet. After the entire family petted Rinny and the mayor discovered that he was privately owned, they continued on into the game. The subsequent Monday Michael received a call from his boss. Mayor Lugar had decided that IPD needed more K-9 units and had promised to finance the increase.

But most of his time was spent as a patrolman including the last 23 years in Haughville and Stringtown. When asked if he felt uncomfortable working in his neighborhood as a law enforcer, he laughed and noted that he asked to be assigned there and it was like "Brer Rabbitt asking to be thrown into the Briar Patch," in reference to the Disney movie "Song of the South." He greatly enjoyed his job and the rapport he developed with the kids as well as adults on his beat, he said.

Michael had married 1964 GWHS graduate Marie Gray in 1965. They had six children all of whom attended North Central High School. The eldest, Jounice class of 1983, was a member of the North Central State Championship 400-meter relay team in 1982 winning with the time of 48.41 seconds. Younger sister, Margaret, was an accomplished hurdler on the team also. Marie and Michael were married for 29 years.

In 1999 he remarried to a fellow IPD officer, Donna. She continues on the job entering her 28th year as a patrolwoman in 2010.

In the second decade of the 21st century, Michael works part-time at the Indiana Law Enforcement Academy in Plainfield as a guest instructor. He teaches Basic Firearms Training. When he won the annual "Jim Baugh FOP State Shoot" in 2009 after finishing 3rd the year before, the youngsters at the Academy who chided him as "Danny Glover" had to admire his proficiency with his revolver and 63-year-old eyes.

A self-proclaimed "loner," Michael lost his single best friend in April of 2009. Kirk Watkins, Attucks class of '64, died. Kirk had been his buddy since 1956. In the early 1990's they became committed hunters, fishermen and scuba-divers. But Mike continues to enjoy hunting and fishing in Hendricks County. His jerky made from geese is a delicacy as he maintains a strict, Spartan-like lifestyle.

Officer Highbaugh's reputation as a committed police officer was always beyond reproach. And he's a lot more handsome and grounded than Danny Glover.

The third son of the Highbaughs put the bar at a very high standard. Larry traveled in the summer of 1964, after his freshman year at Washington High, to the famous Mansfield, Ohio Relays with a group led by coaches Orman and Bradley.

Larry shattered legendary American Jesse Owens' 100-yard dash record when he ran a 9.2, albeit noted as "wind-assisted." Owens became a legend in United States history for his exploits during the Berlin Olympics of 1936. And Highbaugh remains as one of a handful of Americans to have run a 9.2 in track history. American track records vacated yards for meters in 1980. Ironically, the same year that Jesse Owens died.

Highbaugh returned to the Westside with much fanfare for his sophomore year in high school. ABC's "Wide World of Sports" followed him and interviewed his family for a special report on high school star athletes. In the fall of 1964 he became a top running back for the Continentals while receiving two touchdown passes from this author. Thus becoming the third Highbaugh in three years to tally TD catches on the field with "the planes and the trains." He was also a sophomore member of the State Championship basketball team in March of 1965.

Larry won the City Championship and Sectionals in both the 100 and 220-yard dashes for three years. At 5'8" he once played center for Jerry Oliver's basketball team and tallied 29 points in the second half alone, that's 16 minutes, against Attucks in a first round game during the Butler Sectionals in 1967.

The State Championship Track Meet in June of 1967 was another marquee event in his life. He won the 100 in 9.6 as well as setting an all-time 220 record at 20.5.

Along with teammates Ricky Thompson, Bobby Canady and Charlie Walton he was selected for the very first Indiana football All-Star game in August of '67, which included a game in Bloomington as well as one at old Victory Field. He was awarded a full football-track scholarship, as was Thompson, to IU by Coach John Pont.

But his career went into a brief stall amid allegations of racial preferences and an African-American walkout during the fall of 1969 in opposition to the football staff a year after IU's Rose Bowl appearance. Larry did not participate in the walk-out but still his reputation temporarily suffered. He continued his IU education but traveled to Dallas for a try-out with the Cowboys in the summer of 1970.

Yet his legacy would be with the Canadian Football League. His career began as a member of the British Columbia Lions in 1971. In 1972 he signed with the Edmonton Eskimos. He would be one of only three Eskimos (one was a place-kicker and the other was a QB named Warren Moon) when they won five consecutive CFL Championships through 1982. In fact, the Eskimos played in the Grey Cup, the Canadian equivalent of the Super Bowl, in nine of ten seasons from 1973-82. They won six titles, including the 63rd in 1975 and then the 66th through the 70th ('78-'82) in Cup history. He had been named the team's MVP in 1977, the year before Moon joined the team.

(In what would be an interesting trivia question one could asked, "name two Haughville football players who were teammates of NFL Hall of Fame quarterback Warren Moon?" Corey Harris, who grew up just around the corner from the Highbaugh home, led Ben Davis to their very first State Championship in football in 1987. He won a scholarship to Vanderbilt and was initially drafted by the Houston Oilers who had Moon as their QB in 1992. Harris was the starting free safety for the World Champion Baltimore Ravens by 2000.)

Listed at 5'9" and 165-lbs. Larry clearly had learned to use his speed and quickness to offset his lack of size. And he quickly adjusted to the Canadian rules as a punt-KO-return specialist. During most of his years catching punts, any blocking for the receiver was not allowed and the "fair catch" was not permitted.

Yet, he established a great legacy in Edmonton. On October 17, 1976 he sprinted to a record-setting kick-off return of 118-yards from the 20-yard deep end zone. He was a three time All-Star and was named to the Eskimos Wall of Honour in 1996 before his 2004 induction into the

Canadian Football Hall of Fame. Moon and Doug Flutie are two other notables whose busts reside there along with Larry's.

When he retired in 1983 he was the second all-time interception leader in Canada football annuals with 66. And he was voted as the 38th greatest player in that northern nation's football history by the Canadian Sports Network in 2006.

In 1981 Tom Keating, the respected Indianapolis Star columnist, had reached Larry's wife, Patricia who was a Crispus Attucks graduate, in their fashionable Edmonton suburban home in Sherwood Park. She noted, "We've been very lucky. Larry has worked hard in the off seasons and now has two businesses. One is a sporting goods store in Edmonton and the other is called 'Highbaugh Enterprises'…..this corporation was formed when Larry acquired the exclusive marketing rights for the Eskimo logo."

In the late 1980's the Highbaugh family temporarily moved back to Indianapolis, settling in Lawrence Township. Their daughter was a Lawrence Central cheerleader circa 1990. Currently Larry lives in suburban Atlanta while teaching at South Gwinnett High School in Snellville, Georgia. Larry's grandson, Tre Roberson, is the star quarterback for Lawrence Central's squad in 2010. He is headed to IU on a football scholarship.

From Indianapolis to Norfolk to the Virgin Islands to Edmonton to Atlanta to the Indianapolis Police Department, the Highbaugh family remains a family of lofty success and noble character.

JOE SHIRES

The Shires family was present in the form of Joe's mom and dad at the beginning of the school in 1927. And, the Shires family was instrumental in the organization for the closing celebration of our school in 1995. In between Joe was center stage as teacher, coach, Dean and Athletic Director from 1965 through June of 1994.

Elizabeth Belle Huffman graduated in the first four-year graduating class in 1931. Her boyfriend and future husband, Charles Norman Shires, had dropped out of GWHS to begin to earn a living as many did while our nation slumped into the Great Depression. Mrs. Shires' younger brother, Joseph, would be severely injured by five bits of shrapnel at the World War II battle of Anzio beach in Italy. He would live into the 1970's but remained disabled as a result of his Purple Heart injuries. But his sister Elizabeth and Charley Shires produced a younger Joe. Those two Valley residents and School 47 graduates would set in motion the fate that would produce the man that many consider one who bleeds the most purple of any Continental.

Norman Joseph Shires was born November 2, 1937. He was the oldest of three boys. His older sister Gloria graduated in 1952. Younger brothers Chuck and Greg would graduate from Northwest High more than ten years after Joe's 1955 GWHS graduation. Chuck would gain much notoriety as a high school basketball coach in Michigan for both boys and girls. At his induction into the Michigan basketball Hall of Fame in the 21st century, he would introduced older sibling Joe as his hero and role model as brother, athlete and coach. And youngest brother Greg would establish golf records at both Northwest High and Marion College. Joe stuck to fishing. And coaching.

Joe had entered Washington High School the day after Labor Day in 1951. For four years he would excel as a hurdler and sprinter on Amos Slaton's track teams. One highlight was when 5'8" Joe won a close high hurdles race in 1955 against 6'5" junior Oscar Robertson from Attucks. Joe was disappointed when he refused to shake hands.

Joe was junior class Vice-President with President Delbert Gregory as his energetic personality garnered him much popularity among the student body.

But Joe also was accomplished in wrestling and football. In the late fall of his junior year in 1953 Joe went out for Washington High's first wrestling squad. Coach Johnny Williams, who had played on the very first Indiana basketball All-Star team in 1939 and was President of the Indianapolis Officials' Association, was an unlikely wrestling coach. But his aggressive, assertive nature was to the liking of young Joe. Once he smacked Shires in the locker room for his unruly behavior. Joe was the varsity 127-pounder for two years. And he finally broke into the starting football line-up in 1954 teaming with fellow end Ray Duncan after Bob Forsythe was injured. Bill Purichia was their quarterback while Carl Ragland and Slavie Lalioff churned out the rushing yards.

Along with Coach Johnny Williams, Joe's Washington High hero was 1953 graduate Phil Peterson. Phil had been All-City in both football and basketball before he headed south to Hanover College.

So, when Les Fox approached Joe about attending Hanover he jumped at the opportunity. Mr. Fox, who had grown up in the Valley, sent three daughters to our school. But he was a father-figure to many Washington boys as he mentored Joe and others offering educational opportunities that were not all that widespread in those days.

When Joe graduated from the southern Indiana school in 1959 he had been co-captain of the football team and conference champion in four track events. His sub-10-flat in the 100-yd. dash along with wins in the 180-yd. low hurdles, 120-yd. high hurdles and the long jump (called broad jump in those days) put him among the all time elites at Hanover. He also ran the 220-yd. dash and was on the 880-relay team while acting as captain.

Running against Louisville once Joe, at 5'9" 160-lbs., broke from the blocks well ahead of future Baltimore Colts defensive back Lennie Lyles. But the 6'1" 190-lbs. Lyles nipped Joe at the tape for Shires' biggest disappointment in college sports.

Then he was hired as assistant football coach at Greenwood High School by 1952 Washington graduate Leonard Scotten. While at that Johnson County school for four years he met beautician Kathleen Leonard. Kathleen had once been the teenage babysitter for future Christmas song-icon Bobby Helms ("Jingle Bell Rock"). In 1962 they welcomed their first child, Susie. Then the Shires family moved north.

In 1963 Joe took an assistant football coaching job at Goshen High School. Joe "Chonky" Springer was head man. Chonky had graduated from Tech High School and was once, as a 300-lber, on the New York football Giants roster. But maybe more importantly, Chonky was the older brother of Washington High coach Bob.

The 1963 and '64 football staff also included Bill Doba, who would become head coach for Mishawaka against the Continentals in the 1974 state championship game and Washington State University head coach in the 21st century, and Ken Mirer, who would become the head coach after Chonky at Goshen and whose son would be Notre Dame's quarterback and future #2 draft pick in the NFL by Seattle in 1993.

With Joe in charge of the junior varsity in '63 they lost to South Bend teams in consecutive weeks 0-49 and 0-47. So, when they lost to South Bend St. Joseph's 0-42, Chonky expressed to Coach Shires that they were improving. Much like the city teams in Indianapolis in those days, the South Bend teams were more populated and funded than the smaller rural teams of like-size in Goshen's conference. So, Joe noted, he was proud of the conference championship that the varsity experienced in 1964.

Coach Mirer shared a story with me in the '70's concerning Coach Shires during the '63 season. According to Mirer, there were only 20 junior varsity game jerseys and Joe had close to 30 players. His solution: throw the jerseys in a pile and order a scrum. The 20 players most able to acquire the 20 jerseys would suit-up. Hopefully, at least one skinny quarterback snatched a shirt. Coach Shires' leadership and personality were contagious and almost always positive for aggressive male athletes of that era.

When an Indianapolis Public School opportunity arose Joe left Goshen in January 1966 after 2½ years. Until the 1980's IPS was the highest paying and most reputable school district in the state so Joe's assignment initially to Howe High School was a step up for his career. Teaching P.E. and arriving at the end to help in the wrestling program, along with assistant Jim Arvin also from Washington, Joe respected the professionalism but not the idea that he had to don a shirt and tie to walk 50 yards to pick up his mail in the office before returning to his coaching outfit. So, when Continentaland beckoned it was an easy choice to accept the head wrestling job and an assistant football position replacing his old coach Johnny Williams.

For the next 29 years Coach Shires would become one of a select few iconic figures in the Washington High School history book.

During his first year in the fall of 1966 Washington High would become the mythical State Champions in football with a 10-0 record. Joe's "bonsai" leadership as backfield coach was seen by all players as inspirational. And in early 1970 Heavyweight wrestler Philip Leslie would win the State Championship held at Southport for Joe.

Joe seemed to be Principal Julian's jack-of-all-trades and jobs by the 1970's. He was assistant dean of boys for Girdley and Perry before becoming the head dean in 1972. But, with Russell McConnell's retirement mid-year, Joe was named Athletic Director in January of 1973. His unique paddling style was not easily forgotten by those so blessed by that accepted discipline following the turbulent '60's. But sports leadership called.

The 1974 football championship in only the second year of the tournament was perhaps the highlight of his AD career. And the girls' state championship in track in 1975 was the final Continental championship under Shires' leadership.

But the constant hassle to make a living sometimes put Joe behind the eight ball in lack of time. His second child, Sherry, was born in 1964 and son Bric was born in March of 1969 during the McGinnis led championship run. For more than a few years he was in attendance as AD or coach at about every GWHS athletic contest while also working on the truck docks on Morris Street. And, he returned to help good friend Bob Springer in the 1980's through the 1993 football season. His classroom abilities have often been acclaimed by many non-athletes while Government, Economics and Health & Safety were just a few of the academic classes that Joe seemed to master.

And, in 2010, he sports a National Championship ring as big as a Super Bowl band on his finger. It's compliments of daughter Sherry. Her coaching abilities led to a nationally prominent cheerleading squad working out of Plainfield. And she too affirms that her dad has been the single most significant role model in her life as a competitive cheerleading coach.

With his 15-year companion, Missy, Joe continues to enjoy his social life. And some have proclaimed him the jitter-bug champion of the west side as his life-long love of fishing continues while he brags about his four grandkids. Susie's two daughters, living in Avon, along with Bric's son and daughter, who live near Moorseville, also enhance Coach Shires' active life.

BALDWIN family

Don Baldwin was born in Indianapolis in 1912. He was a top-notch student and was elected Senior Class Secretary. Don graduated from Washington High in 1931 before attending Butler University. When he was drafted in America's first peace-time draft on March 27, 1941 he was assigned to the 551st Parachute Infantry Battalion which included American and British personnel.

After serving one tour of duty, after the Pearl Harbor attack thrust our nation officially into war in December 1941, Corporal Baldwin decided to re-enlist. His younger brother, Kenny, warned him "don't do it. You're committing suicide!" But his commitment to his conscience was too much. He re-upped with the Airborne and became a medic with the 551st.

After heavy fighting during the Battle of the Bulge in December-January 1944-45, which severely decimated the 551st, Don and some of his buddies regrouped at Juslenville, Belgium. Jack Affleck, Dewey Bentley and Wesley Richard along with Don took some well-deserved rest and recuperation. They were entertained by a local family for two weeks. Then the 551st was deactivated.

On January 23, 1945 Corporal Baldwin was transferred to a unit of the 82nd Airborne. He was killed in action on February 9, 1945 when a mortar shell landed nearby. Don was initially buried in Belgium but his family moved his remains to Crown Hill Cemetery in 1947. His service record includes three Purple Hearts and a Presidential Unit Honor Citation.

It is estimated that up to 78,000 service personnel during World War II, including those in the Pacific and European Theaters, continue as Missing In Action. Real events are more complicated than any Hollywood movie. Don was almost 33 years old when he died, older than the 29-years-of-age average in WW II but still way too young.

Don's younger brother, Kenny, would graduate in 1932. He played football for four years aspiring to be as good as year-older neighbor and football star Ishmael Lawlis. Don and Kenny's Baldwin grandparents lived on South Elder near the New York Central tracks just two blocks east of Washington High.

One summer evening in the late 1930's, Kenny would stop his car in front of Louise Liebenderfer's home just two doors from Clark's Pharmacy at Tibbs and Michigan Streets. The older Liebenderfer girl, Mary, was soon to marry her high school boyfriend, athlete Jim Leeper. But Louise's good friend, Chryssanthy Zoitos, was sitting on the front porch swing with her. The Zoitos family had come to the United States from Greece after World War I and found a house on North Berwick. Their two oldest sisters had graduated from Manual High School. But brothers Constantine and Crist had both graduated from new Washington High School in 1935. Little sister Chryssanthy had graduated in 1937. All three had attended School #67. And, with her dad's encouragement, she had legally changed her name to an Americanized-Connie.

Dark-haired Connie Zoitos caught the eye of Kenny Baldwin and he asked her to go on a coke date to the North Pole. Not the extreme north latitude North Pole but the North Sheffield North Pole at 16th Street. Twenty-five years later both of their kids would frequent the still popular Washington High School hangout then known simply as The Pole. Connie obviously accepted the proposal and thus began a love that led to their marriage on June 21, 1941.

Constantine, known as Dino, moved to California to work for Standard Oil. Crist married next-door neighbor Doris Cripe in 1940 and followed his brother to California.

After the Baldwin-Zoitos wedding, Ken and Connie would buy a home on Alton Ave. one block west of Tibbs south of Michigan Street. Their eldest, Kenneth Joseph, was 1960 Senior Class President at GWHS. He played on Frank Luzar's varsity baseball team. Kenny, known as Joe, most regrets a football injury that prevented him from playing on the record setting 1959 undefeated team. After graduation he attended Indiana University where he played one season of baseball. Then he worked on the new Interstate system during the 1960's before choosing the trucking industry as his profession in 1967. In 1966 he married the love of his life, Pam, from Bluffton. In 2010 they have four children and five grandchildren.

Sister Donna Elaine, born in 1945, would also graduate from Washington High. She was Senior Class Treasurer in 1963 when she was voted "Martha Washington" as the most typical female at our high school. Clark Dickerson was voted as "George." Donna was also chosen for the prestigious May Queen Awards Day Court. And she had been on the Homecoming Queen Court during the 1962 Ben Davis football game.

Second year Journalism teacher, Mrs. Anita Morris, would choose Donna for the Surveyor staff (school newspaper) as well as the Post staff (the yearbook). The Washingtonians, the senior girls' service club, was another organization in which Donna was an active participant. Junior Vaudeville and the Talent Show were two others.

Donna married classmate and GWHS athlete George Sipe. Although they have separated, Donna and George had four kids who have blessed them with 14 grandchildren by 2010, including triplets recently delivered by Michelle in suburban Detroit.

From 1957 through 1964 Kenny and Donna's mom, Mrs. Connie Baldwin, was one of our school's secretaries. Connie resigned in '64 because of her mother's illness. After her mom died, Connie began working in the Education Center downtown. She eventually retired after 26 years in IPS. In 2010, Connie at age 91 lives below her 93-year-old sister at Crestwood Village on the Westside. And their aunt by marriage, Mrs. Nellie Baldwin, was our school's Social Worker, who was sometimes called the Truant Officer, from the 1940's into the 1970's.

The Baldwin family continues to honor the ultimate sacrifice that Uncle Don made for our nation's freedoms so long ago on the battlefields of Europe.

JOE TOFIL

Joe Tofil arrived in the late summer of 1951 as Washington's second football coach. He had just completed four years at Columbia City High School in Indiana. But it all began in Ohio.

Even as a sophomore in the fall of 1934 Tofil was a star fullback/linebacker under Coach Dick Barrett in Mahoning County, Ohio for Campbell Memorial High School. The following two seasons he was co-captain for new Coach John Knapick's first teams. The 1935 season ended with an 8-3 record. Fullback Tofil spearheaded an offense that tallied 132 points while holding their opponents to 47 points in eleven games. Then his senior season of 1936 ended at 8-0-2. The two scoreless ties against powerhouse teams from Elyria and East were the only slight blemishes on a near-perfect season. The Memorial Red Devils scored 185 points while allowing only one TD the entire season to their opponents. Only Struthers H.S. had scored in the Red Devils 27-6 victory. And young Joe was a unanimous choice for the Mahoning County All-Star team.

So his 1937 high school graduation set the standard for the Tofil reputation of "tough competitor and relentless performer." Brothers Al, Stan, Rudy and Ron continued the tradition of football prominence as Joe was destined for the Ohio Football Hall of Fame.

From CMHS Joe accepted a football scholarship to Indiana University to play under legendary coach Bo McMillan. In the fall of 1940 he was named All-Big Ten. Joe had been the powerful fullback in the potent single-wing offense.

One game in particular gave Joe an IU reputation that endured for years. He was injured in mid-season and told by doctors and coaches that he would not be making the trip to Iowa to play the Hawkeyes. But Joe devised a plan. He talked the student equipment manager into packing his game gear. Then he hitchhiked to Iowa City.

He quietly changed in the locker room and slipped out to the bench. With the Hoosiers trailing in the fourth quarter, Coach McMillan turned to the bench and spotted Joe. Instinctively he ordered him into the contest. Joe led the drive and scored the game winning touchdown. In the newspaper reports on the game he was labeled the "Hitchhike Hero" much to the admiration of his teammates.

After his 1941 graduation, as the first peace-time draft in U.S. history began in earnest, he decided to answer an invitation from the Brooklyn "football" Dodgers in the NFL under Coach Jock Sutherland. "I was going into the Navy after the season in early 1942," Tofil recalled, "and Jock managed to delay my entrance until December after the season was to end." But Pearl Harbor occurred on December 7.

He did finish the season for the Dodgers playing end next to tackle Bruiser Kinard. The pair blocked for Pug Manders, one of Minnesota's reknowned ball carriers along with an earlier Bronko Nagurski.

Joe was assigned by the Navy to San Francisco as the U.S. entered World War II. While serving as Lt. Jg. he read a newspaper article about tryouts for the Frisco Clippers. The Clippers played in a ten-team league rated the same caliber as the Continental League. Team officials were impressed but naval officers could not play for pay. So he adopted the moniker Bill Robbins. "Robbins was my wife's maiden name and Bill was easy to remember," noted Joe.

For two years Lt.jg Joe Tofil, alias Bill Robbins, was stateside on duty from 8 AM to 4 PM. He played football two fall seasons in the later afternoon and on game Sunday. Fullback-end Robbins played alongside former college All-Americans Paul Christman (Missouri), Kenny Washington (UCLA), Joe Stydahar (West Virginia) and Bob Suffridge (Tennessee).

After the war Joe returned to Indiana and began his career in education. First at Columbia City and then to Indianapolis Washington. In eleven years as head coach he garnered a .527 percentage with a record of 48-43-10 highlighted by an 8-1 record vs. Ben Davis and winning records against Shortridge, Manual, Scecina, Noblesville, Brazil and West Lafayette. His son, Gary, was the All-City quarterback who led Cathedral in victory against his father in his last game as head coach in 1961. Gary would attend the Air Force Academy before transferring to his father's alma mater IU as a football man.

In 1965 Coach Tofil transferred to Shortridge as the Athletic Director. His physical education department replacement at Washington was Shortridge's ex-coach Tom Rosenberger. On May 10, 1973 Joe suffered a massive heart attack in the hallway at Shortridge. Football and wrestling coach Dick Boarman, who starred at Washington on Coach Tofil's 1959 and 1960 teams, reached him too late. His wife, Phyllis, died almost exactly a year later.

Joe served the Indianapolis Public Schools for 22 years. He was described by Shortridge principal Bob Carnal as "a serious, hard worker who tackled assignments willingly and thoroughly. He also had time for a friendly smile for students and encouraged every one of his pupils to set high goals and try to exceed them."

The Joe Tofil Memorial Award was established at Shortridge H.S. to honor the school's outstanding athlete with a 3.5 or better grade point average, is recognized at city or state level, letter in two or more sports and have a good mental attitude.

RICK LEON HIGHTOWER

When the name Rick Hightower was announced as the winner of Washington High School's prestigious "Rowland Jones Mental Attitude Award" at the May Day festivities in 1977, Rick felt the emotions of a defining moment in his life. But no one was surprised with the choice. For two years Rick had walked the 1½ miles from South Hiatt Street north on Belmont Street to Washington High before hitching a ride with the Cox brothers. During his junior year his dad gave him a '66 Newport and then a nice church lady let him consistently borrow an older model Gremlin during his senior year so that he could meet a spiritual calling virtually every week day morning his final two high school years. He traveled 20 miles round trip to 900 E. Stop 11 for his Church Seminary class. Then he'd meet Washington High's AM welcoming bell for period one.

Rick's consistent and serious demeanor seemed to predict academic success, although he struggled in Algebra. His athletic success was less consistent, but he was always a rugged competitor. Yet Rick seemed to really excel in the arts, especially as a singer with the Continentalaires. And his participation in speech and debate seemed to foretell a future in public broadcasting.

Byron and Imogene Hightower had migrated to the Valley during World War II from Bowling Green, Kentucky. Although Byron had only a 4th grade education, he was a literate and well-read man. Imogene graduated from the 8th grade but gained a significant job at Western Electric. Father Byron was known as "Uncle Hightower" as a country music singer/musician/MC working with Little Jimmy Dickens and Lattie Moore. Rick was born in 1959. By the mid-1960's and into the '70's little Rick was a regular backstage with his dad at Coliseum concerts rubbing elbows with Loretta Lynn, Marty Robbins, and others.

His older brothers, Larry and Bill, didn't complete all four high school years but his sister, Barbara, had graduated in 1961. Rick's family moved from the Valley to the Hill area north of Morris Street on Hiatt Street before he was born. He attended old Daniel Webster Elementary #46 near Richland and Miller. Consequently, Rick walked six blocks daily to grade school while he participated on the softball, basketball and track teams. The football far-throw was his favorite track and field event. He was the only boy who could throw the football over the school's fence. Rick was also a Traffic Boy. But when he gave a well-received 8th grade commencement speech, his love for writing and public speaking became obvious.

Rick had thrived as an 8th grade basketball player at 6'1" and 165 lbs. He first tried football as a freshman at Washington High but only played basketball and baseball his final three high school years. But he did meet a good friend on the football team, Gary Glaze. And he continued his grade school friendship with Dennis "Bookie" Sharrette as well as Mike Hamilton, both from School #46. Rick didn't have many dates but he does remember two Continental cuties that he was sweet on, Candace Langford and Amy Black. His two years as a reserve starter for Coach Bopp then Coach Pearson saw him score a high of 14 points in one reserve city tourney game. And the highlight of his high school years in sports was the Ben Davis Basketball Sectional Championship in 1977 and the subsequent regional game against Southport at Hinkle Fieldhouse. A game in which he contributed in both points and rebounds for Coach Sfreddo.

But his education was most important to him and he had a number of significant influences. One was Ms. Carole Fisher. She encouraged Rick to become a member of the Speech and Debate team. So, along with his buddy Hamilton, they led a Debate team which placed in state-wide competition. And, when Rick was elected Student Council President, his confidence level rose under a young Ms. Marsha Russell who taught him about leadership and "how to treat people."

Rick's involvement with the singing Continentalaires gave him a venue for his emotional self-expression. A young Mrs. Bessie Colvin encouraged him to sing and dance, especially during the holidays, at school and around the city at special events where they performed. Mrs. Colvin was the mother of future Broad Ripple and Purdue football standout Roosevelt Colvin who became a Bears linebacker in the NFL before he signed with the Patriots where he won two Super Bowl rings as an OLB.

Hightower had represented his school at Hoosier Boys State at Terre Haute in the summer of 1976. And Rick was another Continental who was affected in a positive way by Coach Shires. The day after Rick had quit the baseball team late in his senior year, Athletic Director Shires called him from class and encouraged him to "go back and ask Coach Pearson for your uniform, get on the bus, go to the game today, and finish out the rest of the season." Advice that he accepted from Mr. Shires, advice that taught him a lesson about commitment and perseverance, and advice that lead to the Rowland Jones Award. Coach Shires' direct, assertive demeanor served many Continentals well.

His post-high school life would most reflect his family's life. His grandparents in Richardsville, Kentucky in 1917 were taught by The Church of Jesus Christ of Latter Day Saints and became what people east of the Mississippi River call Mormons. It was an unusual conversion as the Roarin' Twenties were beginning but today it is the fastest growing Christian faith in the world with over 14 million members.

Rick began giving talks, prayers, and scriptures at church when he was only three years old. So, when he applied to two universities he had a choice to make. IU's letter of acceptance arrived along with one from Brigham Young University. Bloomington, Indiana was a lot closer than Provo, Utah. But BYU was a lot closer to his personal and religious beliefs. Consequently he headed west.

The ethics and moral code contract that students signed as freshmen included a vow to avoid alcohol, smoking, and premarital sex. Two of Rick's dorm mates his freshman year were future Boston Celtic Danny Ainge and future Chicago Bear Jim McMahon. Rick doesn't think that McMahon signed the school's contract.

After his freshman year at BYU, Rick served a two-year mission in the Philippines. He spent a year in Manila and a year in the barrios as well as jungle areas on the island of Luzon. Rick suffered through a critical fever with dehydration during a severe illness caused by parasites. But he considers his mission, as he served in the highest position as assistant to the mission president, as the most significant action in his life. That is, second most significant; his subsequent marriage to Cathy in 1983 being the paramount event in his life.

But his two-year mission "literally made me who I am. It took my focus away from 'me' and put it on others," Rick explained, "I learned what it meant to serve God by serving my fellowmen." Unfortunately, Rick's father was killed in a tragic accident while Rick was in the Philippines.

After Rick returned to Brigham Young University, he received a B.A. degree in Broadcast Journalism with a minor in World History in 1984. As a young married man and with the job market being tight, especially in broadcasting, he took on a variety of jobs. Driving a UPS truck then an electrical supply truck, selling men's clothing in a department store, and even running the shipping and receiving in a warehouse all served him well financially but not so much in relationship to his degree.

His first big break presented itself when he was offered the anchor reporter position on TV-news on an Idaho Falls, Idaho station in 1985. Halloween was his premier day at KIFI-TV-8 Idaho Falls/Pocatello. After three years as a weekend anchor/reporter/weather man/producer/editor he moved on to main anchor position at his parents' roots in Bowling Green, Kentucky. Spending four years there before his job was downsized, he headed back west to Boise, Idaho in 1992.

When he finally landed in the "Bigs" at WISH-TV-8 in December of 1993, he returned to his own roots in Indianapolis. As a back-up for respected anchor Mike Ahern, Rick spent 12 years as a reporter and weekend morning anchor in the North Meridian Street building. He decided on another career path in 2005 when he hired on as public relations manager for ATA Airlines in Corporate Communications. Working there for over a year he missed the broadcast industry, so when he was offered another in-the-field reporter position with WRTV-6-News, he jumped at the opportunity.

His marriage to Cathy Creek from Longview, Washington has yielded six children. They met at Brigham Young and, after two years of friendship and one year of dating, they married in Seattle in their church's temple. Their two oldest children, Brandon and Heather, have graduated from BYU in 2007 and 2009 respectfully. Caitlin in 2010 is a sophomore there. All graduated from Southport High School. Holly, age 16, is currently ranked #1 in her Southport class. Harvard and Stanford are two possible colleges she may attend but BYU is also on the short list.

Eleven-year-old Hunter is already a three year veteran of football as a lefty quarterback, Steve Young style, as well as playing on the 5th grade basketball team. And the baby, Alyssa age 8, loves art and singing while hoping to audition for American Idol some day. The Hightower legacy will continue for many years to come.

Rick claims Washington High athletes Keller, Bopp, and McGinnis along with teachers Carole Fisher, Joe Shires, and Bessie Colvin as idols while noting Senator Lugar as his political hero. But the greatest men in his life include his spiritual dad Delbert Leon Stapley, the young missionary who taught his grandparents the Gospel years ago and is his namesake "Leon," and his mission president Stephen K. Iba of Salt Lake City.

Richard Leon Hightower holds the Priesthood in the Mormon Church and is an ordained High Priest, the highest position at the local church level. Others across the nation who hold the same position include: Mitt Romney, Sen. Harry Reid, Sen. Orrin Hatch, Dale Murphy, Steve Young, former Pacers Devon Durrant and Greg Kite, Danny Ainge, Donny Osmond, Glen Beck, three other U.S. Senators, and two pro golfers.

Hightower has written two books. "The Church Bench" is a family/children book about generations of a family growing up on their favorite church pew. "It Doesn't Get Any Better Than This" is a narrative about raising children, a story he is well versed to tell. And he is proud of his volunteer work with the Arthritis Foundation.

Rick's mother, who continues to live in the family homestead on Hiatt Street, is the rock of his life. She has sacrificed much for Rick's life experiences and opportunities. And he considers himself a "blue collar broadcaster," someone who has always had to work hard to be successful. Public Relations jobs as well as teaching in high school or college about broadcasting continue to be possibilities for this virtuous, diligent, and accomplished Continental. (Rick's mom died in August 2010)

LARRY AUSTIN, class of '63

Hollis Austin, one time Tech student, walked outside to his '62 Chevy Impala one clear May morning at 150 S. Traub in 1963. His son Larry had borrowed the family car for the Junior Prom held in the school's gym the previous night. With his date, junior Vicki Wright, senior Larry had doubled with a younger couple. "Who was in the back seat?" his dad asked. "Why?" Larry responded. "Where did all those White Castle boxes come from?" his father laughed. In 1991 Mr. Austin would repeat that story to this author. We both laughed. The culprit in the back seat the night before had been the junior class President-elect and his date (and future wife) was freshman Regina Such.

Larry Austin always seemed to have a modest smile on his face, which reflected his pleasant personality as well as his physical similarity to his father. His mother, the former Dorcas Bain, had attended Washington High. One of her brothers, Alvie, had married Maxine Gilbrech from South Warman Avenue. They were both killed in a traffic accident on early Labor Day in 1953 at Girls School Rd. and 10th Street. Larry's other two uncles, Ralph and Paul Bain who live on in 2010, had been POWs during World War II. They, too, had been Continentals. Little brother Jerry graduated in 1968 and his future wife, Sharon Chandler, graduated in 1970. Larry's older sister married Mike Kerr from Lawrence Central later in life. She had attended Washington High in the mid-'50's.

At School 30 Larry's buddies were Bernie Reamer, Charles Welding, Kenny Gibson, Jimmy Denton, and two of the 14 Morgan boys who lived across the street, Tommy and Denny. Ernie Cline, later Tech High School's basketball coach, was his junior high coach. Larry traded his 2½ block walk to School 30 for a 1½ block walk to Washington High in the fall of 1959.

His favorite, and most influential, high school teacher was charismatic football coach Bob Springer who arrived at the beginning of Larry's senior year. Playing offensive guard and defensive tackle, he may have found a person who didn't like him. That person being the boy playing across from him each game who suffered at the hands of his aggressive, football techniques. One can't find anyone from Washington High who didn't find Larry's personality as amicable.

Baseball coach Frank Luzar was another Austin favorite. Larry played 3rd base as well as sharing catcher duties with Jerry Sanders and Bill Keller. And, predictably, wrestling coach Johnny Williams was unforgettable. Once, well more than once, Johnny flung a rope around a wrestler's neck and pushed him down the stairs. Only in those days could a coach do some of the things many have noted that Johnny Williams did. And Jerry Oliver was Larry's line coach in football for three years. Larry only remembers Latin teacher Mrs. Erwin from his academic endeavors. But he was no dummy as his professional record shows.

Larry only dated four girls in high school that he remembers, varsity cheerleader Vicki Wright, Cheryl Swartz, Carol Brandt, and sophomore reserve cheerleader Carol Beets. Although he liked cheerleaders, he would marry Cheryl in 1964 when she traveled to Oklahoma as he began a year of training in pararescue/recovery. But she headed back to Indianapolis during one of his extensive training missions and they later divorced.

His enlistment in the U.S. Air Force on September 15, 1963 extended 27 years until his retirement on September 30, 1990. He experienced Basic Training at San Antonio and then on to Supply Specialist School at Amarillo, both in Texas. School 30's Jimmy Denton started at Washington High but then went with his mom to California. He returned to Indianapolis and then went into the Air Force on the "buddy program" to Basic Training with Larry. After

October 1963, Larry had never once heard from Denton until January of 2010. He received an e-mail query and the memories continue to be exchanged for the first time in over 46 years.

Larry was assigned to Clinton-Sherman AFB in Burns Flat, Oklahoma where he was married to Cheryl. Then his Pararescue Training extended from Jump School at Ft. Benning, Georgia to Emergency Medical School at Montgomery, Alabama to Survival School at Reno, Nevada to Scuba-Divers' School at San Diego, California and then to Pararescue/Recovery Technician Transition School at Ft. Walton Beach, Florida.

Then he was ordered to Tachikawa Air Base near Tokyo were he served for 18 months while training for emergency recovery of space capsules. Then it was six months at Clark AB, 80 miles from Manila in the Phillipines. His year at Pease AFB at Portsmouth, New Hampshire was when he continued a focused training for emergency recovery for the Gemini and Apollo Space Capsules. He did 20 practice jumps on capsules but did not participate on either of the two actual recoveries.

Next he spent four years just outside Panama City in Central America before another year in Thailand on the Cambodian border where he was involved during a rescue mission on a "Jolly Green Giant Helo." Into the mid-1970's Larry was ordered to Sheppard AFB at Witchita Falls, Texas where he supervised those attending Emergency Medical Class for 1½ years. At Hill AFB in Ogden, Utah he taught medical training.

Albuquerque, New Mexico's Kirtland AFB was home to Sgt. Austin for three different tours between 1976 and 1990. He was an instructor for Emergency Medical, Parachuting, Survival and Combat Tactics, and Mountain Rescue Techniques. Larry's expertise in many areas traveled with him to Iceland (for 12 months at Keflavic), Okinawa (a year and a half at Kadena AB), and then back to Kirtland where he retired.

Chief Master Sergeant Austin had been Director of Training and Commandant as well as saving several lives. Once, in Panama, he delivered a baby. Larry also earned his AA in Work Center Management, a BS in Business Administration, and two MAs in Human Relations and Public Administration. Quite a resume that he presented to the New Mexico Department of Public Safety in January 1991. His second career started in Sante Fe, where he began as an emergency planner before moving up as director in the Bureau of Emergency Management. Then he became the deputy division director who supervised and managed the New Mexico Crime Lab, Law Enforcement Records, and the Emergency Management Bureau. The events of nine-eleven, 2001 was accompanied by a name change from the BEM to Homeland Security.

Career number three saw Larry as a contractor in the development and practice of homeland security drills as well as exercises and evaluations for the Department of Energy, the Coast Guard, and several adjacent state's National Guard units.

His last job was with New Mexico's Department of Homeland Security & Emergency Management as the Border Security Liaison while working along his state's counties bordering Mexico. He retired in November 2008. His biggest benefit from his years working for the New Mexico state government was meeting his wife, Kathleen, who continues serving society as a New Mexico State Trooper. Larry had a daughter with his second wife. Stacy, who is 27 years old, lives in Tucumcari about 150 miles east of her dad. In 2010 Larry has one granddaughter, Makenzi, who is seven years old.

Playing golf three to five days each week in balmy Rio Rancho near Albuquerque, with a handicap that fluctuates between eight to two, is a well-deserved benefit for one of our school's finest and most successful student-athletes.

JERRY OLIVER

The son of two parents who prospered in farming homes on opposite sides of the small town of Rochester, Jerry Oliver would become a success story with national prominence. Thanks, in large part, to his associations evolving from Washington High.

Jerry was married to Ann Miller on August 7, 1955 just eight days before his official arrival on the west side of Indianapolis as Joe Tofil's football assistant. Tofil's other assistant was Bruce Hammon who would become the first coach at Northwest High School in 1963. And Coach Oliver would also take the reserve basketball spot from Economics teacher Richard Hedges for Head Coach Dave Hine the same year Russell McConnell replaced Amos Slaton as frosh coach. High school coaching positions in IPS, at the time, weren't considered significant stepping-stones to better jobs but times were beginning to change, at least until the busing turmoil of the '70's and '80's took its toll.

Coach Oliver arrived into the world on November 3, 1930 in the same small town where both of his parents had been raised in northern Indiana intersected by Highway 31. His younger brother Jack would be born a year later. Jack would eventually follow in his big brother's footsteps as a Rochester High School basketball star before attending Ball State. He became Nashville, Indiana's high school basketball coach in 1953. But he soon headed to Arcanum, Ohio as Head Coach. Eventually Jack would retire from the Ohio State Legislature after his earlier retirement from teaching.

Jerry graduated from his hometown high school in 1948. He worked for a year before entering Ball State in the fall of 1949. J.O. played on both the football and basketball teams as an undersized freshman. But he was a four-year golf star for the Cardinals from Muncie. His four years as a business and physical education student in the School of Education offered an introduction to the major perk of his life, lovely Ann Miller. Ann, who had graduated from Broad Ripple High School in Indianapolis, was a skilled artist who also earned a teaching degree. She began teaching art in IPS in the fall of 1955 soon after her college graduation and marriage. Her dad, Paul, was Assistant Superintendent for the Indianapolis Public Schools. In 2010 Ann still has one of her murals adorning a stairway in the Speedway Christian Church, dated 1968.

A week after Jerry's 1953 graduation, he received a call from Uncle Sam. Basic training at Fort Knox preceded his deployment to Germany, but after his engagement to sophomore sweetheart Ann. He was assigned to the 7th Army in the Tank Corps. Luckily his commander at Fulda, Germany was one who appreciated athletics. Jerry's leadership skills became apparent immediately. He was ordered to Augsburg, Germany where he was a halfback on the camp football team and player-coach of the basketball squad. Their best football man was the Detroit Lion's fullback, Stan Campbell. And his best roundballer was Holy Cross star Wayne Kongee. His two big men (both at 6'9") headed home when their enlistments ended. Unfortunately it was just before the European tournament. Coach Oliver would see better luck in future years. He returned to the States as a Corporal. His wedding day was soon thereafter.

Their son Bryan was born in December of 1960 followed by Mark in January of 1963 while living on the southeast corner of Lyndhurst and Winton directly across from brand new Speedway High School. In 2010 Bryan resides with his family, consisting of two teenage boys, in St. Louis while Mark lives in Avon. Mark and his wife have a daughter and son who are both in their early 20's.

But in the mid-1950's life was much different. As struggling young educators, Jerry and Ann first lived with her parents in Broad Ripple as Coach Oliver began his illustrious career. His circuitous route home after the very first August 15th practice from the westside to Broad Ripple was indicative of his life's journey. Carl Ragland, Washington's first African-American All-City player, was the senior star halfback Coach Oliver's first athletic season. And, Jerry was sitting next to Coach Hine when Jerry Lawlis tallied a Marion County record 48 points in January 1956. The lessons that he experienced that first year seemed unprecedented.

Coach Oliver began attending junior high games, usually in the Continental gym on Saturday mornings, and developed a positive relationship with nearby grade school coaches like Bill Mattingly, Guy Fish and Ernie Cline among others. Mattingly and Fish had been star athletes at GWHS ten years earlier. Jerry also was guest speaker at junior high award banquets during the last half of the 1950's. According to all relevant participants from 1956, Washington High's new principal Mr. Walter was not interested in athletics. So, it was another stroke of happy coincidence that Curly Julian returned to Continental-land as Jerry began his second year as a typing teacher and assistant coach. Curly was given the reigns of leadership in GWHS sports. He had been working in the downtown office for four years as the junior high "feeder" programs for athletics were first developed. Along with George Farkas, Mr. Julian can be said to be the main source of the original athletic "program" development in IPS. Not until the "super school district" programs of the 1980's exploded on the local scene, in parallel with forced busing and financial superiority, did Marion County see the athletic domination by one high school like the singular domination of Washington High. Jerry Oliver was Mr. Julian's first, and perhaps most significant, choice to lead the charge forward. Coach Oliver was chosen to replace 12-year coach and former Washington star Dave Hine by Assistant Principal Julian. The Continentals finished his first season at 10-11 but pulled off a big upset over North Central in the Hinkle Sectionals of 1961. But there were bigger fish to fry.

When Curly Julian was named the school's fourth principal in January of 1961 the foundation had already been established. And, in the fall of 1961, Coach Oliver saw the obvious potential of future greats Ralph Taylor from School 5 and Billy Keller from School 67. Oliver had already coached Bill's older brother Bernie in two sports and he proved himself to be a great judge of talent as he salivated over their future possibilities.

The first state-wide glory years of Washington basketball began with Jerry Oliver in the lead. Behind seniors Clark Dickerson and Clovis Stinson, along with leading scorer and rebounder Taylor, the Continentals won their first City Championship in 14 years. But the devastating loss to Blackie Braden's Southport team in our school's second Southport Sectionals on Louie Dampier's last second shot was disheartening in 1963. In November of 1963 the new season began with an 85-59 thumping of Howe in their gym. Later the City Championship game pitted two undefeated teams, Washington and Tech, against each other in Tech's gym. Coach Oliver's Continentals prevailed, 73-71, behind five long baskets by emerging super-star Keller in the final three minutes of the game. John Dowdell, Bob Komlanc, Sam Kitchens and Taylor all contributed heavily to what became a 20-0 beginning to the season. The rematch between Tech and our school took place at Hinkle Fieldhouse before over 13,000 fans that saw the junior varsity teams as the preliminary. Tech pulled out a 71-69 squeaker. But it seemed clear that both Tech (with the largest enrollment in the state) and Washington High (which had lost half of its enrollment to brand new Northwest High School) were both legitimate challengers for the State Championship. Unfortunately, one of the most perplexing losses in school history denied the Continentals for the third consecutive year in the Southport Sectionals final. Taylor had torn cartilage in his knee in the afternoon victory over Wood but most felt it was a given that Washington would defeat opponent Howe, even without Taylor. But it was not to be as the Hornets scorched the nets before cutting them down in a shocker.

The Final Four banquet that year witnessed Evansville Rex Mundi's coach making the statement that "Indianapolis Washington is 'by far' the best team we played this year." The Continentals had traveled to Evansville in December, winning 92-69. So again it was "wait 'til next year." Coach Oliver couldn't wait.

The first two games of the 1964-65 season were played at second year Northwest High School. The fan base was too large so there were no games scheduled for our 1938 gym, which seated only 1,400. Coach Oliver's Continentals avenged the Sectional loss to Howe followed by a 102-60 drubbing of Northwest. But talented Manual defeated the Continentals on January 2 at Indiana Central College's gym. Coach Oliver's unprecedented 3rd consecutive City Championship against a 17-team field, with a win over 1946 Mr. Basketball Jumpin' Johnny Wilson's Wood Woodchucks at Butler Fieldhouse, reflected the leadership of the Washington program under Jerry. Principal Julian soon decided, for the sake of some tradition, that we would play one game in our old gym. We beat Shortridge in our only home game of the season. When high-energy coach Evan Fine of Ben Davis led his Giants to a win over his friend Jerry Oliver's team in early February by two points, it seemed unusual for the opposing coach to enter the losing team's dressing room to console them while predicting our State Championship.

J.O.'s squad ended the season at 20-2 ranked fourth and third in the State polls. The subsequent nine-game winning-streak included the evasive Southport Sectional crown and concluded with the prestigious State Championship. Coach Oliver's team had avenged both defeats during the tournament run, becoming only the second Marion County school to win in the 55th year of the tourney, and was only the second school to sweep both individual awards (Trester Award and Mr. Basketball) as State Champions. Jerry's 102 wins in only five seasons made his name synonymous with "winner."

Coach Oliver's next season saw his first loss in the City Championship game to Howe at the recently re-named Hinkle Fieldhouse. The rest of the regular season left the westsiders with only that single defeat. So, after four tumultuous years at Southport, Washington returned to the Butler campus Sectionals. After defeating Tech during the latter part of the schedule, Coach Oliver's five suffered a first round loss to the eventual State Runners-up Titans. The Continentals were led by Championship holdovers Marvin Winkler, William Rogers and Mark Gladson who were complimented by guards Bill Ott and Roger Law. "Feets" Rogers was handicapped with the stomach flu and got sick on the Fieldhouse floor. His replacement, freshman George McGinnis, was an untested rookie and 5'8" junior Larry Highbaugh also couldn't quite fill the scoring and rebounding void left by Rogers. So Washington ended the season at 19-2. Winkler had broken legendary Oscar Robertson's ten-year single-season scoring record and was Coach Oliver's third All-Star in two years. In 1966-67 sophomore McGinnis began to exhibit the talent and intensity that the nation would one day see on display but the varsity season saw a somewhat disappointing record of 16-7.

During McGinnis' junior year, along with a growing Steve Downing and three-sport athlete Bob Jones as well as shooter Jim Arnold, Coach Oliver's team won his fourth City Championship in six years. And they won the Butler Sectionals for the first time since 1948. But Washington grad George Theofanis, who had played on the '48 team, led a quick Shortridge team to the

Regional Championship win over his friend Oliver. Jerry ended his career at Washington High with 161 victories and 34 losses in eight season as head man and another five as an assistant. He also had continued as an assistant football coach for two seasons under new coach and continuing friend Bob Springer for the 1962 and 1963 football seasons.

Indiana University gave Jerry an offer he couldn't refuse. He traveled to Bloomington as assistant to Lou Watson. Coach Oliver's second year saw both of his high school super-stars, McGinnis and Downing, accept scholarships to IU. But freshmen couldn't participate at the varsity level at the time so, when Watson fell ill and Jerry was the interim Head Coach for a time in 1969-70, he couldn't use their talents.

Big George's sophomore year in 1970-71 saw him lead the Big Ten in scoring and rebounding. Then he left to join the Pacers and Watson left coaching. Coach Oliver was one of two finalists for the Head position. A young coach from West Point who had played at Ohio State won the position. His name was Bob Knight.

So, in 1971-72, Oliver accepted a one-year job at his old high school. He taught Business and Typing at Indianapolis Washington. But he was named the All-Star coach for the summer series in June 1972. IU recruit Bobby Wilkerson was probably his best player. In the fall he was named Head Coach at Warren Central High School and following that year he again coached the Indiana All-Stars, becoming the first high school coach to do so. He was assisted both summers by Globetrotter and 1953 Mr. Basketball Hallie Bryant. Their star in June 1973 was IU-bound Mr. Basketball Kent Benson.

After two mediocre years at Warren Central, Jerry was hired by Bobby Leonard as an assistant coach for the Indiana Pacers. His eight years with the Pacers cemented his relationship with Indianapolis' movers-and-shakers. In early 1983 Indianapolis Sports Corporation President Sandy Knapp, who had worked for the Pacers, recommended Oliver as the first Sports Director for the brand new Hoosier Dome. The Colts arrived in May 1984. Jerry's six years with the Hoosier-RCA Dome led to his hiring as the General Manager of the Florida Suncoast Dome, which was soon re-named the Thunder Dome. He retired in 1992, at age 62, but not before the Thunder Dome was awarded the NCAA Final Four. Jerry and Ann spent one year in Madeira Beach before returning to Indianapolis and a condo in Brownsburg. Into 2010 they spend three months at their other condo on Dolphin Island. Jerry plays golf 11 or 12 months of the year, as does Ann. J.O. maintains a 7-handicap as he approaches age 80.

Coach Oliver's admonition that "girlfriends ruin more athletes than cigarettes and drinking combined" would be an anachronism today. But his line to "do as I say not as I do" was not accurate. More Continentals should have followed his example of consistent success and social networking in an athletic setting marked with strong self-confidence.

Jerry Oliver's energy, ambition and personality clearly reflected his reputation as an all-time legend in Indiana basketball and Washington High School history.

DAVE & JERRY SANDERS

Living near Blake Street on the south side of New York Street just west of Military Park, the Sanders brothers were assigned to School 5 at California and Washington Streets and then to the high school on the National Road about a mile west. Older brother Dave would set a high bar of excellence as perhaps the best Continental football player of the 1950's. He would be unanimously named one of only eleven All-City grid stars in both 1956 and 1957 at halfback. So, when Jerry entered GWHS in January of 1959, he had big shoes to fill. He did so admirably.

Jerry played football, basketball and baseball through his junior year of '62. His football ability was most apparent in his gutsy performance against future Purdue and New York Giant starter Randy Minniear from Broad Ripple during the Homecoming game of 1961. With mud and blood and a cracked helmet, Jerry couldn't single-handedly pull off a victory but his hard-nosed "never say die" attitude was just what new coach Bob Springer gleaned from watching the film from that game as he arrived in the fall of 1962. Along with fellow captains Malcolm Marlow and George Sipe, Jerry would welcome Coach Springer with his first five Continental victories, including an emotional win over Sacred Heart in game four. But the season ending Cathedral game tie on a rainy November night, which denied the Irish their fourth consecutive City Championship, was the highlight of a dramatic season.

Dave's 1957 season ended at 6-2 with big wins over Sacred Heart, Ben Davis and Howe and a combined score of 119 points scored to 33 points allowed in those games. And Dave was probably a faster runner but he didn't have any more determination, drive or leadership than that of little brother Jerry. But Dave would join the United States Marine Corps in August of 1958 in the same recruitment class as Southport's Jack Cottey, the future Marion County Sheriff and IPD Assistant Chief. Two of Cottey's IPD buddies were Continentals Don Campbell and undercover partner Jimmie Highbaugh. Dave would serve through 1968 and gained distinction on the Camp Lejeune football team playing halfback and cornerback for that North Carolina based squad.

While Dave was serving his country, Jerry was becoming a reputable Continental athlete. In the summer of 1961 while playing summer baseball, the Parks Department leader of baseball drove up to one of Jerry's games. Frank Luzar, who was preparing for his first year as an NFL official and 27th year as a Washington High teacher and coach, approached Sanders with catcher's glove in hand. Since Luzar was baseball coach his words carried weight. He told Jerry that he needed him to begin practicing the art of being a catcher. Sanders concurred and began a two year high school run behind the plate. He was both "good hit and good glove" as sometimes the lead-off hitter and sometimes the clean-up stick. His football aggressiveness served him well.

A year after Jerry's high school graduation, he traveled to upstate Powell, Wyoming to Northwest Community Junior College to play football. Continentals Jim Rhodes, Louie Craig, Clovis Stinson, Calvin Schaffer and John Dowdell were the starting five for their basketball team. An unusual occurrence to say the least. The 20-hour drive found Jerry 80 miles from Billings, Montana and about 50 miles from Yellowstone National Park but with few social opportunities. After a year Jerry would return to Indianapolis and semi-pro baseball with the Southside Saints.

As the Tet Offensive was concluding in Vietnam, Jerry was drafted into the U.S. Army in July of 1968. He spent 14 months in South Vietnam, mostly at the Chu Lai base camp of the American Division which also served as a Marine Corps airfield. Chu Lai was 56 miles southeast of Danang along the east coast and just five miles from the infamous My Lai Massacre, which had occurred in March of 1968. It was a trying time for many. Jerry's two closest friends in the

137th Engineer Battalion were killed within three months. PFC Charlie Hughes (from Edenton, North Carolina) died on the 14th of July and Corporal John Sterling (from Concord, California) was mortally wounded September 5th, both in 1969. They served as Combat Engineers with the job of Mine Sweeping. E-4 Sanders returned to the states in late 1969. In the 1980's Jerry would honor his two friends when he named his adopted special-needs-son, Jonathan Charles.

Washington High had at least 15 boys killed in Vietnam. But Jerry, Mark Gladson, Dannie Johnson and quite a few others from our school carry the scars of an intense early adulthood with them into their civilian lives.

Jerry had two older sisters along with older brother Dave. Jerry was born October 2, 1944. When his family moved to a home across from South Grove Golf Course in the summer of 1958, he was confronted with the reality that he would attend Sugar Grove School #44 which, during that period, had their graduates assigned to Shortridge High School. Ironically, a year younger Calvin Schaffer found himself in the same predicament. Both School 5 boys decided that they would continue at their old school under their previous addresses so that they could attend Washington High. And both would have a large positive impact on Continental athletics during the early 1960's.

Jerry would marry Sacred Heart graduate Mary Ann Murphy in June of 1986. As mentioned, they adopted her grandson at his birth. Sanders would work 35 years for General Services Administration at the Indianapolis Federal Building then ten more years as a general contractor doing the same job after retirement.

Older brother Dave married his high school sweetheart in 1958, Venetta Etty, and they had four kids. Dave died in 1999 of a heart attack while residing in Greencastle. Venetta died a year later while driving near Bainbridge on Rockville Road when a deer leaped through the windshield of her car from the side of the road.

Brothers like the Carters, the Deems, the Bransons, the Tillerys, the Highbaughs, the Howards, the Boswells, and the Portens may have had a better player or two but none could claim to be any more football-intense than the tenacious Sanders brothers.

BILL NIEMANN, ALL-STAR

Bill was born April 11, 1930 and graduated from Washington High in 1948. He lived a modest existence at 833 S. Warman Avenue and attended grade School #49. His walk to the Morris Street school, which was 13 city blocks to the east and south, was not unusual by the standards of the day. His mother fed him lunch at home every day. But Billy's Continental history had resulted from an unfortunate personal situation.

Bill's dad had died when he was 8-years-old and the family lived on the eastside. His sister soon graduated from Tech High School, the school that little Billy had dreamed of attending. His mother remained a widow for almost four years but eventually married John Warner, who became a good provider and kind step-father to Bill. Mr. Warner owned two pieces of property on South Warman Avenue on the Westside. The move west was not initially embraced by 12-year-old Billy Niemann. But he was enrolled in the 6th grade by his mother and his fate on the Westside was sealed. Yet athletic competition, especially basketball at Rhodius Park Community Center, intrigued the young Niemann.

He attended the State Finals at Butler Fieldhouse in March of his sophomore year and watched Anderson win the night game against Ft. Wayne Central, 67-53. But what had most impressed him was the Anderson player with the "cool" nickname, Jumpin' Johnny Wilson. Jumpin' Johnny had a strange looking shot for that era. It was called a turnaround jump shot. Wilson scored a then record setting 30 points in the championship game.

But Bill had to have a summer job to help with family finances. So he acquired a job at Indianapolis Power & Light after his second year in high school. Bill worked the "underground," running electrical cables underneath the downtown streets, for the next three summers.

Next to the Niemann abode was a vacant lot owned by his step-father. Bill was given the approval to put a basketball goal on that dirt lot in 1946. But first he needed a pole. He asked one of his supervisor's if he could take possession of one of the many discarded telephone poles from his summer job. Getting it to South Warman and putting it erect was harder than digging the hole. But the job was completed and Niemann's obsession with developing a turnaround jumper, during the era of two-handed set shots, made him unique in central Indiana. Bill is considered central Indiana's first jump shooter, with the exception of Johnny Wilson according to Niemann himself.

Billy's first official organized team was as a freshman at Washington High in the late fall of 1944. New teacher-coach Johnny Williams, who transferred from School 50, had played on the initial basketball All-Star team in 1939 and many expected him to be a basketball coach. But Leo Rosasco remained as the leader of the frosh team. Jack Woodson and Kelly Strange, a School 49 classmate of Bill's, were the two stars of their freshmen team. Bill broke his wrist during game two as a freshman. Woodson continued to be the top all-around basketball player into his sophomore season in 1945-46, according to both Bill and George Theofanis, even though senior Buckshot O'Brien made all the headlines. Strange also was a top contributor his sophomore year and is considered, by Bill, to be the best ball-handler he ever saw in high school. Unfortunately, both Woodson and Strange quit school in 1947.

The first game against Southport in 1947 ended with a one-point loss. Billy had scored 21 points but had missed four or five free throws. The next week, while practicing the traditional under-handed free throws, Coach Jones challenged his star Niemann that "I don't care how you shoot 'em, just make 'em." So Bill changed his method to the new-fangled bent-elbow shot. It served him, and the team, well. After 18 games he had scored 224 points and he finished the season as the city's leading scorer.

In the Butler Sectionals the Continentals defeated Broad Ripple, Warren Central, Decatur Central, and then Lawrence Central to win our first IHSAA tournament crown in the 21st season of our school's existence. The first game Regionals opponent was Speedway. We won 60-44 but lost a close four point game with Anderson. The dream season was over. Two weeks later Anderson would lose in the afternoon of the Finals to eventual champs Lafayette Jeff.

But in the spring of 1948, track coach Curly Julian used Niemann's speed and skill to claim another City Championship. Bill ran on the winning 880-relay team along with Charley Trotter, Don Carlyle, and Bob Reuter. Bob Stewart, who had been the fastest track-man in 1947, tore up his knee in football and was permanently sidelined. But Bill also won the broad jump at 20'6" on Tech's field. Coach Julian had convinced Bill that he should focus on the broad jump rather than the 440, which Niemann claimed was his best event. Tech's track, at the time, was the premier venue in the state.

Winning an athletic scholarship to Purdue didn't bode well for young Bill. Athletes were expected to join a fraternity but he was not a joiner and he soon left Purdue for the more friendly surroundings at Butler University. With frosh coach Herb Schwomeyer and Washington teammate Maurice Wilhoite, Bill enjoyed the limited basketball schedule but still needed a steady income, he felt. So, he took a summer job at Allison's Division of General Motors. The money was good but the benefit of reacquainting with his high school sweetheart down the hallway from his job station was a temptation he couldn't resist. Joann Linville accepted his marriage proposal and they were wed on August 27, 1950. Their union produced four sons: David, Jeff, Tim, and Bill. All became Speedway basketball stars, much like their dad. Eldest son David's 1973 team lost in the Butler Semi-State to Franklin High School as Dave fouled out with five offensive fouls. Franklin H.S. was coached by eight year Washington High assistant Dick Harmening who had left in 1967.

Bill retired in the early '90's after 41 years at Allison's in management. The Niemanns spend winters in Florida but enjoy their three grandchildren ranging in age from six to 27 in their Brownsburg condo.

Mr. Niemann's many happy memories bolster his image of his strong family life: working at old Victory Field as World War II began with his best grade school buddy Kelly Strange, leading the city in scoring his senior year, winning the Butler Sectional and outplaying his future friend from Lawrence Central Bob Harper (who led the county in scoring that year), winning two events as Mr. Julian won another City in track, working the "underground" for IPL, and watching his kids grow and play sports. The pole that his step-dad helped him elevate which then elevated Bill's shooting skills was a pivotal event in his life. But his most emotional memory is the day he reconnected with the Linville girl, his high school sweetheart, down the hall at his new job.

BASIL SFREDDO

In September of 2009 this author had an unplanned lunch with Coach Sfreddo, his wife Carolyn and their daughter Susan. Basil had just endured his first chemotherapy treatment for prostate cancer. He would die in August 2010. Following is a eulogy published in the Indianapolis Star on August 23 written by Washington High's greatest athlete, George McGinnis, titled "Never a finer person than Washington coach Sfreddo."

Basil Sfreddo passed August 13 at the age of 79. It has been a tough week as I reflect on the impact coach Sfreddo made not only on me, but on all the kids that he mentored at Washington High School in Indianapolis. He coached basketball from 1965 through 1989 and retired from teaching after transferring to Tech after our school had closed.

During the four years I attended Washington, I crossed paths with many fine people but never a finer person that coach Sfreddo. He was a Christian, honest, sincere, dedicated to his profession and a devoted husband and father.

As I got to know coach Sfreddo, I became aware of how he cared more about the total person, not just the basketball player.

The year 1969 was special for us at Washington. Our basketball team went 31-0 and won the state high school championship. There are a few great memories about that season, one of which was our practice sessions. They were extremely competitive. Steve Downing and I always played on opposite teams, with assistant coach Sfreddo coaching Steve's team, and head coach Bill Green with my side. Coach Sfreddo and Downing won most of those games and I always left practicve upset with both of them, but the experience elevated our game.

The other memory is that coach Green told us before the season that for every game we won, the coaches would take us to White Castle. What a treat it was on Friday and Saturday nights after every game that year. Coach Sfreddo's wife, Carolyn, was our second mother, and their sons, Bobby and David, helped with the transportation to White Castle.

When Downing and I entered Indiana University in the fall of 1969, we missed our home and our Washington High School family. To our surprise Steve and I would receive incredible care packages from Carolyn every month. What a treat and what a great family.

To his wife, Carolyn, sons Bobby and David and daughter Susan, and the entire family you're in all of our prayers. We'll always remember how coach Sfreddo enriched our lives, making us better basketball players but, more importantly, better men.

Author's note: Coach Sfreddo arrived at Washington High from Plainfield High School to teach in Carl Zenor's Social Studies department in the fall of 1966. He replaced Russell McConnell as freshmen basketball coach. Basil also became tennis coach then baseball coach in 1969.

In the fall of 1967 Bill Green replaced Dick Harmening as the junior varsity coach under Jerry Oliver. Coach Harmening had been named head coach at Franklin High School in Johnson County.

When Coach Green left for Marion High School in the fall of 1970, Coach Sfreddo became our fifth head coach as our school opened after Labor Day for the 44th year. He finished his head coaching career after 1989 with 222 wins over 19 seasons as the winningest coach in Continental history. He also won five Sectional Championships, more than the previous four coaches combined.

Coach Sfreddo had served in the Armed Services during the Korean War era on the Army basketball team before returning to Indiana State Teachers' College to complete his varsity basketball career.

After graduation and his marriage to Carolyn, he became head coach in Kansas, Illinois. Then he took the Plainfield job.

His two boys both graduated from Washington High School. Bob is currently a police officer in Atlanta, Georgia. Dave works for the CIA in Washington, D.C. Susan has recently suspended her business career to become a stay-at-home mom. She graduated from Plainfield High.

Basil and Carolyn had seven grandchildren by 2010 ranging in ages from 22 to 8 with five boys and two girls.

GOLF STATE CHAMPIONS 1961

	Bill Becker	Rob Clark		Jim Knobel	Denny Dennett
team members:	78	79		77	77

Toby Frost, Skip Crawford, Dave Mahler, Frank Ivancic, Pete Clark, L. Lewis, P. McCoun, L. Roe

1965 BASKETBALL STATE CHAMPIONS

back: Principal Julian, Larry Highbaugh, Leroy Dill, A.D. Jones, Harvey Holmes, Richie Sumner, Coach Harmening

middle: John Wesseler, Rick Blake, Roger Law, Bill Ott, Coach Leedy, Coach Oliver, Nelson Byers

front: William Rogers, Mark Gladson, Eddie Bopp, Ralph Taylor, Bill Keller, Marvin Winkler

1966 MYTHICAL STATE CHAMPIONS

front: Coach Springer, D. Watson, J. Finnerty, J. Hill, R. Sylvester, R. Marlowe, R. Thompson, B. Canady, C. Walton, L. Highbaugh, M. Cummins, R. Davidson, J. Neely
row 2: Ath.Dir. McConnell, Coach Shires, D. Maberry, D. Derringer, D. Phillips, B. Wooten, M. Doll, H. Carpenter, L. Cannon, M. Bradley, B. Jones, G. Baker, T. Noland
row 3: Coach Harmening, E. Smith, T. Ragland, M. Unversaw, D. Jones, B. Beard, L. Day, L. Shaw, D. Weaver, J. Green, R. Williams, G. McGinnis
row 4: Coach Rosenberger, J. McClure, D. Semenick, F. Miles, D. Schroeder, D. Daugherty, M. Newland, D. Deakin, B. Thomas, J. Vaugh, R. Rose, C. Russell, J. Hayes, J. Austin
not pictured: Coach England, M. Robinson, T. McGrevy

STATE CHAMPIONS 1969

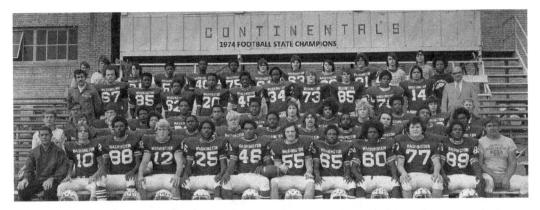

front: Coach Springer, J. Receuver, A. White, D. Butler, K. Weatherby, E. Branson, D. Beets, D. Wilburn, P. Mayfield, R. Heinrich, D. Sides, Coach Poehls

row 2: Coach Bopp, T. Davidson, S. Gorman, T. Leslie, R. Branson, B. Dishman, R. Smith, N. Abney, J. Cobbs, J. Powers, J. White, T. Palmer

row 3: Doc Rather, G. Glaze, K. Pullins, M. Jenkins, D. Harris, F. Cole, S. Newland, T. Kent, D. Smith, C. Gilbert, D. Ingalls, Coach Rosenberger

row 4: AD Shires, A. Pack, J. Sanders, D. Bradham, E. Hoskins, P. Lawrence, C. Thomas, S. Stamatkin, C. Shelley, W. Henry, A. Carpenter, Mr. Julian

back: P. Hamilton, D. Rees, L. Milliner, C. Marble, M. Gibbs, L. Jones, Darrell Ballou, J. England, J. Fields, David Ballou, M. Thompson, G. Porter

not pictured: C. Stamatkin

1975 TRACK STATE CHAMPIONS

front: Joene Bailey, Debbie Quarles, Donna Pope, Mardine Quarles, Gertrude Springfield, Vanessa Tate, Brenda Welch

middle: Principal Julian, Jean Bradham, Tonya Slaughter, Paula Williams, Karen Filer, Rhonda Quarles, Lisa Hill, Bonita Rice

back: AD Shires, Gail Arterburn, Amy Black, Gloria Johnson, Eddie Scott, Kathy Gaddie, Coach Marti Reece

1948 BUTLER SECTIONAL CHAMPS

front: Don Masterson, Maurice Wilhoite, Bill Niemann, Chris Theofanis, Bob Kikendall

middle: Leo Lentz, Bob Young, Leo Little, Ralph Lollar, Stan Benge, Dick Crittenden

back: Ass't Coach Amos Slaton, Dick Lipscombe, George Theofanis, Head Coach Rowland Jones, Bob Tillery, Bob Trinkle, Charlie Trotter

1959 UNDEFEATED TEAM 8-0-1

row 1:   L. Glaze, L. Compton, L. McClellan, M. Baker, D. Brunner, D. Hoffa, B. Cook, S. Peterson, F. Heinzmann, J. Dill, J. Reinbold

row 2:   K. Corey, B. Clark, R. Tyler, B. Leeper, W. Beliles, B. Snowberger, L. Meador, B. Wainscott, C. Prince, T. Frost, Line Coach Jerry Oliver

row 3:   Head Coach Joe Tofil, V. Combs, C. Harris, R. White, G. McGowen, D. Lawson, T. Taylor, D. Hazelwood, J. Thompson, S. Moorefield

row 4:   R. Mitchell, B. Hattiex, J. Purichia, F. Johnson, D. Shepard, N. Donovan

not pictured: D. Boarman

1930'S

EMERSON CARTER
1930 Pole Vault
State Champion

MARION "RED" CARTER

Kersey and Carter led the football and basketball teams to two City Championships each in their junior and senior years. At Purdue each lettered in football their sophomore and junior years before joining the military after Pearl Harbor. Bob was a Pacific pilot. Red was killed in training in New Mexico. Bob attended School 50. Red attended School 30.

ALVIN CASE
Class of 1938

VIRGINIA GARRABRANDT
Class of 1938

Gladys Huddleston Radcliffe
1938 graduate
PTA President 1958
mother of Trina Radcliffe

Bob Kersey

Ralph Chambers
1937 football captain

Georgie Enyert
class of 1938
Enyert's Cafe
wife of Harry Cherry

Mary Jane Howell
married classmate Ray Funk
mother of Elaine Funk
long-time school secretary

1937 FOOTBALL TEAM

Bogue at left, Luzar and Julian at right. #15 Roger Hoffa, #7 Bob McCalif, #20 Marshall Read, #16 Bob Kersey, #18 Ralph Chambers, #12 Red Carter, #22 Harry Rickenback, (2nd row) #23 John Sipe. New Gym being built in background.

SCHOOL #50 Graduation JUNE, 1935

from left: front #1 Rosella Woods, #3 Annabella Anderson, #5 Evelyn Woods, #7 Lillian Watson, #8 Bennie Lewis, #9 Thelma Bloomenstock

middle #4 Thelma Damer, #11 Virginia Sage

back #5 Lenore Miller, #6 Lester Butts, #10 Bill Sipe, #12 Joe Friger, #13 Norman Fuller

Jim Carter, class of 1930, with LaVerne Conway Crafton, class of 1932, and Jeannette Arnold, class of 1930 at November 2008 re-dedication.

Thelma Bloomenstock, class of 1939. HaywardBarcus city-wide essay contest, second place.

1935 COLLEGE ALL-STAR TEAM

Our Jim Carter #99 with Touchdown Twin Duane Purvis #88 in row 2. Back row far left #70 future Green Bay Packer coach Phil Bengtson. Also, over #24's left shoulder future Packer Hall of Famer Don Hutson (#14) & over #4's right shoulder future U.S. President Gerald Ford (#23).

Purdue's #95 below, Dutch Fehring from Columbus, Indiana. Fehring became the long-time Stanford baseball coach. He recommended his friend, John Wooden, to UCLA as basketball coach in 1948.

Touchdown Twin Jim Carter turns the corner vs. Ohio University in opening game win 13-6 in 1933.

LAUTER BOYS' CLUB

front: Ralph "Buckshot" O'Brien, Bud Hoagland, Evan Fine,
Eddie "Peanut" Miskoweic
back: Jack Woodson, Red Morgan, Coach E.B. Kelley, Gerald
Leslie, Bob Sheehan

BABE DIMANCHEFF
Class of 1940
Purdue All-American 1944
Chicago Cardinals
World Champs 1947

SCHOOL 50 JAN. 1949

front: Emma Lou Chandler, Arlene Gray, Carolyn Perry, Anita Bloomenstock,
Shirley Riggin
middle: Doris Neville, Lois Andes, Betty Lou Miller, Lila Pleasant, Jean Ann
McKinney, Annie Dosseff, Meredith Bomgardner
back: Tom Ferguson, Patty Hoffner, Rosemary Taylor, Don Williams, Ann
Kinnard

Bogue's next-to-Last team, 1949

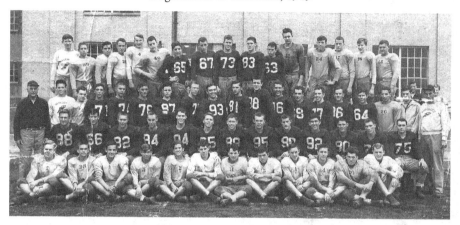

front: 88-B. Lalioff, 66-M. Purichia, 82-E. O'Riley, 84-D. Cozart,
       94-B. Short, 85-L. Lord, 89-G. Totten, 95-R. Schroeder,
       90-J. Hodson, 92-F. Fieser, 80-A. Cooper, 79-P. Maschino,
       75-B. Kelley with coaches Bogue and Luzar

middle: 71-C. Fender, 74-S. Miller, 78-E. Lowery, 97-B. Borneman,
        75-S. Tillery, 93-H. Nothern, 81-P. Harding, 98-J. Marshall,
        96-B. Cook, 68-J. Lee, 77-W. Ornsby, 86-D. Whitmore,
        64-R. Beasley

back: 6S-J. Petercheff, 67-E. Kernodle, 73-J. Burke, 83-D. Hensley,
      63-R. Ourrett

First Female Cheerleaders 1947-48

Patty Whitmore   Sue Wilson
         Betty Voege

Niemann
scored
224 pts.
in 18 games
to lead the
city in
scoring

1948 Butler Sectionals celebration
front   Lollar, Masterson, Wilhoite, Niemann, C. Theofanis, Don Edwards
back   G. Theofanis, Little, Kikendall, Coach Jones, Young, Crittenden

128

School 49 Kids in 1953

Sharon Wycoff ('62), Kenny Wolfe ('66), Terry Sylvester ('64), Betty Eadens ('63), and John Chapman ('66)

Purichia boys

Joe ('62), Nick ('59), Steve ('65), and Carol ('57) with nephew Mike (Ritter '70) in 1953

Larry Pyatt (center front) at 10th birthday party in 1957 with Stevie Sears and Paul Fair. back: Garry King, Mike Fair, Eddie Bopp & Ronnie Sears

Steve Kuszmaul ('66) and Terry McGrevy ('67) with retired undefeated Heavyweight boxing champion Rocky Marciano at Municipal Gardens in 1958

SCHOOL 50 KINDERGARTEN 1952-53

Anita Bloomenstock ('53) and Nula Purichia ('52) in 1952

at Belleview & Ohio Streets
front: Judy Weekly, Marvin ?, Cheryl Roberts, Kathy Lomen
row 2: ??, Eddie Bopp, Mark Masariu, ??
row 3: ??, Jimmy Smith, ??, Karen McDonald, Kenny Strong
row 4: Charles Crain, Judy Danner, Evelyn Utley,
Diane Felber, Margaret Morris, ??
row 5: Howard Bennett, ??, ??, Garry King, Alva Smith, ??
back: Dan Froedge, Janie Willoughby, Linda Johnson,
John Lee, Ronnie Broadstreet, Nancy Higgins

Spin-the-bottle party in 1957 with class of 1964 School 67 kids Kay Heriter, Mike Boyd, Nancy Phillips and Gary Baugh

Williard Sylvester, class of 1934, with son Terry ('64) sledding at Rhodius Park in 1951

1957 RHODIUS PARK SWIMMING & DIVING TEAM

front: Denny Schafer, Ricky Schafer, Mim Harris, ??, Linda Leak, Sheila Hamilton, Ann Allison, Nola Havens, Jeannie Such, Bobby Crist
middle: Mike Havens, Jimmy Johnson, Corky Smith, Danny Schafer, Larry Cullivan, Billy Keller, Steve Allison, Chuck Crist, Dick Funk, ??, Richard Such
back: Coach Ernie Medcalfe, Bob Brouse, Coach Bill Kratowska, Dave Donovan, Elaine Funk, Richard Bumps

An Indianapolis Times article noted that over 400 swimmers and divers had participated in the weekly meets from six pools: Rhodius, Ellenberger, Willard, Broad Ripple, Douglas and Garfield. Other Rhodius Park kids named in various acquatic articles in 1957 were:

Charlene Gosnell, Bernie Keller, Charlene Houchins, Kay Pate, Sandra Henthron, Nancy Reynolds, Mildred Butler, Mike Foster, Jim Thompson, Jean Potts, Fred Tingle, David Jared, Jim Montgomery, Mike Bruce, Tamara Tingle, Jo Ellen Jared, Maxine Kennedy, Jesse Cox, Richard Phillips, Diedre Fisher, Larry Medcalfe, Billy Jared, Joyce Manley, Connie Henderson, Benny Cook, Paul McCormick and Nelson Mattingly

Dave Sanders ran for two TDs and 132 yards in ten carries against Ben Davis in 1957 victory, 53-14. Younger brother Jerry had a similar game in the 1962 35-0 win.

Terry, Bruce, and Tim McGrevy with Chicago Bears fullback Rick Casares at St. Joseph's College training camp in 1959

SCHOOL 75 FOOTBALL 1959

front: R. Cesnik, M. Wild, B. Tsakrias, S. Lewis, D. Green, T. McGrevy, W. Stout, B. Knobel
back: J. Wampler, R. Dalton, P. Myers, C. Benson, M. King, C.B. Durr, ??, ??, L. Bartlet, N. Shelley and Coach Joe Draughn

Carnine Little League Home Run leader Harvey Holmes with no-hit pitchers Gary and Ricky Sylvester

Dannie Johnson ('65) and Eddie Bopp ('65) with Johnny Bopp ('71) on South Warman Avenue in 1956

Jeannie Such & Bea Ann Gill with Louie Stamatkin, class of 1974

Steve Purichia in Miss Zook's 6th grade, 1957

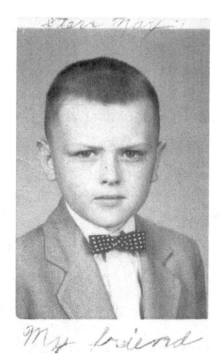

Steve May ('65) in Mrs. McKee's 4th grade class, 1956-57

1960 UNDEFEATED SCHOOL 50

from left: G. Hiese, J. Schabel, M. Parker, T. Anderson, R. Marlowe, R. Holtgrave, D. Koch, M. McAllister, D. Pritchard, D. Johnson, B. Apple, E. Bopp, B. Crist, J. Sowers, K. Strong, D. Rose, B. Neff, B. Sowers, M. McKee, J. Whittle, E. Griggs, D. Froedge, B. McCoy
not pictured: B. Lohrmann and Mr. Guy Fish

SCHOOL 50 GRADUATION 1959

front: M. Cogell, B. Anderson, ?, G. Blevins, V. Gasper, C. Watkins, L.A. Bainaka, H. Veza, R. Herndon, L. Kenley, C. Neff, D. Gray, D. Tice, G. Terry, F. McCain

middle: Miss Linehan, S. Higgins, B. Boring, P. Marlowe, R. Such, R. Boston, S. Green, J. Lucas, M. Talbot, J.A. Davis, P. Parks, D. Green, V. Strong, K. Hill, R. Wiles, B. Ausbrooks, K. Griggs, H. Crawley, B. Russell, R. Morris, I. Tincher, M. Durham, Miss Peck, Miss Starost

back: T. Eisele, D. Frame, M. Marlowe, C. Parmely, L. Morgan, M. Vaughn, C. Watkens, B. Sowers, E. Morrow, M. Lomen, R. Smith, J. Fultz, J. Wilbur, A. Derringer, J. Koons, G. Opp, E. Horton, R. Harrington, C. Crist

Majorettes in 1959--Jeannie Such, Charlotte Doll and Sherry Benson

Dannie Johnson in Miss Herman's 3rd grade, 1955

Jimmy Smith ('65) in Mrs. Schiffman's 5th grade class in 1957-58.

133

SCHOOL 50 GRADUATION 1961

front   J. Wheeler, G. King, B. Crist, D. Bollinger, S. Cheung

row 1   B. Matesick, R. Jones, A. Smith, M. Gott, B. Baker, L. Richardson, M. Wolford, N. Higgins, S. Neff, L. Holtgrave, K. Lomen, B. Apple, T. Anderson, M. McKee, E. Griggs

row 2   B. Mitchell, K. McDonald, C. Roberts, G. Mayes, E. Utley, T. Brown, L. Reed, S. Wesseler, C. Trotter, M. Morris, J. Durham, B. Haas, J. Weekly, J. Myrick, M.L. Bridgewater

row 3   M. Goff, E. Bopp, J. Wesseler, K. Strong, J. Smith, R. Sparks, L. Pyatt, B. McCoy, J. Phillips, D. Pritchard, B. Shelton, D. Ludlow, D. Rose, R. Hawblitzel, J. Cooper

8th grade dance
June 1961--Eddie Bopp
& Jeannie Such

DD SOCIAL CLUB, LAKE SCHAFFER 1962

front   Bobbi Morgan, Cindy Allen, Patty Miller, Karen Hessel, Diane Wyland, Maxine Kennedy, Carol Beets

back   Cheryl Roberts, Donna Baldwin, Beverly Carpenter, Judy Cobb, Marilyn Findley, Deanna Johnson, Janie Leeper, Suzie Carpenter

PONY LEAGUE ALL-STARS 1961

Six Ben Davis boys & Six Washington boys

front   Johnny Bath, Bobby McCoy, Eddie Bopp, Mike Tibbetts, Mike Dees, Bobby Villegas

back   Coach, Dick Koker, Mike Noble, Harvey Holmes, Mark Gladson, ??, Danny Carnes

SPRINGER'S FIRST TEAM, 1962

Phil Smith ('65)
longtime Speedway
Ass't Police Chief.

row 1:   E. Bopp, L. Austin, S. Shouse, R. Payne, J. Sanders, G. Sipe, G. Marlow, J. Arvin, J. Highbaugh, R. Weaver, L. Shotts, L. Lewis, W. Lanker, Coach Oliver;

row 2:   Coach Springer, B. Anderson, B. McCoy, N. Shelly, B. Collier, J. Blake, S, Midkiff, D. Garver, M. Coffey, M. Lloyd, M. Parker, S. Purichia, G. Sylvester, M. Highbaugh, Coach Harmening;

row 3:   G. Lawson, M. King, G. Bland, J. Cartwright, B. Lemmons, B. Brown, B. Sandusky, D. Johnson, T. McGrevy, M. Furimsky, P. Cook, B. Apple, S. Unversaw, M. Tibbetts, J. Turner, K. Strong, G. Opp, Coach England

1963 TEAM

row 1: M. Tibbetts, R. George, K. O'Brien, B. McCoy, H. Tibbetts, D. Brown, E. Bopp, B. Keller

row 2: Coach Luzar, J. Cox, L. Austin, G. Sylvester, M. Lloyd, J. Sanders, F. Komlanc, B. Komlanc, C. Dickerson, G. Leet

Sandy Dulla ('63), Gary Sylvester ('64), Donna Baldwin ('63) and Rob Clark ('62) at 1962 Junior Prom.

Jackie Flowers ('65) and Denny Morgan ('64) in 1963

1963 Jamboree Queen Regina Such

Jim Chase ('62) and Steve Midkiff ('64) in 1962

Darlene Beasley ('65) and Gerry Smith ('64) at Lake Freeman in 1963

Bill Keller Mr. Basketball 1965

135

Eddie Bopp scores winning X-P in 1963 Homecoming. Broad Ripple defenders are Mike Perry and Ricky Lee.

1963 CITY CHAMPIONS

C. Dickerson, S. Slauter, R. Taylor, S. Kitchens, C. Stinson, B. Keller, Coach Oliver, G. Sylvester, C. Schaffer, B. Komlanc, J. Belser, J. Dowdell, S. Midkiff

1965 May Queen
Karen McDonald

Grider Wins Title; Team Ends Eighth

CHAMP AND COACH—Posing for The Surveyor photographer are State Champ Dennis Grider and Mr. John Bradley, cross-country coach.

1962 and 1963 Cross Country State Champion Dennis Grider with Coach John Bradley.

Guard Bob Jones cuts the nets after 1968 Hinkle Sectional championship game.

1964 CITY CHAMPIONS

row 1: J. Wesseler, D. Brown, B. Keller, S. Kitchens, E. Bopp, C. Rowland, G. Sylvester, B. Personett
row 2: Coach Harmening, C. Schaffer, B. Komlanc, H. Holmes, R. Taylor, J. Dowdell, S. Slauter, Coach Oliver

Richard Such and George Terry
class of 1963

136

with Voice of 500 and high school basketball Tom Carnegie, 1965 Cheerleaders Nancy Parks, Barbara Brunt, Regina Such, Phyllis Abbott, Bobbi Morgan, and Nancy Adams. not pictured: Donna Burkert

Eddie Bopp puts Washington ahead by five points with 1:02 vs. Attucks in City Tourney in January 1965 at Northwest

Eddie Bopp with boss Dick Lugar at trailer home before football game at GWHS in 1965

Bopp and Plump before Butler pre-season game in November 1965

Two former Washington High quarterbacks, freshman Eddie Bopp and senior Joe Purichia before Butler Blue vs. White game in September 1965

1969 State Champs:
front   Principal Julian, Harvey Galbreath, James Riley, Steve Stanfield, Louie Day, Paul Donald, Jim Winters
back   Coach Walton, Steve Downing, Abner Nibbs, Ken Carter, Ken Parks, Head Coach Green, Wayne Pack, George McGinnis, Jim Arnold, Coach Sfreddo, Alan Glaze

1932 QB Hop Howard with 1964 QB Eddie Bopp on May 8, 1976 before 1965 vs. 1969 game. Hop's grandson, future ESPN race reporter Vince Welch, took the picture.

1965 STATE CHAMPIONS

Wesseler, Rogers, Ott, Taylor, Holmes, Gladson, Winkler, Oliver, Julian, Highbaugh, Law, Keller, Bopp, Dill, Blake, Harmening, Jones

Continental State Champs, 1965: Ralph Taylor, Mark Gladson, Marvin Winkler, Eddie Bopp, Bill Keller, and William Rogers before Semi-State.

Inaugural 1967 Football All-Stars Bobby Canady, with his wife, and Charlie Walton at Coach Springer's Hall of Fame induction in 1991.

with 1934 graduate Harry Cherry

1995 School Closing with Mrs. Hine, Jim Arvin, Mrs. Julian and Mr. Julian

Final basketball game 1995 at Butler Bob Tillery ('48), Charlie Rice ('52), and Thelma Bloomenstock Bopp ('39)

Curly Julian and Johnny Williams at 1990 Silver Anniversary game between 1965 and 1969 Champs

Mrs. Connie Baldwin and daughter Donna at Coach Springer's 1991 Hall of Fame induction.

Texas Tech Coach Bob Knight and Ass't Steve Downing ('69) with Mary Hooser Woodson ('47) at Lincoln, Nebraska in 2002

School 50 teacher Mrs. Bopp with former student, cadet teacher, and student teacher Diane Kenley Arnold, class of 1971.

Tony Allen-Cooksey, class of 1974, World Record Pentathlon

1970 Westlake Beach Club card. Westlake closed after 1973.

At Chuck Dulla's 50th birthday party in 2002 with sister Sandy, class of 1963

Banners rededication 2004: Donnie McCoy, John Wesseler, Harvey Holmes, Mr. Julian, Ralph Taylor, Jim Arnold, Bill Keller, Mike Cummins, George McGinnis, Basil Sfreddo, Gary Sylvester, Eddie Bopp

Mr. Guy Fish, 1945-46 Student Council President and All-City Right Tackle, in 1988 at Regina Such Bopp birthday party.

1983 State Runners-Up
#87 K. Stinis, #78 D. Stamatkin, #60 M. Baber, #59 B. Seargent,
#63 C. Fitzgerald, #76 J. Cunningham, #85 T. Chandler
Coach Newland, #40 G. Carpenter, #45 D. Luter, #8 J. Overstreet,
#1 T. Weeden, Coach Shires

Miss Basketball 1981
Cheryl Cook
State Champ Hurdles
1981

Jim Carter ('30), Dick Lugar ('50)
& Curly Julian ('28) in Nov. 2008
at school re-dedication.

Ralph Taylor's Hall of Fame
Induction in 2001 at New Castle
with School 5 Coach Robinson
and teammate Eddie Bopp

Jim Clevenger ('70) with Gary
Sylvester ('64) at Chuck Dulla's
50th birthday party in 2002.

1965 Senior Class President Fred
Hulser with newborn Eddie
Tom Bopp. Fred graduated
from Columbia University and
became a corporate lawyer in
Puerto Rico.

Jerry Sanders, class of 1963, on
cover of last Indianapolis News
October 1, 1999. Selling papers
in 1955. Jerry starred in football
and baseball at GWHS

Ass't Coach Bopp with Coach
Springer and 1974 State Champion
QB Danny Butler at Springer's
1991 Hall of Fame induction.

Jerry Oliver and wife Ann with
Gary Sylvester in 2001.

With Joe Shires ('55) and Steve
Sermin (Howe '65 and GWHS
teacher) at school closing 1995.

IV.

WORLD WAR II

COMMITTEE of CORRESPONDENCE

The following two verbatim "letters to the troops" were written by two of our schools most notable personalities during World War II. The first was written by our first principal, Mr. Gingery, and the second by our first football coach, Mr. Bogue. The capitalization of "Greatest Generation" was by me, the author. It seems that Mr. Gingery was well before his time in that characterization. The named captain of the 1943 football squad was a boy who actually was serving in the military at the time.

GWHS Committee of Correspondence
Newsletter
Volume II   Number 2
May, 1943

Dear Continentals,

It is always a welcome privilege to use the facilities of the correspondence committee to reach all you former Continentals with a message. However, it is not easy to compose a letter that fits all of you equally well. Some of you left in the middle of your schooling, some finished high school, others have some college training, and some have graduated from college. Still others left jobs or businesses in which you were established. Some of you expect to make the armed forces a profession, while the rest want to get this job done in order to take up life where you put it down to go to war.

What I am about to say all of you already know; yet it may not be amiss to call attention to it again. Even before you entered the service, your generation, in America, was better educated than any other generation anywhere has ever been. Now I am told that better than 60% of all the men and women entering the service are given additional education. Some receive many months of high pressure instruction that in peace time would have taken much longer.

It is true this education is highly specialized and technical. That phase of it is at least partly balanced by the great amount of traveling and mingling with people from other parts of the country and world that you folks are doing. Travel has always been one of the accepted liberalizing factors of an education.

I'm saying all of this because I believe it means that you have a chance to be the GREATEST GENERATION the world has known. The problem of establishing an improved world-order is great---probably the greatest problem the world has faced. I believe that you can do it.

My suggestion is that you take advantage of every opportunity that comes along to learn something more. Keep always on the constructive side. Let this period of military service be, also, a further opportunity for growth.

Sincerely yours,
W.G. Gingery (signed)

Dear G.W.H.S. Service Men Everywhere,

What's left of the athletic Department sends you greetings and wishes you good luck. The "Three Musketeers"—Jones, Marshall, and Bogue—are all that's left of the old gang of coaches and gym teachers that were around when this war started. Rosasco was in and is out teaching soldiers; McNerney is a chief petty officer; Slaton is a chief petty officer; Luzar is an ensign; Julian is a lieutenant J.G.

Many of the seniors of this year's class are already in the service. A lot more will go just as soon as they receive their diplomas. Several older juniors are now in the service. Others will go before next fall. We just do not know what our prospects for good teams will be for next year until we hold the first practice.

Here at Washington we have always tried to provide the best uniforms, the best equipment, and give you the best training that was in our power. Sometimes we were overmatched, but everything being equal, we know that victory went to the team with the best spirit and the greatest desire to win. You won plenty of times here at Washington. We believe you will go right on to victory now that you are playing in the big leagues.

We trust that your contact with the Athletic Department has proven an asset to you. We will hit the ball a little harder and do that extra bit to get more boys ready for Uncle Sam.

Stay in there and pitch!

Yours,
Henry Bogue

Final note: Jack Hensley, class of 1948, helped create the "Veterans Memorial Plaza and Parkway" located in the Raymond Park Campus in Warren Township between Franklin and Post Roads on East Raymond Street. Included in that memorial is a plaque dedicated to Washington High School veterans and includes a quote from Mr. Gingery's "Committee of Correspondence" note repeated above and including his "Greatest Generation" prophetic designation. That plaque is at the base of an American flag and also reads: "This flag pole and flag are dedicated in honor of all the students and faculty of George Washington High School who have served their country honorably in times of war and peace."

JACKTOWN HEROES
Five Boys Within Five Blocks

I believe in ghosts. At least ghosts from the Greatest Generation that presided in my childhood neighborhood. My Uncle Bob Bloomenstock was born May 1, 1923 in a corner of his grandparents bedroom at 514 S. Warman. When he died on D-Day of 2007 I was compelled to think of the 95 names in the entranceway of Washington High/ Community School of "Those Who Gave All" during WW II. Uncle Bob fought on Peliliu and Okinawa.

After I talked with Harry Northern in 2007 I realized again that he, Sonny Roberts, Fred Medenwald and two of the four Pyatt brothers were maybe the only Jacktown area residents left who served our country in the early 1940's (Harry Pyatt died in 2008). Mr. Northern currently resides in Danville. His wife of 61 years is struggling with her health (she died in 2009). Her brother, Bob Cooke, was killed in France on October 26, 1944 serving with the 44th Infantry. And Harry's younger brother, Virgil, was killed on Saipan on July3, 1944 with Company K, 3rd Battalion, 23rd Marines, 4th Division. Those were two of the five boys who lived within five blocks of each other who walked to School 50 and Washington High perhaps side-by-side but would never again see Indianapolis or experience the joys of young adulthood.

A house is not a home but to think that in the 1930's the Cooke family at 2409 W. Jackson St. and, just around the corner, the Northern family at 41 S. Warman would both lose boys to war seemed improbable. But within five blocks lived Eugene Heicken at 435 S. Harris, Lloyd Posey at 501 S. Warman, and Charles Bradshaw at 526 S. Holmes. Eugene was killed in a wartime plane crash, Lloyd died in Germany on February 19, 1945 when a comrade stepped on a land mine killing them both (he had survived being wounded on D-Day with the Rangers), and Charles died on Okinawa in February of 1945 not long after being featured by Ernie Pyle for his heroism on New Britain Island. None would enjoy the freedom of post-war America that my generation would take for granted.

As a "walker" to School 50 then Washington High in the '50's and '60's from South Warman Avenue I walked the same route all of those boys did. At School 50 Miss Linehan and Miss Zook began teaching at the conclusion of World War I, the War to End All War. Miss Peck started not long after in the early '20's. All three would retire in the 1960's. And Miss Baumgart taught from 1935 until her 1970 retirement. My classmates of 1961 and those of the Greatest Generation had at least four of the same teachers. Miss Baumgart Goodman died in early March of 2007.

At Washington High Curly Julian, Frank Luzar, Barbara Jean Sullivan Hine, Jim Otto, Lloyd Mann, Margaret McWilliams (Miss Peck's sister), Leo Rosasco, Rowland Jones, Justin Marshall, Vivian Ely, Hester Baker Bock Erwin, Anne Burge, Paul Carmichael, Samuella Shearer Sands, Mary Laatz, RJ Weaver, Orrell Negus, Mabel Loehr, Elizabeth Hatfield, and Margaret Hannan were the 20 personnel who served both generations. Mrs. Hine died this year (2007) and Mr. Julian lives on.

I've often wondered what those two dozen educators thought about those five heroes or any of the 95 KIA from World War II as compared to my generation, including at least 15 of my contemporaries who died in Vietnam?

History has a way of re-writing itself. I hope that no revisionist is able to erase the spiritual footprints of so many. And, every time that I see the file photo of those ten American soldiers holding a large Nazi flag on the History Channel I think of my old neighborhood. Because that's Lloyd Posey on the far right with his left thumb hooked in his belt maybe as he had stood after a Washington High track meet three years earlier when he was one of Curly Julian's captains on the old cinder track.

WORLD WAR II WASHINGTON BOYS

The first four years of the 21st century I sponsored four seminars over four Aprils at the school in which I was a history teacher. The Wayne Township Education Foundation twice refused to give any financial help when I sent a written request. One rejection letter began "I regret to inform you…." It seemed quite ironic. Yet I honored 25 different living men over the four years including two Tuskegee Airmen, Louis Garfield and Walter Palmer. Both have since died in 2008 and 2009. Jim O'Donnell and Dick Mote attended all four years. Mr. O'Donnell is a survivor of the U.S.S. Indianapolis disaster. Mr. Mote was with the 82nd Airborne arriving on D-Day plus 1. He also was a history teacher at Haughville's School 75. Both men live on into 2010. I had student sponsors for each man and their wives, fed them, and awarded each with a small memento. Nine men had a Washington High School connection. Students also read short biographies of five other men. Two were killed in action during World War II and the other three died in the late 20th century.

After studying the chapter on WW II we had three intense days of non-textbook instruction. Day one we presented a video collage, specific reading selections, and the presentation of specific era items that included a samurai sword, kamikaze plane part, an oil soaked dollar bill from the U.S.S. Indianapolis, a cricket-clicker from the Normandy invasion, and a fighter pilot helmet. On day two the men presented themselves at our convocation in the school's auditorium before traveling to four separate classrooms. One for Marines, one for the Army Air Corps, one for the Navy, and one for the Army men who honored us with their presence. On day three we had a school sponsored field trip to downtown Indianapolis. We took a walking tour visiting seven different memorials including the Medal of Honor and U.S.S. Indianapolis monuments on the canal, the Civil War museum in the basement on the Circle, and the four war displays in the American Legion Mall. Students had a series of questions to answer. (note: with the exception of Washington, D.C. Indianapolis has more war memorials than any U.S. city)

Obviously, the 1,900 men including the 95 who "Gave All" cannot all be honored here. But the 14 following biographies, which were read by junior high students in the 21st century, hopefully can represent all from the Greatest Generation. As their individual biographies were read their 1940's pictures were projected onto a large screen.

Written and read in 2003:

FRED MEDENWALD graduated from Public School 50 and then Washington High in 1941. He lived on the alley on the east side of Tremont St. just north of Washington Street. His mother could watch him walk all the way to school.

As a 16-year-old he worked at the Holt Road National Guard Headquarters under the direction of Major Stout. He was commended in the Indianapolis Star for quick action and thinking which saved a number of planes during a fire at what became Stout Field. He then enlisted in the Army Air Corps in 1942 as a pilot cadet at the University of Tennessee. Lieutenant Medenwald became a Flight Test Engineer as well as a single-engine fighter pilot.

Mr. Medenwald was on Tinian Island in August 1945 when the plane (the Enola Gay) lifted off with the first atomic bomb which was dropped on Hiroshima.

After the war he was recruited into the new Air Force where he worked on the secret U-2 project on both Saipan and Guam. He was also involved with the first post-war atomic bomb test on Kwajalein Atoll.

He was married at the little white church at Patterson Field in Dayton, Ohio in 1947. He and his wife were married for 55 years before her death in 2002. They had three daughters who graduated from Speedway High School. He has seven grandchildren in 2003. (Mr. Medenwald showed his fighter pilot helmet)

HOLLIE COX graduated from Washington High in 1935 and comes to us highly recommended by our Media Specialist, Mrs. Smith (at Fulton Junior High), who is his daughter.

He was inducted into the U.S. Army in 1941 during America's first peace time draft. First Sergeant Cox's service with the 75th Division, 275th Engineer Battalion saw action in the Battle of the Bulge in December of 1944. The 75th was then ordered to Colmar, France from which they pushed the German Army back across the Rhine River.

Then they were ordered to the Ruhr region in occupied Germany. The 75th won three Battle Stars during the liberation of Fortress Europa. Hollie won a Bronze Star.

Mr. Cox was honorably discharged in December 1945. He married in 1948 and has two children and three grandchildren. He worked 44 years at International Harvester as a Patternmaker. His kids attended Ben Davis High School. (Mr. Cox wore his original "Eisenhower jacket" which fitted him perfectly 58 years later)

HARRY NORTHERN and his good friend Bob Cooke graduated from Washington High in 1942. Both were drafted in 1943. Mr. Northern would eventually marry Bob's sister, Betty, who is with us today. Unfortunately, young Bob was killed in action with the 44th Infantry in France on October 26, 1944.

And Mr. Northern's younger brother, Virgil, was killed on Saipan in the South Pacific on July 3, 1944 with Company K, 3rd Battalion, 23rd Marines, 4th Division. Both the Northern and Cooke families paid the ultimate price for our freedoms.

In the states, Mr. Northern was assigned to Fort Benning, Georgia and the 82nd Airborne. On June 6, 1944 at 2:30 AM Staff Sergeant Northern and his comrades were dropped at Saint Mere Eglise behind German lines just inland from Omaha Beach. He was wounded on June 7 in the hedgerows at twilight losing his thumb.

In December '44 he watched, by bright moonlight, as German Panzers moved into Webermont as the Battle of the Bulge began. Sergeant Northern was also involved in the liberation of Belgium and reached the Elbe River.

Mr. & Mrs. Northern celebrated their 57th wedding anniversary on March 10 (2003). They have four kids and two grandkids. (In early 2009 Betty died.)

PAUL HAYES graduated from Fayette High School near Terre Haute in 1939 and began working in the Gary Steel Mills. In 1942 he enlisted in the U. S. Marine Corps. He was ordered to Tank Training near San Diego where he trained as a Driver, Loader, Assistant Driver, and Gunner on the M-4 A-3 Sherman tanks.

Corporal Hayes landed under fire in the Marshall Islands, on Kwajalein Atoll, on Saipan, at Tinian, and finally on Iwo Jima. On Tinian Island his tank was hit five times by anti-tank 37-millimeter shells. One piece of shrapnel entered their tank injuring all five men although none were seriously harmed.

His crew landed on Iwo Jima at 9 AM on February 19, 1945. Of the 15 Marine tanks landing there only eight made it to the air field. Corporal Hayes watched the famous flag raising on Mount Surabachi from the air field. After 30 days on Iwo over 6,000 Marines had been killed.

Corporal Hayes' younger brother, Verlin, was listed MIA during the Battle of the Bulge in Europe but eventually was found alive. Verlin was then sent as a 330th Infantry Regiment replacement and was killed in action in January of 1945 with the 83rd Division.

After the war Mr. Hayes graduated from Indiana State Teachers' College in 1950. He became a Machine Shop teacher at Indianapolis Washington High School in 1951. In 1964 he was promoted to the Downtown Central Office as Director of Cooperative Education. He retired in 1984 from Marshall High School as Supervisor of Evening School and Director of Placement.

Mr. Hayes and the former Ruth Rosser (she was Continental Choir director in the early 1960's) have two children. Their daughter is Supervisor of Eastern Asian Studies at Indiana University. Their son begins teaching Military Science at West Point Military Academy this week (April 30, 2003) as a career member of the U.S. Army.

(His son accompanied him and headed to the airport after our convo)

CARL SONNY ROBERTS graduated in 1943 from Washington High School while playing varsity basketball for Coach Rowland Jones. He joined the Army Air Corps in October of '43. His first overseas assignment was as a Gunner on a B-17 stationed at Kimbolton, England. Between August 1944 and April 1945 he survived 24 bombing missions but not without incidents.

On December 8, 1944 near Mannheim, Germany his plane was shot down and he had to parachute behind enemy lines. He and a comrade commandeered a jeep and by December 16 had reached American lines. Little did he know that he had arrived in the middle of the famous Battle of the Bulge. Sergeant Roberts was given a rifle and immediately became an infantryman.

On January 23, 1945 after returning to his base in England, Staff Sergeant Roberts' twin-engine plane crashed on take-off killing six of the nine-man crew. He did not see the co-pilot from that crash and assumed that he had been killed. In October 2002 at a reunion in Texas he was shocked to see his friend alive 57 years later.

Mr. Roberts was married in 1945 and had one daughter. He currently has three grandchildren with five great-grandkids. His daughter, Cheryl, graduated from School 50 and then Washington High in 1965. Mr. Roberts was a teacher, coach, principal, and Central Office Supervisor for Health, Physical Education & Safety for the Indianapolis Public Schools for 34 years. He retired in 1985.

PAUL LAYTON was born in 1920 and attended Washington High School before joining the Indiana National Guard in 1940. His 38th Infantry Division was Federalized in January of 1941. They marched from the Armory on South Pennsylvania Street to Union Station on their way to Camp Shelby, Mississippi.

After the Pearl Harbor Sneak Attack, Master Sergeant Layton's unit traveled through the Panama Canal to Schofield Barracks on Oahu near Pearl Harbor. Their first mission was to secure Oro Bay which was 90 miles from Australia as it was then threatened by the Japanese. Next, Sgt. Layton and his men were sent to Leyte, Philippines to help General MacArthur keep his "I shall return" promise. From Leyte they made an amphibious landing at Subic Bay. He was involved in the liberation of Bataan, Corrigador and Manila all in the Philippines. It is Mr. Layton's strong belief that the Atomic Bomb shortened the war and saved many lives, American and Japanese.

Mr. Layton was married in 1946 to Evelyn who is with us today along with one of their three children, Mrs. Cora Johnson, who is our favorite Audio-Visual Specialist at Fulton. The Layton kids graduated from Ben Davis but started school at IPS #67.

They also have seven grandkids and six great-grandkids. Mr. Layton retired from Indiana Bell after almost 38 years in 1982. He moved his family near Girls School Road in 1960.

EDWARD BOPP was born on the east bank of Eagle Creek just north of the National Road in 1919. His mother died in May of 1922 and his father gave three children up to adoption. His new Bopp family lived at 301 S. Harris.

He attended School #50 and Washington High and was drafted in our nation's first Peace Time Draft in the spring of 1941. PFC Bopp trained at Ft. Sill, Oklahoma but was guarding the water tower at Ft. Leonard Wood, Missouri on Pearl Harbor night. Our troops were so poorly equipped that he had to "hand off" his 45-pistol to the next guard.

Most of his 52 months of service was on Kiska, Attu and Kodiak Islands in the Aleutian Island Defense off the coast of Alaska. Mr. Bopp took a two week leave in October of 1944 to marry his sweetheart, Thelma Bloomenstock, at the Methodist Church at Ida and Holmes Ave. When he died in 1992 he had two children, Eddie (class of '65) and John ('71), and two grandchildren.

LLOYD POSEY was born and lived at 501 S. Warman. He was a captain of Mr. Julian's 1942 track team. He was drafted into the Army in 1943. Corporal Posey was wounded on D-Day with the Army Rangers and recovered in a private home in Scotland.

Staff Sgt. Posey was killed in combat in Germany on February 19, 1945 while attached to the 75th Division of the American 1st Army. He had four brothers and one sister when he died at age 21. A comrade who visited Indianapolis in 1950 told brother Chet and friend Bob Bloomenstock that Lloyd was killed when another soldier stepped on a land mine which exploded hurling shrapnel into his neck.

His picture is seen often on History documentaries (including "Making of Band of Brothers") in a famous picture of GIs who captured a Nazi flag. He is on the far right.

WILLIAM ROBERT BLOOMENSTOCK was born at 514 S. Warman in 1923. He enlisted in the Marine Corps in February, 1943. PFC Bloomenstock was with the 1st Marine Division "A" Company 1st Motor Transport. He saw action on Peliliu and Okinawa. Mr. Bloomenstock's good friend Lloyd Posey was killed in the European Theater and is buried in Luxembourg. He also found and photographed another friend's grave on Okinawa. That friend, Charles Bradshaw who lived one block east at 526 S. Holmes, was a decorated sniper in the South Pacific.

Mr. Bloomenstock continues to work at Ford Navistar in 2003. (He retired in 2006 at age 83 and died on D-Day June 6, 2007.)

GEORGE SUCH was born in the Romanian tenement houses in 1914 in the area of home plate inside today's Victory Field. He was a track star before graduating from Manual High School in 1932. Classmate Norm Bepley, who was the PA voice of the Indianapolis Indians for 50 years, once called George "the best centerfielder in softball in Indianapolis in the 1930's." He was also a locally prominent swimmer and played amateur basketball.

He was married in May of 1939 at the original Indianapolis Romanian Church. Today a plaque commemorating the church is found near the Medal of Honor Memorial on the canal north of the IMAX theater.

Corporal Such enlisted in the Marine Corps in September of 1943 and served mostly stateside in California until his honorable discharge in 1946. He had two children, Richard (GWHS class of 1963) and Regina (class of '66), and five grandchildren when he died in 1987.

(In 2009 his picture from the mid-1920's can be seen inside the Indiana History Museum-Imax Theater under the banner of "Making Americans." That display case recognizes School 5 students and Mr. Such is pictured next to George McGinnis.)

HARRY PYATT attended School 50 and Manual High School before the war but graduated from Washington High later. Machine Shop classes at both schools helped him perfect skills he used in the Army as well as during his post-war career.

He was drafted in 1943 and eventually was assigned to the 9th Army, 29th Division, Northern Section under General Omar Bradley. His rank was Technician-5. His division was involved in the liberation of Holland, Belgium and Germany from Nazi domination. T-5 Pyatt constructed anti-aircraft optical instruments and altitude fuses.

His unit also acted as guards for liberated cities similar to the Iraq cities today.

After the war he worked in Job Shops as a Pattern Maker at Allison General Motors among others including the old Federal Foundary. His first job paid 75-cents an hour. He retired in 1990.

Mr. Pyatt married his childhood sweetheart in July of 1944. Betty, who graduated from GWHS in 1943, is with us today. They have one son and four grandchildren. One of their grandson's was co-Valedictorian at Carmel High School in 1996 (along with Amy Morris whose mother was Journalism teacher Anita Morris from 1961-65). (Mr. Pyatt died in 2008. His funeral was exactly one year after his wife's death.)

PAUL McGREVY was a Torpedo-man 2nd class on the U.S.S. Murphy during the November 6, 1942 invasion of North Africa. It was the first United States' offensive in the European Theater during World War II. They attacked at the port of Fedahla just north of Casablanca in French Morocco. His K-gun counterpart on the starboard side was killed along with four others on their ship during the attack when French and German guns fired on U.S. ships.

He returned to the U.S. and underwent submarine training. Then he was stationed at the Panama Canal Zone for the duration of the war.

He was married in 1945 to Barbara Spilbeler who accompanies him today. They had three boys and one daughter and five grandchildren. Their two oldest boys, Tim ('65) and Terry ('67), graduated from Washington High but have died in recent years. They both played on their school's football team.

Mr. McGrevy was an Indianapolis Fire Fighter from 1948 until 1968. He accompanied the Attucks State Champs of 1955 around the Circle as the city leaders supported Marion County's first State Champs. The jubilant celebration continued at today's Watkins Park but descended into a bottle and rock throwing incident as well as the serious injury to a young lady by a motor vehicle. The city's only hook and ladder truck had its "spine" broken, according to Mr. McGrevy, thus the following year the city did not participate in the 1956 State celebration. In 1968 he became the first Art Department director as the official Illustrator of St. Vincent's Hospital on Fall Creek Boulevard. (Mr. McGrevy died in February 2009)

In early 2010, Mr. Medenwald, Mr. Hayes, Mr. Cox, Mr. Northern, Mr. Roberts and Mr. Layton all survive. (note: Mr. Cox died on Flag Day 2010)

LLOYD POSEY

The following is a replication of three newspaper articles given to the author by Lloyd's brother-in-law Bernard Garver, himself a Navy veteran of the Korean War.

Article 1 Wounded—Sergt. Lloyd Posey, 20 years old, son of Mr. And Mrs. Noble Posey, 501 S. Warman Avenue. Sergt. Posey, who was employed formerly at the J.D. Adams Company, was wounded "seriously" in France on June 8, according to the War Department. However, his parents have since received a letter in which he stated that he is recovering in a hospital in England. Sergt. Posey is a graduate of George Washington High School.

Article 2 "New Friend in Scotland" writes to Indianapolis soldier's mother—Mrs. Noble Posey, 501 S. Warman Avenue, whose son, Corporal Lloyd Posey, is now in Scotland, has received a letter from her "new friend from Scotland," Mrs. Peter Currie while he is recovering from wounds. Mrs. Currie, whose address is Seaview, Lighnabriauh, Argyll, Scotland, has entertained Corporal Posey several times and wrote to tell Mrs. Posey that "he is the first American soldier I have ever spoken to, and believe me, if they are all as nice and mannerly as Lloyd, they will be a fine set of boys."

"This is a quiet place we live in," Mrs. Currie wrote, "we have not much entertainment for boys who are used to city life, but we have all the fresh air, green fields and a lovely stretch of water, so we really can't ask for anything more."

Mrs. Currie's husband is in the British merchant marine and they have a daughter 11 months old. Her sister lives with her, while working in one of the women's war organizations, and her brother is in the police force at Glasgow, which, she says, is about 100 miles from Lighnabriauh.

"I hope you will take this letter as from a friend," she concluded, "and I hope and pray that your son will arrive home sooner than we can hope for, and all others who are away from home; and that this dreadful war will be over soon."

Corporal Posey, who entered the army in March, 1943, has been overseas four months. He is a graduate of Washington High School.

Article 3 Monday, March 26, 1945 Hoosier Heroes Dead—A Ranger S. Sgt. Lloyd Posey, was killed Feb. 19, in combat in Germany. He was with the 75th division of the 1st army. Wounded on D-Day in the Normandy invasion, Sgt. Posey had been overseas 15 months. He was the son of Mr. and Mrs. Noble J. Posey, 501 S. Warman.

Surviving besides the parents are four brothers, Chester, Floyd, Gene and Russell, and a sister, Thelma.

CHARLES BRADSHAW

The following is a replication of three newspaper articles given to the author by World War II veteran Harry Pyatt. Cpl. Bradshaw was killed about the same time that famous Hoosier correspondent Ernie Pyle was also KIA. The author has not been able to verify reports from many people that Ernie Pyle wrote an article on Charles.

Article 1 The Indianapolis Star Saturday, May 27, 1944—"Y"-Trained Local Marine Braves River, Jap Guns to Save Buddies by Staff Sgt. Gerald A. Waindel, Marine Corps Combat Correspondent—Notes from New Britain—(NANA)—Private First Class Charles C. Bradshaw, 18 years old, of Indianapolis, learned to swim at the Y.M.C.A. He liked to swim, but this time was different.

It was growing darker. They were giving wounded marines morphine and plasma. They were burying the dead. Private First Class Bradshaw shivered in the sharp sea breeze. He was naked except for a cord around his waist and the two hand grenades that hung there. His clothes, battle-torn, sweat-stained, lay in a heap at his feet, in his foxhole at the edge of the river.

Marines had to cross the river. But first someone had to swim across and reconnoiter. Bradshaw was silent, like the men who covered his crossing with automatic fire. He slipped into the dark, sullen waters of the Natamo. The Japanese on the other side didn't open fire. They were waiting for more marines.

But the marine column didn't cross that night. Bradshaw had signaled them back before drifting downstream to safety, away from the Japanese machines gun he had discovered.

Article 2 Private Bradshaw Cited—Private first Class Bradshaw is the son of Mr. and Mrs. Charles C. Bradshaw, 526 South Holmes avenue. He attended Washington High School and has been overseas since October, 1943, after entering the marines a year ago. He was graduated from boot training second highest in his platoon, and holds the sharpshooters medal. He has also received a letter of commendation for previous meritorious action from Gen. W. H. Rupertus.

Article 3 May 1945—Cpl. Bradshaw was killed May 7 on Okinawa. A graduate of George Washington School, he was employed by the Pennsylvania railroad prior to enlisting the Marine Corps in May, 1943. Since going overseas nineteen months ago he had been commended in a dispatch from New Britain for swimming the Natamo river in a scouting feat that saved his buddies from a hidden Japanese machine gun.

A member of the 1st Marines, he had graduated second highest in his platoon after recruit training. He received the Sharpshooter's Medal and a letter of commendation for meritorious service.

(A picture of Charles Bradshaw's grave in the Marine Cemetery on Okinawa is included in this book. But the author also discovered on a 3x5 card at Floral Park Cemetery that his mother in 1949 had paid to have his body moved to Indianapolis. He is buried next to his mother directly southeast of the Wishing Well at Floral Park.)

WILLIAM SATTERFIELD

William Satterfield graduated from Washington High in 1939. His son, Steve (Northwest class of 1968) who died suddenly in early 2006, supplied the author with three news articles and a picture of his dad as well as an 8th Air Force patch. During World War II Lt. Satterfield was pilot or co-pilot on 28 bombing missions over Germany including the first daylight raid over Berlin on March 4, 1944. He served with the Army 8th Air Force, 95th Bomb Group. Mr. Satterfield went to the 8th grade at School 50 after the family moved into the house next to West Park Christian Church. He died in 2001.

Article #1 Local Pilot Survives Plunge with Plane into Channel—An Indianapolis pilot and seven other surviving crewmen of a Flying Fortress which plunged into the English channel near the French coast told the story of their rescue today at a U.S. bomber station.

The local pilot was Lt. William Y. Satterfield, 16 N. Addison St. The crew was rescued by an R.A.F. Walrus seaplane, which taxied 70 miles at night through heavy seas because it was unable to take off with its heavy load.

The Fortress "Liberty Ship," piloted by Capt. Perry L. Huie, 23, Urbana, Ill., was participating in a mission when fire broke out in the cockpit. Capt. Huie and his co-pilot, Lt. Satterfield, attempted to beat out the flames with their hands and flying jackets, but failed. Huie nosed the plane into the sea. One waist gunner was killed by the impact and another went down with the plane when it sank.

One life raft did not inflate and for three hours Lr. Satterfield, 1st Lt. Cecil M. Peacock, the navigator, Crescent City, Fla., and Sgt. John P. Ische, ball turret gunner, Brooklyn, N.Y., treaded water while they blew it up with lung power. They drifted 12 hours until a Walrus rescue plane alighted near their flares. A Junker 88 began to circle the Walrus but was driven off by two British night fighters while the eight clambered aboard. The Walrus then battled headwinds and seas until dawn when a patrol boat picked the men up.

Other survivors included: 1st Lt. William A. Toth, 22, the bombardier, Cleveland, Ohio; Sgt. Fred Canfield, 21, top turret gunner, Manton, Mich.; Sgt. Donald Jervais, 19, radioman, Antigo, Wis.; and Sgt. Edwin A. Levorchick, 22, tail gunner, Uniontown, Pa.

Article #2 Mother Here Unaware of Rescue at Sea—Mrs. Lena Satterfield, mother of Lt. William Y. Satterfield, the co-pilot, was unaware of the stirring drama her son had participated in when a Times reporter contacted her this afternoon.

"He tells me so little in his letters. He doesn't want to worry me," she said. She and the lieutenant's twin sisters, Lena and Lenora, hung on every word of the dramatic vignette of war.

Lt. Satterfield, who is 22, has been overseas six months and has completed about 24 missions. In service for 20 months, he received his wings and commission last July in Stockton, Cal. He is a graduate of Washington High School where his twin sisters are now in their senior year.

Lt. Satterfield learned to fly at the Hoosier airport. "Unbeknownst to me," said his mother. The son of Mr. and Mrs. Mike Satterfield, he has two other sisters, Betty Lou of Indianapolis and Mrs. Mary Golay, Chicago, and a brother, S.Sgt. Clarence E. Satterfield, now serving with the engineers in Ireland. He has been overseas three years.

Article #3 Lt. William Satterfield receives D.F.C.—Word has been received recently that Lt. William Y. Satterfield....has received the Distinguished Flying Cross for "extraordinary achievement" while participating in more than a score of heavy bombing assaults on Nazi targets.

Lt. Satterfield already holds the air medal with three oak leaf clusters. Before entering service August 5, 1942, he was employed by the Indianapolis Forwarding Co.

(The initial story from the Indianapolis Times was accompanied by two pictures. One of Lt. Satterfield and the other a picture of his mother and twin sisters which reads: "They hung on every word of the rescue story....twin sisters Lena and Lenora....")

THE PYATT FAMILY

As World War II continues to fade more and more to the past, another Continental family which exemplifies the selfless nature of the "Greatest Generation" was the Pyatt family. By 2004 with fewer than four million of the 16 million who served in that war surviving (it has been noted that over 1,000 WWII veterans are dying throughout the U.S. every day) two of the four Pyatt boys survived. Bob died in 2002 and Walter died in 1990. Bill and Harry along with their wives, Thelma and Betty, continue their monthly attendance at the World War II Round Table dinners at the North Side K of C at 71st & Keystone into 2007. The famous Sullivan brothers numbered five; the Pyatt brothers four. Luckily, they all survived the war.

William Wilson Pyatt's family was from Washington Court House, Ohio but he was born in Indianapolis in 1887. He married Pearl Wilson from Jennings County in southern Indiana. They would have five children. All would attend School 50 and Washington High School.

The oldest Pyatt was named Walter at his 1914 birth in their home on North Warman Avenue. Next was Charles Robert (Bob) who was born in 1917. The middle child, a girl they named Mary, entered the world in 1920. Then Bill and Harry who were born in 1923 and 1925 added to the Pyatt chow line. All were born at home with the help of mid-wives. By the time Harry arrived the family lived on North Addison St.

The Tinsley Grocery at Addison & Ohio Streets was the neighborhood store. And the kids played ball in Hawthorne Park or at the nearby Settlement House (Hawthorne Community Center).

During the war Walter served with the 395th Infantry in the U.S. Army during the D-Day invasion as well as the equally famous Battle of the Bulge. A copy of his Bronze Star citation reads:

Headquarters 99th Infantry Division
APO 449 c/o Postmaster
New York, New York

AG200.6 4 August 1945

Subject: Citation

To: Staff Sergeant Walter W. Pyatt, 35571702

Following is citation for Bronze Star Medal awarded

You per General Orders No. 1, this headquarters, cs:

Staff Sergeant Walter W. Pyatt, 35571702, 395th Infantry, United States Army, for heroic action in connection with military operations against the enemy on 18 December 1944, in Germany. Enemy attacks penetrated the area destroying critically essential communication lines and threatening to annihilate the entire defense. Disregarding concentrations of both enemy and friendly artillery, with steady courage and encouraging soothing words, Sergeant Pyatt passed from fox-hole to fox-hole assuring and organizing his men. Through these efficient and heroic actions, the platoon became solidly organized and in the ensuing attack, the enemy was repulsed and communication lines restored. Entered military service from Indiana.

By command of Major General Lauer:

L. P. Sullivan
Major, AGD
Asst Adjutant General

Second oldest son Bob enlisted in the Army Air Corps and served state-side. Bill landed on Pelilieu and Okinawa with the 1st Marine Division. And young Harry served under General Omar Bradley during the invasion of Germany.

An Indianapolis newspaper article titled "Brothers Will Meet After Months At Front" reads:

"S/Sgt. Walter W. Pyatt, who was wounded in Germany in December, and his brother, Pvt. Harry J. Pyatt, who returned from Germany Wednesday, will have their first reunion in two and a half years when Walter arrives home from Mayo General Hospital, Galesburg, Ill., this week.

Walter Pyatt, who was discharged from the Army last week, is the husband of Mrs. Evelyn Pyatt, 244 North Belle Vieu Place. He has the Combat Infantryman's Badge, Purple Heart, Bronze Star Medal and Good Conduct Medal.

Another brother, Sgt. William J. Pyatt, is serving with the Marines on Okinawa. Harry served overseas 10 months with a maintenance ordinance unit."

Mary Pyatt Russell, like almost all Americans of that era, contributed to the war effort on the home front as manufacturing increased 800% during the war effort. With over 400,000 Americans killed from 1941-1945 most families were dramatically affected.

And at the peak of the war effort one U.S. plane rolled off of the assembly line every five minutes and one ship per day was completed.

Walter left a legacy of two kids (Mike, GWHS class of '62, and Judy), six grandkids, and one great-grandkid at his death in 1990. Two of his grandkids are Brownsburg policemen (along with one's wife) thus service to our society continues in the Pyatt name. Bob died in 2002. He had a son Bill (class of '63) who I remember as a good pitcher for Hawthorne's summer baseball team at Rhodius Park. Unfortunately, Bill would die in the early 21st century of a lung disease that his family felt was a result of his long-time service in the U.S. Navy. Bob also had five grandchildren. Mary has two daughters, Susanne and Lucinda Russell, as well as two grandkids. Dave, Danny and Bob are Bill & Thelma's kids with a total of three grandkids. Harry and Betty's only child, Larry, was a classmate of mine from kindergarten through high school graduating in 1965. Larry has four kids. One of his boys was Co-Valedictorian of the Carmel High School class of 1995 along with Washington High's Journalism teacher from 1961-65 Anita Morris' daughter was also a #1 student at Carmel. Amy Morris is currently a medical doctor after her Academic All-American recognition in Track at William & Mary University. She was an 800-meter specialist.

(Betty Pyatt died Nov. 10, 2007. Harry Pyatt was buried alongside his wife on Nov. 10, 2008)

Staff Sgt. Harry Northern, at left, class of 1942. Northern parachuted into St. Mere Eclise at 2:30 AM on D-Day, June 6, 1944.

Torpedo-man 2nd class Paul McGrevy fought in the North African invasion in November 1942. Two Continental sons who served during the Vietnam era.

T-5 Harry Pyatt served in Gen. Bradley's 9th Army in Europe.

Leatherneck Sgt. Bill Pyatt landed on Pelilieu and Okinawa with 1st Marines

Bronze Star recipient Walter Pyatt after the war in 1946

Cpl. Paul Hayes landed in the Marshall Islands, Kwajalein Atoll, Saipan, Tinian and Iwo Jima in the tank corps. He taught Machine Shop at GWHS from 1951-1964.

Lt. Fred Medenwald, class of 1941, as a fighter pilot in the Pacific during WW II.

Sgt. Hollie Cox, class of 1935, with 75th Division 275th Engineer Battalion during the Battle of the Bulge.

Newlyweds Harry Pyatt and Betty Housefield, class of 1942, in 1944.

Lloyd Posey, at far right, with captured Nazi flag. This picture is shown often during World War II documentaries.

S/Sgt. Lloyd Posey

Bob Pyatt and wife in later years. Four Pyatt brothers served in World War II.

William Y. Satterfield was pilot or co-pilot during 28 bombing raids against Germany including the first day light raid on March 4, 1944.

First Marine Division Fleet Marine Force Okinawa Shima Cemetery

Gravesite #493 Charles Bradshaw (moved to Floral Park in 1949)

PFC Bob Bloomenstock landed with the 1st Marines on Pelilieu and Okinawa. Here with sisters Thelma and Anita at 514 S. Warman.

Cpl. George Such, Manual 1932, with Marine Corps. Father of 1963 GWHS graduate Richard and 1966 graduate Regina.

PFC Eddie Bopp, class of 1937, at Ft. Sill, Oklahoma in the summer of 1941.

Staff Sgt. Carl Sonny Roberts survived 24 bombing missions as a gunner on a B-17 over Germany.

Cpl. Don Baldwin, class of 1931, as a medic with 82nd Airborne. He was KIA in 1945.

World War II convocation in April 2002. Fred Medenwald ('41), Harry Northern ('42), E. Bopp ('65), Hollie Cox ('35), Harry & Betty Pyatt ('43), and Betty Cooke Northern ('44) with Monica Bopp-Osburn ('89) and son Austin ('20).

Master Sgt. Paul Layton, class of 1938, served with 38th Infantry Division at liberation of Leyte, Subic Bay, Bataan, and Corregador in the Philippines.

3rd class Petty Officer E-4 Billy Apple ('65) served four years of duty at ports-of-call in Vietnam, Philippines, and Japan.

Two days before the Pearl Harbor Sneak Attack in December 1941, Senifta Such was the official RCA host for band leader Tommy Dorsey on the Indianapolis east side.

Sgt. E-4 Harry Miller, GWHS night school 1972, with 3rd Army at Ft. Jackson, South Carolina during Vietnam era.

E-4 Dannie Johnson, class of 1965, as driver of 52-ton M-48 tank at Pleiku during Tet Offensive, 1968

Marines Terry McGrevy ('67) and Phil Myers ('64) at Danang during 1968 Tet Offensive. The neighbors attended the same church near School 75.

Sgt. Richard Such, class of 1963, with the Air Force at Tuy Hoa, Vietnam in 1969.

155

Master Sgt. Chester Dotson ('66) and SFC Dennis Ludlow, School 50 and GWHS but Danville '65 grad. Both served over 30 years in National Guard.

Ludlow with Sgt. Major Mike Lucas, at left, class of 1973. Lucas had just returned from Bosnia in the 1990's.

Spec-5 Mike Tibbetts ('65) served on Okinawa from Dec. 1966 until July 1968. Mike was Sectional Champ in wrestling in 1965 and started two years on the football and baseball teams at GWHS.

Martin Lomen ('63) and Dannie Johnson ('65). Butch returned from Korea and Dog from Vietnam in late 1968.

Lt. Col. Larry Muncie ('65) enlisted in Indiana National Guard in 1969. After 9-1-1 he was called to active duty. In 2005 he was Deputy Commander at Camp Atterbury in Edinburgh with 600 to 8,000 troops on site daily.

Chief Master Sgt. Larry Austin ('63) served in the Air Force from Sept. 1963 until Sept. 1990.

Barbara Spilbeler & Paul McGrevy's 50th wedding anniversary in 1996 with son Tim. Tim was a medic and brother Terry served three tours in Vietnam.

Bob Tillery ('48) served in the 4th Air Force, 78th Fighter Wing at Hamilton AFB near San Francisco

Newlyweds Thelma and Eddie Bopp in 1944. Eddie was on a month furlough. He was best man in friend Bill Sipe's wedding.

Lugar family in mid-70's. Char, John, Dick, David, Bobby, and Mark with Bassett Hound Samantha. Mr. Lugar served in the U.S. Navy for Adm. Burke.

Best friends Ruth Bloomenstock and Jane Posey at 501 S. Warman. Both had sons serving overseas. Bob Bloomenstock lived until 2007. Lloyd Posey was killed in Germany in 1945. He had been wounded on D-Day June 6, 1944.

PFC Marvin J. Austin fought with the 95th Infantry as one of the Iron Men of Metz along the French-German border in Nov. 1944 in the 378th Regiment, Co. E called the "bravest of the brave." Father of Judy ('65) and Jennie ('76).

Newlyweds Louise Rus and Bill Sipe ('39) in 1944. He was best man in friend Eddie Bopp's wedding.

Jerry Sanders, class of 1963 at right, in 1969 at Chu Lai in Vietnam with friend Charlie Hughes from North Carolina. Charlie was killed on July 14.

Spec-4 Gary Sylvester, class of 1964, served in Korea with an Artillery unit in the 7th Army. His son graduated from the Naval Academy in 2002 as a Sea Hawk helicopter pilot serving into 2010.

Sgt. Mark Gladson preparing for an ambush on Hong Kong Mt. in Vietnam. Mark was in the Army unit called the Short Range Ambush Patrol (SRAP) in 1968.

V.

Washington Boys Killed In Action

WORLD WAR II
THOSE WHO GAVE ALL

IRVIN L. ALLEE	CHARLES L. GOERKE	CARL PEARSON
DONALD H. BALDWIN	C. WILLIAM GREENWOOD	JOSEPH PEAY
ROBERT BALDWIN	RICHARD C. HAMILTON	G. JACK PEYTON
WILLIAM E. BLACKWELL	DONALD E. HARRIS	JAMES G. PHILLIPS
EDWARD B. BOSWELL	EUGENE L. HEICKEN	NORMAN W. PHILLIPS
CHARLES C. BRADSHAW	EDWIN HELTON	RAYMOND PLEASANT
NOBLE BREWSTER	HERSCHEL C. HENDRICKSON	LLOYD F. POSEY
NORMAN BROCK	DELBERT B. HERALD	BERT RAINSFORD
SHIELIE BROWER	J. LOHRMAN HOFMANN	TED RINKER
HARRY BROWN	WILLIAM HOLLINGSWORTH	HAROLD E. SCHENK
NORMAN J. BROWN	CHARLES S. HOWARD	WILLIAM SHIPMAN
VIRGIL BRYSON	RONALD HOWARD	LYNN A. SHOTTS
CARL BUCHANAN	H. RAY HUCK	E. CURTIS SMITH
FRANKLIN BURGESS	HERMAN KAMPOVSKY	GEORGE SORTWELL
JAMES CALDWELL	ROBERT KEITH	WALTER SOUTH
MARION CARTER	RICHARD KRATOSKA	RICHARD STONE
JULIAN COMMONS	JOHN LaMAR	JAMES STOVALL
ROBERT L. COOKE	JOSEPH LAMBERT	ROBERT E. STUTSMAN
WILLIAM E. COOLEY	JOHN R. LENTS	DONALD SULLENBERGER
RUSSELL CRAIG	RICHARD T. LENTZ	JAMES R. TUCKER
DONALD CRAWFORD	GORDON E. MATHER	ROBERT VAUGHN
EUGENE CRIBELAR	FREDERICK McREE	H. GEORGE WALKER
THOMAS CROSLEY	WILLIAM MILLS	DANIEL WEINBRECHT
ROBERT C. DAVIS	DAVID MINNICK	CHARLES F. WEST
MARTIN DUFFY	PAUL E. MITCHELL	G. ALLEN WHITE
GERALD EAGAN	WALLACE MORTON	DONALD E. WILLIAMS
NORMAN R. EWING	ROBERT L. MOSIER	MANLEY WINKLEY
ROBERT A. FLACK	JOHN G. MURPHY	LEE A. WOODALL
BRUNO FLOREANCIG	VIRGIL NORTHERN	JOSEPH L. WRIGHT
DALE E. FORTUNE	NELSON OVERDEER	LOUIS ZNIDERSICH
CHARLES FOX	WILLIAM A. PARKER	CHARLES E. MARTIN
LEROY KURRASCH	ROBERT MELLINGER	

The author personally asked Mrs. Hine, Mr. Julian, Mr. Carter, Mr. Case and a number of other Continentals if all of the above 95 boys were killed during World War II or if some died during the Korean Conflict. No one could give me a definitive answer. I do know that among the 1,900 other names on the impressive memorial inside the school's entranceway that there are veterans listed who served in Korea but not during World War II. Donald Gilbrech, the father of 1970's graduates Vicki and Donna, is listed and he was too young to serve during WW II but was wounded in Korea. In any event, most of those 95 listed above died in the early 1940's before they could experience the joys of young adulthood and the resulting freedoms from which the world has benefited as a result of our nation's leadership in the defeat of national socialism and imperialism.

WASHINGTON HIGH SCHOOL ----VIETNAM DEATHS 1965-1973

Date of Grad.	Rank, Name, & Service	DOB	Date of Casualty
1964	PFC DONALD R. BARRETT Army (worked at Dairy Queen just before Vietnam duty)	8 June 1946/	18 Aug. 1969
1966	CPL STEPHEN M. CARNINE Army (worked at Lugar's Thomas L. Green Co., summer '66)	20 Dec. 1946/	12 Aug. 1968
1966	PVT CHARLES M. GOFF Marine Corps (lived at 322 S. Holmes; School 50)	17 Feb. 1948/	21 Sept. 1967
1965	PFC DAVID C. KAYS Army (came to GWHS during '64-65 year; dad Coleman Kays, teacher School 75)	12 July 1948/	10 April 1970
1966	SP4 DAVID O. ROBERTS Army (School 49; 1961 Pony League Braves)	30 May 1948/	31 January 1968
1966	CPL ROBERT R. SMALL Army (killed by mortar fire near Hue; School 47)	29 April 1948/	4 May 1968
1964	PVC IVAN R. SMITH Marine Corps (death, at the time, said to be first Marine from Indiana; funeral at church on Washington St. & Miley; School 50)	14 Feb. 1946/	13 May 1965
1965	PFC LESLIE R. SMITH Army (School 46)	13 July 1945/	29 June 1966
1969	CPL THOMAS H. TAFT Army (played on Hawthorne's American Legion team in '69; School 47; moved later to first block on S. Warman)	8 August 1950/	24 April 1971
1966	SP4 JUNIOR L. WHITTLE Army (School 50 football team 1960; child with wife Luana Robey, class of '66)	8 Nov. 1947/	24 Sept. 1966
1959	SGT. HORACE G. MITCHELL Jr. Army (left-handed pitcher, class of 1960; earlier served as Marine)	10 Oct. 1941/	7 July 1965
1963	PFC WILLIAM J. HUNT Marines (worked in Audio-visual room at Washington)	25 Dec. 1944/	6 Nov. 1965
1963	CPL MELVIN SINK Marines (School #49)	22 Dec. 1944/	13 Oct. 1967
1968	LCPL RICKY HALL Marines	15 Nov. 1948/	23 Aug. 1969
1967	LCPL HERMAN ELLIS Jr. Marines	24 Aug. 1948/	4 Oct. 1967

Any and all personal family stories would be gladly accepted by the author as well as any unfortunate additions to this historical list. Future generations should not forget.

VI.

COMMUNITY STORIES

THE GIST

Beginning in 1933 when every freshman student entered Washington High School they were given a 5½ " x 3½ " eighty page booklet with all of the information known to man, or so it seemed. That booklet was called "The Gist."

An introductory paragraph included the following comments: the booklet was to "give better understanding of the school organization and a finer appreciation of the high scholarship and clean sportsmanship for which the school stands. Read these pages carefully and consider your work seriously. Let noble and right ideals direct your life to the best of your ability. We earnestly wish for you happiness and success in your school years and in the future for which you are now preparing." Mrs. Margaret McWilliams, whose sister was School 50's Miss Gertrude Peck, was the faculty advisor of the school's chapter of the National Honor Society. Mrs. McWilliams was mainly responsible for the creation of that highly informative booklet. She had begun as vice principal.

Christopher Gist was an American trailblazer who had descended from the Gist and Oliver Cromwell families who had come from England and settled in Maryland in 1682. In 1749 fur trader and frontiersman Gist was sent by the Ohio Company to explore 200,000 acres as far south as present day Louisville. The path that he trailed over the Appalachian Mountains was known as Nemacolin's Path then Gist's Trace then Braddock's Road then the Cumberland Road and finally the National Road. In Indianapolis we call it Washington Street or Road 40.

In 1753 when Virginian George Washington was sent to give a message to the French to vacate the Ohio Valley, Christopher Gist was the man chosen to lead the group. It was said that once while crossing the Allegheny River that Gist had saved the life of young George. Thus the inspiration for the name of our school's booklet.

Principal Gingery noted in the early pages that "like a person, a school possesses personality, character, and feelings. We hope that this school may always have a friendly, intimate, helpful personality; a loyal, courageous, uncompromising character; and sympathetic, responsive feelings." The school's motto: Exitus Acta Probat means "The goal is worthy of the Effort." And the self anointed pledge includes "I will strive never to bring disgrace to George Washington High School, my alma mater, by any act of dishonesty or cowardice, nor ever be unkind to a citizen of my school city…." The Code was adapted from The Ephebic Oath.

A one page history of Washington High is much abbreviated. But it does state that "approximately a century after the opening of the Cumberland, or National Road, (our school) was built on twelve acres…" My mother told me once that the National Road was paved for the first time on the Westside in 1927, the year our school opened.

Pages 10-12 in The Gist explains "The Code." Prefaced with "In God We Trust" followed by the admonition that "If I want to be a happy, useful citizen, I must have: " the code notes ten characteristics. A paraphrasing of the ten follows: 1. Courage and Hope—I must be brave (to control what I think and say), 2. Wisdom—I must act wisely (to choose the good, and how to avoid the bad), 3. Industry and Good Habits—I must make my character strong (when I am busy doing good, I shall have no time to do evil), 4. Knowledge and Usefulness—I must make my mind strong (the better I know myself... the happier and more useful I shall be), 5. Truth and Honesty—I must be truthful and honest (know what is true...to do what is right...be honest in all my dealings and in my thoughts. Unless I am honest, I cannot have self-respect), 6. Healthfulness and Cleanliness—I must make my body strong (my whole body must be healthy so that my mind can work properly. I must keep physically and morally clean), 7. Helpfulness and Unselfishness—I must use my strength to help others who need help (If I am strong, I can help others, I can be kind, I can forgive....I can help and protect the weak...the young and the old, and dumb animals), 8. Charity—I must love (I must love God, who created not only this earth but also all men of all races, nations, and creeds, who are my brothers. I must love my parents, my home, my neighbors, my country, and be loyal to all these), 9. Humility and Reverence—I must know that there are always more things to learn (to respect all who have more wisdom than I....know how and whom to obey), 10. Faith and Responsibility—I must do all these things (... because I am accountable to God and humanity for the way I live and help my fellows, and for the extent to which my fellows may trust and depend upon me).

The school flag, coat-of-arms, and seal were then explained. The Code became obsolete by the 1960's when a new liberalism bolstered by a social civil libertarian attitude made most of the above guide to a common culture no longer acceptable, at least in the changing atmosphere of a modern definition of public schools as secular.

Awards Day along with the May Queen and Strawberry Festival activities were then explained. Attendance, scholarship, and athletic awards were defined.

The $120 annual tuition for "pupils whose parents live outside the city" noted that IPS was the top of the pecking order in relationship to the township schools in the days before social engineering doomed much of IPS. About 100 students paid tuition in 1933.

The early 1930's time schedule with 40 minute periods and a ten minute roll call after period two remained intact into the 1970's. Classes began at 8:15. Athletes and others ended their day at 2:25 after 8th period and the 9th period ended at 3:10. In the early '60's with the peak of our school's enrollment schedules were staggered with many arriving for their first class the 3rd period and continuing into a 10th hour ending at 3:45.

Pages 18 through 61 explained and clarified room numbering, visitor's rights, attendance, school terms (like "admit slip" and lunch pass), home room, marking system, senior honor roll, rules ("there should be no loud and boisterous talking...."), the book store, lockers, telephone rules (no cell phones in those days), the cafeteria, study halls, the library, street car conduct, fire drills, outside employment, automobile and bicycle regulations, curriculum, full and ½ credits, graduation and college entrance requirements, the requirements to enroll in elective subjects, clubs (including the Men's Club for local businessmen, aircraft club, Camp Fire Girls for "All-American" girls, HI-Y for high standards of Christian character), and the National Honor Society.

The next six pages define eligibility and requirements for athletics and military training. One rule noted that a boy could not have reached "his 20th birthday."

"School Songs and Yells" comprise the last four significant pages of The Gist. The Washington Hymn, with words by Mr. Gingery and music by Ross Campbell, was emphasized for the early years of our school. But the Pep Song, with words by Bess Wright, seems to be the continuing most popular. The official version: "We're loyal to you, Washington, We're always for you, Washington, The best in the land And for you we will stand. We will honor and praise you, Washington. In victory we'll love and adore you. And when our good days are gone by, We'll always remember, those dear days together, In dear old Washington." Rah Rah. Coach Bogue is credited with "Oh, we're from Washington, Washington. The Purple and the White….."

The original school schedule read as follows:

Period	Time
1	8:15-8:55
2	9:00-9:40
3	9:45-10:25
4	10:30-11:20
Session Room	11:25-11:35
5	11:40-12:20
6	12:25-1:05
7	1:10-1:50
8	1:55-2:35

Period 4 was 50 minutes long; other classes were 40 minutes long with some classes in shop, home economics and journalism accounting for double periods.

When 1,000 freshmen entered Washington High in 1961, there were ten class periods with some students (freshmen and sophomores but with athletes attending periods 1-8) attending periods 3 through 10 and others periods 2-9. Home Room was then after period 2. The basic 40-minute period then looked like this:

Period	Time
1	8:15-8:55
2	9:00-9:40
Home Room	9:45-9:55
3	10:00-10:40
4	10:45-11:25
5	11:30-12:10
6	12:15-12:55
7	1:00-1:40
8	1:45-2:25
9	2:30-3:10
10	3:15-3:55

Too bad that the "personality, character, and feelings," that Mr. Gingery stated that he felt public schools possessed as a reflection of our democratic heritage in our then-Common Culture, seem to have vanished in the modern world.

FIFTY YEARS at HAWTHORNE CENTER (1923-1973)

My family's relationship with Hawthorne Community Center began in the 1920's and effectively ended when my mother resigned from the Board of Directors in 1988 after being Secretary for almost 30 years. I began attending the Community Center in 1953, began playing baseball there in 1956 under Tommy Anderson's dad, coached the D-league baseball teams (and two C-league teams) from 1967-1977 (except in '76), officiated basketball games from '67-'78, and served on the Board from 1974-1978. The "kid friendly" environment was enhanced when former Indiana Middleweight Boxing Champ and Parks Department leader Wallace Baker arrived in 1960. Soon he had hired George Waning from Marion College via Cleveland, Mr. Indiana 1958 Loren Comstock from Hofmeister's Gym (Mr. Universe Harold Poole from Shortridge H.S. often followed him to the Center's weight room), and southsider Tom Stevason from Manual H.S. who coached the 1969 American Legion A-league State Baseball Champions out of Hawthorne. By 1970 the basketball league for junior high players was second to none in central Indiana. Teams from Tabernacle, Carmel, Northwest Youth Athletic Association (NYAA), St. Patrick school, and School 66 Center were regulars in the traveling teams league organized by Tom. In 1967 a three- point line was incorporated mimicking the brand new ABA Pacers, one of the first of its kind in Indiana.

But in the 1950's Hawthorne had been the center of activities for grade-schoolers with things like the Bear Club, Wolf Club, skating, Brownies, Blue Birds, Girl Scouts, Cub Scout group meetings, Boy Scouts, dance lessons, baseball, and many School 50 sports and banquets. The Pre-High Friday nights which included dodge ball, basketball, and (required) dances as well as nightly "free hour" basketball for different age groups on different nights was incorporated under Mr. Baker's leadership. By 1974 I know that we had over 100 boys (and three or four girls by '75) involved in D-league baseball between the ages of five and twelve thanks to Harry Miller, Bob Weaver, John Doyle and Tommy Strong. We once had 23 baseball games in 12 days (not counting Sunday) that I helped coach, umpire, or organize. Sadly, I understand that the diamond at Belleview & Washington Streets that we cooperated with the Parks Department to develop by 1974 is no longer used by an "organized" program. But soccer thrives three blocks to the west in the changing neighborhood culture. Today the Center seems to primarily serve the Senior Citizens of the area in a much needed way serving free lunch among other amenities.

The three buildings owned by "Hawthorne" between Belleview and Mount Streets on the north side of Ohio Street focused on 2440 W. Ohio.

The following facts and stories were compiled by Mrs. Alma Lemen and Mrs. Marie Kenley for the Golden Anniversary celebration before the untimely fire which destroyed the original building in February of 1975.

The seven pages of information included:

HISTORY

Neighborhood concerns over a strip of land, once know as Flack's pasture, between Ohio St. and Turner Ave. and directly north of the newly built Nathaniel Hawthorne Elementary School #50 led to the formation of the Hawthorne Community Association on November 30, 1921. Fifty neighbors met in the community room of the Hawthorne Library east of the new school to map plans to obtain this ground, now known as Miniature Park, to keep it from becoming a railroad switch yard and coal dump, as was being rumored. The group also proposed to form another association to build a community center on the south end of the land across the street from and facing the school.

The West Park Social Service Association became a reality when it was certified by Secretary of State Ed Jackson on July 26, 1923 as a "not-for-pecuniary-profit" organization. Charles H. Royster was elected the first President of the Board of Directors. On October 1, 1923 the Reverend Clarence G. Baker was hired as the first Superintendent, a title later changed to Executive Director. Both men served in their respective capacities for twenty-five years. Mr. Baker's contract directed him to raise funds "to erect, equip, and maintain a community house, plan and supervise activities there, cooperate with the Board of Directors, and prepare a monthly report in writing," all for the munificent sum of fifteen hundred dollars.

So well did Mr. Baker fulfill his contract, the West Park Social Service House, costing $20,000 was dedicated on Sunday, March 2, 1924 in its own Gym-Auditorium. The 66' x 110' building consisted of eight rooms; the Auditorium seated one thousand persons.

Funds for the building were raised entirely by subscription and it was a superb example of community cooperation with residents, industry and business, churches and schools, all taking part. Each of these groups was represented on the Board of Directors which, then as now, was local in character. Board members often co-signed notes for loans so there would be no liens against the community house. Operating funds were obtained from the new Community Fund and by some earnings from memberships and rentals. Shortly after the dedication ceremony, the name of the organization was changed to the Hawthorne Social Service Association though the change was not certified until May 25, 1929. The plan was to make the area into a "Hawthorne" civic center. The school, library and community house combination was an excellent start to a neighborhood dream.

By July of 1928 Hawthorne had acquired the property adjacent on the west at 201 N. Belleview Place. That building, called the Annex, was used for children's activities. For many years it housed a free kindergarten under the auspices of the Indianapolis Free Kindergarten Society and offices of the Family Service Association.

The 25th Anniversary in 1948 was a landmark in Hawthorne's history. By now it had acquired a third building to the east at 202 N. Mount Street and known as the Cottage. It was used for adult activities including the Board of Directors monthly meetings and, in the 1960's, as the home for the Director and his family. The high point of the celebration was the burning of the mortgage. Hawthorne was debt-free. A sad note was the retirement of Mr. Baker and Mr. Royster, both having served almost three decades.

After several years of study and planning, Hawthorne became one of the first affiliated of the newly-formed Indianapolis Settlements Inc. along with Concord, Christamore and Mary Rigg Centers. By the 1970's the Cottage is now the home of the Central Office of ISI. Each Center's Board delegates four of its members to serve on the ISI Board of Directors.

Disaster struck Hawthorne on the evening of April 27, 1966 in the form of a fire which did extensive damage to the roof above the Gym. Fearful of losing their beloved Community House, children began bringing their savings to the office and organized their own talent show, donating the proceeds to insure that Hawthorne would be rebuilt.(note: the roof was soon rebuilt after the '66 fire and the Hawthorne "odor" remained. After the total-loss fire in February 1975 the entire building was re-built, albeit with much hesitation. A completely new Hawthorne opened in August 1978.)

Through the leadership of Mr. Baker and the cooperation of the Hawthorne community, George Washington High School was obtained for the West Side and opened in the fall of 1927. Also, Hawthorne Park and the playground was established between School 50 and the National Road as street lighting was installed for the area along with the creation of Little Eagle Park. Hawthorne's influence was credited with an immediate drop in juvenile delinquency in the neighborhood. Hawthorne has much to be proud of and commended for during its fifty golden years.

WE SALUTE

Clarence Garfield Baker

Rev. Baker was born in Canfield, Ohio on July 28, 1881. His father, a minister, was a personal friend of President Garfield. The President had been shot on July 2 and died in September of 1881. Mr. Baker attended Hiram College to prepare for a teaching career and became a superintendent of township schools while still a sophomore but found that he enjoyed the pulpit more when he substituted in a chum's pastorate. Eventually he came to the West Side of Indianapolis by way of Chicago to serve as minister of West Park Christian Church. He founded the West Side Messenger, the city's first community newspaper, because he felt that it would be a cohesive force in his beloved adopted community. He believed wholeheartedly in neighborhood involvement and community loyalty.

Mrs. Robert Lemen---50 years of service

Alma Lemen is the first and only Secretary and Bookkeeper that Hawthorne has had. She started on a half-time basis in late 1923. She put in many additional hours as director of girls' and women's activities. She was leader of Girl Scout Troop 42 and was well known city-wide for Scout activities. An entire volume could be written about her association with Hawthorne. The thousands of people who have passed through Hawthorne's doors—members & staff, patrons & friends—she has seen them all and can call most of them by name. Is it any wonder that she is so often called affectionately "Mrs. Hawthorne."

Rowland Jones---50 years of service

Rowland was a charter member of the first official Board in 1923. He is the 1973 Board's Treasurer. He was the coach of Hawthorne's first program which was naturally basketball. A graduate of Butler University, Rowland taught at Manual High for two years then came to Washington High in 1927. He taught mathematics, was the first basketball coach, and became Athletic Director in 1948, retiring in 1966. He has always had time for Hawthorne activities and has contributed countless hours over fifty years.

Robert Groth

"Uncle Bob" officially was supposed to maintain the building and grounds on a half-time basis but, being a natural-born social worker, he became director of boys' and men's activities, a basketball coach, and the first Scout Master of Troop 58. Uncle Bob died February 13, 1950.

Program

The program is evaluated and updated periodically with the needs and interests of the community in mind.

"Our idea is not merely to make this a place for education and exercise alone," Rev. Baker once noted, "but it is a social center as well where old and young can gather and get acquainted with their neighbors."

The Gym has been a popular place for team, league or free-hour basketball, roller skating, dances, flower shows, civic meetings, weight control classes, talent shows, large dinners, wedding receptions, and other functions. The stage can be partitioned into smaller rooms and has a kitchenette at one end. It buzzes with ballet and tap classes, club meetings, card parties, and other activities for which a smaller space will suffice.

Board of Directors meet in the Annex which has been the scene of Scout meetings, sewing and craft classes, a library, and weddings performed in front of the fireplace. The Cottage was intended for adult activities and was so used for many years.

"Off campus" activities include swimming and camping in the summer, day camps, entertaining other organizations with talent shows, educational trips to industries and cultural trips to places such as Clowes Hall and the Circle Theatre.

Service to one's fellow man will always be a large part of the program, whether a by-product or intended: Christmas baskets, Christmas and other holiday celebrations, transportation to shopping centers for the elderly without autos, and the old "Red Feather" basketball league. And, during World War II, bandages for the Red Cross as well as emergency day care for the children of working mothers along with the "Victory Gardens." There has also been referral services to professionals for serious problems.

Support

Hawthorne receives its major support from the United Way, formally called the United Fund.

An expanded Senior Citizens Program is made possible by a share of Community Services Project (CSP) funds.

There is some self-generated income from memberships, small fees, and special activities as well as gifts and bequests.

HAWTHORNE HAPPENINGS
(just a few happenings of members of the Hawthorne "family" over the years----1923-1973)

The termite treatment in the '30's that we have never been able to forget….Mae Vaughn, Board member, and her Berean class which has prepared so many of our annual dinners….Judge Harold N. Fields, steady on the bench of Juvenile Court since 1952….Diane Elam, Teen Service Club, a "500" Princess and 1973 Marion County Queen….lovely Ensign Marjorie Lytle, girls' worker…. the Ladies Auxiliary "cooling it" on the stage with the gift of an air conditioner….the handcrafters' Easter eggs, elegantly decorated, which won seven prizes in a contest at Crossroads….Harold Negley, musician and Eagle Scout who grew up at 66 N. Pershing, now State Superintendent of Public Instruction….the cake made by Uncle Bob which had Camp Fire girls from all over the city jumping out of it….the Happy Taps on the WTTV Cancer telethon….Cascade High School which adopted Hawthorne for Easter egg hunts and came bringing eggs, prizes, and treats for the children....Billy Keller, pro basketball with the Pacers.... ....Eddie Bopp, Trester Award winner, Washington basketball State Champs....Les Kersey Esarey, staff member before and after World War II, now with the FBI....the "paint in" in 1954 when Local #47 of the Painters and Decorators Union of the AF of L gave the three-story Annex a complete paint job while Landscape Artist J. Paul Dunn planted two trees and 25 shrubs donated by Hobbs Nursery, all done within three hours....the tragic losing fight to keep the Hawthorne Library on Mount Street....the Capitol City Casting Club, dry dock fishermen and, much to their chagrin, a couple of expert fisherwomen....Zeta Phi Zeta, a helpful sorority....1930's WPA Children's Theatre Group....Martha Carmichael, Camp Fire Girls Club and sister of Hoagy Carmichael, who still keeps in touch with Mrs. Lemen.... the Pageant of Progress in 1937 in the gym with numerous big companies displaying their products all week plus music, picture shows, and souvenirs with 700 people attending opening day, a triumph for the tireless Rev. Baker....this must come to an end, but there's you and you and you, whoever and wherever you are, who have been among the thousands who have helped make Hawthorne a great West Side institution.

Presidents of the Board of Directors 1923-1973

Charles R. Royster	1923-48
Roscoe Conkle	1948-50
A. K. Jones	1950-53
Mrs. Harry (Lydia) Litchfield	1953-55
A. K. Jones	1955-58
Justin H. Marshall	1958-60
Judge Harold N. Fields	1960-62
Joseph Bright	1962-63
Justin H. Marshall	1963-66
William Mattingly	1966-68
Gerald Lawlis	1968-71
Phillip Brundage	1971-73

Directors

Rev. Clarence G. Baker	1923-48
Frank Hopper	1948-60
Wallace Baker	1960-63
Gerald Stout	1963-67
Thomas Stevason	1967-71
Mrs. Ernest (Marie) Kenley	1971-73

1973 Board of Directors

Phillip Brundage, President
Ray Durham, Vice-President
Mrs. Edward (Thelma) Bopp, Secretary
Forest Hutton, Treasurer
Darryl Adkins, Mrs. Alvin (Etta) Aue, Ray Backus, Steve Burris, Weldon Fultz, Albert Glaze, Dale Johnson, Rowland Jones, Cloyd Julian, Coleman Kays, Gerald Lawlis, Mayor Richard G. Lugar, James Mahan, Mrs. Ralph (Martha) Schafer, Joe Shires, Mrs. William (Dorothy) Shaw, Mrs. Garnetta Thacker

1973 Staff

Mrs. Ernest (Marie) Kenley	Director
Mrs. Robert (Alma) Lemen	Secretary-Treasurer
Mrs. Homer (Louise) Gibson	Program worker
John Doyle	Program worker
Clarence G. Baker	Executive Director Emeritus

and ten to twelve part-time staff, some seasonal, who serve as special instructors, program workers, coaches, chauffeurs, and in maintenance; Mrs. Dorothy Unger, Executive Director of Indianapolis Settlements, Inc.

Article II of the Constitution of Hawthorne Social Service Association

"The purpose of said association is to operate a community center to provide recreational opportunities and to develop skills and attitudes which will improve the citizenship, ideals, and individual moral, educational, ethical, and social responsibilities of its members in the community."

Special Note: Mrs. Lenore (Miller) King, Washington High School Class of 1939 and School #50 class of 1935, continues her presence attending Senior Citizen activities into the year 2009. She began her commitment to Hawthorne in the 1920's. Her daughter (Sharon) and son (Garry, class of '65) both attended activities at Hawthorne in the 50's & 60's.

MY SCHOOL 50 DURING THE FIFTIES

My School #50 class of 1961 spent most of the Fifties as Hawthorne Hornets and graduated exactly 50 students. My mother was also a teacher in the 3rd and 4th grades from 1953 until her retirement in 1985. She had begun her career at School #22 in 1943 just southwest of Meridian and Morris Streets where the new Concord Center now stands. Tom Stevason and Mason Bryant were two of her students there. But she also had connections to School #50 dating to the first decade of the 1900's.

Her family—the Bloomenstocks, Gilbrechs, Atkins, and eventually Bopps—all attended the neighborhood icon at 75 N. Belleview on Ohio Street just 1½ blocks north-west of Washington High. Edna Ruth Atkins, Mrs. Bopp's mom, enrolled in kindergarten in 1903. Mrs. Bopp's grandkids, Eddie Tom and Monica Bopp, transferred from there in 1978. The 75 intervening years showed an Atkins, Bloomenstock, Gilbrech or Bopp as either a student or teacher on the roster at 50.

Before World War I Belleview was known as Gardenia St. and Ohio was Flack St. but prejudice against German names prevailed. My mother actually began school in School #5 at California St. and the National Road. Her dad maintained a restaurant between West and California Streets. But in the fall of 1931 the family of four moved in with mom's grandparents at 514 S. Warman and she enrolled as a 4th grader at School 50. My dad, who lived at 301 S. Harris, graduated from 50 in 1933; mom in 1935.

I entered half-day kindergarten in the fall of 1952 in the Hawthorne annex building on the northeast corner of Belleview and Ohio Streets. Mrs. Polk was our teacher. After I kissed Cheryl Roberts just before nap time, Mrs. Polk always kept a careful eye on me.

Garry King, Mark Masariu and Marvin (I can't remember his last name) were my best buddies. In 1961 as the freshman QB at Washington High we hosted Cathedral. Both teams were 4-0. Masariu was their QB. We beat them 18-0 for Coach Johnny Williams' first ever win against Cathedral. John had started his teaching career at School 50 but transferred to Washington High in the fall of 1944.

We moved into our small brick house at 321 S. Warman as it was completed in the spring of 1953. I took the blame from Billy Homan and Bernie Stinnett for ruining their vacant lot football field which our new home displaced. So they turned me into a prize-fighter by forcing me to fist-fight. I believe that $1.25 was wagered once on a return bout with Skippy Lewis at Harris & Ida Streets. But Moose Smith dethroned me in another classic rematch in the alley between Harris and Warman.

In the "big house" school most elementary grades had two teachers. The first grade had three rooms with some mid-term students at 1A when I entered as a 1B. Mrs. McMillan, Miss Wright (later Mrs. Bourne) and Miss Burge (her sister-in-law, Mrs. Burge taught at Washington High) were the three teachers. The first semester I had a very pregnant Mrs. McMillan. I remember our "Dick and Jane" reader and losing out to Judy Danner in our Christmas recitation from the Bible. "And she brought forth her first born son, and wrapped him in swaddling clothes, and laid him in a manger….And the angle said unto them, Fear not, for behold, I bring you good tidings of great joy, which shall be to all people…" was memorized by Judy and presented in a more poised manner. She won the role. In January I was transferred to Room 8 from Room 6 (the southeast corner of the building) to Miss Burge's class. I don't think I had tried to kiss any other girls? I remember Jim Phillips and Richard Deem as my buddies in 1A. There were some

2B students in our room also. That school year was the first year that my mother had become a School 50 teacher. I didn't like that reality at the time.

Mrs. Beckert's grade two in Room 9 next to the Teachers' Lounge in the south-west front of the building was a fun year. She seemed very sensitive to kids. But once I was unable to thread some darn through holes in a paper plate-and-a-half which was to be given to one's mother as a Christmas present. As I tried to hide my frustration-tears, good old Bonnie Ledbetter from South Hancock Street came to my rescue. She had the pot-holder-holder threaded together in short order. Third grader Stevie Sears and I both were sweet on Bonnie. Once we carried a football to within ten feet of her front door and practiced tackling one another while trying to impress the black-haired, seven-year-old. She was probably inside watching "Beanie & Cecil" or "Sky King" or maybe even "Mighty Mouse" as her two mighty-boys performed their macho actions. Her cousin Linda Chastain lived just a block away. In the 1990's I had Bonnie's daughter as an 8th grade student. She looked just like her mom.

Miss Whitehead, a colleague of mine at Washington High from '69-'76, was our physical education teacher. We skipped, hopped and galloped in the basement room near the boys' restroom, which later became Mr. Fish's Science room.

The move upstairs to Room 13 in the northeast corner was Miss Walker's room. I thought that she was the prettiest teacher in the school. Near the end of the school year her picture was on the front page of the Wedding Section among twelve other brides-to-be. I was disappointed. I remember that we had a "Reading Station" in the back of the room. But I also remember the fear I felt when Mr. Crites called me into the hallway. I had punched 7th grader Herb Downton going home to lunch one day. I guess Billy and Bernie had turned me into a bully. Tommy Anderson was with me and I was trying to "show off." I was disciplined with a "talking to" as I escaped a possible paddling. Dale Bollinger and Richard Hawblitzel, both from the Salem Park area near Eagle Creek, became two good friends who went to the Belmont Theater with me. If one arrived early for the 1 PM Saturday or Sunday matinees or the 6 PM Friday showing, the same three songs were played. "Volaire" by Sergio Mendez, "Midnight Gambler" by Frankie Laine and "All Day, All Night, Mary Ann." George, who owned the Belmont Movie House in the 1950's and '60's, died of a heart attack while running behind GWHS in the mid-60's.

Mrs. McKee's 4th grade classroom in '56-'57 seemed to be filled with her adept piano playing with much classroom singing. The connecting door between our #15 and Mrs. Shiffman's #14 saw many a Lorna Doone cookie and shared coffee between the two. Maybe even a Hot Totty or so. More than once over two years when I arrived early from home lunch, one of the two would send me to the confectionary catty-corner across the street to buy one type of cookie or another. Every Friday Rooms 14, 15, 16 and 17 would gather in the upstairs gym and sing with Mrs. McKee on the piano and Miss Zook directing. Christmas time was always filled with great songs in the days when public schools could still practice our Christian heritage. "O Come, All Ye Faithful," "Joy to the World," "Good King Weneeslas," "The First Noel," "Silent Night," and "Little Town of Bethleham" were mainstays. We started that year with the old desks attached to the floor but ended it with movable desks slightly larger than the ones we had in the primary grades. But Miss Linehan's Room #1, next to the Main Office, still had attached seats when students attended the Student Council meetings. Billy "Bird" Apple became my best friend and would continue to be into the 1990's.

What was the first Indianapolis community newspaper, "The West Side Messenger," was delivered in the Haughville, Hawthorne, and Jacktown area by an eccentric, seemingly old, man who was always confronted by kids as he walked the neighborhoods. He was known as "Haboush" and would consistently bite his thumb while being taunted by the unkind, area kids. Political correctness, even common decency, was sometimes not the norm in our less sympathetic society of street kids.

Although the chimes next to the office continued to announce the end of the morning session and the end of school at 3:15, room intercom boxes appeared high on the wall which served as an informational device for the principal. The ink wells located in the top right corner of the old desks gave way to the new technology of the disposable ink cartridges. By the 5th grade students were allowed the new ball-point pens. My Cub Scout Den Mother was Mrs. Frank Russell, she had graduated from GWHS in 1938 as Virginia Garrabrandt. She continues to live independently into 2010. And we attended Weekly Religious Education class after walking to West Park Christian Church.

Mrs. Shiffman's room was rife with student government type activities. Mrs. Shiffman, maiden name Miss Pauley, had married a north side chiropractor in the mid-'40's and continued her stern, no-nonsense demeanor. During one of our campaigns for class president, we had to stand at a large metal fake-microphone to give our speeches. I lost my train of thought and Mrs. Shiffman scolded me for not projecting my voice enough. "Don't stand there with you mouth hanging open, looking stupid listening to me," she demanded. I obeyed. What would be considered "negative" today was common practice in those days. The "new" administrator in the modern era would ridicule the teacher. But I know that I learned to gather my poise and parse my mouth in most public speaking situations. When I was the "color commentator" with Don Fischer as the play-by-play man for the very first football game announced from the Hoosier Dome in 1984 (the high school All-Star game in August), I thought of Mrs. Shiffman.

Our desks were organized in four or five circles. After October 4, 1957 and the Soviet Union's satellite Sputnik's orbit, Mrs. Shiffman announced that science would be over-emphasized in our curriculum. We had been studying Latin American history; Simon Bolivar had been my book report. Now the Cold War became most important.

In the spring of 1958, I had a minor operation and was assigned a room with three other boys in Methodist Hospital. A two year younger kid, John Hill from School #49, was undergoing a tonsillectomy. His mom was in charge of TV distribution in the hospital. We both got good ones. John would become tri-captain of the football State Champs at GWHS in 1966. Mrs. Shiffman sent me a "Sugar Foot" comic book based on the television series. And Judy Durham moved into our neighborhood. Bobby Crist immediately started "going steady" with her.

With Jimmy Hodges, Stevie Sears or Stevie Purichia I attended most Continental home football and basketball games as well as School 50 Saturday morning games in the Washington gym or on the football field. Once we followed Joe Purichia, Eddie Morrow, Bill Sowers and Bob Bundy from Bahr Park football practice south on Warman Ave. as they sang "M-I-C-K-E-Y M-O-U-S-E" from the popular TV afternoon series in 1957.

Since all kids who attended School 50 walked to school, if one lived within ten blocks of school they were expected to walk home for lunch. I lived eight blocks away and Rose Johnson, Dannie's grandmother, was my noon cook. Her grilled cheese were classics. The school chimes rang out at 11:40 dismissing students for lunch. Probably 90% of students went home. Afternoon class began at 1 PM. Mrs. Kersey, who lived one block north of school on Belleview, was one of a few who were hired as a "lunch at home" provider. The few kids that ate at school in the small cafeteria, next to Mrs. Hodson's Home Ec. Room in the basement, were hostage to Miss

Scott's dictatorship. Room #3's Miss Scott, the strict art teacher, was small in physical stature but mighty in moral-suasion. Her toughness wouldn't have made it in the students' rights era.

I was lucky to have Billy Apple, Dannie Johnson, Clifton Butler, Butch Lomen, Charlie Neff, Mike Parker, Kenny Strong, Tommy Anderson, Steve Purichia, Robbie & Moose Smith, Bill McKenna, Bones & Russy Morris, Dennis Ludlow and Richard Daugherty among others that walked probably three miles daily (to school, home for lunch, back to school then home after school). During decent weather, Mr. Fish was normally playing basketball with the school lunch boys and nearby school kids as most returned to afternoon school. I was always envious of those able to play especially watching Mr. Fish with his famous fake hook-shot as he cradled the ball in his belly. And to be a traffic boy was quite an honor. Strong and I were 6th grade lieutenants under captain Crist. "Old" Gabe Anderson, who lived in the last house on Harris Street, was the chief crossing guard. He was briefly replaced by an unfortunate man who had his jaw bone removed, probably because of cancer. Too many smart alec kids chided him as "slobber jaws." Mrs. McCoy, Bobby's mom, replaced him in 1960.

Crist, like his older brother Chuck, always seemed to be the "movie projector" specialist for the Friday movies in the upstairs gym or the occasional film in classrooms. And they both "ran" the basketball clock at Hawthorne. Was it in their genes?

Mrs. Starost, who had been a teacher at our school, was named principal in the fall of 1957. She replaced long-time principal, Mr. Johnson. Mr. Johnson was "forced" into either retirement or transferring. (Mr. Johnson ridiculed the "Downtown Doctors," as my mother later explained to me, saying to his teachers in his "going away" meeting that "there are no 'doctors' in education.") Soon after his departure he ran his auto inside his home garage and died of carbon monoxide poisoning. Mr. Sturm, another well-respected principal, was also forced to transfer as busing began in the early '70's. Of course, a "Downtown Doctor" eventually closed Washington High in 1995 then School #50 in 1997 then reopened GWHS only to eliminate the football program in 2010.

Miss Baumgart was probably my favorite classroom teacher. Her 6th grade room always displayed excellent writing on the blackboard. Most teachers took pride in their writing skills in those days and promoted the same attitude to students. Miss Baumgart enjoyed poetry readings like "Poor old Jonathan Bing…." and stories like "The Emperor's New Clothes." She held weekly spelling bees with students lined up on opposite walls leading up to the Friday spelling tests. She always seemed consistent and effective. Her legendary fussing with student Janie Willoughby in the cloakroom once ended with a door slammed and a window broken. "Doggie-Doggie, your bone's gone" was a relaxing relief from academic stress.

Although Mr. Fish had tried to get me to practice basketball when I was in the 5th grade (I did a few times in blue jeans since I refused to show my skinny legs), the fall of 1958 was when I first played on an organized school team. The four or five years of "street-ball" in front of the Purichia house and many other lightly-traveled streets as well as on Washington's field and Hawthorne Park had prepped me for football. While pick-up basketball games at Hawthorne's Free Hour complimented individual shoot-arounds at home-goals maintained by Dickerson, Chastain, Stockoff, Sears, Garver and Stoneking.

Lou Moneymaker was my first teammate-mentor. As an 8th grader he was the left end on the football team. I had known Lou while playing "flies & grounders" in Hawthorne Park and behind the Center. He was the only kid with two baseball gloves. He seemed rich. His dad owned the Checkered Flag Tavern. And his uncle, Bob Potter, was one of the three well known cops from the 'hood along with Karen McDonald's dad, Curly, and Mr. Veza on West Jackson Street. I watched every move that Lou made while blocking and running the "down and out." When he was sick our last game against Manual Junior High played on Manual's field and coached by Cheryl Roberts' dad Carl, I started my first game as a 6th grader. My most intricate skill was to first communicate with left tackle Bob Easton. If we wanted to cross block the defensive tackle and end, Bob was to make a line call of "Chester." Chester, played by Dennis Weaver on the top TV show "Gunsmoke," was the limping sidekick of Marshall Matt Dillon. We won but, if I would have known that I was going to play that Saturday AM, I wouldn't have gone to the McDonald Halloween Party the night before. But then I would have missed out on "spin the bottle" and "bobbing for apples" that Mrs. Grace McDonald had set up for us. What sacrifices I've made and almost made for sports.

Lou became a successful administrator at the Indiana Blind School after he coached the wrestling team for years. In 1958 we were the only team in IPS that played without face masks. It was our unique "badge of courage." But buddy "Bird" Apple lost his front teeth during practice one day while tackling "Dog" Johnson.

Washington High's assistant football and basketball coach, Jerry Oliver, was our banquet speaker at Hawthorne Community Center. 8mm film of Lou water-skiing was a highlight of the banquet. I knew he was rich.

We often had "Air Raid Drills" when the entire school would proceed to the basement with coats or books to cover our heads to protect us from a nuclear attack by the Russians. "Duck and cover." Times were different.

Mr. Crites, in Room 4 on the main floor in the northeast corner, was held in high esteem as well as high fear by everyone that I knew. He always seemed to wear a suit and tie. He specialized in math and was my 7th grade teacher. We were now in junior high and would travel from room-to-room for classes. English with Miss Peck, Social Studies with Miss Linehan, Art with Miss Scott, physical education with Mr. Fish for the boys or Mrs. Dawson for the girls, and Home Economics for the girls with Mrs. Hodson or Shop for the boys with Mr. "Andy" Andrews. Life was good.

Once when we were headed for restroom break, Tommy Anderson and Donnie Dudley slammed their bodies on purpose against the metal sight-barrier inside the restroom door. The sound caught the attention of Mr. Fish who came from his room with paddle in hand. Two whacks each brought tears and the awareness of everyone else.

Andy's Shop class was separated into Wood Shop, Metal Shop, Print Shop and Mechanical Drawing. A serving tray, a two-level wall shelve with dowel rods and the famous wall horse with sheet metal legs are three that I still have although one was done by brother-in-law Richard Such and another by my son in Andy's class in 1978. My wife's first married meal was a "Mrs. Hodson fried chicken" recipe. Mr. Andrews also had the unique distinction of paddling both me and Steve Purichia within seconds of each other after we had teased Alva Smith and Alva smacked some soap in Steve's mouth. Steve retaliated and I laughed. We both learned a lesson not related to academics.

Sometime in 1960 Mr. Crites was diagnosed with cancer. He would die within a year. Mr. Little became his permanent sub in the late spring into 1962. Mr. Fish was the dominate non-family adult figure in my life for three years. Football, basketball and track (along with girls) dominated my thoughts along with summer baseball for most of the time. I had broken Ken Corey's class-B high jump record by clearing 4'7" with a scissors jump in 1959. In late May of

1961 Mr. Fish, I'm sure in a slyly motivating way, announced in his Science class that "Martin Lomen's 5'1" class-A high jump record is one that will not be broken today." I took the bait. After traveling with Mr. Fish to get the lime-chalk machine from Johnny Williams at Washington High at noon, I belly-rolled 5'3" (officially 5'2") over a sagging cane pole into a sand pit. Corey held the high school pole vault record at the time, along with another School 50 boy Tommy Benson, and Butch Lomen would soon set three track records including the high jump at 6'2" for Washington High.

In October of 1960 I had carried my small black and white portable TV to school on the last day of the World Series. Miss Peck, my 8th grade teacher in Room 2, allowed us to watch the final game in class. But our class was due to travel to Mr. Little's room for math as the ninth inning began. I couldn't take the TV with me. I missed the famous Mazeroski home run over left fielder Yogi Berra's head. I've never forgiven them.

The previous summer of 1960 had been the summer of the Indianapolis Indians for me. Jimmie Hodges had moved to the School 30 area, next door to the Morgans, yet continued his friendship with me and Stevie Sears. Jimmie's best buddy at 30 was Ronnie Dill. The four of us walked the long distance to Victory Field on 16th Street about three times for Indians games as we drudged across the railroad bridge spanning White River. My favorite players were Ron Jackson, Jim Woods, Cloyd Boyer, Jim Snyder, Ted Beard, and Lennie Johnston. Lennie later became a regular subsitute-teacher at Washington High in the 1970's and a good friend. But I often think of Dill's unique talent. Once, when we stopped at his house, he was the first "kid" I ever saw who made his own hamburger, pressing it out like a real cook. He even gave me a bite.

Instrumental music lessons were given during the school day by Mr. Ray Funk and Mr. Edison in the old kindergarten building across Ohio Street. Mr. Funk was band director at Washington High and was the father of Dick and Elaine. Mr. Edison had his own dance band in the real world continuing into the 1990's.

Mr. Lashbrook had been named principal in 1959 and left in 1961 to be replaced by Mr. Sturm. And Miss Peck continued to lead the Friday chorus in the upstairs gym as she had done since the 1920's. All four of the military songs along with other traditional patriotic music as well as the continuing Christmas music defined our Common Culture.

School 50 had two undefeated football teams going 4-0-1 in 1959 and 5-0 in 1960 but we could never beat School 5 in basketball. With Calvin Schaffer in '60 then Ralph Taylor and Teddy Williams in '61 they were tough. In the fall of '59 Dick Parks was our best athlete. His dad was the minister at the Washington Street Methodist Church on Warman Avenue. They lived in the house directly south of the church. The last play of our final game I threw a desperation post-pattern pass to Dick. He ran for the 50-yard winning touchdown. In the spring of '60 he moved away. I never saw him again.

Bobby McCoy was our move-in star athlete my 8th grade year. I scored a running TD late in the game in our final game vs. School #21. We played most of our grade school football games and all of our basketball games at Washington High. For over twenty years that was the tradition. But after a fight between Schools 67 and 52 athletes and fans in 1972, there was never again to be a junior high football or basketball game allowed at GWHS. Not until the school re-opened and the first game was played after Labor Day in 2001 against Tech as a somewhat "junior high" game. I attended the game. It ended in a fist-fight between the freshmen teams.

January of 1961 saw some of my buddies (namely Danny Johnson, Steve Purichia, Mike Parker and Gary Hiese) graduate at mid-term to Washington High. We took a bus trip downtown, ate at the sub shop on the Circle then attended a movie at the Indiana Theater. "Journey to the Center of the Earth" starring James Mason and Pat Boone was the show. In June of '61 we also headed downtown on the bus. We ate at the Big Boy restaurant located on the southeast corner of Market and Illinois at the time. Then we attended "Swiss Family Robinson" at the Circle Theater. I allowed my cute little 7th grade girlfriend to go with me. I first "fell" for her on May 5 at Pre-Hi. It was the same day that Alan Shepard became the first American in space that I went into "space." We walked home from downtown all the way to 246 N. Pershing.

When Wally "Kid" Baker, as he was know while Indiana middleweight boxing champion in the 1930's, came to Hawthorne Community Center as the Director he instituted Pre-Hi for junior high students on Friday night. We were allowed to play basketball for an hour if we promised to stay for the dance, with girls, to follow. So, when I slow danced with Jeannie Such, my fate was sealed. Fast dancing was dominated by regulars like Jeannie, Bea Ann Gill, Brenda Baker and Sherry Benson. Bea Ann was the benchmark for the "Bristol Stomp." Jeannie had a contagious personality and pierced ears. She was neat. After I walked her home, we watched her brother and George Terry climb the Such garage then she gave me a kiss. And her mom liked me.

The graduation dance in June of '61 was emceed by Loren Comstock. He had been Mr. Indiana body-builder in 1958 (and first became a teacher at Ben Davis Junior High in the mid-60's before becoming a criminal lawyer into the 21st century). He turned down the lights inside the Center for the last dance. The Marcels song "Good-bye to Love" (the flip side of "Blue Moon" on their 45-speed record) was very exciting for me, age 14. Washington High loomed just two blocks away but School 50 was a great school in the Fifties and before. The neighborhood schools in Indianapolis seemed godlike.

Miss Zook had retired in 1960. A testimonial dinner was held at the Murat. Long-time Marion County Juvenile Court Judge Harold Fields, who had been in her first class in the early '20's, and Regina Such, who was in her last 6th grade class, were guests along with the teaching staff. Long time teachers during the last quarter of the 20th century included Mrs. Derthick, Miss Mohr (GWHS class of 1948), Gail & Bob Smith, Mrs. McGilliard, Mrs. Green, Mrs. Sulkoske, Mrs. Soloman (Mr. Julian's daughter), Mrs. Goler, and Mr. Bryant. Mr. Bryant was the first African-American teacher at School 50 and his daughter was the first such student there starting in 1970. Mason had been a 6th grade student of my mother's at School 22 before he graduated from Cathedral H.S.

When Miss Baumgart (who became Mrs. Goodman) died in early 2007, she was the last living teacher from the '50's. I talked to her in 1998. She had been guest of honor of Nichols, of Reis-Nichols fame, in '97 at the 50th reunion of the School 50 class of 1947. She noted to me that she had a condo in Hawaii and had a different bikini for each day of the week, into her 80's. Andy died in 1997, Mr. Fish in December 1994, Mrs. Dawson in the fall of '92, and Mrs. Shiffman in August 1996. Miss Linehan had taught at 50 from 1918 until 1962.

My mom died the same month, June of 1997, that St. Anthony parish officially bought School 50's building. They renamed it All Saints School. In the early 21st century our building was sold to the national chain of schools called Providence Cristo Rey High Schools. I assume that the "Hawthorne" across the top and "50" on both sides remain engraved in the limestone behind the Cristo Rey nameplates.

Most kids will always remember "Musical Chairs," "Red Rover, Red Rover" and dodgeball among other bits of our common culture. The last two are considered too dangerous today. But Tinkertoys still prosper along with video games.

When the principal in the early '80's destroyed the old file-record-cards of former students some history was lost forever. One cynic suggested that he needed room for his real estate sales records as he worked at his other job during the school day. Nonetheless, our memories cannot totally be erased. Hopefully this journal will help.

One final note: School 30 junior high kids walked to School 50 for Shop and Home Economics. Mrs. Russell shared a story with me. She stated that John Jackman from School 30 and a Washington High graduate in 1938 and his wife Mildred (GWHS '37) bequeathed $200,000 from their estate to St. Anthony's parish. They both died in the mid-'90's. Evidently, their money was used to buy School 50. The Jackmans were living in John's childhood home near Miley and Washington Streets when they died.

1931 Marion County Sectionals

Al Hamilton arrived as a teacher at Washington High School in the fall of 1959 after four years at Purdue University. He had graduated from Lawrence Central High School in 1955. Al was a Science teacher for 36 years until our school closed in 1995. But he was best known as the equipment man, statistician, and official basketball scorer for Washington athletics. He replaced his Science Department Head Jim Otto on the scorer's bench initially alongside future principal Leon Hunt. John Bradley (who arrived in 1961 and retired in 1989) and Al were the foundation of the loyal core of Continental "team-players" who made the tradition rich athletic programs so significant during their years of unselfish participation.

Mr. Hamilton supplied the author with a copy of a full-page pictorial of the 16 Marion County basketball teams that vied for the 1931 Marion County Sectional. Al was also the official IHSAA scorer for the Girls' Basketball Tournament for the first 21 years (State Finals only) through 1996 as well as for the Boys' Tourney from 1970-1995 where he would start at the Hinkle Sectionals then through the Regionals and Semi-State before the State Finals. (note: his first two State Finals were held at Hinkle Fieldhouse before three years at IU's new fieldhouse in '72, '73, & '74 then on to Market Square Arena and then the Dome in 1989. The multi-class finals are currently held at Conseco Fieldhouse.)

In 1931 the two Marion County Parochial schools, Cathedral and Sacred Heart, participated in a Catholic tournament and Crispus Attucks also played in a separate tourney. It's interesting to note that there were only five IPS schools and the names of some of the other "population center" rural areas are not household names today (I don't think that "suburbs" was a widely used term at the time).

The sixteen teams were: West Newton, Castleton, Acton, Washington, Technical, Ben Davis, Shortridge, Manual, Beech Grove, Broad Ripple, Lawrence, New Augusta, Oaklandon, Valley Mills, New Bethel, and South Port. I believe that the Marion County Sectional in 1931 was played in the Cow Barn at the State Fairgrounds.

Oaklandon, Lawrence, and Castleton consolidated in 1941 to become Lawrence Central and a year later LC would reach the Sweet Sixteen in the State Tourney. By 1976 the Oaklandon area would then be the center of the new Lawrence North H.S.

Arsenal Technical, better known as Tech, was the powerhouse team since it was the largest high school in the state as they also won five consecutive city championships from the late 1920's into the early 1930's. West Newton and Valley Mills would become Decatur Central in later years. Acton became the foundation for Franklin Central and New Augusta became Pike.

Although we have not re-produced the actual full-page picture, the players and some coaches names that were published on Friday, March 6, 1931 in the Indianapolis News are as follows:

WEST NEWTON---Clifford Christy (co-captain), Wilbur Rhoades, Charles Byers, Robert Jordan, Milo Mendenhall, Robert Fields (co-captain), Fonnie Blankenbaker, Dick Dininger, Kenneth Butler, Nelson Nunamaker.

CASTLETON---Curtis Justus, Max Deford, George Beaver (captain), Glenn Dooley, Donald Sowers, Coach Kyle Peters, Russell Morgan, Glen Bolander, John Robison, Myron Zook, Andrew Smith.

ACTON---Steve Spear, Jerry Rabourn, Jim Hicks (captain), Harold Toon, Herman Schnier, Clarence Smith, Harry Pritchard, Paul McFarland, Bud Smith, Clarence Adams, Coach W.G. Kellam.

WASHINGTON---John Foudray, Worth Pullen, Donald Bright, Clarence Hogue, Robert Hedge, Harry Lewis, Coach R.H. Jones, John Blankenship (captain), Harry Sanders.

TECHNICAL---Earl Overman, Clarence Jones, David Jordan, Kermit Bonnell, Howard White, Howard Pursell, Earl Townsend, Raymond Gladden, Paul Boyer, Leroy Edwards.

BEN DAVIS---Lex Wood, Harold Willsey, Farland Wallen, Norman Uhrig (captain), Lloyd Starnes, Harold Simmons, Coach G.W. Gerichs, Orville Toler, Frank Gill, Morris Gray, Albert Thompson (mgr.).

SHORTRIDGE---Lorrein Bulleitt, Arthur Gage, Marion Heckman, Herman Berns, Bob Dewess, Ralph Brafford, Bob Brown, Bob Sutherlin, Herbert Hays, William Reed, Coach Kenneth Peterman, Bud Underwood, Spud Johnson.

MANUAL---Edwin Beeson, Carl Hanna, Raymond Kleppe, Eugene Stuart, Charles Stuart, Eugene Loeper, Nathan Regenstreif (captain), Fred Brant, Mark Armour, Frank Welton, Coach Oral Bridgford.

BEECH GROVE---Coach O.L. VanHorn, Woodrow Worrell, Welbon Britton, Charles Terhune, Richard Clapp, Maurice Mitchell, Harry Shelby, Laurence Lambert, Bud McElroy, Raymond Maines, Byron Rutledge.

BROAD RIPPLE---Eugene Goss, Carl Rauh, Jack Dearinger, Rich Lee, Rickey Murbarger, John Ammerman, Harvey O'Brien, Gordon Everson, Bill Nelson, Coach Ed Diederich, George Ferguson, Kenneth Olvey, Gene Bisinger.

LAWRENCE---Coach D.K. Beaver, Robert Bragdon, Harrison Smith, Charles Bruce, Ronald Roberts, Allen Sutton, Thomas Herman, Paul Raab, John Rector, Charles Garrison.

NEW AUGUSTA---Edward King, Oscar Stewart, Donald Duncan, George Monniger, Frank Collins, Edward Fults, Droyson Whitesell, Richard Hayes (mgr.).

OAKLANDON---Ross Harold Apple, Harold Riley, Elbert Apple (captain), Dave Hockett, Florin Huntley, Coach S.B. Todd, Henry Torrence, Komer Klepfer, Thomas Morris, Huston Offenbacker, Ernest Uhlmann, Frederick Teter.

VALLEY MILLS---Coach F.C. Foley, Charles Riddle, Francis Busald, Vernon Copeland, George Baldwin, Edward Wampler, Maurice Barnett, James Woods, Curtis Munson, Morris Routon, Walter Taylor (captain), Maurice Furnace, Charles Kugleman, Carl Portch (mgr.)

NEW BETHEL---Edward Sutherland, Fred Fox, Earl Williams, Richard Willsey, Tom Smith, Coach O.J. Smith, _____ Van Dyke, Frank Kline, Charles Fisher, Robert Lehnert, Albert _____.

SOUTH PORT---Maurice Riser (mgr.), Jess Smithey, Francis Harding, Robert Mayer, James Lamb, Crafton Waddell, Robert Anderson (captian), Harry Fox, Bill Orme, Spencer Richards, Calbert Cox, Gene Wayman, Coach A.C. Pitcher.

Most of the above "boys" were born between 1913-1916. Obviously, most are not alive. But they were grandfathers and great-grandfathers of many living descendants. Traditionally, Hoosier basketball teams were a reflection of a school's public personality.

An Indiana State Basketball Champion was first crowned in 1911 at the Indiana University Fieldhouse. The finals continued there through 1920 with the exception in 1919 when Purdue hosted the championship tournament. The next four years the finals were held at the State Fairgrounds Coliseum. Wayne Fuson, the long-time News sports editor, once wrote that the 1925 through 1927 final games were played at the Fairgrounds Exposition Building, popularly called the Cow Barn. In 2010 Jim Carter (GWHS class of 1930) claimed that the Final game, which was won by junior Johnny Wooden's Martinsville team, took place at the Riverside Park roller-skating rink on 30th Street. Semi-final games may have been played there. In any event, the Final games were first hosted at the new Butler Fieldhouse in 1928. With the exception of the war years of 1943-45, the Final Four tournament continued on the Butler campus through the 1971 finals. From 1972 through 1974 the Finals moved to the new IU Assembly Hall. In 1975 the final three games moved to Indianapolis' Market Square Arena. In 1990 the games were held at the massive RCA-Hoosier Dome. Since 2000 Conseco Fieldhouse has hosted the Finals.

THE WORKINGMAN'S FRIEND

As the Balkan Wars raged in southeastern Europe just before the Great War of 1914, Macedonian immigrant Louie Stamatkin traveled to the United States through Ellis Island on a Turkish passport. Eventually he settled in Indianapolis and in 1918 opened a restaurant-bar as the Prohibition era was beginning post-World War I. The Belmont Lunch was born. Located on the southwest corner of Belmont & Turner adjacent to the B & O Railroad, it was a boon for the many workers nearby from J.D. Adams, Link-Belt and Thomas L. Green & Company owned by the Lugar family. But the many railroadmen, particularly those working in the Round House directly to the northeast of the luncheon, were the first "regulars." Louie allowed many to run a weekly tab to be paid on Friday.

Louie's "Belmont Lunch" began as a one-room eatery with a dirt floor and no roof. The original three posts, used to support the new 1920's roof, still stand in the center of the current building albeit with a fresh coat of green paint. Louie had married a Shelbyville girl and brought her to the big city. They had two boys, Carl born in 1921 and Earl born in 1923. Both Carl and Earl would attend nearby Washington High.

During the Great Depression of the 1930's many of the railroad workers and other laborers were usually short of money. So Louie would often allow them to eat lunch on credit. One worker labeled Louie as "the workingman's friend." Thus, a name was born.

When founder Louie died in 1946 his boys would take charge and began a "new" building. As the new facility was built around the original building, pieces of the old bar were transported out of the north side door and business continued as usual. The Grand Opening of the tavern took place in 1952. Not until 2005 were the tables, chairs and restrooms replaced. The 60-foot bar, which still stands, was once considered the longest in Indianapolis.

A printed menu from the mid-50's offers 32 mixed drinks ranging from Gin & Tonic at 60-cents to the Singapore Sling at $1.25. Ice Cold Frosty beer was priced at 15-cents. The Big Cheese Double Deck Cheeseburger went for 65-cents and Pizza cost from $1 to $2 for a large "Around the World." The top menu item was the 18-oz. T-bone Steak with salad, baked potato or French fries and roll for $2.75. And one could get Buttermilk for 15-cents and Coca Cola or 7-Up for a dime. And all of that before Democrat Governor Matthew Welch and the General Assembly introduced the first Indiana sales tax in 1961.

Mary Alice Gill, class of '51, began working in the Stamatkin bar in the mid-50's as she continued her job at Bell Telephone Company until 1956. A one-armed piano player, who marked time with his stump, was a popular mainstay of the '50's. Retired Colonel Robert Fischer, who continued his weekly Wednesday night visits into the 21st century, first enjoyed the vittles and libations in the '50's also. And Buddy Boy would often open the bar for the Stamatkin brothers. Once he had to be carted home in a wheel-barrel after a long day on the job.

Carl and Earl didn't always agree on business decisions and in 1965 Carl became the sole proprietor. So Earl gained individual ownership of the property at the south side corner of North Tibbs and Washington Streets, just east of the street-car turnaround, until his death in 1994. Once each summer into the '60's, a carnival rented the open lot before Burger Chef signed a lease with Earl in 1962. A proposal for a restaurant to be called the "Ranch Drive-In" was shelved. So Burger Chef's 15-cents for a hamburger, fries and small drink became the first "fast food" joint in the immediate Washington High area. Fire Station #18 was directly across the street. Earl, who had no children, willed the property to two of Carl's kids. The Hardee franchise prospered until closing in '08.

During the 1960's Mary Alice took the lead in managing the famous menu. Sizzling Steaks, Beef Stew, Balkan salads and Big Johns were the forerunners of the award winning Double Cheeseburgers. Submarine or "Poor Boy" sandwiches, as they were called in the late '50's, were being sold at Workingman's. Once when Carl noticed a surplus of the large buns in stock, he ordered Mary Alice to make a Hot Ham & Cheese which would fit the bun ("you have to know how to perfectly burn the corners of the melding of cheese and ham," Mary Alice once noted). The Big John was named after the 1959 #1 pop song "Big Bad John" sung by future-sausage-man Jimmy Dean.

Beer ranging from the 32-oz. Fish Bowl to the small stein in the frosted mugs as well as iced cold bottles continue as staples for the drinking crowd. Braunschweiger on rye with cheese and/or an onion slice, the Diet Platter, Chili and Bean soup are also featured on the wall-window menus with Fish and Tenderloin among other delicacies.

Larry, class of '65, began the next generation of Stamatkins working the bar and he still maintains his Wednesday night presence. Becky, class of '82, became the head cook at noon replacing her mom by the late 1990's. Terry Stamatkin normally reigns over the patrons in the afternoon until 6 or 7 PM. Becky's partner, Shelly Groover, displays a staunch professionalism behind the bar. And, along with waitresses Shannon Napier and Cindy Lindsey, they continue a conscientious dependability of over a dozen years that the original Louie would appreciate.

A stroke in the early '90's limited Carl's presence. He died in December 2004. And Mary Alice died peacefully in April 2008 while at home.

All of Mary Alice's kids have worked in the bar. First was Louie, class of '74, followed by the twins, Steve and Chris. Earl, who has his own catering business in the new century, first experienced food service working at the family establishment. His tour in the U.S. Navy as a chef was somewhat predestined. And Danny, class of '85 who works at the State Office Building, is known by many as he displays a strength of presence while often subbing behind the bar. The twins played on the '74 State Championship football team while Danny was a tough tackle on the '83 runners-up.

But Becky and Terry seem to carry the consistent work-load into the decade of the centennial anniversary. In the 21st century the "Indianapolis Monthly" magazine has voted the Workingman's Double Cheeseburger as #1 in Indy based on taste and price. Earlier on December 30, 1994 Star Special Writer Steve Mannheimer wrote that the Workingman's Friend is the "oldest eatery in Indianapolis continuously owned by one family" and he quotes sports personality Robin Miller that the bar has "the absolute best in town" double cheeseburger. Spoken like a true regular.

As its name suggests, the Workingman's seems to promote the image of being a Democrat Party bar. Recent governors O'Bannon and Kernan both often enjoyed the ambiance of the Westside gathering place. When the state of Washington elected Maria Cantwell as United States Senator in 2000, the local Democrats held a reception for her in town. Guess where?!? The Workingman's Friend. And one of Indiana's U.S. Senators, Evan Bayh, along with recent Mayor Bart Peterson have attended gatherings there.

On the other side of the political coin, in early 2004 almost 40 Republican legislators "walked out" of the Indiana General Assembly in protest only to travel the short distance west on Washington Street then north to 234 N. Belmont to set their strategy while munching on a Stamatkin-grilled sandwich.

Marion County's most famous defense lawyer, Jimmy Voyles, along with ex-Pacer Rick Smits, quite a few local TV personalities, many uniformed policemen, basketball icons Larry Bird and Quinn Buckner and George McGinnis, as well as Jacktown's longest resident Tooter Rice all appear often for lunch. The Workingman's has transcended the Round House Railroad workers daily lunches to serving many young office-worker professionals and medical students.

The St. Patrick's Day celebration continues as one of the largest in central Indiana. And nephew Ronnie Joe Sears, son of Bea Ann Gill and Ronnie Sr., concludes the March 17 party with his infectious personality along with Karaoke entertainment. The one-arm piano player hasn't shown up lately.

And it all began with a Macedonian immigrant named Louie who the railroaders considered the workingman's friend.

FIRST SECTIONAL CHAMPS 1948

In 20 previous attempts to win Washington High's first basketball sectionals Coach Rowland Jones' teams came up short.

Of course, until 1967 and the first baseball state tournament, boys' basketball was the only purely team-sport tournament in Indiana. Wrestling and track had sectionals, regionals, semi-state, and state but the emphasis was on the individual champions. Basketball, in the Indiana "common culture," was THE one and only tourney.

Mr. Jones had won four City Championships but never a sectional. The year 1948 was going to be different. The Continentals had lost in the City Championship game to Shortridge by a score of 38-36. And we were one of the dark-horse favorites in the always brutal Butler Sectionals.

The regular season had ended with a 9-6 record and one of the Sectionals favorites, Broad Ripple, loomed as the opening game opponent. The Jonesmen squeaked out a 39-37 win then handily defeated Warren Central, 57-48. Decatur Central was the round three foe. We spanked them 48-39. Then in the championship game the Continentals thumped Lawrence Central by almost 20 points, 62-43.

Marion County's first jump-shooter, Bill Niemann, was our consistent leading scorer as the right-forward. He would later be named to the 10th annual Indiana All-Star team. Baseball star Maurice Wilhoite was the starting left-forward and second leading scorer, Ralph Lollar was the leading rebounder, with Chris Theofanis as the back-guard and captain Don Masterson the floor-general. One-handed shots were just becoming common.

The other varsity players were George Theofanis, Robert Kikendall, Leo Little, Stanley Benge, Richard Crittenden, Lowell Lentz, Robert Trinkle, and Robert Lehr.

An all-girl cheerleading squad was new from the previous year lead by Mildred Sue Wilson. Twenty-three years later Sue's daughter, Connie Higgins, would be a sophomore cheerleader for the 1969 undefeated State Champs.

In the four team Butler Regionals, Washington defeated Speedway 60-44 in the afternoon. But that night the Continental dream was shattered by the Anderson Indians, 45-41. Anderson even then was a central Indiana powerhouse having been State Champs two years before with Jumping Johnny Wilson. But, in 1948, Lafayette Jeff would win State. And future Congressman Lee Hamilton, from Evansville Central, would win the coveted Trester Award.

Indianapolis Washington ended the season with a 14-7 record. In future years Chris Theofanis would become a long-time Public Relations Director for Butler University. Niemann would retire from Allison's Division of General Motors while his sons would become star athletes at Speedway. Masterson would become a leader as principal of Wayne Township's Chapelwood Elementary. Wilhoite became a brick-mason. Kikendall owned a used parts store as an adult. Benge's son, Stan Jr., would become the long-time multi-State Championship coach of girls' basketball at Ben Davis High School. And his other son, Kurt, was girls' coach at Plainfield High. George Theofanis became head basketball coach at Avon High then transferred to Shortridge as an assistant before becoming their highly successful head coach. In 1968 his smaller team defeated the McGinnis-Downing Continentals in the Regionals. Eventually, he replaced legend Tony Hinkle as Butler University's coach.

But in 1948 Coach Jones' last team set a precedent that was not to be met again until 17 years in the future. It was truly a magical year for the Continentals.

Tom Stevason, adopted Continental

As part of the Indianapolis Star "Life Lines" series the author wrote a testimonial to Tom Stevason. It was published April 13, 1991 on page F-2. Tom was diagnosed with renal cell cancer in January 1991 and died in January 1996. He graduated from Manual High School in 1954 and Indiana Central College in 1970.

"A Coach, a Friend, a Teen's Hero"

The year 1961 became my most memorable. "Falling" for little Jeannie, playing on Mr. McCoy and Mr. Anderson's Pony League team and leaving the friendly confines of School 50 for the dominating presence of Washington High all affected my 14-year-old life.

Our social life on the near-Westside was dominated by Hawthorne Community Center activities. House director Rosey "Kid" Baker, once the Indiana middleweight boxing champ (who some said had fought Gary's future World Champ Tony Zale), hired Loren Comstock in 1960. Loren had been 1958's Mr. Indiana body builder from Hofmeister's Gym. Both men knew how to defer to kids.

But in the late fall of 1961 a young hook-shot artist from the Southside found his way to Hawthorne after serving Uncle Sam and began a 10-year journey on his way to his dream of becoming a high school basketball coach. What a group those three were for an aggressive bunch of kids.

Tom Stevason spent money without hesitation. He once bought a Hawthorne kid Converse basketball shoes with "built-in" weights at the old Em-Roe store downtown served by local baseball legend Joe Kelly.

But what Tom mostly spent was *time*. Time with teen-agers obsessed by basketball and baseball; time to listen to typical and not-so-typical teen-age problems; time to take kids to his sister's picnics, or to their first golf course, or to Wagner's swimming pool, or to their first college football game.

"You can't fool kids," he used to say. And he spent time to prove that he practiced what he preached.

From Regina, Connie and Diane to Butch, Billy and little Gary and many others Tom made an indelible mark that can only be made on impressionable teens. He posted his rules for basketball on the wall: "Know where the basket is" and "follow your shot" and "warm up like Oscar."

Billy Keller was the best player to come under Tom's tutelage but not necessarily the most intense. In the early '60's Tom showed up in the end zone at Washington High more than star Ricky Thompson. He seemed to attend so many activities that people asked his brother James if Tom had a twin. Coleman Kays and John Wirtz were two of his buddies that helped him lead Hawthorne to the American Legion Baseball State Championship in 1969 with boys from Washington, Cathedral, Ritter, and Ben Davis.

His strong family life extended to the Hawthorne family of the Potters, the Garvers, the Stamatkins and many others. Tom's energy and foresight created a Tuesday night basketball league second to none for junior high kids. Carmel, NYAA, Tab and St. Pat's were just a few of the teams that traveled to the House just off of the National Road on Ohio Street on Tuesday nights.

Yes, the year that saw Roger Maris hit 61 homers, A.J. Foyt win his first 500 and Ernie Davis become the first black Heisman Trophy winner was more important for a lot of Westside kids because Tommy Stevason became a player in their lives.

As my wife says, Tom had a way of making people feel that they were an important part of his life. He knew how to listen. Chatard High School has had the benefit of having Tom since the spring of 1971. Many Westsiders are envious.

Tom found out he was a little sick this January and most who know him share his anguish. I still think he's the best third baseman in softball. And a pretty good basketball coach, too.

The Coliseum Disaster and the JFK Assassination

On Thursday, October 31, 1963 a football game was played at CYO Field on West 16th Street. Scecina Memorial, an eastside Catholic school named after Indianapolis hero-priest Thomas Scecina who was killed during World War II, had beaten traditional powerhouse Cathedral for the first time ever in 1962 and was favored to repeat. A simple 4' x 4' poster board sign reading "Kill" held by a student in the northwest corner of the grandstands seemed mild by the standards of the day. Later, the irony of that typical scene was noted by at least one high school student. Since Washington High was to play Cathedral in the traditional tenth game the next Friday on November 8, many Continental football players were in attendance that rainy Halloween night. Cathedral dominated the game and remained undefeated at 8-0-1. Indianapolis high school football seemed more relevant in the days when the old Victory Field, directly across the street from CYO, was home for the only professional sports team in town until 1967. But that was a story that soon seemed unimportant.

A little over an hour after the game ended Indianapolis would experience the worst disaster in its history. A short distance to the northeast, inside the Indiana State Fair Grounds, it was opening night for "Holiday on Ice." It was an ice skating extravaganza of much repute. As the grand finale began while workers were preparing popcorn for the following night, an enormous explosion erupted. A leaking valve on a propane tank had built up its power and sent fire and concrete flying. Many humans were propelled up to 60' into the air. In moments 65 people were dead from severe burns or crushed by large chunks of concrete. Within hours another eight died and one unfortunate individual lived for over three months before succumbing to infection. The final death toll was 74. There had been over 4,300 people in attendance. It seemed that the Fairgrounds Coliseum was forever doomed as a venue for group activities. Ironically, when the Pacer franchise was born in 1967 they became the first significant booking for the Coliseum since that fateful Halloween night. It became the Pepsi Coliseum in 1991.

But just three weeks and one day later, the United States would experience a traumatic event which changed American history.

Friday, November 22 was another rainy, dreary day in Indianapolis. But in Dallas, Texas the sunshine of the noon hour seemed to reflect the optimism of America with our young, personable President. JFK persuaded his Vice-President Lyndon Johnson to accompany him on a political party trip. Democrat Governor John Connally and Johnson were close philosophical allies. But the U.S. Senator from Texas, Ralph Yarborough, was characterized as "too liberal" and more of a Kennedy friend. Therefore, the two Democrats who didn't always see eye-to-eye, Johnson and Yarborough, were to ride together two cars behind the President's limo. The 1964 reelection needed a united front for the party. The Deep South had long been a Democrat stronghold but the matter of race relations threatened the cohesiveness of the so-called Solid South. In any event, it would be the last time in American history that a President and his Vice-President would travel together. And never again would a President travel in an open motorcade through masses of people.

The four days between Friday's assassination, the nighttime arrival of JFK's casket, Sunday's noontime murder of Lee Harvey Oswald by Jack Ruby, and the somber funeral on Monday was a national occurrence that seemed surreal. For the only time in United States television history all programming on the three national channels focused on our common tragedy for four consecutive days.

Along with 9-11 for the younger generation and the Pearl Harbor Sneak Attack for our oldest citizens, the assassination of President Kennedy was extremely shocking and oddly unifying. Those of a certain age will never forget where they were or how they felt during those three events of extreme national awareness.

And most Indianapolis residents will long remember the Coliseum disaster.

RICHARD G. LUGAR

When President Kennedy was assassinated on November 22, 1963, 31-year-old Dick Lugar was shocked like most Americans. Although he and his brother, Tom, were heading a prosperous baking machinery company on the Westside of Indianapolis, he was inspired into public service by that national trauma. And he was well prepared for such an endeavor.

Early in 1964, a group of Westsiders came to Dick's office and strongly encouraged him to become a candidate for election to the Indianapolis Board of School Commissioners. They felt he was the best qualified for Westside schools to obtain appropriate fairness and attention. Encouraged by the words of these new friends, Dick became a successful candidate in the May, 1964 School Board election.

Richard Green Lugar was born April 4, 1932 in Indianapolis to Bertha and Marvin Lugar. He attended IPS #84, #60, and Shortridge High School. He was active in Methodist Youth Fellowship and joined Central Avenue Methodist Church. Dick attained the rank of Eagle Scout in the Boy Scouts and was the very first winner of the God and Country award in the Central Indiana Council. And as a Blue Devil football player for George Gale, he exhibited a competitive zeal that would follow him throughout his active life.

Then Dick traveled east to Granville, Ohio to attend Denison University on a full tuition academic scholarship. He finished at #1 in his college class of 1954 while serving as co-President of the Student Government. His co-President was a young lady from Detroit, Michigan named Charlene Smeltzer. On September 8, 1956 she would become his co-partner for life. Their honeymoon suite was in a little farm house on South Mann Road in Indianapolis' Decatur township on the Green-Lugar farm property of 604 acres.

But first Dick had sailed across the Atlantic Ocean as Denison's initial under-graduate to win a Rhodes Scholarship to Oxford University. While at Pembroke College, one of the colleges at Oxford and studying as the only American, he was elected President of the Student Body. Eventually he served as President of the 250-man American Students Association of Oxford University before receiving a Bachelor of Arts Honours Degree in Politics, Philosophy, and Economics. A few years later, he was awarded a Master of Arts degree from the highly reputable British university.

While in England, Dick volunteered for active duty in the United States Navy and was ordered to Officer Candidate School in 1957. He served on active duty for three years and four months. During most of his Naval service, Dick was a personal intelligence briefer for the Chief of Naval Operations, Admiral Arleigh A. Burke.

Returning to Indianapolis in May of 1960, Dick and his brother Tom assumed the top management position at the family business, Thomas L. Green & Company on North Miley directly north of IPS #30 and three blocks northeast of George Washington High School.

Green & Company manufactured automated food machinery for companies like Nabisco and Schultze-Burch among others. Business tripled between 1960 and 1967. Dick and Tom led a resurgence in the family business that continued under Tom's leadership after Dick was elected Mayor of Indianapolis in 1967.

Mr. Lugar had already been active in the nearby high school's Businessmen's Association including periodic luncheons at Washington High under the directorship of Principal Curly Julian. So it was coincidental that his arrival on the IPS Board of Directors in 1964 would just precede the basketball State Championship year of '64-65. Mr. Lugar naturally became a devotee in time and energy during that victorious season.

When he mentored one particular student-athlete during the summer of 1965 in preparation for his Butler football freshman and sophomore years, three days per week at 6:00 AM, he continued to display both his compassion and work ethic. The workouts included a quarter mile run as well as pass receiving duties for the Shortridge grad.

But Dick's life would take a dramatic turn in late 1966 when he sought the backing of the new Marion County Republican Chairman, L. Keith Bulen. He was encouraged to become the Republican candidate for Indianapolis Mayor in 1967. Incumbent John Barton seemed beatable but was still the favorite against 35-year-old Dick Lugar. A vigorous campaign strongly supported by John Mutz, John Benbow, and Fred Armstrong as well as Chairman Bulen resulted in both Republican Primary and General Election victories. The first elected Republican Mayor in 16 years.

The Lugar family at 3333 Highwoods Drive, just west of Kesseler Blvd., would never be the same. Along with wife Char and boys Mark, Bobby, John and David as well as Bassett hound Samantha, His Honor the Mayor was headed toward a great destiny. By 2010 the four boys had helped add 13 grandchildren to Char and Dick's legacy.

Mayor Lugar's initiative sought passage by the 1969 General Assembly of legislation re-organizing Indianapolis and Marion County civil government. After court tests, the Unified Government (UniGov) was voted into law and went into effect on January 1, 1970. The unification of "old" Indianapolis with the surrounding eight Marion County townships into a consolidated and efficient City-Council with one Mayor set the foundation for the immense growth of downtown Indianapolis. This included the Market Square Arena, a new host for the Indiana Pacers in the early 1970's, as well as the basis for the next mayor's, Bill Hudnut's, enticement of the Colts franchise to central Indiana in 1984. Dick became known as President Nixon's "favorite mayor" based on the conservative concept of revenue sharing of tax dollars, which was a policy which empowered local communities and seemed to diminish federal bureaucracy.

When Mayor Lugar left office in January of 1976 after eight years he immediately was met with another challenge. While still our mayor he had lost in 1974 to incumbent Democrat Birch Bayh. But Dick successfully unseated the other incumbent Democrat Vance Hartke in November, 1976. And he has been successfully reelected in 1982, 1988, 1994, 2000 and 2006. When he won in '94 he became the only Hoosier Senator in American History to be elected to a fourth term. In 2000 he received over 85% of the popular vote and he tallied 87% of the vote in '06.

Senator Lugar was on the short list for Vice President for Richard Nixon in 1972, for Ronald Reagan in 1980, and George H.W. Bush in 1988. He sought the Republican nomination for President in 1996.

But his statesmanship and bipartisanship as Senator is what has secured his positive reputation in American history. In 1991 he and Senator Sam Nunn, a fellow Eagle Scout and a Democrat, persuaded the former Soviet Union to deactivate more than 5,900 nuclear warheads. As Chairman of the Agriculture Committee, Senator Lugar led a federal farm program reform which ended the 1930's-era federal production controls.

In 2008 he and the ranking Democrat on the Committee on Foreign Relations, Sen. Joe Biden, received the Hilal-I-Pakistan (Crescent of Pakistan) Award from the government of Pakistan for their continued support of Pakistan. During the recess of 2005, Senator Lugar and freshman Senator Barack Obama visited Russia to inspect nuclear facilities there and in Azerbaijan as well as the Ukraine. They were detained for over three hours in the city of Perm near the Ural Mountains before Russian authorities released them with an apology. The Lugar-Obama Proliferation and Threat Reduction Initiative was signed into law by President Bush in January 2007.

In April 2006, TIME magazine dubbed Lugar as the "Wise Man" of the Senate in its list of American's ten best Senators. He has been nominated for the Nobel Peace Prize every year since 2000. During the final 2008 Presidential debate, Democratic candidate Barack Obama noted that Lugar was one of the individuals "who have shaped my ideas and who will be surrounding me in the White House." Again, rumors arose that either Senator McCain or Senator Obama would offer Dick the position of Secretary of State. But Senator Lugar announced his intention of being able to do more for our country as Indiana's senior Senator.

On March 18, 2009 Lugar cast his 12,000[th] Senate vote. This vote put him 13th on the all-time Senate votes list. In 33 years Senator Lugar has a better than 98% attendance record. From 1985-1987 and again from 2003-2007 he was Chairman of the Senate Committee on Foreign Relations.

Into 2010, he is the senior Republican Senator and has only Democrats Byrd(1958), Inouye (1962) and Leahy (1974) ahead of him on the Senate seniority list of 100 members. (Byrd died in June 2010)

Little did Marvin and Bertha realize that their little boy, born in the final year of Herbert Hoover's presidency, would become Indiana's most famous and prolific Republican since President Harrison. And old Washington High claims him too.

JIMMIE ANGELOPOLOUS

Sportswriters for the three Indianapolis newspapers in the 1950's and '60's all seemed dedicated to their jobs. Dick Mittman's steady professionalism, Dick Denny's quiet sincerity, Bob Williams' confidence, Bob Renner's personable attitude and Wayne Fuson's competent leadership left their vocation in a better place when they all retired. But of all of the Indianapolis sports writers over the years, Jimmie Angelopolous may have been the most enthusiastic and personable. He was a man dedicated to human interest stories as they related to high school athletics. He was pushy for the best story but not intrusive. And he was a true friend to the less privileged student-athletes in IPS.

Jimmie's mom arrived from Greece in 1916. His dad had settled near the "immigrant school," known as School 5, a year or two earlier. Jimmie's oldest sibling, Aglaia, was born in 1918. Brother Angelo arrived in 1919. Jimmie was born December 13, 1920. He had followed older sister Mildred. Youngest of the family was Katherine who was born in 1928. The family homestead was on Geisendorff Street about two blocks west of Military Park probably about center court on today's IUPUI tennis field.

The Holy Trinity Greek Orthodox Church could have fielded an all-Angelopolous basketball team. But the "Making Americans" school on the north side of the National Road beckoned as the educational opportunity for the many early-20th century westside immigrants. Jimmie received his grade school diploma in 1934 and began his four years of high school at old Manual Training High School within walking distance on South Meridian Street.

Social life for the kids in that area mostly consisted of trips to the Indiana and Circle Theaters as well as baseball games in Military Park. During the racially segregated era of the '20's and '30's Colored kids from Michigan Street's School 4 participated with the Greeks, Romanians, Italians, and others at the park on West & New York Street.

His college years, like most in his generation, were interrupted by the American commitment to defeating the Germans and Italians in Europe and the Japanese in the South Pacific. Jimmie served 21 months in the Pacific Theater of war with the U.S. Navy. He served mainly as physical education instructor for troops on the islands that were procured by our many amphibious landings.

Jimmie had been a wrestler for legendary Billy Tom at IU before the war. After the war he achieved his diploma by 1947 on the GI bill. His first journalistic endeavor was for the Ft. Wayne News Sentinel from '47-48. But then he returned home and the Indianapolis Times. Older brother Angelo was already a top writer for the News. Angelo had been a Navy pilot during the big war. When he died of leukemia in 1962 his family felt that his wartime experience of flying over Hiroshima to detect the radiation damage was the cause of his deadly disease 17 years later.

For almost 18 years Jimmie was a mainstay for the Times until they closed in October of 1965. His much anticipated "Angie Picks the Preps" was highly popular among high school football and basketball players and became part of the pop-culture in Indianapolis. His assertive personality was reflective of his honesty.

And his creativity led to renting four horses upon which the Manual High School backfield of 1958 (which ended the season at 10-0) was pictured in a much publicized photo emulating the Four Horsemen of Notre Dame fame from 1924. He couldn't find seven mules for the linemen.

Jimmie also touted the professional career of light-heavyweight Champion Marvin Johnson from Attucks High School.

Jimmie had a special place in his heart for Manual, Washington, Attucks, Cathedral, Sacred Heart and the poorer kids in Indianapolis. He had two younger cousins attend GWHS in the early 1950's. The DeMoss sisters who lived on Rockville Road.

Angie worked for the News from 1965 until his retirement in 1991. At his retirement dinner he gave a classic characterization. He said, "you know what the definition of an All American is......someone who's been out of school for 25 years." He was one of a kind in his self-deprecation and story-telling ability.

Jimmie was proud of his induction into five Indiana Halls of Fame including the Indiana Sports Writers and Broadcasters Hall of Fame in 1999. He also had been a certified wrestling official for 14 years as well as an Associate Director of the Indiana Basketball Hall of Fame.

When he died on July 23, 2009 at age 88 Jimmie was memorialized thus:

> Longtime News Managing Editor Wendell Trogden wrote affectionately that Jimmie was a "sports department icon" on the News staff and noted Jimmie's "favorite daily greeting" of "Hey, pal."
>
> Warren Township administrator and one-time Washington High quarterback Tony Burchett stated, "Jimmie was a great voice for student-athletes....He promoted kids, programs and schools."
>
> Nula Purichia Harmon noted that "It was a pleasure to read about so many local athletes in such a constructive manner."
>
> Dr. Elliott said that Jimmie was "a kind man who always had interesting stories" and was much enjoyed by his staff.
>
> From the late Wayne Fuson's family came the admonition that Jimmie had been a "friend and colleague" as well as a "fine and loyal man." Fuson had been the long-time sports editor of the News.
>
> And Jack Overmeyer, retired publisher of the Rochester Sentinel in New York state, wrote a significant testimonial that included that "Jim was an IU wrestler when I was doing publicity for the team. Our friendship continued from IU to Indianapolis where I was a sports writer for the Star until 1946. He was one of the kindest men I ever met, a sincere friend and talented writer. We occasionally would meet on my trips to Indianapolis and invariably an engrossing conversation would follow, for that was one of his many talents....I know too few like him now."

And he was always a friend of Washington High School and the Westside.

1959 Unbeaten Football Team

All-City end Larry Glaze compiled a detailed analysis of the 1959 football season as well as short biographies of most of the players. Our city's three newspapers at the time with their top high school beat writers were: The Times' Jimmie Angelopolous, The News' Wayne Fuson, and The Star's Bob Williams. They generated positive and accurate descriptions of all ten games. Yet, Washington High's own Ron Ellis was also a main source of information. Through the mid-1960's the Times and News would pay a small stipend to a journalism student from each area high school who usually reported their school's home game since only a featured game or two was covered by a professional correspondent. The following is the author's interpretation of the facts from all nine games as printed in one of the three newspapers along with some personal additions.

Game number one was played on the Continental field on Friday, September 11. Noblesville, coached by Bill McClain who would become the Ben Davis head coach in 1963, had been undefeated in 1958 and had beaten Lawrence Central 34-0 on September 4. They were ranked in the pre-season top ten in the state football poll. But on the fourth play of the game #72 Bob Leeper would sprint 45-yds. to make it 6-0. After two Millers' TDs in the second quarter, fullback Larry Compton would high step for a 17-yd. score followed by Bennie Cook's PAT tying it 13-13. A Charlie Prince pass to Larry Glaze in the end zone from 5-yards out in the fourth quarter with Cook's kick made it 20-13. Noblesville scored late but missed the extra point ending the game at 20-19. There were no two-point conversions in those days.

Opening the City Series competition against Manual on our home field was a chance to avenge the previous year's loss to the Redskins, 55-0. Often seen as the best Indianapolis team ever by "old school" pundits, the 1958 Manual team destroyed all comers defeating Cathedral 44-0 or so and handing Sacred Heart's Bob Springer a 61-0 loss in his very first varsity head coaching endeavor. But 1959 was to be different. In fact, oddly different, Manual ended the season at 0-9-1.

Quarterback Prince jogged into the end zone from 5-yards out after a 43-yard drive making it 7-0 for the Continentals after the kick. Halfback Ken Corey, on the first play of the second quarter, ran a 2-yard TD. He had run for 37-yards on the last play of the first session. But Manual followed up with an 80-yard scoring drive culminated by Don Kleppe's plunge tightening Washington's lead to 14-6. Manual's Dave Schieb would then throw to end Ed Stiegelmeyer making it 14-12. Another Kleppe run, this one for 67-yards, would put the Redskins ahead in the third quarter, 18-14. With 3:29 left in the game, Compton would match Kleppe's run with a 67-yarder of his own making it 20-18. Then end Steve Peterson's "scoop 'n score" for a 49-yard TD run on defense made it 27-18 after Cook's kick. Washington out-rushed Manual 246 yards to 232 and the passing was about even at 95 compared to 96 yards in favor of the home team. Punter Denny Hoffa, who was tutored by basketball coach and 1935 Washington graduate Dave Hine, would keep the Redskins pinned in their own territory most of the game.

An unfortunate side bar to that game carried over to the 1960 Washington-Manual game on the southside. In September 1960 their star, Kleppe, suffered a recurring concussion during the game and later died of a cerebral hemorrhage. Kleppe is the only known high school football player in Marion County to die as an active participant.

Rated number three in the state of Indiana football polls, unbeaten Shortridge loomed on the horizon. But three minutes into the game Corey returned a Blue Devil punt 76-yards for a

TD and a 6-0 lead. Shortridge star John Charleston passed for a TD to Sylvester Williams tying it after they had recovered a Continental fumble. In the second quarter Leeper scored a 5-yard TD after a 36-yard drive and Cook's kick made it 13-6. A 53-yard Shortridge scoring drive culminated in a Mel Jeter TD but the run for point was unsuccessful so Washington still led 13-12. But with only 59-seconds left in the first half the Blue Devil's ran an 81-yard sweep and kicked the extra point to put them ahead, 19-13. The ensuing kick-off was caught by Compton who summarily sprinted 80-yards for the score. Cook's kick put the score at 20-19 with only 47-seconds left until halftime. During the intermission, according to Prince in 2010, defensive captain Weldon Beliles suggested to Coach Tofil that the team should "widen" the outside LBers in our 5-4 front to neutralize the speed of the team from 34th & Meridian. Neither team scored in the second half. Prince, the QB, played right outside LBer on defense.

Washington was out-gained on the ground 123-yards to 210 and completed only one pass for three yards but the Continental defense, led by Beliles, intercepted three Charleston passes and their special team kick returns were the difference. At the time, the 4,000 fans along the New York Central railroad tracks witnessed what may have been Washington's biggest victory ever over a George Gale coached Shortridge eleven.

Game number four was to be the biggest disappointment. Coached by second year coach Bob Springer, the Spartans of Sacred Heart would only gain 31 yards on the ground and 86 in passing but when they recovered a Continental fumble with 3 minutes left in the game they drove 50 yards for the tying score with extra point making it 7-7. An Art Beck to Pete Speth 3-yd. pass followed by Ted Fields' run for point shattered hopes for a perfect season. The Continentals had first scored in the 3rd session on a Prince to Compton 23-yard pass followed by a Cook kick. Left end Glaze noted that the "35X" off-tackle, cross-block between him and tackle Jim Dill ("which paid for Compton's full-ride to Louisville" according to Glaze) didn't work since he was unable to block Sacred Heart's Joe Spitznagel.

The October 9 game with Scecina at GWHS ended 39-0 in our school's favor and allowed for some rejuvenation of spirit. Three touchdown passes in the first half, added to a Compton run, found the score 25-0 at halftime. Leeper caught two TDs from Prince of 29 and 58 yards while Glaze caught the first TD of 15-yards. Corey ran 65-yards early in the 3rd stanza and a quarterback sneak ended the scoring at 1:06 of the 3rd quarter. The defense only allowed Scecina 49 total yards causing three fumbles.

Homecoming against Broad Ripple was an every-other-year occurrence. The statistical game was in favor of Ripple with their 181 rushing and 83 passing yards compared to our 153 rushing and 58 passing. But our hard-nosed defense recovered five fumbles and Compton's 82-yard kick-off return opening the second half finalized the score at 20-0. Beliles had opened the scoring in the first quarter when he picked up a fumble and ran 49-yards for a 6-0 lead followed a few minutes later by a 68-yard dash by Corey with the kick showing 13-0 on the east-end scoreboard. A 78-yard Corey run was called back on a clipping penalty.

For the sixth consecutive year (of what would become ten), the Ben Davis Giants were victimized by the Continental eleven. The 350 total yards for Washington as compared to BD's 105 yards was indicative of the 40-0 final score. Leeper scored the first two TDs, a 13-yarder followed by a 5-yard jaunt. Then Corey scored on a short off-tackle run before sophomore Joe Purichia threw his first varsity TD pass to Steve Peterson for 15-yards making it 27-0 at halftime. The second half saw Larry Meador scoring his only 1959 TD followed by a TD pass from defensive leader Beliles who took the snap and tossed a "halfback down the middle" to his best buddy, Billy Snowberger.

The same Snowberger who had scored two TDs against Ben Davis his sophomore year in 1957's 53-14 thrashing of the Giants.

Playing Anderson north of Indianapolis put the Connies face-to-face with Washington High's first great athlete. Jim Emerson Carter, class of 1930, was head football coach for the Indians through 1964. But his magic could not deny a victory for our Westside school. Two touchdown passes from Prince, one to Leeper and the other to Glaze both for 30-yards, and one PAT by Cook made it 13-6 at halftime. Fullback Compton's 4th quarter dive put the final score at 19-6 and the team's record at 7-0-1.

Howe High School on the eastside opened in 1937. Its very first football city championship in 1959 seemed inevitable. At 8-0 they were ranked 5th in the State UPI and AP football polls. Only Washington High stood in the way.

According to those present, the practices for the Westsiders leading up to the Howe showdown were the worst days of preparation all season. Bookies, and there were many bets put on most high school games in Indianapolis in those days (coaches traditionally warned athletes to shy away from phone calls and personal inquiries from those with questionable reputation), made Howe the prohibitive favorite. The game was to be played on Tech High's field Friday, November 6.

On the way to the game Marion Baker demanded, "It's up to the defense. If they don't score, they can't win!" Howe star Darlan Billups had scored 110 points in eight games (and finished with 128 after Howe's tenth game with Scecina). So it seemed that the defensive side of the ball was where the Continentals needed to brace for action as the field temperature neared zero.

But it was the offense that took charge by scoring the first four times they had the ball in the first half. A five-play drive concluded with Corey crossing the goal line from the three immediately after his 50-yard run only a minute and 25 seconds into the game. A "crushing block by Compton" was reported by both the Star's Williams and the News' Fuson on Corey's TD run. Then Howe answered with their own drive to the Continental ten before Corey intercepted an errand pass. Howe's "double lonesome ends," which copied Earl Blaik's Army phenomena of 1958, didn't fool Washington. The subsequent 60-yard drive was bolstered by runs of over 20-yards by both Leeper and Compton. And Corey scored his second of three TDs making the score 13-0 after Cook's kick. In the second quarter Prince got hot completing passes to Snowberger and Leeper before scoring himself on a 22-yard run. Then Tom Taylor picked off another Howe aerial at the Hornets' 46 leading to a 35-yard gallop by Compton making it 26-0 at halftime.

In the third quarter Beliles picked off the third of four Washington interceptions at Howe's 32. Two plays later Prince lofted a 22-yard TD pass to Corey at 8:56 finalizing the 33-0 drubbing. The Continentals finished with 237 rushing yards while adding 127 passing yards with seven completions. Corey had nine runs for 117 yards and Compton tallied 60 yards in six carries.

Linebacker Beliles snatched the game ball at the final buzzer but had to surrender it to Coach Tofil minutes later on the bus. Howe needed it for week ten. But the bus driver was persuaded to circle the Pole Drive-in on the route home diverting from Washington St. to 16th St.

After the Sacred Heart game, over the final five games, the 1959 team scored 151 points while allowing only a first half touchdown by Anderson.

Only leader-quarterback Charlie Prince was named All-City in all three Indianapolis newspapers in the "old school" days when only eleven boys were so honored. Guard Bernie Wainscott and halfback Ken Corey were named first team in the Star while Wainscott and end Larry Glaze made the top eleven in the Times. By today's standards of naming 22 to 24 players the following Continentals would most certainly have been designated as All-City or All-Conference in the unquestioned top league in central Indiana at the time: fullback Larry Compton, tackle Jim Dill, and halfback Bob Leeper. Leeper scored seven touchdowns including three receiving TDs. Compton chaulked-up eight TDs including two kick-off returns of over 80-yards. Corey also tallied eight TDs including a 76-yard punt return while Prince threw six TD passes to go with his two running scores. And in the many biographies gathered by Glaze, Weldon Beliles at 140-pounds is consistently noted as the defensive middle linebacker and leader of the undefeated Continental eleven. Even then 26-year-old line coach Jerry Oliver noted that he was running a pass route on the Scout Team, week-nine, and was "absolutely killed by Weldon Beliles, our MLB.....I couldn't walk for a week." That fall was also when Greenfield's future Hall of Fame basketball man Dick Harmening was added to the football coaching staff.

The continuing camaraderie for many from the team of 1959 seems to exhibit the cliché that there is no I in team. And Coach Tofil's admonition in the News' preseason article seemed to sum up the year. "Let the others do the boasting. We'll do the playing."

Although Cathedral became the official City Champs with their subsequent 10-0 record, rumors that there would be a game between Washington and Cathedral was intriguing. With Coach Tofil's son, Gary, as a sophomore QB at Cathedral and with Cathedral's Coach Dezelan being a 1933 Washington High grad as well as friend of Coach Tofil the friendly rivals could logically have played, some thought. But the season ending contest with Manual would have needed to have been cancelled. Father Higgins, superintendent of Cathedral, was quoted by Jimmie Angelopolous as saying, "We had a tremendous gate last year because of Manual; we want to help Manual the same way this year." One wonders if the 40-0 loss in 1958 to Manual had helped someone's tongue to become placed in someone's cheek? In any event, the 1960 season saw Washington High adding Cathedral the tenth week of the season on the schedule a date which continued as a tradition through 1972. That '72 season ending game was rumored to be the very last Cathedral football game ever since their school was to close at year's end.

Many of the team members recalled two non-statistical things. One was the only pre-game meal at the Chicken Shack across from Municipal Gardens on Lafayette Road. The greasy chicken gravy sat heavily on their stomachs throughout the Homecoming game. Tiny Taylor, in particular, may have set an all-time chicken-gravy and biscuits eating record many noted. And, the atmosphere that those of that era experienced with freshmen coaches Johnny Williams and original head coach Henry Bogue will never be forgotten. Bogue's declaration "do you want this size 11 up your butt" might not be accepted in today's more liberal coaching methods but they were effective in the '50's.

Perhaps there were Continental backfields that were better. The T-formation city champs of 1944 led by Deem, Byfield, Hodges and Bauer or the single-wing '37 team with Carter, Kersey, Reed and McCalip or Butler, Weatherby, Branson and Smith in 1974 or Overstreet, Carpenter, Luter and Weeden in 1983 as well as the 1947 backfield that had good speed with unusual size in Reuter, Lipscombe, Lentz and Jent and the three speedsters from the '66 team named Highbaugh, Cannon and Thompson with Neely as their QB all of which had great chemistry as well as talent. But the 1959 backfield was a very well-rounded group. They combined the leadership of Prince, the versatility of Corey, the hard-running and blocking of Compton and the outside speed of Leeper to become one of Continentaland's greatest backfields ever on one of the best teams in the school's 68 year history.

VII.

Scores, Records & State Champions

WASHINGTON HIGH FOOTBALL 1927-1994

HENRY BOGUE (1927-1950)

1927			1928			1929		
0	KIRKLIN	20	41	LOGANSPORT	6	7	BLOOMINGTON	6
13	BRAZIL	38	0	KIRKLIN	6	6	TECH	12
6	CRAWF'LLE	26	19	KNIGHTST'N	6	13	KIRKLIN	0
6	FT.WAY.SO'H	58	6	CATHEDRAL	31	34	MANUAL	0
7	NOBLES'LLE	26	25	WESTFIELD	7	27	BROAD RIPPLE	13
6	CARMEL	6	13	CRAWF'LLE	7	32	JEFFERS'LLE	0
0	LEBANON	20	46	LEBANON	0	27	RENNES'LEAR	12
6	BOYS PREP	18	29	GREENFIELD	0	0	SHORTRIDGE	8
			13	SHERIDAN	20	13	GREENFIELD	0
						6	SHERIDAN	7
						39	CATHEDRAL	0

(AD Bruce Morrison
coached first game)

	Record	0-7-1		Record	6-3		Record	8-3
	Pts.	44-212		Pts.	192-83		Pts.	204-58

1930			1931			1932		
13	SOUTHPORT	0	33	SOUTHPORT	0	104	CARMEL	0
0	CATHEDRAL	6	6	CARMEL	0	21	KIRKLIN	0
27	KIRKLIN	6	13	KIRKLIN	6	13	MARION	13
27	MANUAL	0	0	MANUAL	14	26	MANUAL	0
6	BLOOM'TON	6	20	HAM'T'N(OH.)	0	7	LIBBY(TOL.OH.)	30
12	SHORTRIDGE	7	69	NOBL'SV'LLE	0	27	SOUTHPORT	0
41	BR.RIPPLE	0	40	SHORTRIDGE	6	7	SHORTRIDGE	0
14	SHERIDAN	12	63	SHERIDAN	0	40	SHERIDAN	0
14	TECH	0	46	BR. RIPPLE	6	25	TECH	7
0	ELKHART	33	14	TECH	13			

	Record	7-2-1		Record	9-1		Record	7-1-1
	Pts.	154-70		Pts.	304-54		Pts.	270-50

1933

14	MARION	0
2	BLOOM'NTON	7
0	SOUTHPORT	27
27	SHELBYVILLE	0
0	SHORTRIDGE	7
14	SHERIDAN	0
7	TECH	6
7	MANUAL	0

Record: 5-3
Points: 71-47

1934

13	BLOOM'NTON	13
6	SHELBYVILLE	0
27	CATHEDRAL	0
0	SOUTHPORT	0
15	SHORTRIDGE	0
13	ELWOOD	7
14	TECH	7
0	MANUAL	0

Record: 5-0-3
Points: 88-27

1935

16	BLOOM'NTON	2
7	SHELBYVILLE	0
6	CATHEDRAL	38
13	SOUTHPORT	35
6	SHORTRIDGE	27
7	KIRKLIN	26
0	TECH	13
7	MANUAL	0

Record: 3-5
Points: 62-141

1936

45	BLOOM'TON	0
33	SHELBYVILLE	0
28	CATHEDRAL	0
0	SOUTHPORT	0
14	SHORTRIDGE	12
44	KIRKLIN	0
0	TECH	7
26	MANUAL	0

Record: 6-1-1
Points: 190-19

1937

40	KIRKLIN	0
40	SHELBYVILLE	0
12	CATHEDRAL	0
13	SOUTHPORT	7
6	SHORTRIDGE	12
21	CRAWF'DV'LE	0
21	TECH	19
45	MANUAL	0

Record: 7-1
Points: 198-38

1938

48	KIRKLIN	0
26	SHELBYVILLE	6
6	CATHEDRAL	12
7	SOUTHPORT	13
6	SHORTRIDGE	23
12	CRAWF'DV'LE	0
0	TECH	23
12	MANUAL	6

Record: 4-4
Points: 117-83

1939

33	RUSHVILLE	6
27	SHELBYVILLE	7
13	CATHEDRAL	0
7	SOUTHPORT	13
0	SHORTRIDGE	6
34	CONNERSVILLE	0
13	TECH	13
46	MANUAL	0

Record: 5-2-1
Points: 173-45

1940

20	RUSHVILLE	20
13	SHELBYVILLE	0
40	MANUAL	0
47	SOUTHPORT	0
0	SHORTRIDGE	6
0	T.H.GERSTM'R	12
0	TECH	0
0	CATHEDRAL	13

Record: 3-3-2
Points: 120-51

1941

20	NEWPORT,KY.	0
22	SHELBYVILLE	6
13	MANUAL	0
13	SOUTHPORT	7
12	MISHAWAKA	13
27	T.H.GERSTM'R	2
6	TECH	7
39	CATHEDRAL	0

Record: 6-2
Points: 152-35

1942

0	MISHAWAKA	19
46	SHELBYVILLE	0
0	MANUAL	7
13	HAMILTON,OH.	25
0	SHORTRIDGE	19
6	SOUTHPORT	6
0	T.H.GERSTM'R	0
13	TECH	0
13	CATHEDRAL	7

Record: 3-4-2
Points: 91-83

1943

0	W.LAFAY'E	38
18	WARREN CEN.	0
6	MANUAL	6
6	CATHEDRAL	19
0	SHORTRIDGE	27
45	SOUTHPORT	0
0	MANUAL	19
6	TECH	14
6	CATHEDRAL	7

Record: 2-6-1
Points: 87-130

1944

26	W.LAFAY'E	6
27	WARREN CEN.	0
6	MANUAL	6
7	SHORTRIDGE	0
59	WESTFIELD	0
33	SOUTHPORT	0
0	CLINTON	25
6	TECH	0
6	CATHEDRAL	0

Record: 7-1-1
Points: 170-37

1945

14	W.LAFAY'E	18
7	WARREN CENT.	28
6	MANUAL	7
6	SHORTRIDGE	9
7	EVANS.REITZ	26
12	SOUTHPORT	28
20	CLINTON	7
25	TECH	18
20	CATHEDRAL	38

Record: 2-7
Points: 117-179

1946

6	W.LAFAY'E	6
38	WARREN CEN.	0
13	MANUAL	6
7	SHORTRIDGE	7
14	EVANS.REITZ	32
14	SOUTHPORT	0
7	T.H.GERSTM'R	25
0	TECH	19
0	CATHEDRAL	20

Record: 3-4-2
Points: 99-115

1947

24	W.LAFAY'E	13
6	SO.BEND C.	24
33	MANUAL	0
13	SHORTR'GE	13
0	EV.REITZ	20
34	SOUTHPORT	0
13	HOWE	0
7	TECH	0
7	CATHEDR.	13

Record: 5-3-1
Points: 137-83

1948

6	CATHEDRAL	21
6	W.LAFAYETTE	14
6	MANUAL	0
14	SO.BEND CENT.	44
6	BROAD RIPPLE	20
13	EVANS. REITZ	38
0	SHORTRIDGE	26
20	SOUTHPORT	7
6	HOWE	14

Record: 2-7
Points: 77-184

1949

7	CATHEDRAL	7
0	MANUAL	12
6	W.LAFAY'E	21
14	T.H. WILEY	28
7	BROAD RIPPLE	6
7	SHORTRIDGE	14
13	T.H. GERSTM'R	12
14	HOWE	6
20	TECH	20

Record: 3-4-2
Points: 88-126

1950

7	NEW ALBANY	6
0	CATHEDRAL	7
12	MANUAL	19
13	W.LAFAY'E	20
19	T.H.WILEY	16
0	BR. RIPPLE	24
7	SHORTR'GE	13
25	T.H.GERSTM.	25
7	HOWE	13
0	TECH	25

Record: 2-7-1
Points: 90-168

Head Coach JOE TOFIL (1951-1961)

1951			1952			1953		
7	CATHEDRAL	19	6	CATHEDRAL	24	7	BRAZIL	0
27	MANUAL	0	6	MANUAL	7	33	MANUAL	6
0	SHORTRIDGE	20	6	SHORTRIDGE	25	20	SHORTRIDGE	7
14	T.H. WILEY	16	6	T.H. WILEY	24	0	SACRED H'RT	0
7	W. LAFAYETTE	0	12	W. LAFAYETTE	14	12	W. LAFAY.	0
7	BROAD RIPPLE	12	18	BROAD RIPPLE	0	25	BR. RIPPLE	0
6	T.H. GERSTMEYER	20	12	T.H. GERSTM'R	0	6	BEN DAVIS	20
0	TECH	25	6	TECH	34	6	TECH	7
0	HOWE	20	0	HOWE	26	13	HOWE	6

Record: 2-7	Record: 2-7	Record: 6-2-1
Points: 68-187	Points: 72-154	Points: 122-46

1954			1955			1956		
27	BRAZIL	6	14	BRAZIL	0	20	BRAZIL	6
13	MANUAL	0	0	MANUAL	0	0	MANUAL	0
19	SHORTRIDGE	19	7	SHORTRIDGE	7	13	SHORTR'GE	14
6	SACRED HEART	7	20	SAC. HEART	13	7	SAC. HEART	20
20	W. LAFAYETTE	7	7	W. LAFAYETTE	7	13	W. LAFAY'E	7
7	BROAD RIPPLE	7	7	BROAD RIPPLE	13	13	BR. RIPPLE	14
34	BEN DAVIS	7	13	BEN DAVIS	7	33	BEN DAVIS	6
21	TECH	6	6	TECH	7	20	TECH	33
14	HOWE	28	12	HOWE	0	32	HOWE	6

Record: 5-2-2	Record: 4-2-3	Record: 4-4-1
Points: 161-87	Points: 86-54	Points: 151-106

1957			1958			1959		
12	MANUAL	0	13	EAST CHICAGO	34	20	NOBLESV'E	19
14	SHORTRIDGE	6	0	MANUAL	55	27	MANUAL	18
31	SACRED HEART	12	6	SHORTRIDGE	0	20	SHORTR'E	19
7	SCECINA	6	28	SACRED HEART	7	7	SAC. HEART	7
7	BROAD RIPPLE	26	7	SCECINA	13	39	SCECINA	0
53	BEN DAVIS	14	12	BROAD RIPPLE	35	20	BR. RIPPLE	0
13	TECH	21	6	BEN DAVIS	0	40	BEN DAVIS	0
35	HOWE	7	27	BROWNSBURG	6	19	ANDERSON	6
			18	HOWE	25	33	HOWE	0
			12	TECH	35			

Record: 6-2	Record: 4-6	Record: 8-0-1
Points: 172-92	Points: 129-210	Points: 225-69

1960			1961		
26	NOBLESVILLE	14	18	COLUMBUS	7
20	MANUAL	14	0	MANUAL	21
14	SHORTRIDGE	6	6	SHORTRIDGE	6
13	SACRED HEART	34	7	SACRED HEART	27
19	SCECINA	7	12	SCECINA	24
12	BROAD RIPPLE	14	18	BROAD RIPPLE	40
26	BEN DAVIS	6	31	BEN DAVIS	7
14	ANDERSON	18	13	ANDERSON	33
0	HOWE	0	27	HOWE	33
14	CATHEDRAL	19	0	CATHEDRAL	36

Record: 5-4-1
Points: 158-132

Record: 2-7-1
Points: 132-234

Head Coach BOB SPRINGER (1962-1993)

1962			1963			1964		
26	COLUMBUS	7	19	COLUMBUS	14	40	COLUMBUS	6
13	MANUAL	13	13	MANUAL	6	20	MANUAL	7
13	SHORTRIDGE	7	20	SHORTRIDGE	7	21	ELKHART	27
14	SACRED HEART	13	0	SACRED HEART	7	6	SOUTHPORT	41
13	SCECINA	39	12	SCECINA	59	7	SCECINA	27
6	BROAD RIPPLE	14	27	BROAD RIPPLE	19	19	BR. RIPPLE	14
35	BEN DAVIS	0	31	BEN DAVIS	12	20	BEN DAVIS	27
12	TECH	20	0	TECH	28	14	TECH	13
49	HOWE	20	13	HOWE	6	19	HOWE	0
13	CATHEDRAL	13	0	CATHEDRAL	20	0	CATHEDRAL	7

Record: 5-3-2
Points: 194-146

Record: 6-4
Points: 135-178

Record: 5-5
Points: 166-169

1965			1966			1967		
13	COLUMBUS	13	40	COLUMBUS	18	6	COLUMBUS	6
6	MANUAL	27	33	MANUAL	13	33	MANUAL	12
33	CLARKS.PROVID.	7	31	ATTUCKS	7	22	ATTUCKS	0
14	SOUTHPORT	6	19	SOUTHPORT	0	34	SOUTHPORT	7
25	SCECINA	22	27	SCECINA	0	27	SCECINA	20
7	BROAD RIPPLE	25	28	BROAD RIPPLE	20	34	BR. RIPPLE	13
27	BEN DAVIS	7	34	BEN DAVIS	0	20	BEN DAVIS	26
0	TECH	14	46	TECH	6	27	TECH	7
6	HOWE	7	34	HOWE	0	7	HOWE	14
13	CATHEDRAL	13	32	CATHEDRAL	17	40	CATHEDRAL	6

Record: 5-4-1
Points: 144-140

Record: 10-0
Points: 324-81

Record: 7-2-1
Points: 250-111

1968

35	COLUMBUS	21
39	MANUAL	7
51	ATTUCKS	7
53	SOUTHPORT	12
20	SCECINA	12
14	BROAD RIPPLE	7
34	BEN DAVIS	6
34	NORTHWEST	6
41	HOWE	6
7	CATHEDRAL	20

Record: 9-1
Points: 328-103

1969

14	COLUMBUS	25
12	MANUAL	6
42	ATTUCKS	18
28	SOUTHPORT	22
20	SCECINA	18
6	BR. RIPPLE	14
14	BEN DAVIS	20
26	NORTHWEST	12
0	HOWE	12
16	CATHEDRAL	26

Record: 5-5
Points: 178-173

1970

30	COLUMBUS	0
16	MANUAL	32
26	ATTUCKS	0
14	SOUTHPORT	14
22	SCECINA	7
28	RIPPLE	6
6	BEN DAVIS	12
34	NORTHWEST	0
48	HOWE	18
2	CATHEDRAL	6

Record: 6-3-1
Points: 226-95

1971

19	COLUMBUS	0
24	MANUAL	0
37	ATTUCKS	0
35	SOUTHPORT	7
37	SCECINA	14
42	BROAD RIPPLE	0
10	BEN DAVIS	13
48	NORTHWEST	6
36	HOWE	6
32	CATHEDRAL	0

Record: 9-1
Points: 320-46

1972

50	COLUMBUS	6
52	MANUAL	18
44	ATTUCKS	0
30	SOUTHPORT	0
32	SCECINA	0
20	BROAD RIPPLE	2
44	BEN DAVIS	6
44	NORTHWEST	0
20	HOWE	8
14	CATHEDRAL	20

Record: 9-1
Points: 350-60

1973

0	CATHEDRAL	5
48	ATTUCKS	0
36	MANUAL	0
14	SHORTR'GE	15
28	SOUTHPORT	21
62	RITTER	28
46	WOOD	16
40	BEN DAVIS	0
14	NORTHWEST	7
28	RONCALLI	0

Record: 8-2
Points: 316-92

1974

26	CATHEDRAL	0
40	ATTUCKS	7
40	MANUAL	12
40	SHORTRIDGE	6
33	SOUTHPORT	8
50	RITTER	12
56	WOOD	0
45	BEN DAVIS	6
27	NORTHWEST	7
32	RONCALLI	0

AAA Playoffs

21	RICHMOND	14
19	MISHAWAKA	12

Record: 12-0   Pts. 429-84

1975

18	HOWE	7
36	ATTUCKS	18
28	MANUAL	8
32	SCECINA	12
22	SOUTHPORT	8
34	TECH	6
12	CATHEDRAL	28
14	BEN DAVIS	23
6	NORTHWEST	21
6	RONCALLI	32

Record: 6-4
Points: 208-163

1976

20	HOWE	7
27	ATTUCKS	0
14	MANUAL	7
12	SCECINA	7
15	SOUTHPORT	7
24	TECH	0
14	CATHEDRAL	28
6	BEN DAVIS	13
0	NORTHWEST	7
21	RONCALLI	35

Record: 6-4
Points: 153-111

1977

0	SHORTRIDGE	6
46	ATTUCKS	14
14	CHATARD (OT)	13
14	NORTHWEST	7
28	SOUTHPORT	7
26	BROAD RIPPLE	0
2	RONCALLI	0
8	BEN DAVIS	24
12	MARSHALL	20
12	CATHEDRAL	15

Record: 6-4
Points: 162-106

1978

39	SHORTRIDGE	0
18	ATTUCKS	0
6	CHATARD	7
16	NORTHWEST	8
6	SOUTHPORT	0
42	BROAD RIPPLE	6
12	RONCALLI	21
8	BEN DAVIS	35
8	MARSHALL	14
32	CATHEDRAL	7

Record: 6-4
Points: 187-98

1979

32	ATTUCKS	0
14	NORTHW'T	41
46	ARLINGTON	0
40	CATHEDRAL	22
20	SOUTHPORT	21
26	MANUAL	22
6	BR. RIPPLE	21
22	BEN DAVIS	28
8	RONC'LLI(OT)	7
12	HOWE	6

Record: 6-4
Points: 226-168

1980

50	ATTUCKS	8
8	NORTHWEST	14
28	ARLINGTON	0
24	CATHEDRAL	0
16	SOUTHPORT	8
6	MANUAL	13
36	BROAD RIPPLE	20
30	BEN DAVIS	14
6	RONCALLI	27
52	HOWE	16

Record: 7-3
Points: 256-120

1981

12	BLOOM. SOUTH	6
14	NORTHWEST	0
42	ATTUCKS	0
44	TECH	12
24	SCECINA	28
20	MANUAL	14
46	ARLINGTON	14
14	LAW. CENT. (OT)	11
8	MARSHALL	24
28	HOWE	12

Record: 8-2
Points: 252-121

1982

44	BLOOM. SO.	7
14	NORTHWEST	29
34	ATTUCKS	0
32	TECH	6
32	SCECINA	10
18	MANUAL	22
14	ARLINGTON	27
30	LAW. CENT.	0
22	MARSHALL	14
8	HOWE	0

Record: 7-3
Points: 248-115

1983

58	BLOOM. NORTH	0
34	BROAD RIPPLE	8
8	DECATUR CENT.	0
28	MANUAL	14
38	TECH	0
48	ATTUCKS	0
28	BEN DAVIS	6
32	HOWE	2
22	NORTHWEST	0
36	ARLINGTON	0
32	LAW.NORTH	9
30	NORTH CENT.	3
22	BLOOM. SOUTH	0
14	MISHAWAKA PENN	25

Record: 13-1   Points: 430-67

1984

30	BLOOM. NORTH	7
2	DECATUR CENT.	6
44	MANUAL	0
16	TECH	3
54	ATTUCKS	3
18	BEN DAVIS	11
12	HOWE	3
20	NORTHWEST	12
38	ARLINGTON	6
32	BROAD RIPPLE	7
18	WARREN CENT.	20

Record: 9-2
Points: 284-78

1985

34	HOWE	20
5	NORTHWEST	0
44	ARLINGTON	6
31	TECH	0
50	ATTUCKS	0
17	RONCALLI	35
7	BEN DAVIS	0
35	MANUAL	0

Play-offs
| 9 | BROWNSB'G | 22 |

Record: 7-2
Points: 232-83

1986			1987			1988		
6	HOWE	7	12	HOWE	13	22	HOWE	25
6	NORTHWEST	0	16	NORTHWEST	8	37	N'THWEST	0
20	MANUAL	7	20	MANUAL	27	35	MANUAL	7
30	TECH	6	8	ARLINGTON	30	26	ARL'GTON	7
6	ARLINGTON (2OT)	12	14	TECH	0	36	TECH	6
6	RONCALLI	14	0	BROWNSBURG	19	13	BROWNSB.	6
0	BEN DAVIS	13	0	BEN DAVIS	28	14	BEN DAVIS	35
12	BROAD RIPPLE	7	20	BREBEUF	12	44	BREBEUF	15
	Play-offs							
16	DECATUR CENT.	0	0	PERRY MERID.	9	33	SOUTHPORT	34
14	AVON	13	14	BROWNSBURG	11	14	CHATARD	28
	Record: 7-5			Record: 3-6			Record: 6-3	
	Points: 144-118			Points: 90-137			Points: 227-101	

1989			1990			1991		
22	COLUMBUS NOR.	20	14	COL. NORTH	0	24	HOWE	14
12	NORTHWEST	0	34	NORTHWEST	0	38	NORTHWEST	0
18	SCECINA	0	12	SCECINA	15	14	CATHEDRAL	0
30	BR. RIPPLE (OT)	24	6	BROAD RIPPLE	20	27	BR. RIPPLE	13
28	TECH	6	14	TECH	24	6	RONCALLI	14
16	RONCALLI	14	6	RONCALLI	21	38	TECH	0
40	ARLINGTON	21	12	ARLINGTON	24	41	ARLINGTON	0
30	MANUAL	0	14	MANUAL	28	28	MANUAL	0
	Play-offs		8	TECH	16	27	BR'NSBURG	19
26	CARMEL	28				20	LAF.H'RISON	13
						18	AVON	21
	Record: 8-1			Record: 2-7			Record: 9-2	
	Points: 196-85			Points: 120-148			Points: 281-94	

1992			1993			1994 Head Coach Myron Newland		
29	HOWE	27	55	HOWE	13	27	HOWE	0
35	NORTHW'T	0	35	NOR'WEST	0	35	NORTHWEST	32
0	CATHEDRAL	16	17	CATHEDRAL	14	0	CATHEDRAL	36
22	BR.RIPPLE	28	26	BR.RIPPLE	0	33	BR. RIPPLE	14
14	RONCALLI	35	12	RONCALLI	24	6	RONCALLI	21
35	TECH	0	52	TECH	12	13	TECH	12
42	ARLINGTON	6	44	ARL'GTON	0	20	ARLINGTON	6
39	MANUAL	6	41	MANUAL	21	50	MANUAL	12
28	LEBANON	13	54	GR'NWOOD	7	39	MOORESV'E	27
12	LAF.HARRISON	13	30	MANUAL	0	26	FRANKLIN	18
	Record 6-4		42	GR'NFIELD	7	27	GR'NF'D CEN.	20
	Points: 256-144		21	CATHEDRAL	16	20	McCUTCHEON	19
			0	EAST CENTR.	7	15	EAST CENTR.	56
				Record: 11-2 Pts. 429-121			Record: 10-3 Pts 311-273	

some notable Assistant Coaches over the years:

FRANK LUZAR	CURLY JULIAN	GARY BROWN
JOE TOFIL	HENRY BOGUE	JAMES SHOCKLEY
JOHNNY WILLIAMS	GARY BAKER	BILL SPRINGER
FRANK MUNSHOWER	JOHN HAYNES	JIM PHILLIPS
BILL PERRY	JOE SHIRES	
TOM ROSENBERGER	RALPH POEHLS	
EDDIE BOPP	CARL SHORT	
MYRON NEWLAND	JOHN BRADLEY	
WALT STAHLHUT	LEONARD CANNON	
TONY BURCHETT	BRUCE HAMMOND	
JERRY OLIVER	GENE ROBERTSON	
VASCO WALTON	JERRY ENGLAND	
DICK HARMENING	HOWARD LEEDY	
LEO ROSASCO	CLIFF SEDAM	
DAVID EASTON		

Coach Bogue	24 seasons	110-81-20	.576
Coach Tofil	11 seasons	48-43-10	.527
Coach Springer	32 seasons	227-94-5	.707
Coach Newland	1 season	10-3	.769

overall:	68 seasons	395-221-35	.607
	651 games	48 winning seasons/15 losing seasons/5 even	

For both football & basketball every yearbook did not have all relevant information. Some didn't even have player picture names. Most had All-City players and the "City Champs." But others did not mention any specifics. At least by 1961 the Downtown Kiwanis Club requested an official MVP in football through the 1980's. Thus, the 20 "consultants" that I talked with over two weeks (see their names on the basketball history document) helped me with my consensus choices.

One interesting point is that our school's 48 game record against Cathedral can be broken down like this: against non-Joe Dezelan coached teams we were 15-14. Joe Dezelan, of course, was a star tackle on our school's 1932 City Championship team who grew up in Haughville. Coach Dezelan was 13-3-3 coaching against his alma mater.

CITY CHAMPS, CO-CHAMPS & IPSAC CHAMPS:
1930	1932	1934	1936	1939	1944	1959	1966
1971	1974	1983	1984	1985	1989	1991	1993

MYTHICAL STATE CHAMPS---1966
STATE TOURNAMENT CHAMPS---1974 STATE RUNNER-UP---1983

Most Valuable or Most Outstanding Football Players 1927-1994:

1927 PHIL BAYT
1928 PHIL BAYT-JIM CARTER
1929 JIM EMERSON CARTER
1930 GARLAND BURRIS-
     EMIL UNSER-FRANK LUZAR
1931 NORMAN LONG-H. CHERRY
1932 HARRY CHERRY-JOE DEZELAN-
     CLIFF BAUMBACH
1933 HARRY CHERRY-HOP HOWARD
1934 ALEX YAVONOVICH
1935 BOB FLACK-DON JAYNES
1936 RICHARD POTTENGER-
     MARION "RED" CARTER
1937 RED CARTER-BOB KERSEY
1938 BOB McCALIP
1939 KENNY JAYNES-
     BABE DIMANCHEFF
1940 BILL KEERS-DANNY ROTH
1941 CLIFF LANDRY-DON MARIS
1942 LOWELL SCOTTEN-
     MAX HUTTON
1943 CARTER BYFIELD-
     FRANK HINES
1944 BILL DEEM
1945 JIM CLEVENGER-GUY FISH
1946 BOB WOLFLA
1947 BOB TILLERY-BOB TRINKLE
1948 CARL BARNES
1949 MIKE PURICHIA
1950 JIM PETERCHEFF-BILL COOK
1951 REX DURRETT-
     EDDIE KERNODLE
1952 PHIL PETERSON-TOM FIGG
1953 DAVE PORTEN-DICK LAHR
1954 BILL PURICHIA
1955 CARL RAGLAND
1956 DAVE SANDERS-
     CAROL PURICHIA
1957 DAVE SANDERS-BILL GREEN
1958 LARRY COMPTON-
     BERNIE WAINSCOTT
1959 LARRY GLAZE-
     CHARLIE PRINCE-
     WELDON BELILES
1960 DICK BOARMAN-KEN COREY-
     BOB LEEPER

1961 DENNY TROTH-
     JERRY SANDERS
1962 MALCOLM MARLOW-
     JERRY SANDERS
1963 EDDIE BOPP-MIKE HIGHBAUGH
1964 EDDIE BOPP-BILLY APPLE
1965 LARRY HIGHBAUGH-R.THOMPSON
1966 L. HIGHBAUGH-BOB CANADY
1967 LEN CANNON-BOB JONES
1968 GEORGE McGINNIS-LOUIE DAY
1969 STEVE STANFIELD-E. BOSWELL
1970 EDDIE BOSWELL-T. BURCHETT
1971 BRUCE SMITH-
     MARCUS AVERITTE
1972 RONNIE HAYES-DON MALLORY
1973 BOB HICKS-ROCKY DEAKIN
1974 KEVIN WEATHERBY-
     EARL BRANSON-
     DANNY BUTLER
1975 RICKY SMITH
1976 FRANKIE COLE-
     DONNIE HARRIS
1977 JEFF COLE-
     TOM RAMIREZ
1978 KERRY NOBLE
1979 TRACY WINSTON
1980 CURTIS KIMBROUGH
1981 LAVELL POWE-BOBBY WILSON
1982 IVAN BOWENS-JOHN DISHMAN
1983 JIM OVERSTREET-
     HARVEY STORMS-
     CALVIN FITZGERALD
1984 TONY WEEDEN-KENNY WEBB
1985 LAWRENCE TURNER-
     MARK BROWN
1986 JAMES MILLER-RICKY HOLT
1987 MARK BRAY
1988 LAMONTE DEAN-STEVE SCOTT
1989 LAMONTE DEAN-
     MONTERRIO HOLDER
1990 ELI RASHEED
1991 TED DERRICOTE
1992 ADRIAN CRENSHAW-
     BOB JONES
1993 QUINTIN DAVIS
1994 JACK OWENS

Records against City/County/some notable teams for each era:

Bogue Years:

vs. Tech	10-8-3	vs. Southport	11-5-3
vs. Broad Ripple	4-2	vs. Warren Central	3-1
vs. Shortridge	6-13-2	vs. Noblesville	1-1
vs. Manual	14-5-3	vs. Carmel	2-0-1
vs. Howe	2-2	vs. Bloomington	3-1-2
vs. Cathedral	8-11-1	vs. Sheridan	4-2
vs. West Lafayette	2-5-1	vs. T.H. Gerstmeyer	2-2-2
vs. Shelbyville	10-0	vs. Kirklin (Ohio)	7-3

Tofil Years:

vs. Tech	1-7	vs. Scecina	3-2
vs. Broad Ripple	3-7-1	vs. Sacred Heart	3-4-2
vs. Shortridge	5-3-3	vs. Ben Davis	8-1
vs. Manual	6-3-2	vs. Noblesville	2-0
vs. Howe	5-5-1	vs. Brazil	4-0
vs. Cathedral	0-4	vs. West Lafayette	4-1-1

Springer Years:

vs. Tech	17-5	vs. Marshall	1-3
vs. Broad Ripple	17-6	vs. Chatard	1-2
vs. Shortridge	4-2	vs. Roncalli	5-10
vs. Manual	24-6-1	vs. Wood	2-0
vs. Howe	20-6	vs. Bloomington So.	3-0
vs. Cathedral	10-11-2	vs. Law. Central	2-0
vs. Arlington	11-4	vs. Law. North	1-0
vs. Northwest	20-5	vs. Bloomington No.	2-0
vs. Attucks	20-0	vs. Decatur Central	2-1
vs. Scecina	12-5	vs. North Central	1-0
vs. Sacred Heart	1-1	vs. Brownsburg	3-2
vs. Ritter	2-0	vs. Avon	1-1
vs. Ben Davis	12-13	vs. Warren Central	0-1
vs. Southport	14-3-1	vs. Brebeuf	2-0
vs. Columbus	10-1-2	vs. Carmel	0-1
		vs. Perry Meridian	0-1

Newland Years: see scores for 1994

over 68 years

vs. Tech	28-20	vs. Broad Ripple	24-15-1	vs. Howe	27-13-1
vs. Shortridge	15-18-5	vs. Manual	44-14-6	vs. Carmel	2-1-1
vs. Cathedral	18-27-3	vs. Bloomington*	8-1-2	vs. Southport	25-8-4
vs. Warren C.	3-2	vs. Noblesville	3-1	vs. Sheridan	4-2
vs. Scecina	14-7	vs. Ben Davis	20-14	vs. Northwest	20-5
vs. Arlington	11-4	vs. Columbus	11-1-2	vs. Ritter	2-0
vs. Attucks	20-0	vs. Marshall	1-3	vs. Chatard	1-2
vs. Wood	2-0	vs. Lawrence*	3-0	vs. W. Lafayette	6-6-2
vs. Brazil	5-0	vs. Sacred Heart-Roncalli	9-15-2	vs. T.H.Gerstmeyer	3-3-2

TEAM OFFENSIVE POINTS & TEAM DEFENSIVE POINTS (Fewest)
1927-1994

Overall Points Scored

1.	430	(1983)	14 games
2.	429	(1974)	12 games
3.	429	(1993)	13 games
4.	350	(1972)	
5.	328	(1968)	
6.	324	(1966)	
7.	320	(1971)	
8.	316	(1973)	
9.	311	(1994)	13 games
10.	304	(1931)	9 games
11.	284	(1984)	11 games
12.	281	(1991)	11 games
13.	270	(1932)	9 games
14.	256	(1980)	
15.	256	(1992)	
16.	252	(1981)	
17.	250	(1967)	
18.	248	(1982)	

Points in FIRST TEN games
(Circa. 1960 Washington's regular season schedule was normally 10 games. From 1985 until the 1994 closing, the "regular season" consisted of 8 games followed by the tourney.)

1.	389	(1974)	
2.	366	(1993)	
3.	350	(1972)	
4.	332	(1983)	
5.	328	(1968)	
6.	324	(1966)	
7.	320	(1971)	
8.	316	(1973)	
9.	304	(1931)	
10.	270	(1932)	9 games
11.	266	(1984)	
12.	263	(1991)	
13.	256	(1980)	
14.	256	(1992)	
15.	252	(1981)	
16.	250	(1967)	
17.	249	(1994)	
18.	248	(1982)	

Fewest Pts. Allowed overall

1.	19	(1936)	8 games
2.	35	(1941)	8 games
3.	37	(1944)	9 games
4.	38	(1937)	8 games
5.	45	(1939)	8 games
6.	46	(1971)	10 games
7.	46	(1953)	9 games
8.	47	(1933)	8 games
9.	50	(1932)	9 games
10.	54	(1931)	10 games
11.	58	(1929)	11games
12.	60	(1972)	10 games
13.	67	(1983)	14 games
14.	69	(1959)	9 games

Fewest Points in first 10 games

1.	30	(1983)
2.	46	(1971)
3.	54	(1931)
4.	58	(1929)
5.	58	(1974)
6.	60	(1972)
7.	73	(1991)
8.	81	(1966)
9.	91	(1993)
10.	92	(1973)
11.	95	(1970)

Regular Season Winning Streaks with losses at both ends of streaks

1973-1975	22 games	Shortridge	Cathedral
1965-1967	17 games	Howe	Ben Davis
1982-1984	14 games	Arlington	Decatur
1984-1985	13 games	Decatur	Roncalli
1971-1972	12 games	Ben Davis	Cathedral
1988-1990	11 games	Ben Davis	Scecina
1967-1968	10 games	Howe	Cathedral
1931-1932	10 games	Manual	Libby-Toledo, Ohio

1973-1975	24 games through State Championship (two play-off wins)
1982-1983	16 games through State Runners-up (three play-off wins)

Undefeated Teams

1934	5-0-3	Bogue
1959	8-0-1	Tofil
1966	10-0	Springer
1974	12-0	Springer

Most wins   1983   13   Springer

INDIANAPOLIS WASHINGTON BASKETBALL----1928-1995

Head Coach ROWLAND JONES 1928-1948 (20 seasons) (four City Champs
one Sectional Champs)

1928-29	10-12		1938-39	8-14	
1929-30	10-14		1939-40	13-7	
1930-31	4-17		1940-41	1-17	
1931-32	17-7		1941-42	15-8	City Champs
1932-33	12-4		1942-43	13-7	
1933-34	8-8		1943-44	2-17	
1934-35	13-5	City Champs	1944-45	3-15	
1935-36	7-9		1945-46	14-9	
1936-37	19-3	City Champs	1946-47	9-12	
1937-38	12-10	City Champs	1947-48	14-7	*

Head Coach DAVE HINE   1948-1960 (12 seasons) (one City Champs)

1948-49	8-12	City Champs	1954-55	11-7	
1949-50	9-11		1955-56	12-8	
1950-51	11-9		1956-57	7-13	
1951-52	9-12		1957-58	7-12	
1952-53	14-7		1958-59	11-8	
1953-54	10-11		1959-60	10-9	

Head Coach JERRY OLIVER 1960-1968 (8 seasons) (four City Champs, two Sectionals
& one State Champs)

1960-61	10-11		1964-65	29-2	City Champs****
1961-62	21-3		1965-66	19-2	
1962-63	19-4	City Champs	1966-67	16-7	
1963-64	23-2	City Champs	1967-68	24-3	City Champs *

Head Coach BILL GREEN   1968-1970 (2 seasons) (one State Champs)

1968-69	31-0	City Champs****	1969-70	8-14

Head Coach BASIL SFREDDO 1970-1989 (19 seasons) (one City Champs & five Sectional Champs)

1970-71	17-6		1980-81	16-6	
1971-72	14-9		1981-82	19-5	*
1972-73	15-6		1982-83	9-13	
1973-74	16-8		1983-84	5-14	
1974-75	17-8	**	1984-85	5-15	
1975-76	14-9		1985-86	7-15	
1976-77	11-14	*	1986-87	5-15	
1977-78	19-5	City Champs	1987-88	2-18	
1978-79	15-8	*	1988-89	1-19	
1979-80	15-10	*			

Head Coach JOE PEARSON 1989-1995 (6 seasons) (one Sectional Champs)

1989-90	7-13		1992-93	10-11	
1990-91	4-16		1993-94	20-3	City Champs
1991-92	5-17		1994-95	24-2	City Champs *

* Sectional Champions   **Sectional & Regional Champions
****Sectional, Regional, Semi-State & State Champions

1000 Point Club

1. GEORGE McGINNIS   2070   (1969)
2. JOHH WILLIAMS   1456   (1982)
3. MARVIN WINKLER   1132   (1966)
4. RALPH TAYLOR   1116   (1965)
5. DOUG WHITE   1029   (1976)
6. STEVE DOWNING   1026   (1969)
7. DONNIE McCOY   1004   (1979)

1000 Rebound Club

1. GEORGE McGINNIS   1589
2. RALPH TAYLOR   1085
3. STEVE DOWNING   1077

notable Assistant Coaches over the years:

JERRY OLIVER	RUSSELL McCONNELL	FRANK LUZAR
DICK HARMENING	HOWARD LEEDY	JOHNNY WILLIAMS
EDDIE BOPP	JOE PEARSON	BRAD GOFFINETT
BILL GREEN	BASIL SFREDDO	JOE ELLIOTT
VASCO WALTON	RALPH TAYLOR	RICHARD HEDGES
CARL SHORT	CURLY JULIAN	
AMOS SLATON	DAVE HINE	
LEO ROSASCO	DAVID DONALD	
JAMES RILEY	BILL PERRY	

Coaching Records:

ROWLAND JONES   204-202   .502
20 Seasons   4 City Champs   1 Sectional
ten winning seasons/nine losing seasons

DAVE HINE   119-119   .500
12 Seasons   1 City Champ
six winning seasons/six losing seasons

JERRY OLIVER   161-34   .826
8 Seasons   4 City Champs   2 Sectional
1 Regional   1 Semi-State   1 State
seven winning seasons/one losing season

BILL GREEN   39-14   .736
2 Seasons   1 City Champ   1 Sectional
1 Regional   1 Semi-State   1 State
one winning season/one losing season

BASIL SFREDDO   222-202   .524
19 Seasons   1 City Champ   5 Sectionals
1 Regional
eleven winning seasons/eight losing seasons

JOE PEARSON   70-62   .530
6 Seasons   2 City Champs   1 Sectional
two winning seasons/four losing seasons

---

overall:
67 seasons with 1448 games; won 815 & lost 633 (.563);
37 winning seasons/29 losing seasons/one even
13 City Champs, 10 Sectionals, 3 Regionals, 2 Semi-State
and 2 State Championship Teams (1965 & 1969)

People who were consulted in the choices of the MVPs and Best Players for Football and Basketball:

Mr. JULIAN '37-'77	Mrs. HINE '36-'80
HAROLD NEGLEY ('40)	BASIL SFREDDO '66-'95
JOE PEARSON '72-'95	PHIL PETERSON ('53)
BILL SNOWBERGER ('60)	CARL ROBERTS ('43)
LAFAYETTE HOOSER ('35)	BOB TILLERY ('48)
HARRY CHERRY ('34)	GEORGE THEOFANIS ('49)
CAROL PURICHIA ('57)	MYRON NEWLAND ('69) '76-'95
JERRY GEARRIES ('60)	LARRY COMPTON ('60)
TOMMY RAMIREZ ('78)	JOHN BRADLEY '61-'89
TONY BURCHETT ('71) '76-'81	DANNY STAMATKIN ('85)

Consensus MVPs or Best Players (1929-1995) in Basketball

1929	PHIL BAYT	1961	BOB LEEPER-JOE PURICHIA
1930	JIM LEEPER-EMERSON CARTER	1962	LOUIE CRAIG-JIM RHODES
1931	HARRY SANDERS-JIM LEEPER	1963	CLARK DICKERSON-
1932	JOHN FOUDRAY-DON BRIGHT		RALPH TAYLOR
1933	EDWIN "HOP" HOWARD-	1964	RALPH TAYLOR-BILLY KELLER
	CLIFF BAUMBACH	1965	BILLY KELLER-RALPH TAYLOR
1934	LAFAYETTE HOOSER-	1966	MARVIN WINKLER
	HARRY CHERRY	1967	LARRY HIGHBAUGH
1935	LAFE HOOSER-BOB DIETZ	1968	GEORGE McGINNIS
1936	JAMES HARDIN	1969	GEORGE McGINNIS-
1937	BOB KERSEY-RED CARTER		STEVE DOWNING
1938	LOUIE LEERKAMP-	1970	STEVE STANFIELD
	BOB KERSEY	1971	ABNER NIBBS
1939	COURTNEY GERRISH	1972	JAMES HARRIS
1940	COURTNEY GERRISH-	1973	DON MALLORY-
	BORIS "BABE" DIMANCHEFF		BOB WOODFORD
1941	CARL PETERCHEFF	1974	ARDITH WEARREN
1942	WALLER & WALTER O'BRIEN	1975	RICKY SMITH-
1943	WALTER & WALLER O'BRIEN		ARMOND WHITE
1944	BUD JONES	1976	DOUG WHITE
1945	RALPH "BUCKSHOT" O'BRIEN	1977	WINFRED O'NEAL
1946	"BUCKSHOT" O'BRIEN-	1978	WILLIE CARTER
	JACK WOODSON	1979	GEORGE HARRIS-DON McCOY
1947	ROY JACOBS	1980	CURTIS KIMBROUGH
1948	BILL NIEMANN-	1981	RICKY JOHNSON
	MAURICE WILHOITE	1982	JOHN SHERMAN WILLIAMS
1949	GEORGE THEOFANIS	1983	DARREN FITZGERALD
1950	BOB BORDER	1984	TONY WEEDEN
1951	ROY McDOUGALL	1985	BRYAN BURGESS
1952	TOM DOBBS-BILL SPRINGER	1986	JOHN ROBINSON
1953	PHIL PETERSON	1987	STEVE RUTHERFORD
1954	CARL MEADOR	1988	MIKE PARKS
1955	DON MARTIN-DON CARTER	1989	LAMONTE DEAN
1956	JERRY LAWLIS	1990	LAMONTE DEAN
1957	ERNIE SLINKER	1991	JOHNNY MILES
1958	BERNIE KELLER-	1992	DANNY ADAMS
	EDDIE WILLIAMS	1993	JACK OWENS
1959	EDDIE WILLIAMS	1994	JACK OWENS
1960	EARLE STINNIS-BOB LEEPER	1995	JACK OWENS-R.J. WILLIAMS

WASHINGTON Individual Athletic Achievements

Indiana Basketball All-Star team
1948	Bill Niemann
1959	Eddie Williams
1965	Billy Keller*
	Ralph Taylor
1966	Marvin Winkler
1969	George McGinnis*
	Steve Downing
1981	Cheryl Cook**
1982	John S. Williams
1995	Jack Owens

*Mr. Basketball
**Miss Basketball

(long time GWHS coach Johnny Williams was on the inaugural 1939 All-Star team with Mr. Basketball George Crowe, Ray Crowe's brother, from Franklin H.S. Johnny played at Southport H.S.)

IHSAA Trester Award (basketball)
1965	Eddie Bopp

IHSAA Mental Attitude (track)
1975	Debbie Quarles

City Athlete of the Year
1967	Larry Highbaugh
1969	George McGinnis
1979	Kerry Noble
1980	Bonnie Harrington
1981	Cheryl Cook
1991	Eli Rasheed
1995	Jack Owens

Indiana Football All-Star team
1967	Larry Highbaugh
	Bobby Canady
	Charley Walton
	Ricky Thompson
1968	Mike Bradley
	Leonard Cannon
	Gary Baker
1969	Don Phillips
	Louie Day
1971	Monte Woods
	Eddie Boswell
1972	Tom Jones
	Marcus Averitte
	Bruce Smith
1973	Matthew Blane
	Ronnie Hayes
1974	Bob Hicks
1975	Kevin Weatherby
1976	Ricky Smith
1977	Donnie Harris
1978	Jeff Cole
1979	Kerry Noble
1981	Curtis Kimbrough
1983	Ivan Bowens
1985	Tony Weeden
1987	James Miller
1991	Eli Rasheed
1993	Ted Derricote
1994	Adrian Crenshaw

(inaugural year was the summer of 1967)

Boys Track State Champions

Year	Name	Event	Mark
1930	Jim Emerson Carter	pole vault	12'4.75"
1943	Roy Jacobs, Frank Hines, Norman Dunn, John Jacobs	880 relay	1:33.6
1944	Eddie Jones	high jump	6'0"
1966	Mike Cummins	long jump	23'2.5"
1967	Larry Highbaugh	100-yd. dash	9.6
1967	Larry Highbaugh	220-yd. dash	20.5
1968	Don Phillips	shot put	59'7.5"
1969	Don Phillips	shot put	64'3.5"
1971	George Russell, Ruben Timmons, Steve Officer, Wayne Grace	880 relay	1:27.8
1972	Wayne Grace	220-yd. dash	22.3
1979	Kenneth Gilbert	880-yd. run	1:54.8
1980	Lamont Williams	400-meter run	48.14
1980	Lamont Williams	800-meter run	1:52.84
1983	Kenneth Walker	discus	157'7"
1990	Monterrio Holder	high jump	6'10"
1993	Chris Merritt	400-meter run	48.68
1995	Ibn Rasheed	discus	182'3"

Boys Cross Country State Champion

1963 & 1964   Dennis Grider

Girls Track State Champions

Year	Name	Event	Mark
1974	Debbie Quarles	80-yd. hurdles	10.7
1975	Debbie Quarles	80-yd. hurdles	10.7
1975	Donna Pope	long jump	18'10"
1976	Gertrude Springfield	shot put	42'11"
1981	Cheryl Cook	100-meter hurdles	14.26

Wrestling State Champions

Year	Name	Weight
1958	Frank Opp	154-lb.
1961	Randy White	120-lb.
1970	Phillip Leslie	heavyweight

22 Boys Track Sectional Champions

1933	1938	1940	1943	1944
1947	1948	1951	1953	1955
1963	1965	1966	1967	1968
1972	1979	1980	1981	1983
1987	1992			

Boys State Championship Meet Runners-up   four times

1944	1967	1971	1979

Girls State Champions   1975

VIII.

SPECIAL DISTINCTION

Indiana Hall of Fame Athletes (Washington High connections)

BASEBALL   DON LEPPERT (1950) Major league player & coach; in 1960 he was the 20th major leaguer to hit a homer in first bat; on April 11, 1963 hit three homers for Washington Senators vs. New York Yankees; 1960 World Champion Pittsburgh Pirates catcher; coach for Pirates & Astros

TRACK   DENNIS GRIDER (1964) two time State Champ (1962 & 1963) in Cross Country

LARRY HIGHBAUGH (1967) 1967 State Champ in 100-yd & 220-yd. dash; 1964 broke Jesse Owens' 100-yd. dash record in Mansfield, Ohio at 9.2; Canadian Football Hall of Fame; three time Sectionals & City Champion

DEBBIE QUARLES (1975) two time State Champ in Hurdles; Four straight City Champ; IHSAA Attitude Award winner

BONITA HARRINGTON (1980) High Jump record 5'7 ¾"

LAMONT WILLIAMS (1980) State Champion 400 & 800 meters

WALT STAHLHUT coach at Wood & GWHS to 1994 with five individual State Champions

WRESTLING   JIM ARVIN (1963) coach
    GWHS football and wrestling; Howe coach 1969-1989

FRANK OPP (1958) & family
    CARL (1959), GARLAND (REGGIE class of 1960) & GARY (1963);
    GWHS football, wrestling & track; Frank State Champ at 154-lb.

MARVIN HOMER HAWKINS (1949) 35 years working tourney;
    Introduced 11 man football to Center Grove in 1955

JIM PHILLIPS (1965 Northwest grad after two years at GWHS)
    Coach at GWHS & Manual (1978-2003); official '65-'78

FOOTBALL   HENRY BOGUE   GWHS coach 1927-1950 110-81-20
    record at Washington with six City Champs & two South Central Conf. Champs; coached Phil Bayt, Frank Luzar, Harry Cherry, Joe Dezelan, Babe Dimancheff, Emerson & Red Carter, Bob Kersey, & Cliff Baumbach

FRANK LUZAR (1931) (Official)

    GWHS assistant football coach 1936-1952; head baseball coach 26 years; golf coach; NFL official 1961-1974; major league baseball players Jeff James, Don Leppert & Dennis Jent; football official 1936-1974; in 1965 made the goal line call in Green Bay vs. Baltimore

CLOYD "CURLY" JULIAN (Official) inducted in 1975

    GWHS principal 1961-1977; Washington teacher/coach 1937; Head Coach Track; football & basketball assistant

ROBERT PETRANOFF (contributor)

    Indianapolis Star; High School All-Star game; IU radio and promotionals

JOSEPH DEZELAN (1933) (player-coach)

    1932 All-State; Butler Univ. All-Conference; Head football coach Cathedral 1944-1969; coached Bob Springer, Dick Dullaghan, Mike McGinley, Phil Long, Ron Battreall, Julian Peebles and Gary Tofil

BOB SPRINGER (player-coach) inducted in 1991

    GWHS head coach 1962-1993; 229-94-5 record; Catholic All-American 1951; All-City basketball 1952; State Championships 1966 & 1974; only Marion Ct. State Champs during original 10 years at top level; caught future NFL & College Hall of Famer Len Dawson's first college touchdown pass at Purdue & first Big Ten TD pass

JIM EMERSON CARTER (1930) (player-coach) inducted in 1977

    first GWHS State Champ (pole vault 1930); All-American at Purdue as a "Touchdown Twin" with Duane Purvis; College All-Star game 1935; Univ. of Dayton Head Basketball Coach; Anderson H.S. football coach; Indiana Golf Hall of Fame as Anderson H.S. coach

BORIS BABE DIMANCHEFF (1940) (player)

    Played for Butler 2 years then headed to Purdue; star on Purdue's only undefeated team in 1943; All-American in 1944; scored 17 TDs over two seasons; scored TD in 1947 for Chicago Cardinals in NFL Championship win

GEORGE McGINNIS (2010) (player)

    1968 High School All-American at end; member of 1966 Mythical State Champions

BASKETBALL RALPH "BUCKSHOT" O'BRIEN (1946) inducted in 1987

    GWHS All-State; Butler University 3-yr. MVP & 3-yr. conference MVP; Butler career scoring record

BILL GREEN (Manual H.S. 1952) inducted in 1988

    Six State Championships; first was 31-0 at GWHS; Five more Champs at Marion including 3 in a row

BILLY KELLER (1965) inducted in 1992

    Mr. Basketball 1965; Purdue University Big Ten Champs; 1969 NCAA runners-up to UCLA while scoring 20 pts. in final game; inaugural Naismith Award (#1 player under 6')

JERRY OLIVER (Rochester H.S. 1948) inducted in 1994
> GWHS 1955-1968; Head Coach 1960-1968; State Champs 1965; Indiana University assistant; Indiana Pacers assistant; first Hoosier Dome director

GEORGE McGINNIS (1969) inducted in 1995
> High School All-American in 1969; 1969 Mr. Basketball scoring 53 pts. with 31 rebounds in one All-Star game; Big Ten scoring (30-pt avg.) & rebounding (15 avg.) leader in IU sophomore year; NBA co-MVP with 76ers; All-Time Pacer great

BOB DIETZ (1935) inducted in 1996
> 1935 GWHS City Champs; three year Butler starter; Indianapolis Kautsky in NBA; 24 year Butler assistant

STEVE DOWNING (1969) inducted in 1996
> Indiana All-Star; three year IU starter; 1st round draft pick of Boston Celtics 1973; 1973-74 NBA Champs

GEORGE THEOFANIS (1949) inducted in 2000
> 1948 GWHS Sectional Champs; Butler University player; Head Coach at Avon then Shortridge 1965-1970; State Runners-Up 1968; Butler University Head Coach following Tony Hinkle

BILL SPRINGER (1953) inducted in 2001
> GWHS All-City; Hanover College; 40 year high school head coach at Linton, Seeger, Brazil, Shortridge, Jennings County, Bloomington South and won 8 Sectionals at Southport; State Finals with Southport in 1990

RALPH TAYLOR (1965) inducted in 2001
> led GWHS to 3 straight City Championships; 1005 rebounds; 1965 State Champs; voted as one of four All-Time Purdue fan favorites

JIMMY DIMITROFF (1948) inducted in 2002
> Officiated 35 sectionals, 30 regionals, 22 semi-states & 5 state finals; Hanover College

DICK HARMENING (Greenfield H.S. 1954) inducted in 2002
> GWHS assistant 1965 State Champs; Franklin H.S. to State Finals in 1973 & 1974; Center Grove Head Coach

GERALD "JERRY" LAWLIS (1956) inducted in 2003
> set Indianapolis single game scoring record at 48 pts.; Purdue University; 1981 Silver Anniversary team

JOHN SHERMAN WILLIAMS (1982) inducted in 2007
> two sectional champs at GWHS; All-Star team; Indiana State University All-Missouri Conference 4 years; 27.3 pt. ISU scoring average

LOUIS LEERKAMP (1938)
> Named to the Silver Anniversary team in 1963
> GWHS All-City and All-Sectional
> Franklin College single game scoring record

GWHS ALL-TIME FOOTBALL & BASKETBALL

Football

Offense Defense

E	GEORGE McGINNIS	'68	DE	MATTHEW BLANE	'72
T	JOE DEZELAN	'32	DL	BERNIE WAINSCOTT	'59
T	GUY FISH	'45	DL	ELI RASHEED	'90
G	TERRY NOLAND	'67	DL	MONTE WOODS	'70
C	DON PHILLIPS	'68	DL	GARY BAKER	'67
C	BOB TILLERY	'47	DL	CLIFF BAUMBACH	'32
G	FRANK OPP	'57	DE	DICK BOARMAN	'60
G	RON HEINRICH	'74	LB	HARVEY STORMS	'83
T	ISHMAEL LAWLIS	'30	LB	EARL BRANSON	'74
T	MIKE BRADLEY	'67	LB	JAMES MILLER	'86
E	BILL COOK	'51	LB	BOBBY CANADY	'66
E	TED DERRICOTE	'92	LB	FRANK LUZAR	'30
R	MONTERIO HOLDER	'89	LB	EDDIE BOSWELL	'70
QB	JAMES OVERSTREET	'83	LB	REGGIE WILLIAMS	'68
QB	BILL DEEM	'44	DB	PHIL BAYT	'28
B	EMERSON CARTER	'29	DB	DAVE SANDERS	'57
B	HARRY CHERRY	'33	DB	DAVE PORTEN	'53
B	LARRY HIGHBAUGH	'66	DB	BOB KERSEY	'37
B	BORIS DIMANCHEFF	'40	DB	KEVIN WEATHERBY	'74
B	RICKY SMITH	'75	DB	HOP HOWARD	'33
B	LARRY COMPTON	'59	DB	LEONARD CANNON	'67
B	RICK THOMPSON	'66	DB	RED CARTER	'37
K	LOUIE DAY	'68	Ret.	RONNIE HAYES	'72

Team Captains: Six PURICHIA boys '47-'64, DANNY BUTLER '74, JERRY SANDERS '62, PHIL PETERSON '52, JIM '62 & MIKE HIGHBAUGH '63, JIM CLEVENGER '45 & '69, CHUCK DULLA '69

Coaches: BOB SPRINGER '62-'93
HENRY BOGUE '27-'50

Basketball

'65	BILLY KELLER	'64	JOHN DOWDELL	
'69	GEORGE McGINNIS	'56	JERRY LAWLIS	
'48	BILL NIEMANN	'95	JACK OWENS	
'82	JOHN SHERMAN WILLIAMS	'66	MARVIN WINKLER	
'69	STEVE DOWNING	'35	BOB DIETZ	
'59	EDDIE WILLIAMS	'69	WAYNE PACK	
'83	DARREN FITZGERALD	'35	LAFAYETTE HOOSER	
'46	BUCKSHOT O'BRIEN	'76	DOUG WHITE	
'65	RALPH TAYLOR	'81	RICKY JOHNSON	
'74	ARDITH WEARREN	'79	DONNIE McCOY	
'38	LOUIE LEERKAMP	'33	CLIFF BAUMBACH	
'62	JIM RHODES			

Co-Captains: GEORGE THEOFANIS '49
GEORGE HARRIS '79

Coach: JERRY OLIVER '60-'68

220

ALL-TIME WASHINGTON BASEBALL TEAM

Pitchers	RP	JEFF JAMES '59
	LP	DENNIS JENT '48

Catcher   DON LEPPERT '50

1st   CLIFF BAUMBACH '33

2nd   MAURICE WILHOITE '49

SS   ROY McDOUGAL '51

3rd   BOB KOMLANC '64

OF   LARRY GLAZE '60
                 HOP HOWARD '33
                 BILL MATTOX '52

TOM DOBBS '53, HANK EASTER '57,
MARK GLADSON '66, BILL SPRINGER '53,
HORACE MITCHELL '59, DON MALLORY '73,
TOM STRONG '70, JERRY SANDERS '63,
JERRY LAWLIS '56, BILL KELLER '65,
BOB WOLFLA '47, REGGIE WILLIAMS '69,
BOBBY McCOY '65, GARY SYLVESTER '64

Coach: FRANK LUZAR   30 years

Baseball dropped between 1934-1938 then again 1942-1946
Major League Draft picks:
   Wilhoite (Brooklyn Dodgers), James (Phillies), Jent (Yankees), Leppert (Pirates)

WASHINGTON'S TOP ALL-TIME MALE ATHLETES

1. GEORGE McGINNIS '69
2. LARRY HIGHBAUGH '67
3. BILLY KELLER '65
4. BORIS DIMANCHEFF '40
5. JIM CARTER '30
6. DON LEPPERT '50
7. LAMON BREWSTER '91
8. CLIFF BAUMBACH '33
9. HARRY CHERRY '34
10. DON PHILLIPS '69
11. MONTERIO HOLDER '90
12. TONY ALLEN-COOKSEY '74
13. STEVE DOWNING '69
14. LAMONT WILLIAMS '80
15. JACK OWENS '95
16. DARREN FITZGERALD '83
17. EDDIE WILLIAMS '59
18. RALPH O'BRIEN '46
19. PHILLIP LESLIE '70
20. JERRY LAWLIS '56
21. ELI RASHEED '91
22. DENNIS GRIDER '64
23. MARVIN WINKLER '66
24. FRANK OPP '58
25. LOUIE DAY '69

Qualifications: double state champ; future professional, including top draft pick; college star; world champ or record holder; unique high school or college recognition and accomplishments, including State Champion; (At least 12 professional athletes; at least seven on All-American teams in college or high school)

ALL-TIME MARION COUNTY FOOTBALL & BASKETBALL TEAMS

Football 1945-1997

1   WARREN CENTRAL   1985
    Back-to-back State Champs with back-to-back unbeaten teams; Jeff George is probably best quarterback ever from central Indiana

2   BEN DAVIS   1991
    Mythical National Champs; led by Chris Ings and Perry Meridian transfer Steve Holman

3   MANUAL   1958
    Speedster freshman Leon Harris, Dave Miller and QB Steve Wright with end Ray Schultz led their high scoring offense

4   WASHINGTON   1974
    Only Marion County State Champs under original play-off system; 19 game overall winning streak; led by Kevin Weatherby, Earl Branson, and Danny Butler

5   MARSHALL   1981
    Totally dominated Carmel in 7-3 last minute loss with much inferior city "program" (Carmel steamrolled Castle 42-0 and Ft. Wayne Snider with future All-Time All-Pro Woodson 27-7 to win State); 27-game regular season winning streak which was the longest in Marion County history; led by Eli Garza, Mark Osborne, Eddie Murrell and Steve Miller for three years

6   WASHINGTON   1966
    Led by speedster Larry Highbaugh and tough Bobby Canady; Marion County's 1st Mythical State Champs

7   BEN DAVIS   1988
    Led by Tank Adams and Kent Britt to second consecutive State Championship at the Hoosier Dome

8   CATHEDRAL   1973
    before loss on a fluke play in first State Championship game, went to Bloomington South and smashed their 60 game winning streak

9   WASHINGTON   1983
    lost in Championship game after lopsided wins against Lawrence North, North Central & Bloomington South; led by Jim Overstreet, Calvin Fitzgerald and all-time GWHS leading scorer Glenn Carpenter

10   CHATARD   1978
      survived triple overtime vs. Marshall to reach play-offs losing to eventual State Champs Carmel; five City Champs in the 1970's

Basketball 1945-1997

1   CRISPUS ATTUCKS   1956
      second consecutive State Champs led by the Big O and Stanford Patton; first undefeated ever

2   WASHINGTON   1969
      undefeated led by George McGinnis & Steve Downing; averaged almost 93 points over 31 games

3   ATTUCKS   1955
      Oscar Robertson, Bill Brown, Willie Merriweather & Bill Scott led Tigers to Indianapolis' first ever State Championship

4   WASHINGTON   1965
      led by future Pacer record-holder Billy Keller and Ralph Taylor (1005 rebounds in 3-yrs.); won an unprecedented three consecutive City Championships (only team over 60 years); only played one game in home gym; first integrated area Champs; averaged 78 points per game before 3-point line

5   MANUAL   1961
      VanArsdale twins lost final game after questionable calls late after leading by seven with 1:09 left

6   ATTUCKS   1959
      Larry McIntyre & Jerry Hazelwood were long-range shooters in the school's third Champs drubbing of Kokomo

7   BEN DAVIS   1995
      third straight State Finals for James Patterson (IPS School 108); led by Haughville's Damon Frierson with Pike transfer and first Final's MVP Courtney James

8   LAWRENCE NORTH   1989
      first Marion County township State Champs led by Eric Montross and Todd Leary.

9   BROAD RIPPLE   1980
      led by Stacey Toran and Jeffrey Robinson; first Market Square area champs; last city State Champs

10 SHORTRIDGE   1968
      lost final game after earlier in the tourney beating Washington's McGinnis & Downing; led by Clarence Crain, Oscar Evans & Greg Allen.

11 TECH   1952
      led by Mr. Basketball & Trester winner Joe Sexson to State Finals

12 ATTUCKS   1951
      led by Willie Gardner, Bailey Robertson and Trester winner Bob Jewell with sophomore Hallie Bryant to State Finals

Special Mention: BEN DAVIS   1996
      dramatic last second winning shot by Jeff Poesel after penetration by Keith Patterson rivals the 1954 Bobby Plump shot; unranked in the top 20 entering the tournament; 2nd consecutive State

MR. BASKETBALL from Marion County (1945-1997)

1952	JOE SEXSON	Tech
1953	HALLIE BRYANT	Attucks
1956	OSCAR ROBERTSON	Attucks
1961	TOM & DICK VanARSDALE	Manual
1965	BILLY KELLER	Washington
1969	GEORGE McGINNIS	Washington
1995	DAMON FRIERSON	Ben Davis
(1940	ED SCHEINBEIN	Southport)

TRESTER AWARD winners from Marion County (1945-1997)

1945	MAX ALLEN	Broad Ripple
1951	BOB JEWELL	Attucks
1952	JOE SEXSON	Tech
1961	DICK & TOM VanARSDALE	Manual
1965	EDDIE BOPP	Washington

Gimbel Prize
(1929	EMMETT LOWERY	Tech
1933	JIM SEWARD	Shortridge)

Jim Seward hosted a reception for over ten years starting in 1980 for all Trester-Gimbel winners. This author socialized with men as far back as Walter Cross from Thorntown who won the award in 1919. His daughter, Ina, married Butler star Ed Schilling in 1965. Their son, Edmund, would marry Dick Dullaghan's daughter in the 1980's. Big Ed and I were perhaps the only married athletes at Butler and we became friends for a time.

In Herb Schwomeyer's "Hoosier Hysteria" when the Sportsmanship Award was named for Jake Gimbel from Vincennes in 1928 the criteria in the IHSAA handbook were:

1. The winner may be the weakest player on the weakest team in the tourney
2. Poise and calmness in play under any and all conditions
3. Ready acceptance of decisions of officials
4. Attitude toward members of team, opponents and officials
5. Attitude and conduct as known or observed on floor, in dressing room, on street, in hotels, etc.
6. Briefly, the qualities that go to make a real gentleman are the ones in the mind of the donor

Later, the characterization of the Arthur L. Trester Award winner was stated as:
SCHOLARSHIP, ATHLETIC ABILITY, SPORTSMANSHIP & CHARACTER
along with the participation in the Final Four tournament.

MARION COUNTY 20th CENTURY ALL-TIME FOOTBALL Players

Offense

Position	Name	School	Year
End	GEORGE McGINNIS	Washington	'68
	BOB SPRINGER	Cathedral	'51
	RAY SCHULTZ	Manual	'58
	BILL RALPH	Shortridge	'47
	MARK CLAYTON	Cathedral	'78
	CAP BOSO	Chatard	'80
Tackle	JIM PRESTEL	Sacred Heart	'56
	MARK RODRIQUEZ	Lawrence No.	'77
	DERRICK BROWNLOW	Cathedral	'85
	CECIL FRYHOFFER	Shortridge	'44
Guard	TOM HOLZER	Sacred Heart	'62
	GENE TURNER	Tech	'47
	GARY BAKER	Washington	'67
Center	PETE QUINN	Scecina	'75
	LYNN LYNCH	Tech	'47
QB	JEFF GEORGE	Warren Cent.	'85
	BILLY LYNCH	Chatard	'71
	JIM O'HARA	Cathedral	'76
	CHRIS INGS	Ben Davis	'91
Back	RAY WALLACE	North Central	'81
	BORIS DIMANCHEFF	Washington	'39
	RANDY MANNIEAR	Broad Ripple	'61
	STEVE HOLMAN	Ben Davis	'91
	JIM CARTER	Washington	'29
	GORDON TETER	Law. Central	'61
	WALTER PEACOCK	Shortridge	'72
	LARS TATE	North Central	'83
	FRANK McGRONE	Wood	'59
	HARRY CHERRY	Washington	'33
	ROOSEVELT WASHINGTON	Cathedral	'76
	DAVE SHAW	Manual	'44
	BURT AUSTIN	Franklin Central	'82

Defense

Position	Name	School	Year
End	CHICK LAUCK	Sacred Heart	'64
	KENDALL FLEMINGS	Marshall	'81
	CLIFF BAUMBACH	Washington	'33
Tackle	JOHN VEZA	Chatard	'69
	JAMES FINCH	Marshall	'81
	MO GARDNER	Cathedral	'85
LBer	BOBBY CANADY	Washington	'66
	TOM MARENDT	Howe	'69
	ROOSEVELT COLVIN	Broad Ripple	'94
	PAUL SPICER	Northwest	'92
	DON SILAS	Manual	'66
	KENT SHELTON	Northwest	'82
	DAVE GUTHRIE	Decatur Central	'70
DB	LARRY HIGHBAUGH	Washington	'66
	COREY HARRIS	Ben Davis	'87
	BLAINE BISHOP	Cathedral	'87
	STACY TORAN	Broad Ripple	'79
	DICK NYERS	Manual	'51
	KEVIN WEATHERBY	Washington	'74
	DICK STEVENSON	Tech	'47
	TIM WILBUR	Ben Davis	'77

MARION COUNTY 20th CENTURY ALL-TIME BASKETBALL

Forward	WILLIE GARDNER	Attucks	'51
	GEORGE McGINNIS	Washington	'69
	ALAN HENDERSON	Brebeuf	'91
	TOM VanARSDALE	Manual	'61
	GREG GRAHAM	Warren Cen.	'89
	EMMETT LOWERY	Tech	'28
	STANFORD PATTON	Attucks	'56
	MIKE PRICE	Tech	'66
	HERSHEL TURNER	Shortridge	'56
	KEN BARLOW	Cathedral	'82
	JOE SEXSON	Tech	'52
	DICK VanARSDALE	Manual	'61
	PANCHO WRIGHT	Marshall	'78
	JOHN S. WILLIAMS	Washington	'82
	FRANK KENDRICK	Tech	'71
	MIKE WOODSON	Broad Ripple	'76
	WILLIE MERRIWEATHER	Attucks	'55
Center	ERIC MONTROSS	Lawrence No.	'90
	STEVE DOWNING	Washington	'69
	JIM SEWARD	Shortridge	'33
	RALPH TAYLOR	Washington	'65
	WALT SAHM	Cathedral	'61
	JEFF ROBINSON	Broad Ripple	'80
	GREG NORTHINGTON	Wood	'67
	ED SCHEINBEIN	Southport	'40
	MIKE NOLAND	Howe	'66
	LANDON TURNER	Tech	'79
	COURTNEY JAMES	Pike-B.D.	'95
Guard	JIM PRICE	Tech	'68
	HALLIE BRYANT	Attucks	'53
	BILLY KELLER	Washington	'65
	LOUIE DAMPIER	Southport	'63
	OSCAR ROBERTSON	Attucks	'56
	LARRY BULLINGTON	Marshall	'70
	RANDY WITTMAN	Ben Davis	'78
	MARVIN WINKLER	Washington	'66
	BO CRAIN	Shortridge	'59
	DAMON FRIERSON	Ben Davis	'95
	OSCAR EVANS	Shortridge	'68
	MEL GARLAND	Tech	'60
	JASON GARDNER	North Central	'99
	TODD LEARY	Lawrence No.	'89
	LARRY McINTYRE	Attucks	'59
	RODNEY SCOTT	Arlington	'72
	BILLY O'NEAL	Speedway	'62

COACH BOGUE'S FOOTBALL CAPTAINS

1927	none	1939	Kenneth Jaynes
1928	Phil Bayt	1940	Dan Roth
1929	Emil Unser	1941	Louis Condon
1930	Frank Luzar	1942	Max Hutton
1931	Norman Long	1943	Otto Ferguson (in military service)
1932	Glenn Warren	1944	Charles Hodges
1933	Louis Luzar	1945	Jimmy Clevenger
1934	Carl Emeride	1946	Richard Berry
1935	Robert Flack	1947	Robert Trinkle
1936	Phillip Shoemaker	1948	Carl Barnes
1937	Ralph Chambers	1949	Rollie Schroeder
1938	Robert McCalif	1950	Bill Cook

TOFIL-SPRINGER-NEWLAND CAPTAINS

1951	Bill Powell	1975	Ricky Smith-Bryan Dishman
1952	Tom Figg	1976	Donnie Harris-Frankie Cole
1953	Dick Lahr	1977	Tommy Ramirez-Jeff Cole
1954	Ray Duncan-Bill Purichia	1978	Billy Evans-Kerry Noble
1955	Ancil Wyne-Slavie Lalioff-Carl Ragland	1979	Tracy Winston
1956	Carol Purichia-Hank Easter	1980	Cornelius Quarles-Curtis Kimbrough
1957	Dave Sanders-Bill Green	1981	Robert Wilson
1958	Harold Stockoff-Nick Purichia	1982	John Dishman-Ivan Bowens
1959	Larry Compton-Jim Dill	1983	Jim Overstreet-Danny Luter
1960	Ken Corey-Bob Leeper	1984	Tony Weeden
1961	Denny Troth-Joe Purichia	1986	James Miller
1962	Jerry Sanders-Malcolm Marlow-George Sipe	1990	Eli Rasheed
1963	Mike Lloyd-Joe Blake-Gary Sylvester	1992	Ted Derricote
1964	Kenny Strong-Eddie Bopp	1993	Adrian Crenshaw
1965	Ronny Lewis-Danny Glaze	1994	Jack Owens
1966	John Hill-Larry Highbaugh-Rick Sylvester		
1967	Bob Jones-Leonard Cannon		
1968	George McGinnis-Reggie Williams-Jim Green		
1969	Jim Clevenger-Chuck Dulla		
1970	Eddie Boswell-Steve Stanfield-Monte Woods		
1971	Bruce Smith-Marcus Averitte-Tom Jones		
1972	Don Mallory-Ronnie Hayes-Walter Fultz		
1973	Bob Hicks-Sam Butler		
1974	Danny Butler-Phillip Mayfield-Earl Branson		

IX.

Odds & Ends

HALL OF FAME Editorial

The Indianapolis Star sports section printed a story on March 16, 2005 titled, "Unlike Milan, Hall of Fame won't induct Attucks as a team." I was shocked over the obvious display of both an insensitivity to African-Americans in Indianapolis and the lack of common sense of the individuals who made the decision to keep the 1954 Milan team in a realm all unto itself. I decided to write an editorial response. Initially, I had my "tongue-in-cheek" but concluded on a more serious note. On March 17, the Star printed a reversal titled "Hall of Fame to induct '55 Attucks Champs." My edited comments were published a few days later. The following is my original letter. Within a few months the IHSAA established a rule that all undefeated teams would be inducted.

It was an interesting precedent established last year when the entire Milan team was inducted into the Indiana Basketball Hall of Fame. And it seems obvious to me that the Executive Committee should induct the history-making Attucks team of 1955.

But what about the 1956 Attucks team next year? They were the first team in the then-46-year tournament history to end the season undefeated. How will stars Edgar Searcy and Albert Maxey feel, among others not on the '55 team, if they are ignored? The 1956 team was virtually unchallenged with five point wins over Shortridge and Washington during the regular season as their only close games.

And, in 2015, I will expect our 1965 Indianapolis Washington team to also be inducted. We were the first naturally-integrated team to win State from Marion County. All of our players could, and most usually did, walk to school. There were no school buses. There were 15 elementary schools* that fed into Washington along with three parochial schools that had students attending Continentaland. Bob Komlanc, from Holy Trinity, was one of the best players on the 1964 team. We had racial, religious, and ethnic integration without federal court-ordered busing.

Sunday, February 21, beginning our Sectional week, was the day Malcolm X was assassinated. Sunday, March 21, the day after we won the State Championship, was the final march from Selma to Montgomery led by Martin Luther King. Between those historic events we were disallowed from staying in one (and maybe two) elite fraternity house on the Butler campus because, some said, we had Black players. But the Sigma Nu fraternity accepted us for three weeks. We did not take a motorcade around the Circle. But we did have about 4,000 fans awaiting us on the outside football bleachers in 20-degree weather after our championship win. A Marion County judge, who was a teenager at the time and did not attend Washington High, once wrote that she met her future husband at that rally.

Half of our games we "started" three Black players with two Whites; the other half we "started" three White players with two Blacks. We beat every team that we played as we avenged our two losses along the tourney trail while playing only one game in our home gymnasium. And we were only the second team in the then-55-year tourney that swept all three awards: State Championship, Mr. Basketball, and the Arthur L. Trester Award. Seven of the eight elementary schools that played their league games in Washington High's gym in 1961 were represented on the 1965 champs.

When Dr. King gave his "I Have a Dream" speech on August 28, 1963 I would suspect that he would have had positive thoughts in his mind about the segregated Attucks of '55 and '56 as well as the possibility of an integrated Indianapolis team like our 1965 squad. Both were history-makers that directly affected more lives in the population center of Indiana than any rural ball team, including Milan.

And when are the Franklin Wonder Five from the 1920's and Marion from the 1980's, the only two schools with three consecutive State Champions, going to receive their Hall of Fame inductions? But I wouldn't be surprised if Hickory High from the movie "Hoosiers" is inducted in 2011 for the movie's 25th anniversary.

*Indianapolis Public Schools #44, 46, 47, 49, 50,
and
#52, 61, 63, 67, 75
and
#79, 90, 5, 16, 30
and
St. Anthony's, Holy Trinity, Assumption

FEMALE ATHLETIC SPECIAL MENTION

There is little doubt and no argument that girls were never allowed any distinction as student-athletes at Washington High, or most other schools in central Indiana, until the mid-1970's.

The last twenty years through 1995 did allow for some recognition of Continental girls. The top two have to be two-time hurdles State Champion and Attitude Award winner Debbie Quarles, class of 1975. The other is obviously Cheryl Cook who was chosen as Miss Basketball for the state of Indiana in 1981 the same spring that she won the State Championship in the 100-yd. hurdles. Cheryl also had a successful college career at Cincinnati.

Sandy Spuzich, class of 1955, who became a winner on the Ladies Professional Golf Association tour throughout the 1960's was a professional athlete who was afforded exactly zero opportunities as a high school athlete by IPS. She won the Ladies Professional Golf Association Championship (LPGA) in 1966.

State Champs Gertrude Springfield ('76) and Donna Pope ('75) both were highly successful along with well-respected female athletes like Bonita Harrington ('75), Kathy Gaddie ('76), and speedster Joetta Bailey ('75).

Washington High's first great athlete, Jim Emerson Carter, shared with me his unique viewpoint. He noted that Gertrude Cherry was the best athlete of either sex that he ever witnessed when she was a junior high girl. And Mr. Carter was called Touchdown Carter as an All-American at Purdue in the '30's.

And, in 1980, Washington's class of 1943 Carl Roberts shared a personal story with me. He noted that Regina Such, GWHS class of 1966, would hold the 50-yd. dash junior high record permanently since all Indiana schools went to meter distances in 1980. In May 2006 I contacted Mr. Roberts. I had visited the IPS Central Office where I was greeted with the reality that junior high records no longer existed. Mr. Roberts met with me and stated that "George (Farkas) would turn over in his grave if he knew what had happened to all of his records…I went downtown in the early '90's and discovered the same thing you did (that all records had been tossed in the trash)." So much for history and today's IPS. But "it's a new day," according to one IPS leader.

Mr. Roberts had replaced George Farkas as Director of Athletics in IPS for junior highs. Carl retired in 1985.

Mrs. Mary Nicholson Dawson, the long time girls' coach at School 50 who began her career as a P.E. teacher at GWHS in 1953, had often seemed overwhelmed by her own admonitions concerning Regina's 6.2 record in the 50-yd. dash on three of four stopwatches. That 50-yd. time meant little to me although I had personally witnessed her record setting performance on the cinder track at Washington High in the spring of 1962, perhaps wind-assisted. But I knew it was fast. All of the runners from Schools 49, 46, 52, 5, 67, 75 and 47 were not even competitive with her.

But I was myself amazed when I looked on the website hickoksports.com in 2006, under Indoor Women's Track. It showed that the Indoor 50-yd. dash had been run from 1956-1964 at the collegiate level. In 1959 Wilma Rudolph, who became a female superstar by winning three Gold Medals in the '60 Rome Olympics, won the 50-yd. NCAA at 6.2. Miss Rudolph did run a 5.9 in the 1960 NCAA to repeat her win.

Carl Roberts signed an acknowledgment of the IPS Junior High 50-yd. dash record at 6.2 in 1962, which I have laminated.

Regina had run a 6.3 on School 50's graveled blacktop previous to her Washington High track accomplishment in 1962.

In the 21st century young females have many diverse opportunities in athletic competition at the high school level, unlike girls during most of the 20th century.

What's the common connection for these 30-Triple+ Continentals?

1. Charles Goff, David Roberts & Steve Carnine
2. Don Baldwin, Harry Brown, Bob Flack, Marion Carter
3. Gordon Dempsey, Skip Crawford & Dennis Panarisi
4. Hank Easter, Carol Purichia & Jerry England
5. Gary Baker, Leonard Cannon & Myron Newland
6. Connie Higgins, Carol Waggoner & Diane Elam
7. Red Carter, Al Case & Bob Kersey
8. Joe Pearson, Bruce Hamman & Charlie Leamon
9. Joe Tofil, George Theofanis & Gene Robertson
10. Thelma Bloomenstock Bopp, Jean Mohr & Guy Fish
11. Babe Dimancheff, Bill Keller & Sandy Spuzich
12. Carl Ragland, Eddie Williams & Larry Highbaugh
13. Larry Compton, Bobby Canady, Ron Heinrich, Dick Boarman
14. Harry Cherry, Rick Thompson & George McGinnis
15. Mark Gladson, Dannie Johnson & Jerry Sanders
16. Gladys Huddleston, Mary Jane Howell & Virginia Garrabrant
17. Nancy Ehret, Grace Arvin & Vi Sanders
18. Charlie Prince, Jim Overstreet & Danny Butler
19. Earl Branson, Frank Opp & Eddie Boswell
20. Bill Deem, Bob Wolfla & Mike Purichia
21. George Avery, Mike King & Ray Knight
22. Buckshot O'Brien, Darren Fitzgerald & Bob Dietz
23. Bob Tillery, Don Leppert & Dick Lipscomb
24. Barbara Sullivan, Ruth Rosser & Mary Melick
25. John Arvin, Bernie Keller & Dave Sanders
26. Gary Sylvester, Tim McGrevy & Jimmie Highbaugh
27. Jerry Lawlis, Cliff Baumbach & Ricky Smith
28. Kevin Weatherby, William Rogers & Randy Payne
29. Steve Midkiff, Mike Furimsky & Tom Dobbs
30. Debbie Quarles, Lamont Williams & Dennis Grider

1. Class of 1966, killed in Vietnam War (of 15)
2. Washington football players killed during World War II (of 95)
3. Indianapolis lawyers (+Fred Hulser, Puerto Rico corporate lawyer)
4. Indiana Central
5. players then assistant football coaches
6. cheerleaders; School 50; class of 1971
7. class of 1938; Purdue endearment
8. Northwest H.S.
9. Shortridge H.S.
10. School 50 teachers; Washington grads
11. professional champion athletes
12. first Black All-City, All-State & All-American
13. University of Louisville football stars
14. Indiana University varsity athletes
15. Vietnam soldiers & Continental varsity athletes
16. class of 1938 who married Continentals (Radcliffe, Funk, Russell)
17. long time secretaries
18. championship quarterbacks; undefeated regular season
19. stars in football & wrestling
20. QBs in the 1940's
21. medical doctors
22. Butler basketball stars
23. snapper, holder & first place kicker
24. teachers who married other teachers (Dave Hine, Paul Hayes, and Don Kramer)
25. 1957 football team with younger early-60's athlete brothers (Jim, Bill & Jerry)
26. 1962 football team with younger 1966 State Champ brothers (Rick, Terry & Larry)
27. Purdue athletes (plus Touchdown Twin Jim Carter)
28. Indiana State varsity starters (football, basketball, football)
29. Ball State varsity starters (football, football, baseball)
30. unique double State Champions

Year	Washington History	U.S./World History
1927	first football game is loss to Kirklin	-Babe Ruth hits 60 home runs
1928	future Indianapolis Mayor Phil Bayt becomes first All-City football player	-penicillin discovered by Fleming and Kellogg-Briand outlaws war
1929	Continentals beat Cathedral 39-0 with freshman Joe Dezelan	-Vatican City becomes a nation and Stock Market crashes
1930	Emerson Carter is first state champ	-Max Schmeling wins boxing title
1931	future teacher Frank Luzar graduates	-Japan occupies Manchuria
1932	Washington beats Carmel 104-0	-FDR elected President
1933	The Trist first given to freshmen	-Hitler elected German chancellor
1934	Curly Julian marries Betty Brooks	-Dionne quintuplets born in Canada
1935	first basketball city championship	-Social Security passes Congress
1936	Barbara Sullivan begins 44-year career	-Edward VIII abdicates as King
1937	Strother Martin is springboard champ	-Ducky Medwick wins Triple Crown
1938	Jerry Lawlis is born	-Davey O'Brien wins Heisman
1939	Thelma Bloomenstock graduates	-World War II begins
1940	Babe Dimancheff heads to Butler	-Selective Service Act signed
1941	Bill Deem enters high school	-Pearl Harbor attacked by Japanese
1942	O'Brien twins star in basketball	-Boston nightclub fire kills 491
1943	Red Carter killed in plane accident	-Stan Musial wins MVP as Cardinal
1944	Ed Jones wins State in High Jump	-Normandy invasion on June 6
1945	Guy Fish & Jim Clevenger All-City	-A-bombs end World War II
1946	Buckshot O'Brien heads to Butler	-first Baby Boomers born
1947	Dick Lipscombe first kicker	-Jackie Robinson breaks color line
1948	Continentals win first Sectionals	-modern Israel founded
1949	first African-Americans enter GWHS	-Indy 500 first televised
1950	Mr. Gingery begins final year as principal	-Brink's robbery in Boston
1951	Tofil replaces Bogue as football coach	-Ridgeway replaces MacArthur
1952	Phil Peterson All-City end in football	-Ike elected President
1953	Leon Hunt begins as shop teacher	-Rosenbergs executed in June
1954	Bryan Hudson graduates	-Supreme Court rules for integration
1955	Joe Shires beats Oscar in hurdles	-Churchill resigns as British PM
1956	Jerry Lawlis sets county record	-Khrushchev denounces Stalin
1957	Leon Griffith drop-kicks XP	-Aaron wins first of 4 HR titles
1958	Nick becomes 4th Purichia QB in 10 years	-first Atlantic commercial flight
1959	football team ends at 8-0-1	-Castro overthrows Batista
1960	Oliver replaces Hine as basketball coach	-JFK elected President
1961	Julian is Principal & Luzar is NFL official	-Alan Shepherd into space on May 5
1962	Frank Starkey is Valedictorian	-Marilyn Monroe found dead (Aug.)
1963	Miss Ely retires as Math head	-Colisseum disaster on Halloween
1964	second consecutive basketball city champs	-Ruby sentenced to death in Dallas
1965	Ivan Smith killed in Vietnam in May	-Medicare begins in July
1966	Winkler sets scoring record replacing Big O	-first heart transplant by DeBakey
1967	Bill Green arrives as assistant coach	-Six Day War victory for Israel

1968	Baker, Cannon & Bradley football All-Stars	-King & Kennedy assassinated
1969	only 2nd undefeated state champs	-Armstrong steps on lunar surface
1970	frosh city basketball champs	-four Kent State deaths in May
1971	880-relay team sets state record	-18-yr-olds get national right to vote
1972	Don Mallory is first black QB	-Nixon goes to Red China
1973	segregated Westlake Beach Club closes	-Vietnam War officially ends (Jan.)
1974	first Marion County football tourney champs	-Nixon resigns in August
1975	Debbie Quarles wins Attitude Award	-Ford escapes two shootings in Sept.
1976	Newland arrives as coach	-Uganda's Entebbe airport raided
1977	Sfreddo wins 2nd Sectionals in 3 years	-Elvis found dead in August
1978	new Hawthorne Center opens	-Pope John Paul I dies after 34 days
1979	Kerry Noble named top city athlete	-US embassy in Tehran seized
1980	Lamont Williams wins 400 & 800 State	-Reagan elected President
1981	Cheryl Cook wins Miss Basketball title	-O'Connor is first female top judge
1982	John S. Williams is Sfreddo's All Star	-Falklands War near Argentina
1983	football team loses in state finals	-237 Marines killed in Beirut
1984	last ten game football regular season	-Indira Gandhi assassinated
1985	Springer's 200th win vs. Ben Davis	-Gorbachev secedes Chernenko
1986	Stahlhut's 6th City Track title in 9 years	-Challenger explodes killing 7
1987	James Miller is Springer's 26th All Star	-Judge Bork rejected by Senate
1988	Rhonda Craig is softball MVP	-Dukakis runs for President
1989	Rosenberger & Bradley retire	-Hirohito dies ending 63-year reign
1990	Holder wins high jump championship	-MC Hammer's U Can't Touch This
1991	future Boxing Champ Brewster graduates	-Operation Desert Storm in January
1992	Bill Keller inducted into Hall of Fame	-Arkansas governor elected President
1993	Chris Merritt wins State 400-meters	-David Koresh dies with 75 others
1994	Newland named last football coach	-Reagan has Alzheimer's disease
1995	last second Regional basketball loss	-Forrest Gump wins as Best Movie

GWHS QUIZ (answers in "Indianapolis Washington and the West Side")

1. A 1991 graduate, he defeated Wladimir Klitschko April 10, 2004 to become WBO Heavyweight Champion of the World in boxing. Son of Pam Hardy, class of '74.
2. Name the first City Athlete of the Year from GWHS. He broke a Jesse Owens 30 year old Ohio high school track record in the summer of 1964.
3. Name the only Miss Basketball from GWHS who later played at Cincinnati.
4. Name the 1940's graduate who was a family physician on South Traub into the 1980's. Delivered IU's Randy Wittman, son of Washington High friends.
5. Who was the only man to serve four different principals as vice principal?
6. What was the name of the field upon which Washington High was built?
7. What annual Indianapolis event took place on that field until 1927?
8. Name the early-1940's graduate who was president of the Indianapolis Chamber of Commerce in the mid-1960's.
9. Who was the longest serving principal? How many years?
10. Name the faculty member who served the longest (1936-1980).
11. Name the 1957 graduate who became the mother of two NBA coaches (the Van Gundy brothers).
12. Who was our first Indiana All Star basketball player and first area jump-shooter?
13. Who were the last "official" Johnnie and Connie Continentals in 1961-1962?
14. Name the Continental who would hit three home runs in a single game against the New York Yankees powerhouse team in 1963. Class of 1950.
15. Who is considered the very first consistent place kicker for Continental football?
16. Name the Continental drafted #1 by the Boston Celtics in 1973.
17. Name the offensive guard who drop-kicked an extra point in the 1957 drubbing of Ben Davis, final score 53-14.
18. Name the punter from the 1963 football team who became a reputable obstetrician by the 1970's.
19. Who was our very first Mr. Basketball? He scored 20 points in the 1969 NCAA final game against UCLA. First winner of national Naismith Award.
20. Name our second and last Mr. Basketball who averaged 30 points and 15 rebounds as a sophomore All-American at IU.
21. Name the 1959 star southpaw pitcher who was later killed in the Vietnam War.
22. The Chicago Cardinals last won the professional football championship in 1947. Name the Continental, class of 1940, who scored a TD in that 28-21 win.
23. From the class of 1965, name the family doctor who also serves as a teacher at a major Louisville hospital in the 21st century; family practice in Jeffersonville.
24. What Continental "broke the color barrier" at Southwestern Louisiana as one of five "Little All-American" basketball players? He was also on the 1971 World Champion Milwaukee Bucks with Oscar and Lew Alcindor. Class of 1966.
25. Name the first Washington High State Champion in the spring of 1930.
26. Name the long-time secretary whose son was a 1963 graduate and future member of the Indiana Wrestling Hall of Fame as a coach (name both mother and son).
27. Who was the first African-American varsity athlete at GWHS?
28. Name the first African-American All-City football player from our school.

29. (Opinion with limitations) Who do you consider the single best Washington High basketball player who did NOT make the Indiana All Star team?

30. What faculty member was on the first Indiana basketball All-Star team in 1939?

31. Name the 1965 graduate who would earn degrees from Wabash, Rockefeller University, and Yale including Cell Biology and Immunology then worked at St. Jude Children's Research Hospital in Memphis in cancer research.

32. Who was the first African-American Valedictorian (class of 1962)?

33. From the class of 1969, name the two-time State Champion in the shot put. His record of 64'3 ½" endured for almost 20 years.

34. How many Washington names are engraved under the "Those Who Gave All" as young men who died during World War II?

35. The college All-Star game was a pre-season staple for football fans from 1934 through 1976. Name the Continental who played in the 1935 game with future President Gerald Ford. An All-American "Touchdown Twin" for Purdue.

36. From the class of 1949, name the School 5 and 44 boy who would gain fame as a top high school coach before replacing Butler's legendary Tony Hinkle in 1970.

37. He graduated from Washington High in 1935 and became the first State Champion team sport coach at GWHS in 1961. Nicknamed "Mush" who was he?

38. Name the first African-American May Queen, class of 1971.

39. Who became Washington High's second State Finals Attitude Award winner in 1975 when she won her second consecutive hurdles State Championship?

40. What 1955 graduate later became head wrestling coach, assistant football coach, Dean of Boys, Athletic Director and respected teacher at his alma mater?

41. Name the 1955 graduate who would win the Ladies' PGA U.S. Open in 1966.

42. Our All-City tackle, class of 1933, who would become the iconic Cathedral football coach from 1944-1969 after playing at Butler?

43. Name the 1938 graduate who would be named to the inaugural Silver Anniversary team in IHSAA basketball in 1963.

44. He scored an all time county record of 48 points in 1956 only to be upstaged a week later when the great Oscar Robertson tallied 56 against Sacred Heart.

45. A 1971 graduate he was named Mr. USA body builder from Hofmeister's Gym by 1977. Sister Dorothy and brother Arnold both became State Police Officers.

46. He graduated in 1955 and would marry his high school sweetheart Sherry Easter. He became superintendent of Franklin Township Schools for over 20 years.

47. Graduating in 1940 he would become Superintendent of Public Instruction for the State of Indiana for 12 years, 1973-1985. Three sport athlete at GWHS.

48. This 1937 graduate became a respected character actor and uttered the famous "what we have here is failure to communicate" in the movie "Cool Hand Luke."

49. Name the 1966 Continental pole-vaulter who went on to become a Florida dentist.

50. He would amazingly win the State in both the 400 and 800-meter run in 1980.

51. Graduating in 1946 as an All-City right tackle he would be captain of Tony Hinkle's team at Butler University before his tenure as coach at School 50.

52. Graduating in 1935 he would become a star basketball player for Butler University and later the long time assistant to Tony Hinkle.

53. At halftime of IU vs. Minnesota football game in 2007, this 1934 Washington High graduate was proclaimed as "Mr. IU football."

54. The only Continental back-to-back Cross Country State Champ. Name him.

55. The First Family of Washington High wrestling. Four top grapplers. Name them.

56. Her father was considered one of the founders of Washington High. She was a long time Latin and Spanish teacher through the early 1970's.

57. He was the "bootleg pass" quarterback of the 1974 State Champs who could have been an All-State linebacker with his strength and guts.

58. Name the 1959 Indiana All-Star who was a dust bowl teammate of the famous Big O. His brother was the star fullback on the 1968 football team. Name both.

59. Who was the long time Science department head who died suddenly in 1973?

60. Name the long time Dean of Boys who taught history in the 1930's and retired in 1969.

61. Who was the Washington High Shop teacher who served with a Marine Corps tank crew during the World War II invasion of Iwo Jima? He married music teacher Ruth Rosser. In the 21st century their son teaches at West Point.

62. Born in 1920 in the same house on South Belmont in which she died in 2004, this 1937 graduate worked as secretary and unofficial "queen" at her alma mater until its closing in 1995.

63. An All-City quarterback in 1954, this young Continental died of a cerebral hemorrhage in the spring of 1956 while at Chattanooga spring football practice.

64. Name the 1974 grad who held the World's Record Pentathlon score in 1981.

65. He was a Depauw classmate of Mr. Julian. He taught senior English 1930's-70's.

66. He lived on the N. Tremont alley facing GWHS. In the Army Air Corps he was on Tinian Island when the A-bomb arrived in 1945. Post-war he worked on the U-2 spy plane as well as the post-war hydrogen bomb project.

67. Name the 1995 graduate who, in 2010, is an assistant basketball coach at Purdue.

68. In the sixty-eight years of the original run of Washington High School, along with the six top-level team State Championship teams how many State Champion individuals were there? (counting each person, each year, each event as one in track, cross country and wrestling)

69. He was one of the few linemen, as a center-linebacker, ever named MVP in football. Name the line star of the 1947 Washington eleven. Three sons on IU's 1979 Holiday Bowl winning team.

70. What respected long-time coach as a Purdue receiver caught All-American and future Super Bowl quarterback Lennie Dawson's first college TD pass?

71. Before "soccer style" kickers, what Continental regularly kicked 70-yard kick offs through the goal post in the late 1960's? Also, a 1969 basketball State Champ.

72. What young man from South Holmes Avenue was touted as a war hero in a news story shortly before being killed on Okinawa in World War II?

73. What 1931 graduate and long time Continental coach was an NFL official from 1961 through the 1974 season after his teaching retirement in June of 1974?

74. What well-respected faculty member held Depauw University's two-mile run record from 1932 until into the 1960's?

75. Who won Washington's last State Championship (in the discus) actually after the school had closed in June 1995?

76. Name the man who was married in August 1955 the same month he began as line coach for the Continental football team. In the 1970's he was a Pacer assistant.

77. What 1943 graduate would survive 24 bombing raids over Germany as a B-17 gunner and later become head of IPS' Junior High athletics until 1985?

78. Name the Science teacher who taught at GWHS from 1959 through 1995. He was the official scorekeeper for the IHSAA finals from 1970-1995 as well as the first 21 years of the girls' basketball tourney.

79. Who was the 1954 graduate who became football coach at Wood then Athletic Director at Shortridge and, eventually, Washington High School through 1995?

80. What 1971 graduate coached at our school (1977-1981) but made his biggest mark as principal at Warren Central High School using the "Washington Way" while overseeing Warren's four straight football State Championships?

81. Name the Continental who was a member of the 1965 basketball State Champs and also a Sgt. in the Army's famous Short Range Ambush Patrol (SRAP) in Vietnam in the 1960's as is documented on the internet.

82. What 1938 graduate would return to Washington High as the long time band director from 1951 into the 1970's?

83. One of at least 15 boys killed during the Vietnam War this 1964 graduate worked at the Dairy Queen at our school's main driveway before entering the service.

84. Name the 1953 graduate who was an All City end in football as well as being named All City Tourney in basketball.

85. His dad was an early 1930's athlete at Washington. Name the 1961 graduate who was a star halfback on the 1959 undefeated football team but played basketball at Purdue University.

86. He was head coach for 19 seasons and won more Sectional Championships (five) than all of the previous four coaches combined; 222 wins, the most for GWHS.

87. He was a valued faculty member and coach from 1961 until 1995 (even after his retirement in 1989) as a track, cross country and football coach while maintaining all of the statistics for Continental athletes.

88. Along with Joe Dezelan, this 1933 grad made for an impressive pair of All City tackles. As a sophomore at Purdue he started in football, basketball, and baseball but died of an infection in 1935 when his religious beliefs denied him medication.

89. Our fifth principal, this Industrial Arts teacher was a long time vice principal as well as basketball score-keeper in the 1950's.

90. Name the first three all-female cheerleaders. Their initial season was 1947-48.

91. Why did the 1987 Post yearbook display a green & yellow pinstripe on the cover?

92. Name the TV personality, class of '77 basketball player, who in 2010 appears on WRTV-Channel 6 newscasts.

93. Who was the only three-year starter who led Continental roundballers to three consecutive City Championship titles as well as the frosh championship?

94. Our sixth school principal came from Shortridge High School in 1965 as a teacher & football coach. He was "traded" for an ex-head coach who went to Shortridge as Athletic Director. Name the principal and the ex-Washington coach.

95. Their dad graduated in 1939; their mom in 1951. The family opened the Workingman's Friend in 1918 and still own it. Name the family.

96. Honorable Mention All-American in 1973 at Tennessee Tech. Noted by Pacer Assistant Jerry Oliver in training camp of 1975 as "the best guard on the team."

97. Football Coach Tofil noted that during his 11-year tenure a member of this family, Dave, was his best all-around football player. Younger brother Ed, class of 1957, was also a bruising linebacker. Mary, Rosie and Deloris all graduated from GWHS as did their spouses. Three other siblings attended parochial schools. Name the family from West Indianapolis.

98. This noted Hoosier's family ran a business (Thomas L. Green & Co. just four blocks to the northeast) from the 1880's into the 21st century. Although he graduated from Shortridge in 1950, he became an adopted Continental during his tenure on the Indianapolis School Board in the mid-1960's. Who is he?

99. As brothers-in-law in the mid-1970's this 1971 Male Athlete of the Year at GWHS and 1965 basketball State Champ caught a 56-lb. carp and gained temporary angler-fame before it was declared a Buffalo fish. Name them.

100. Although she left in 1978 she gained national fame as an adult film producer and star known as Hyapatia Lee. What was her Washington High School name?

101. He set an NCAA single-season three-point shooting record in 1987 that lasted until 2008 when Davidson's Stephen Curry broke it in the NCAA tourney. He graduated from GWHS in 1983 and starred for Butler University. Name him.

102. She was a 4th grade student of 1939 graduate Thelma Bloomenstock. She was also Mrs. Bopp's Cadet Teacher and IUPUI Student Teacher. This 1971 grad would marry a 1969 basketball State Champ and become Director of Hawthorne Community Center as well as an IPS School Board member into the 21st century.

103. In his sophomore year at IU in 1968, this Continental sprinted for an 82-yd. TD vs. Baylor tying 1934 QB Don Veller for the fourth longest rushing TD in IU football history at the time. He was on the inaugural All-Star team in 1967.

104. Sportswriter Dick Mittman wrote in 1974 that this Continental was the first Hoosier to win both a football and basketball State Championship ring. His son hit the game-winning HR in the Regionals of 1981 for Marion County's only baseball single-class (1967-1997) State Champs (Ben Davis). First family with three rings in top three sports in Indiana.

105. Washington High's last football coach in 1994. He was a star guard on the Reggie Williams-George McGinnis-led Continentals in 1968.

106. Washington's last basketball coach from 1989 to 1995. He spent his freshman year at Continentaland before heading to brand new Northwest in 1963. Butler grad.

107. Sportswriter Bob Collins wrote that this School 50 & 1938 GWHS grad was the best late 1930's athlete, in his opinion. Purdue single-wing QB.

108. Named to the Indiana Central University (Univ. of Indianapolis) Hall of Fame in 2008 he won 12 letters in four sports and became Avon H.S. first football coach.

109. He caught a TD pass that denied Cathedral the 1962 City Championship. Name Coach Springer's very first All-City Continental.

110. This Washington great was affectionately known as "Swivel Hips" and "Red." He followed in his older brother's big footsteps playing football at Purdue before his untimely death in Roswell, New Mexico in a World War II training collision.

111. All-City halfback in 1956 & 1957. Younger brother, Jerry, a '62 star. Name him.

112. School's first All-City football player in 1928. Elected city Mayor in 1955.

113. School 5 Coach Cliff Robinson, Attucks class of '53, noted that the positive personality of this Continental (along with class of 1962's Louie Craig) would usher in the basketball State Championship era of the 1960's. Class of 1964, his nickname was "Onion."

114. Name the four members of the 1943 State Champion 880-yd. team.

115. Known as "Tex" this Continental would graduate in 1961 and star at the University of Louisville before training camp with Oakland Raiders.

116. The unanimous All-City quarterback in 1959, he would fly helicopters and airplanes for the Indiana State Police until 1988 then continue in the same capacity for the FAA into 2007.

117. A true gentleman, this 1940 graduate would become Northwest's first Athletic Director while living on the NW corner at Jackson & S. Mount streets.

118. This star quarterback led the Continentals to 28 football wins over three years.

119. In 1968 she may have become the only sophomore named Homecoming Queen. Her mother was an "original" females-only cheerleader in 1947-48. She was the Washington High Alumni President in 2009.

120. In 1952 he arrived as an assistant coach from Butler University. He later became the first football coach at Northwest High School.

121. When she graduated from Butler University in 1943 she may have been Jacktown's first female college graduate. Name the 1939 Washington graduate who would teach from 1943 until retirement at School 50 in 1985. Joanne Julian Solomon (Mr. Julian's daughter) and Jean Mohr (GWHS class of 1948) were close teaching colleagues.

122. This 1938 Continental grad was a tough football man for Coach Bogue. He became School Board President in Wayne Township before his 1980 death. His brother, Bill, was Speedway's golf coach and his nephew, George, was a rough fullback-LBer for Coach Springer's first team.

123. This family had a student at either School 46 or Washington High from 1927 until 1945. Although their father died in 1929 all eight kids, who grew up on Morgan Street, graduated from our proud school. Name the family.

124. Arriving from William Penn College in 1927, this Quaker-influenced teacher would be football coach for 24 seasons winning 110 games.

125. This 20-year head basketball coach arrived from Manual High. He retired in 1966 after 18 years as Athletic Director. His son Ed, known also as Bud, was 1944 State High Jump champion clearing 6'0".

126. In 1990 name the GWHS State Champ high jumper who cleared 6'10".

127. During the 227-wins Springer-era, how many Indiana All-Star football players did he mentor?

128. Name the 1982 basketball All-Star who would set Indiana State hoop records.

129. What two Continentals, class of 1964, would both become three-year All-Conference football players at Ball State University?

130. Graduating in 1942 he was drafted along with his neighbor Bob Cooke. After the war he married Bob's sister. This man's brother was killed on Saipan and his future wife's brother, Bob Cooke, was killed in France. Who is this man who lives on into 2010?

131. This member of the State Championship American Legion 1969 baseball team (who grew up in the Valley) was killed in the Vietnam War in 1971.

132. He only coached at Continentaland for seven years before heading to Indiana Central as track coach. He specialized in the shot put. And his son became an NCAA champion at the University of Alabama. Also, an ICC teammate of Carol Purichia, Chuck Hedges and Hank Easter. What's his name?

133. He came to Washington in the 1930's as a Vice Principal in charge of discipline. He had been a teacher at Tech who Barbara Jean Sullivan Hine noted that she was "afraid of" when she had been a student there. Nicknamed "Pinky" for his alleged red face when angry. Name him.

134. The last two-handed jump-shooter who started on two city championship teams as well as being a star pitcher on the baseball team. He had graduated from Holy Trinity in Haughville and died too young in 2002. Name him.

135. His 16 years at GWHS was proceeded by a successful tenure at Wood. He mentored seven State Champions in Track & Field. He died in late 2009.

136. This pair starred in the 1968 summer football All-Star game at Butler's field. They played "both ways" as a lineman-Lber and as a back. Later they would both coach as assistants at Washington High.

137. This 1973 University of Cincinnati football recruit was a star running back and defensive back. He would later mentor young athletes at Municipal Gardens on Lafayette Road. Name this School 75 athlete.

138. A 1938 graduate she would become the mother of three Washington grads: Bill, Marsha and Linda. Her father had been Jacktown's last blacksmith.

139. He may have been Coach Springer's only four year football "starter" as a defensive end and linebacker. Tri-captain of 1966 mythical State Champs.

140. Our first varsity African-American quarterback in 1972 and basketball point guard as well as baseball player. His son would be point guard for a Ben Davis state finals team in the 1990's.

141. When he was killed in May of 1965 news reports stated that he was the first Hoosier Marine and first Indianapolis boy killed in Vietnam. Who was he?

142. The fourth brother in less than ten years to become varsity quarterback. He would tragically die, age 39, at a high school football game in 1979.

143. These two 1969 footballers had fathers who also played football at GWHS. Both their dads had the same name as their Jr. sons. Both from School 49.

144. This 1971 graduate was named in popular newspaperman Tom Keating's column as Indianapolis-Marion County's first Student of the Year.

145. During World War II, Mr. Gingery sponsored a series of periodical acknowledgments directed at "our boys overseas." Football Coach Henry Bogue, Principal Gingery and others "talked to our boys" in their essays. What was that periodical called?

146. He put a Continental smack-down on future pro Lars Tate on the third play of the Regional Championship in 1983 to effectively set the tone for Washington's victory vs. North Central, 30-3.

147. Nicknamed "The President" in 1963, this respected leader & student-athlete played tackle-fullback-LBer before a stellar football career at Louisville.

148. Name the 1955 FB & 1956 city champ wrestler with a great sports name.

149. Future Lilly VP & father-in-law of Ralph Poehls; top student, class of 1935.

150. Who was the highly respected quarterback of the 1944 City Champs?

151. Long time frosh football coach Johnny Williams, who retired in 1974 and died in 2003, called this Haughville stud "pound for pound the toughest player I've ever coached." He was a small '72 halfback and outside LBer on the 9-0 football team which lost to Cathedral after failing to convert a 4th & 1.

152. With Jerry Lawlis injured, these two Hinesmen with the same first name stepped forward as stars of the 1954-55 team. One was a Senior, the other a Junior.

153. Name the 1944 city champ pole vaulter and hard charging fullback of the 1943 football team. Before becoming Decatur Central's head football coach he was an assistant to Jim Carter at Anderson High School. Second in State Pole Vault.

154. Along with Bob Dietz this leading scorer of the 1934-35 basketball team would lead the 13-5 Continentals to our first roundball City Championship.

155. Name the 1953 unanimous All-City football tackle for the 6-2-1 team.

156. Name our last football All-Star for the 11-2 team of 1993.

157. This Basketball Hall of Fame member graduated in 1953. He is best known for his 40 years as Head Coach at Linton, Seeger, Brazil, Shortridge, Jennings County, Bloomington South, and Southport. His 1990 team was defeated by Damon Bailey's team in the afternoon state finals.

158. This 1975 graduate won the Girls' State Championship in the Long Jump. Her dad had been a varsity basketball player, class of 1956. Name both.

159. Name the members of the 1971 record setting 880-yd. relay team.

160. Name the 1974 football State Championship tackle who won a scholarship to Louisville. On Christmas Day 1978 he was captain for the South in the annual Blue-Gray All-Star game.

161. Name the 1958 graduate who has taken the torch from Mrs. Sanders as the new "Miss Washington." Secretary from the early 1970's through 1995.

162. A 1950 graduate who played football and basketball. He gained fame as the long-time golf professional at the Brickyard Crossing golf course. Football captain '49.

163. This 1962 football guard and baseball 3rd baseman became a career member of the U. S. Air Force and eventually retired from Homeland Security in the 21st century. He was a member of the frogman recovery crew team for our Mercury astronauts in the 1960's. He's retired living in New Mexico in 2010 married to a female State Trooper.

164. He graduated in 1951 but became a long-time print shop teacher responsible for the publication of the yearbook into the 1980's. His son-in-law became football coach at Avon High School in 2010.

165. These four brothers all served during World War II. Three had sons that graduated from Continentaland in the first half of the 1960's. Those three cousins were Bill ('63), Mike ('62) and Larry ('65). Name the family.

166. Who is credited with the lyrics for the "Washington Hymn?"

167. Who wrote the music for the "Washington Hymn?"

168. Who did Mr. Julian credit with writing the lyrics for the "Fight Song?"

169. Sue Kepner, class of 1953, has a famous grandchild in the 21st century. Name the grandchild and why she is well known.

170. Within three weeks and a day in late 1963 two events occurred that shocked all residents of central Indiana and beyond. Name those two events.

171. Before running on both the Butler and Indiana Central track teams, this future Continental teacher-coach would run on the Tech H.S. Mile Relay team with future State Superintendent H. Dean Evans.

172. He scored eight touchdowns for the undefeated 1959 team including two kick-off returns of 80-yards. As a Louisville sophomore he scored a long TD the first time that he touched the ball for the Cardinals. Northwest coach by 1970.

173. One of the best basketball players to not be named an All-Star, this 1962 graduate's brother was State High Jump Champ in 1968 for Ben Davis. Name our Continental near-great.

174. Name the 1937 graduate who turned 90-years-old in April of 2010. He has worked at the Indianapolis Motor Speedway since 1946. He's their longest serving employee. Uncle of 1964 scholar Janet Blake.

175. What woman, who was the mother of two Continental graduates from the 1930's, could be considered the person who started businessman Dick Lugar's political career? She approached him in 1964 representing the Citizens' School Committee suggesting that he run for a position on the School Board.

176. Name the 1949 GWHS graduate who is credited with starting eleven-man football at Center Grove in 1955. He was the official scorer 35-years for the Wrestling State Finals and was named to their Hall of Fame.

177. He was All-City halfback for the 1959 team. Along with Tom Benson (both from School 50), he broke our school's pole vault record in 1961. Name him.

178. Name the halfback for the 1983 State Runners-up who set an all-time single season scoring record while breaking Louie Day's mark.

179. Although she didn't win State (the winner cleared 5'7") this female Continental high jumped 5'7.75" to set the Washington High record in 1980.

180. This 1931 graduate re-upped with the 551st Parachute Infantry Battalion as a Medic. He was attached to the 82nd Airborne when he died in combat in 1945.

181. Name the Stringtown boy who played on the 1941-42 Lauter's Boys Club team and later was Head Basketball Coach at Ben Davis coaching a 1965 win over our eventual State Champs.

182. This 1965 graduate was the leading scorer on the 1963 and 1964 reserve basketball teams. He also played left field in baseball and was a leading home run hitter. His dad inspired Tony Burchett to become a baseball catcher after Tony arrived in the Carnine Little League neighborhood as a child.

183. Who was the 1946 Mr. Basketball who coached Wood High School in the 1965 City Championship game against our school? He had begun his career in education, after being a Globetrotter, as coach at School 5 through 1958.

184. Name the 1963 graduate who earned high praise as wrestling coach at the Indiana Blind School and as an administrator in education.

185. What was the name of the booklet given to incoming freshmen starting in the early 1930's? Mrs. McWilliams and the National Honor Society published those informative readings which displayed class times, morals, rules, and Christian-based advice for our west side public school students at the time.

186. Name the 1937 tough football captain who continues to attend alumni events into 2010.

187. Name the family whose husband and wife both graduated in the 1940's. They also had five children graduate from our respected school between 1966 and 1976. Their kids are Darrell, Bobby, Phyllis, Rocky and Candy.

188. This 1961 Holy Trinity graduate was the punter for the 1964 Continental eleven. From punt formation he completed a successful desperation-pass on 4th and 12 from our own 2-yard line in our final game against Cathedral.

189. Twin brothers from Hiawatha Street (where IUPUI's track is located in 2010) who starred for Coach Jones' 1942 City Champs. They graduated in 1943 and played basketball for Tony Hinkle at Butler University. Name both.

190. During the pre-game meal before Homecoming in 1959, this popular footballer consumed more than his share of chicken-gravy and biscuits at the Chicken Shack on Lafayette Road.

191. Who was the first Continental female named as the top city athlete in 1980?

192. Although he was serving our nation in the Armed Services, Coach Bogue named him the football captain in 1943.

193. He was credited with 14 tackles in our Homecoming victory during the 1963 football season. His grade school girlfriend, Clancie Opp, was voted Homecoming Queen the same night. Name that 140-lb linebacker.

194. An Art teacher, she graduated from Broad Ripple High School in 1951 then from Ball State in 1955. Her dad was IPS' Assistant Superintendent. At Ball State she met, then married in August 1955, one of our most successful coaches.

195. These three members of the original faculty of 1927 all retired in the mid-1960's. One in 1963, another in 1965, and the last in 1966. Name all three.

196. This ex-Manual High School head coach arrived in Continental-land in the mid-1950's to teach in the Social Studies department and coach freshmen basketball. In 1966 he became Athletic Director.

197. He was a member of the 1959 undefeated football team but gained prominence as the 120-lb. State Champion wrestler in 1961.

198. The graceful strides of this track star led to his 220-yd. State Championship in 1972 after he had anchored the 1971 record setting 880-yd. relay State Champs.

199. He played on Coach Oliver's first varsity basketball team then was a star on the 1961 Golf State Champs for Coach Hine. Name him.

200. Between 1959 and 1980, only one school in Indianapolis-Marion County won a State Championship in either football or basketball at the top or single-class level. Name the school that won two in each sport between 1965 and 1974.

GWHS MT. RUSHMORE

Football   BORIS BABE DIMANCHEFF
Basketball   GEORGE McGINNIS
Baseball   DON LEPPERT
Track   LARRY HIGHBAUGH

GWHS MT. WASHINGTON

Golf   SANDY SPUZICH
Boxing   LAMON BREWSTER
Cross Country DENNIS GRIDER
Wrestling   PHILLIP LESLIE
Girls Sports   CHERYL COOK

SCHOOL BEGINNING

WILLIAM GINGERY
ROWLAND JONES
HENRY BOGUE

SCHOOL MID-ERA

CLOYD CURLY JULIAN
BARBARA JEAN SULLIVAN HINE
BOB SPRINGER

SCHOOL ENDING-ERA

AL HAMILTON
BASIL SFREDDO
JOE SHIRES

All-Time All-Marshall (1967-1981) Coach Eddie Bopp 1976-1981

Offense   MVP---Eli GARZA

Chuck HAWKINS 1969 E	Ron COLES 1968 T	David OWENS 1977 G	Jim WORSTEL 1967 C	Mark OSBORNE 1981 G	Eddie MURRELL 1981 T	Larry BRYANT 1971 E

	Danny LESSELY 1978 Punter		Steve MILLER 1981 QB		Gerald LEWIS 1980 WR	

	Terry HOCHESANG 1973 HB		Eli GARZA 1981 FB		Keith JONES 1979 HB	

Strong Mention: Mike Gentry '71 QB; Ray Shepard '78 G; Bob Bultman '77 T; Tony Washington '79 R-HB; Jeff Craver '69 FB; Marvin Howard '81 HB; Tony Allen '80 HB; Chris Agee '80 C; Bryant Ingram '81 G; David Williams '78 T

Defense   MVP---William YARBROUGH

James FINCH 1981 DE	Mike McCURRY 1980 T	Danny SCHLUGE 1977 MG	Anthony BLACKWELL 1977 T	Kendall FLEMINGS 1981 DE

	George WEST 1975 LB	Jerry HAWKINS 1979 LB		

Greg AGEE 1978 CB	Thomas HENRY 1977 SS	William YARBROUGH 1980 FS	Rick HARTMAN 1978 Kicker	Bill RECKERT 1970 CB

Strong Mention: Elvin Sanders '81 S-Ret.; Mike Shannon '78 DE; Larry Willan '78 T; Mike Jarosinski '79 DE; Billy Wolf & Joe Knudsen '80 LB; Steve Blanche '80 RB-MG; Larry Jacob '80 DB

Honorary Coaches: Bob Tremain ('69), John Tremain ('70), Dave Harvey, John Veza, Tom Marendt, Lennie Brickens, Mojo Hollowell, Don Glesing

First Graduating Class—1928

Name	Address
FLOYD F. BICKERTON	130 Neal Ave.
KATHERINE LUCILE FARLEY	50 S. Warman Ave.
THELMA GRACE FOSTER	2114 W. McCarty St.
GEORGE W. HARLAN	146 S. Elder Ave.
RALPH K. HEDRICK	220 N. Pershing Ave.
LEROY HEINRICKS	726 Grove Ave.
BEDE J. HITTLE	526 Goodlet Ave.
EVA JOHNSON	1848 W. Maryland St.
ROSCOE E. LAYTON	1172 N. Warman Ave.
MARTHA IRENE LEONARD	5010 W. 10th St.
MARY McELWEE	402 S. Warman Ave.
CLARENCE EARL McGEE	85 N. Addison St.
HELEN MARY McLEOD	5058 W. 14th St.
PHYLLIS MARIE MORRISON	Rockville Rd.
THELMA OGDON	122 Riechwein St.
ARTHUR B. PETERSON	1050 N. Tremont Ave.
JOE M. PRITCHETT	221 N. Mount St.
LEWIS O. RUFLY	16 N. Traub Ave.
EVA O. SIMMONS	2101 W. Morris St.
ROBERT C. SPANGLER	546 N. Tremont Ave.
FRANCES ELEANOR STEWART	4915 W. 15th St.
VICTOR THOMAS	1501 W. 15th St., Speedway City
HARRY WARREN	270 N. Pershing Ave.

Valedictorians and Top Academic Graduates
The Goal is Worthy of the Effort

1931	Virginia Miller	1952	Lois Griffith	1976	Kathie Gaddy
	Marshall Smith	1953	Phyllis Young		Mark Riley
	Ray Allen		Sue Kepner		Kimmy Benge
	Eunice Vestal	1954	Norma Inabnit	1977	Tom Pittman
1933	Mary League	1955	John Hood		Andrea Davidson
	Edith Gingery		Gundrun Ziege	1978	Ellen Phillips
	Hazel Grundan	1957	Margaret Reynolds		Brenda Tretter
1934	Edith Carter		Carsey Gentry		Lisa Marion
	John Dunn	1958	Priscilla Thomas	1979	Lenora Mervar
	Alice Walker	1960	Sandra Durham		Larisa Mervar
	Matilda Sparenblek		Carolyn Lloyd	1980	Sharon Stephens
	Doris Smith		Mary Lou Andrews		Bernard Miller
	Frank Cassell	1961	Sherry Leak		Julie Jones
1935	Thelma Martin		Judy Powell	1981	Mariettia Lawson
	Elmer Koch	1962	Frank Starkey		Mary Schaffer
	Julia Sparenblek		Sherry Selch	1982	Finis Cook
	Janith Ramsey	1963	Carol Gardner		Ken Simmons
	Charles Schwartz		Mary Ann Alexander	1983	Kimberly Smith
	Robert Copeland		Charlene Zeronik		Joyce Shelby
1936	Mary Mellinger	1964	Margaret Knight	1984	Theodore Schaffer
	Lee Townley		Connie Hoschouer		Lynn Reynolds
1937	Mary Haynes		Janet Blake	1985	Umi Chong
	John Goddard	1965	Ray Knight		Rebecca Posey
	Mary Mitchell		Kathleen Roberts	1986	Michael Kelley
	Robert Winston		Gary Gunther		Twana Brinkley
1938	Grace Buchanan	1966	Jennifer Gearries	1987	Emma Derebeef
	Daisy Silverman		Bing Fowler		Dennis Thompson
1939	George Mellinger		Gordon Dempsey	1988	Richard Graves
	Louis Kunstek	1967	Ken Haverstick		Penny Wright
1940	Dorothy Asher		Sharon Ayres	1989	Angela Sisson
	John White	1968	George Alexander		Andrea Meredith
1943	Betty Gaddis		Mary Lafevers	1990	Im Yi
	Martha Metcalf	1969	Everett Kunzelman		Holly Goss
	Helen Katterhenry		Michael Hunt	1991	Sang Yi
1944	Norma Messmer	1970	Sam Williams		Natalie Lewis
	Kathryn Harris		Cathy Vaughn	1992	Tony LeMasters
1946	Fred Behning	1971	Nikki Sanders		Katrina Phillips
	Ruth Greenlee		Ronald Burkhardt	1993	Jeremiah Bwatwa
1947	Martha Overman	1972	Dallas Miller		Zac Stewart
	Gordon Whitaker		Cheryl Myrick	1994	Kimberly Tardy
1948	Lowell Lentz	1973	Michael Mick		Jennifer Hudson
	Robert Snodgrass		Darcia Martin	1995	Trinh Tran
					Naeem Baig
1949	Donna Skyles	1974	Jamie Nichols		
	Magdalene Bosiak		Jeff Finley		
1950	Elaine Demos	1975	Lee Kutz		
	Shirley Newnum		Joe Trice		

SENIOR-JUNIOR CLASS PRESIDENTS & WASHINGTONIAN PRESIDENTS

Yearbook	Sr. Class President	Jr. Class President	Washingtonian President
1928	Arthur Peterson	Thelma Flack	
1929	Robert Carlsen		Ione Tullis
1930	Homer Conner		June Darnell
1931	Emil Unser		Eunice Vestal
	Harry Sanders		Nell Hollingsworth
1934	Edwin Howard/Frank Cassell		
1935	Myron Melvin/Bob Dietz		
1936	Lewis Judd		Ann Mitchell/Jeanne Burning
1937	Richard Pottenger		
1938	Louie Leerkamp	Bob McCalip	Marjorie Ryan
1939			Lois McCreery
1941	Donald Cauble		Regina Nichols
1942	Charles Petranoff		Jean Shelburne
1943	Walter O'Brien		
1944	Tom Carpenter/Carter Byfield	Frank Hines	
1945	Don Agnew		Naida Petranoff
1946	Russell Ward		
1948	Chris Theofanis		
1949	Don VanHook		
1950	Albert Cooper	Finis Jent	Sue Blank
1951	Jim Wyckoff	Don Lickliter	Norma Riley
1952	Rex Durrett	Richard Landrigan	Beverly Fischer
1953	Wayne Lentz	Darold Cook	Annetta Chandler
1954	Ronnie Wise	Delbert Gregory	Nadine Holmes
1955	Ray Duncan		Sherry Easter
1956	Don Martin	Eddie Porten	Julia West
1957	Carol Purichia	Bernie Keller	Peggy Arbuckle
1958	Leon Griffith	Steve Kitterman	Sue Priatchard
1959	Nick Purichia	Larry Glaze	Linda Worrell
1960	Kenny Baldwin	Ken Corey	Linda Martin
1961	Jim Loviscek	Mike Guffin	
1962	Joe Purichia	Clark Dickerson	Sally Worrell
1963	John Fletcher	Jerry Wampler	Carolyn Wise
1964	Sam Kitchens	Eddie Bopp	Jane Leeper
1965	Fred Hulser	Ronny Lewis	Irene Helton
1966	Bob Lowery	Winston Fowler	Gail Trout
1967	Eddie George	Terry Pierson	Jan Ewing
1968	Mark Doll	James Chaffin	
1969	Edgar Tipton	Sam Williams	
1970	Steve Durham	Eddie Boswell	Susan Scotten
1971	John Bopp	Karla Riggs	

1972	Dallas Miller	Karen Morton
1973	Ron Craig	
1974	Doug Sims	
1975	Jody Cusson	Donna Brissey
1976	Phillip DeBruler	
1977	Andrea Davidson	
1978	Brenda Tretter	Gale Summers
1981	James Williams	
1982	Leslie Benson	
1983	Scott Hughett	
1984	Tracy Williams	
1985	Genevia Woods	
1986	Mary Montes	
1987	Emma Derebeef	
1988	Shenia Footman	
1989	Michele Adams	
1990	Twana Griffin	
1991	Natalie Lewis	
1992	Malcolm Webster	
1993	Damon Smith	
1994	Jonathan Young	
1995	Trinh Tran	

Fall Queens

	Jamboree Queen	Homecoming Queen	Military Ball Queen
1951		Mary Lalioff	Gail Comer
1952		Pat Craig	Dorothy Schmid
1953		Jackye Lou Fox	Vivian Tyner
1954	Jackye Fox	Edna Teal	Carole Budack
1955	Carolyn Turner	Janet Shaw	Janet Shaw
1956	Mary Sue Kemp	Marlene Short	Mary Sue Kemp
1957	Diane Luzar	Sue Pritchard	Georgia Clarkson
1958	Penny Guffin	Diane Luzar	Lorelei Williams
1959	Linda Martin	Becky Grimes	Rita Felice
1960	Ruthann Leach	Judy Wampler	Pam Waltz
1961	Sylvia Popcheff	Mary Parker	Janice Nash
1962	Becky Mraz	Sue Douglass	Cheryl Swartz
1963	Regina Such	Clancie Opp	Trena Mervar
1964	Karen Powell	Bobbie Morgan	Peggy Green
1965	Teresa Lewis	Portia Lanham	Janet Ewing
1966	Portia Lanham	Shasta Williams	Marcia Davenport
1967	Gail Horner	Denise Byrdsong	Nancy Persinger
1968	Denise Byrdsong	Connie Higgins	Beth Ann Cook
1969	Diane Elam	Kathy Accomondo	
1970	Carol Waggoner	Renee Featherston	Nikki Sanders
1971		Brenda Collins	Marty Martin
1972	Wanda Waters	Becky Tames	Marty Martin
1973	Debbie Quarles	Terri Mervar	Judy Brown
1974	Karen Filer	Peppi Faulk	
1975	Vanessa Tate	Kathy Gaddie/Lisa Hall	Sherry Moore
1976	Crystal Reeves	Annette Fields	
1977		Gail Arterburn	
1978		Jane Loftus	Regena Marion
1979		Bonnie Harrington	
1980		Renee Shanks	
1982	Joyceline Bray	Cheryl BeBow	Joyceline Bray
1983		Heidi Thomas	

STUDENT BODY PRESIDENT + Surveyor & Yearbook Editor

Yearbook	Student Council Pres.	Surveyor Editor	Yearbook Editor
1929		Jack Schenck	Frank Yarbrough
1930			Jack Schenck
1932			Stanley Lawton
1933		Harold Gunderloy	Mary Wicker
1934			George Powers
1935			Elmer Koch
1936		Bruce Herrin	Edward Cotton
1937			Bill Johnson
1938		Myron Scarbrough	Dollie Abell
1939		Myron Scarbrough	Mary Laue
1940	Harold Negley		Jack Nyland
1941	Robert Millspaugh	Sadie Kretheotis	Mabel Mohr
1942		Julia Allen	Bob Clegg
1944			Charlotte Windisch
1945	Russell Esarey	Shirley Lines	Anna Mae Mohr
1946	Guy Fish		
1947			Marilyn Tirmenstein
1948		June Lalen	Helen Alexander
1949	Glen Homer Hawkins	Francine Camden	Mary Helen Gish
1950	Kenny Ayres	James Moore	Elaine Demos
1951	Finis Gent	Bill Porter	Mary Kay Norman
1952	Eddie Kernodle	Rita LeGault	Mary Lou Strader
1953	Nick George	Patty Moore	Barbara Fox
1954	Darold Cook	Lavon Ammerman	Sue Burton
1955	John Hood	Irene Greenhalgh	Gudrun Ziege
1956	Larry Moore	Anne Kessler	Carolyn Knoebel
1957	Errol Loviscek	Lana Kay Matthews	Cynthia Fendley/ Sandra Parries
1958	John Alexander	Jill Carter	Kay Pence/ Judy K. Smith
1959	Diane Luzar	Grace Edwards	Sharon Smith
1960	David Wright	Linda Hefner	Becky Grimes
1961	David Horner	Ken Turpin	Sandy Adams
1962	Mike Guffin	Evelyn Thomas	Steve Dalzell
1963	Mickey Eller	Charles Spurgeon	Linda Jeter/ Gary McFall
1964	Vicki Wright	Bette Kramer	Carol Boone
1965	Tom Gregg	Ray Knight	Barbara Medsker/ Pat Hansford
1966	Bing Fowler	Charlotte Downin	Peggy Green
1967	Ken Opel	Charlene Sturgis	Patty Medley

1968	Gail Horner	John Schmitt	Charlene Blevins
1969	Nancy Persinger	Ken Cox	Marilyn Kerr
1970	David Lowery	Linda Beetem	Kathy Deakin
1971	Ruth Baird	Rayann Backus	Gary Bryant
1972		Becky Tames	Anita Byers
1973			Anita Byers
1974			
1975	Janice Akers		
1976	Lisa Hall		
1977	Rick Hightower	Carol Mahaney	
1978	Cathy Hommel		
1984		Kim Hankins/ Billy Cole	Patty McGraw

Daughters of American Revolution Good Citizen, Drum Major, May Queen

Yearbook	D.A.R. Good Citizen	Drum Major	May Queen
1938		Edgar Cox	
1939		Jim Caldwell/ Bill Jerome	
1945	Jacqueline Smith		
1951			
1952	Lois Griffin	Bill Simmons	
1953	Sandra Grimes	Bill Simmons	Carolyn Hickman
1954	Ruthann Crippen	Bill Cole	
1955		Errol Loviscek	
1956	Donna Smith	Errol Loviscek	Carolyn Turner
1957	Margaret Reynolds	Errol Loviscek	
1958	Jill Carter	Dave Donovan	Joyce Bright
1959	Trina Radcliffe	Dave Donovan	Diane Luzar
1960	Linda Hefner	Kenny Drake	Linda Martin
1961	Judy Powell	Kenny Drake	Judy Wampler
1962	Sherry Selch	Robert Bremer	Mary Parker
1963	Sue Douglass	Robert Bremer	Sue Douglass
1964	Janet Blake	Robert Bremer	Paulette Frye
1965	Kathleen Roberts	Larry Dodson	Karen McDonald
1966	Jennifer Gearries	David Crane	Donna Burkert
1967	Janet Ewing	Roger Weaver	Shasta Williams
1968	Gail Horner	Roger Weaver	Gail Horner
1969	Patty Vaughn	Roger Weaver	Nancy Persinger
1970		Mike Patterson	Alice Montgomery
1971		Mike Patterson	Ruth Baird
1972	Marite Talbergs	Bob Williams	Lois Johnson
1973	Bob Williams	Anita Washington	
1974	Jamie Nichols	Terry Bryant	Debi Graves
1975	Joetta Bailey	Andre Bryant	Janice Akers
1976	Kathy Gaddie	Andre Bryant	Kathy Gaddie
1977	Caroline Coffin		Annette Fields
1978	Brenda Tretter		Amy Black
1979			Lenora Mervar
1980	Robin Dixon	Bonnie Harrington	
1981	Maria Lawson	Tommy Johnson	Debbie Bingham
1983	Kim Smith	Tim McCreary	Syvaline Miller
1984	Daniel Luter	Pete Schultheis	Tracie Williams

*note: Mr. Ray Funk, class of 1938, was Band Director from 1951 through 1972

Selected Lists

Clean Parks Queen

1958	Jo Ann Cherry
1959	Shirley Vaseloff
1960	Brenda Kemp
1961	Beverly Carpenter
1962	Karen Hazelwood
1963	Janet Blake
1964	Darla Moore

Princess of Light

1960	Pat Bowman
1961	Brenda Williams
1962	Marsha Brown
1963	Cheryl Swartz
1964	Paulette Frye
1965	Marilyn Findlay
1966	Donna Burkert
1967	Janet Ewing

Bible Club President

1951	Betty Darnell
1952	Joanne Ensley
1956	Evelyn Becker
1957	Evelyn Becker
1959	Paul Butler
1960	Nancy Selch
1961	James Strange
1963	Berthamae Dix
1964	Judy Austin
1965	Thomas Allen
1967	Pam Wilson

National Honor Society President

1936	Herbert Russell & Harvey Slaughter
1937	Omer Scott
1938	Mary Alice Waltz
1939	Kenneth Goslin
1941	Phyllis Webb
1945	David Wheeler
1953	Jerry Kerkhof
1954	Delbert Gregory & Tom Payne
1955	Donna Drennan
1956	Jan Guffin
1958	Bruce Barr
1959	Dave Thomas
1960	Carolyn Lloyd
1961	Tom Blair
1962	Gary Bland
1963	Skip Crawford
1964	Janet Blake
1965	Greg Shelton
1966	Gordon Dempsey
1967	Winston Fowler
1968	David Crane
1969	James Chaffin
1970	Joy Tweed
1984	Patricia McGraw

Track Queen

1947	Barbara Shackelford
1952	Betty Poland
1954	Jackye Fox
1955	Merriline Surber
1958	Joyce Bright
1959	Sharon Keithley
1960	Joe Marie VanBlaricum
1961	Tessa Trusty
1962	Sally Reddick
1963	Sandy Lambert
1964	Karen Koon
1965	Regina Such
1966	Gail Trout
1967	Linda Hunter

Dance Kings & Queens, Johnnie & Connie Continentals, George & Martha

Johnnie & Connie Continental/*George & Martha/Capers King & Queen

1950	Albert Cooper & Barbara Vargo*		1955	Bill Riley & Sondra VanWinkle
1951	Bill Cook & Roberta Cubert		1957	Phyllis Doucleff
1954	Ronnie Wise & Pat Brandenburg		1958	Fred Hunt & Susan Wampler
1955	Bill Purichia/Joe Shires & Artie Demos		1960	Bill Snowberger & Hazel White
1956	Wayne Vaughn & Patty Lisby		1961	Jim Arvin & Judy Tackwell
1957	Bob Roark & Judy Oliver		1962	Alan Derringer & Maxine Kennedy
1958	Dave Sanders & Vennettia Eddy		1963	Sam Kitchens & Donna Cole
1959	Reggie Opp & Sybil Milspaugh		1964	Pete Cook & Joanne Reid
1960	Larry Compton & Linda Hefner		1965	Bill Keller & Glenna Fields
1961	Doyle Baker & Sandy Adams		1967	Doug Watson & Darlene Jones
1962	Denny Troth & Sally Reddick			
1963	Clark Dickerson & Donna Baldwin*			
1966	Larry Zore & Teresa Lewis			
1967	Rick Thompson & Patty Medley			

Junior Prom King & Queen · Jack Frost & Christmas Carol

1944	Jacqueline Smith		1951	Bill Cook & Martha Craig
1949	Geraldine Hamm		1952	Rex Durrett & Betty Polond
1950	Beverly Vargo		1953	Bill Springer & Carolyn Hickman
1952	Bonnie Benge		1954	Artie Shaw & Gloria Wycoff
1953	Ronnie Wise & Marilyn Reynolds		1959	Kay Richie
1955	Don Carter & Carolyn Turner		1961	Denny Dennett & Tessa Trusty
1956	Larry Morgan & Mary Sue Kemp		1962	Danny Jaquess & Sandy Marsh
1957	Gary Hesser & Lillie Watz		1966	Ron Davidson
1958	Jim Saylor & Joyce Mount		1967	Jim Sims & Patty Davenport
1959	David Wright & Carolyn Lloyd			
1960	Larry Morton & Mary Martin			
1961	Mike Guffin & Marsha Brown			
1962	Clark Dickerson & Janie Horner			
1963	Joe Blake & Paulette Frye			
1964	Bill Keller & Marilyn Findlay			
1965	Ronny Lewis & Donna Burkert			
1966	Jim Sims & Marilyn Sue Spears			
1967	George Alexander & Gail Horner			
1968	Myron Newland & Cindy Warren			
1969	David Lowery & Brenda Hicks			
1973	Terri Moore			

Graduates from Yearbook pictures or Graduation programs

1928-----23	1951----235	1974----324
1929-----75	1952----241	1975----270
1930----125	1953----210	1976----255
1931----174	1954----208	1977----247
1932----136	1955----251	1978----288
1933----244	1956----243	1979----273
1934----232	1957----258	1980----259
1935----252	1958----240	1981----233
1936----279	1959----357	1982----304
1937----290	1960----324	1983----225
1938----300	1961----338	1984----228
1939----301	1962----290	1985----190
1940----343	1963----394	1986----165
1941----331	1964----445	1987----203
1942----308	1965----317	1988----174
1943----217	1966----322	1989----220
1944----253	1967----363	1990----164
1945----201	1968----347	1991----146
1946----230	1969----348	1992----165
1947----260	1970----364	1993----154
1948----247	1971----310	1994----170
1949----187	1972----359	1995---169
1950----232	1973----328	

Cheerleaders

1948   Betty Voege, Pat Whitmore, Sue Wilson, Barbara Carter

1951   Dorothy Nickoloff, Shirle Fulton, Margie Whitmore, Tom Walls,
Norman Jones, Bill Harrell

1952   Carolyn Hickman, Gail Comer, Eleanor Orebaugh, Marjorie Whitmore,
Betty Poland, Sandra Grimes

1953   Sandy Grimes, Edna Teal, Gail Comer, Charlotte Leak,
Eleanor Orebaugh, Carolyn Hickman

1954   Eleanor Orebaugh, Merriline Surber, Patty Brandenburg,
Edna Teal, Charlotte Leak, Janet Shaw

1955   Sonny Fields, Rosalind Brown, Charlotte Leak, Edna Teal,
Janet Shaw, Cynthia Fendley, Wayne Vaughn, Merriline Surber

1956   Cynthia Fendley, Rosalind Brown, Helen Suddeth, Marlene Short,
Janet Shaw, Jackie Blackwell, Wayne Vaughn, Sonny Fields

1957   Marlene Short, Helen Suddeth, Cynthia Fendley, Joyce Mount,
Jackie Blackwell, Emma Yates, Kay Ritchie, Rosalind Brown

1958   Dave Bowman, Marilyn Harrington, Helen Suddeth, Joyce Mount,
Linda Martin, Kay Ritchie, Emma Yates

1959   Marilyn Harrington, Charlene Houchins, Dave Bowman, Kay Ritchie,
Barbara Keller, Sharon Keithley, Linda Martin

1960   Ken Turpin, Eva Walker, Joe Hendricks, Pat Pritchett, Mary Ann Martin,
Charlene Houchins, Linda Martin, Barbara Keller

1961   Karen Turner, Bonnie Dodd, Mary Parker, Mary Ann Martin, Ken Turpin,
Joe Hendricks, Patty Miller, Eva Walker, Pat Pritchett

1962   Sandy Dulla, Jane Horner, Sylvia Popcheff, Karen Hessel,
Bonnie Dodd, Pat Miller, Vicki Wright, Mary Parker

1963   Karen Hessel, Sue Douglass, Nancy McFall, Vicki Wright, Jane Horner

1964   Suzanne St. John, Vicki Wright, Donna Burkert,
Phyllis Abbott, Karen Koon, Bobbie Morgan

1965   Regina Such, Bobbie Morgan, Phyllis Abbott,
Donna Burkert, Nancy Parks, Barbara Brunt

1966   Donna Burkert, Nancy Parks, Phyllis Abbott, Sue Spears, Portia Lanham

1967   Portia Lanham, Sue Spears, Judy Spear, Gail Horner, Janet Ewing

1968   Betty Coop, Luelda Trieb, Denise Byrdsong, Gail Horner, Debbie Woods

1969   Luelda Trieb, Connie Higgins, Diane Elam, Debbie Woods,
Betty Coop, Cindy Warren, Denise Syrdsong

1970   Nina Tuttle, Carol Waggoner, Diane Elam, Connie Higgins,
Darlene Cross, Becky Weiss, Aletha Chandler

1971   Diane Kenley, Carol Waggoner, Aletha Chandler, Diane Elam,
Connie Higgins, Nina Tuttle, Darlene Cross

1972   Aletha Chandler, Tresa Gorman, Sheryl Gray, Avenell Kesler,
Linda Russell, Wanda Waters, Barb Voelkel

1973   Wanda Waters, Terri Moore, Cheryl Gray, Terri Mervar, Vicki Milliner, Willie Carter

1974   Debbie Seib, Debbie Gaddie, Cheryl Gray, Terri Mervar, Kathy Gaddie, Debbie Quarles

1975	Kathy Gaddie, Debbie Gaddie, Debbie Seib, Crystal Reeves, Donna Pope, Debbie Quarles
1976	Rhonda Quarles, Andre Bryant, Vanessa Tate, Kerri Benge, Leslie Madry, Kathy Gaddie, Crystal Reeves
1977	Lenora Mervar, Lorisa Mervar, Jane Loftus, Kelly Elliott, Billie Moore, Crystal Reeves, Vanessa Tate, Rhonda Quarles, Freida Quarles
1978	Renee Chandler, Nora Mervar, Kim Landers, Risa Mervar, Freida Quarles, Jane Loftus
1979	Freida Quarles, Marianne McCoy, Kellie Benge, Renee Chandler, Diane Imel, Kim Lander
1980	Renee Chandler, Shari Shires, Diana Imel, Pam Lawrence, Marianne McCoy
1981	Rhonda Brattain, Peggy McCoy, Pam Lawrence, Shari Shires, Marianne McCoy, Sheila Livingston
1983	Gail Williams, Sheena Bray, Marcia Stinson, Syvaline Miller, Vonda Browning, Brenda Hoffa
1984	Lynn Reynolds, Amy Davis, Jesse Croney, Trina Miller, Danetta Driver, Sandy Harrison, Carla Davidson

X.

Faculty Over the Years

GWHS Faculty---from the original faculty, listed immediately below, to the faculty listed in yearbooks from the late 1930's, the early 1950's, the mid-1960's, the early 1970's and 1995 I have listed those instructors and support staff (primarily secretaries) that were pictured and some who were only named. With the recent, in 2009-2010, expose of Manual High School in a recurring Indianapolis Star commentary on the demise of IPS the news writer noted that Manual had not had a Yearbook in years. To put one's life in proper perspective during our teenage years we all needed a high school yearbook. From the cocky athlete to the teacher's pet to the despised teacher (who in later years may become one's greatest motivator) to the beloved teacher (who later may or may not be so admired) to the prettiest girl to a fellow student that one treated poorly, everyone in our Common Culture in the USA needed a yearbook to better remember one's perspective if not reality. The Rites of Passage in one's teen years has been missing in too many IPS schools in recent decades with poorly organized yearbooks or even non-existent annuals.

Original Teaching Staff--1927

W.G. GINGERY   principal
MAJORIE WALLS   clerk
英 English
MARTHA DORSEY
CLARICE HEDRICK
Mrs. ETHEL HIGHTOWER
MYRTLE JOHNSON
AMY KEENE
MARGARET QUINZONI
Mrs. BESS S. WRIGHT
History
FRANCES MODER
CHARLES MONEY
KATHRYN D. SMITH
Science
RUTH HASELY
ESTIL VanDORN
BRUCE MORRISON
Shop
HAROLD HARDING
BURTON KNIGHT
OCAL MUTERSPAUGH
J.W. SHELL
Music
ROBERT B. SHEPARD

INA S. GAUL   dean of girls
Math
Mrs. CHARITY H. BROWNING
ROSS T. CAMPBELL
ROWLAND JONES
BRUCE MORRISON
MARIE SANGERNEBO
Foreign Language
WILLIAM BOCK
Mrs. IVA COOPER HEAD
ALICE TREAT
Business
ALICE KOEHNE
MARY E. LAATZ
RUSSELL McCLURG
Art
FRANCIS FAILING
LaVON WHITMIRE
Home Economics
MARY CAMMACK
ELIZABETH DeHASS
INA S. GAUL
Physical Education
HENRY BOGUE
MABEL LOEHR

(Miss Loehr retired in 1963 from the Science Department.
Miss Laatz worked through the 1965 school year. Mr. Jones retired in 1966.)

1938 & 1939

W.G. GINGERY — principal
E.B. HARGRAVE — vice principal
MYRTLE JOHNSON (Dean of Girls) — (Eng.) ELIZABETH MARIE SMITH
ISABEL N. DRUMMOND — VIRGINIA GUYTON
ETHEL H. HIGHTOWER — AMY KEENE
FRANK LUZAR — LLOYD B. MANN
MARY S. McBRIDE — MARGARET McWILLIAMS
MARGARET QUINZONI — LEO ROSASCO
EUNICE SEYBOLD — ARTHUR W. SHUMAKER
BARBARA JEAN SULLIVAN — JEAN H. WOOD
BESS S. WRIGHT — (Math) VIVIAN B. ELY
GRACE H. BARKER — ROSS T. CAMPBELL
ROWLAND H. JONES — H. GLENN LUDLOW
JUSTIN MARSHALL — O.W. NICELY
LILLIAN C. NIEMANN — MARIE S. WILCOX
(For.Lang.) WILLIAM BOCK — HESTER B. BOCK
IVA C. HEAD — ALICE T. KRAFT
(Hist.) CHARLES H. MONEY — ANNE M. BURGE
CLEON O. DAVIES — SHIRLEY HARVEY
CLOYD J. JULIAN — FRANCES G. MODER
LOUISE A. ROSS — KETHRYN D. SCHAKEL
EMMA LOU THORNBROUGH — (Science) ELIZABETH HESTER
GERALDINE R. JOHNSON — J.C. NELSON
JAMES H. OTTO — HARVEY V. RACQUET
ALLAN R. STACY — ESTIL B. VanDORN
(Commer.) RUSSEL McCLURG — PAUL L. CARMICHAEL
JOHN C. CROUSE — GLADYS EWBANK
MARY E. LAATZ — AGNES E. MEEHAN
SAMUELLA H. SHEARER — (Art) FERD BRUMBLAY
FRANCES FAILING — LaVON WHITMIRE
(Ind.Arts) HAROLD HARDING — CLARENCE JACKSON
BURTON KNIGHT — IRA MELVIN
OCAL MUTERSPAUGH — J.W. SCHELL
DEAN SMITH — JAMES SMITH
R.J. WEAVER — (Home Ec.) MARY E. CAMMACK
CATHERINE DeROSSETTE — GRETCHEN MUELLER
ORRELL NEGUS — ELIZABETH RANDOLPH
HELEN WALLICK — (Music) DELBRIDGE
KELVIN MASSON — ETTA SCHERF
ROBERT B. SHEPARD — 1939 (Eng) LYDIA B. THOMAS
FLORENCE GRAHAM (SMITH) — GLENN LUDLOW
O.W. NICELY — LOWELL GOOD
ARTHUY SIMS — ELIZABETH MYERS

VICTOR GRAVES
M.D. WILLIAMS
(SGT. WOLFF)
VELMA SCHAAF
MARJORIE REINHART
CHARLOTTE CRIST
SARAH ANN HARTLEY
MAJORIE WALLS
HENRY BOGUE
MARGARET HANNAN
GERALDINE McCAMMACK

URSA WALKER
MABEL LOEHR
MARY RICH
HELEN WALLICK
MILDRED ROSS
EDWARD EMERY
OPAL BOSTON
ROBERT SHEPARD
ELIZABETH HATFIELD
CAROLYN O'NEAL

1951
JUSTIN MARSHALL VP
AUDIE WATKINS DEAN
HESTER & WILLIAM BOCK
THELMA BROWNEWELL
PAUL CARMICHAEL
MARY ESTES
GLADYS FREUNDT b
CHARLES HAMILTON
ETHEL HIGHTOWER
CORLIE JACKSON (WALKER)
ROWLAND JONES
WILLIAM KIMBERLIN
GERTRUDE LINDLEY
FRANK LUZAR
RUSSELL McCLURG
MARGARET McWILLIAMS
OCAL MUTERSPAUGH
ELIZABETH RANDOLPH he
MAJORIE REINHART
MILDRED ROSS
BARBARA SARTOR
MARGARET SIMONDS
ALLAN STACY
MALVIN WALKER
ROGER WEAVER
MARIE WILCOX
G.L. WOODRUFF
ELIZABETH HESTER
1951-52 WILBUR BARNHART
EDNA LONG
JOE TOFIL

AK JONES VP
MYRTLE JOHNSON DEAN
RUTH AMOS
HENRY BOGUE
ROSS CAMPBELL
ROSS COX
FRANCES FAILING
VICTOR GRAVES
ELIZABETH HATFIELD
DOROTHY HOBSON
GERALDINE JOHNSON
VIRGINIA KASSLER
ROBERT LeMASTER
BARBARA LUCAS
LLOYD MANN
EVELYN McCONNELL
GRETCHEN MUELLER
LILLIAN NIEMANN
JIM OTTO
LEO ROSASCO
SAMUELLA SANDS
JOHN SEEBURGER
ELIZABETH M. SMITH
ESTIL VanDORN
URSA WALKER
BETTY WERTHMAN
JOHN WILLIAMS
BESS WRIGHT
SUE GUTHRIDGE
RAY FUNK
DOROTHY LUTHER he
MARIESUE VANNATTA

GRACE BARKER
ANNE BURGE
FRANK COOK
VIVIAN ELY
THELMA FORD
IVA HEAD
BARBARA HINE
DAVE HINE
JOSEPH JONES
BURTON KNIGHT
MARY LAATZ
MABEL LOEHR s
MARY McBRIDE
ORRELL NEGUS
J.C. NELSON
O.W. NICELY
JEAN OBER
LOUISE ROSS
LOUIS RUTAN
EUNICE SEYBOLD
AMOS SLATON
JEWEL STINGLEY
HELEN WALLICK
LaVON WHITMIRE
JEAN WOOD
NELLIE BALDWIN

PAUL HAYES
BEN SANDERS

1952-53 BRUCE HAMMAN VIRGINIA KASSLER LEON HUNT
KEPHART LINSON BARBARA OWEN JV STINGLEY
MURIEL TUCKER 1953-54 MARY BENEDICT
ROSEMARY BERGMAN CLARENCE BUESKING HILDA DUDZIAK
JAMES EAST MARY NICHOLSON (Mrs. DAWSON)
TOM HAYNES FRANK HAMILTON Principal WALTER

AILEEN DICKMAN MARY JANE FUNK '53 MARGARET HANNAN
MARY KAY MITCHELL EDNA LONG POLLIE KIDWELL
DOROTHY HOUGHTON
'51 MSgt LELAND ANDERSON Sgt.1 CLAY CABE LT.COL. CHESTER LANG
Sgt. 1 JE LaTOURETTE Capt. JULIEN LePAGE
'52 Sgt. DAVID TESS '53 Sgt. DONALD NEAL
'54 Sgt. HARVEY JACKSON
1961 GUY MAHAN LEUNICE HORNE RUTH ARNEY he
ROBERT BADGLEY KATHERINE BARNES he MIKE BARRETT
JASON BOWERS JOHN BRADLEY CHARLES BROWN
ANNE BURGE ss JOLENE CARROLL e ANNE CARTMEL e
BETTY CEDARS b ROBERT CLOYD s VERNES COLLINS s
IRENE COREY e LARRY COX a ROSS COX ia
ELIZABETH CRIDER s ELVA MAE DEER HERBERT DIXON ss
ALLIE DRAGOO JOSEPH DUTTON e MILDRED EDWARDS e
MARIANNE ELLSBERRY he EVELYN FARMER li LAURA FRENCH e
MARY JANE FUNK li ALAN HAMILTON RICHARD HARMENING
CHARLES HAWTHORNE RICHARD HEDGES ss ELBERT HOWELL ss
CARL JENSON a STEWART JOYCE ia
DAVID KETTLER ROSE KING he PATRICIA KIRBY m
DAVID KNOTT DONALD KRAMER LELAND LEMME s
PHYLLIS LOFFLAND s LAURA LYONS e ROBERT McCONNELL m
RUSSELL McCONNELL ss NANCY McCULLOUGH e WALTER MENDEL
MARY MELICK s PERSHING MEYERS ss ERNEST MINTON s
ANITA MORRIS DAVID MUSE b FRANK MUNSHOWER s
JERRY OLIVER HAROLD ORMAN THELMA PARKS
DWIGHT PIERCE NELLIE PITTMAN VIOLA RAMSEY m
HELEN RANSBURG pe MARY RARDON he FIMIE RICHIE l
HERSCHEL ROSS s RUTH ROSSER mu BERNARD SAUTER s
KENNETH SCHUSTER m MARIE SCHAFFER m PAUL SCHNEPF ss
DARLENE SMITH s FLORENCE SMITH e HERBERT SMITH ia
DAVID SPENCER e JANICE SPENCER e COLLEEN STANLEY
MELVIN SOUTHARD b FRANK TARDY m CHARLES THATCHER mu
RONALD THOMAS KEITH WALTZ ia R. J. WEAVER ia
ROSEMARY WHITEHEAD ADA WILLIAMS e MARGARET WILLIAMS e
MARVIN WINZENREAD m EDNA LONG mu GERALD WYMAN
CARL ZENOR M/Sgt. A.R. JENKINS Sfc. BASCON PERDUE

266

1962 JEANETTE AMSDEN
WILLA BEDELL
P.D. BURKHALTER s
NANCY CONGER e
LINDA DOYAL s
GERALD ENGLAND pe
CAROL HOLMES pe
LOUISE LAMKIN ss
MARILYN LeMOND m
JANE McELROY e
ROBERT SPRINGER pe
EDGAR ZIEGE s
1963 WAYNE GIRDLEY m
1964 DONALD COUNTS m
RICHARD SHARP e
Sec. GRACE ARVIN
LORENE HARVEY
NELLIE LaMAR
EDNA LONG
1971 JERRY ARVIN
GAIL OVERPECK a
LOUISE TIMCHAK s
CATHERINE LAMB he
OLIVIA LADD he
ROGER DEAN he
DARWIN SHEA ia
DARLENE BLANFORD b
MIKE WESLEY b
english DORIS SCOTT
GEORGE STUCKEY
NANCY JOHNSON
MARY BENSON
EDDIE BOPP
JULIA BIRGE
WALTER McPHERSON
phys. ed. KATHLEEN KENNEDY
POLLY WILLIAMS
JOHN PERRY
LARRY TODD av
sec. KATHLEEN SILER
ANDERSON DAILEY mu
WALT STAHLHUT
BESSIE COLVIN mu

JANET ARTHUR b
LINDA BOTTORFF e
PHYLLIS CASSON b
DONALD CUNNINGHAM m
JOHN EDWARDS ia
JOE GREENE ia
DAVID HYTEN s
JOHN LEE b
JOHN MANKA pe
RUTH NELSON l
ELIZABETH ULREY l
P/Sgt. ROBERT BOWMAN
ROBERT GURCHIEK s
SANDRA MEYERS m
CYNTHIA THUMA e
DORIS DOWNEY
MARGARET HANNAN
MARY KAY MITCHELL
BERTHA MEDSKER
JOE BENDA m
TIM GILES s
MAUREEN BROWN s
SUSAN BROWN he
MARILYN HEINRICH he
KEN LONG ia
ROBERT WILLIAMS ia
LEONA MOORE b
PAULINE STAGGERS b
DEBORAH SNYDER
KATHRYN ERVIN
MARYANN BRODNIK
social studies SALLY MACY
ROOSEVELT GRIFFIN
for. lang. JOHN BAKER
JUDY SHAW
BASIL SFREDDO
guid. GEORGE PIERSON
TOM ROSENBERGER
JOHN RHODES av
DORETTA THOMAS
ANNE LIDIKAY mu
CHARLES PAYNE ss
EZEL MARS dean

WILLIAM BALDWIN s
JOHN BRIDGES b
LaVERNE COFFIN e
MAUREEN CUNNINGHAM e
JOYCE EHLERT s
BEVERLY HARLAN e
ROCHELLE KROOT he
HOWARD LEEDY
C. THOMAS McCORMICK m
JOSEPH REYNOLDS a
STEVE YERICH e
RUTH KING mu
MARIAM LOVEJOY m
SARA SAGRAVES b
WALLACE WEBB s
VI SANDERS
MARIAN KUSZMAUL
EVELYN FARMER

BOB WHITMORE a
BILL HOWARD s
SUSAN COSTER he
MARY DAVIS he
BRAD WEST ia
DAVID BRAY ia
BOB GOLER ia
RUTH McLEISH b
STEVE LAWSON b
BETTY MALONEY
KIM ROSKI
CAROLE FISHER
RALPH TAYLOR
MARILYN NOLL
SUSAN HUFF
RUDY DOTLICH
RALPH POEHLS
VERNES COLLINS
WILLIAM SUMLIN vp
KEN EILER vp
DONA NOGGLE
ROSEMARY BROOKS mu
JOHN HANLEY ss
Mr. FREEMAN m

1995---final yearbook of original school

To Be Or Not To Be (yearbook name)
Only 27 pictures with 64 faculty members not pictured

CHERYL LEWIS	JERRY LUCAS	RICHARD MARONE
TERRY MAY	MYRON NEWLAND	ALVIN PANNELL
POLLIE PAYNE	STEPHEN PROCTOR	SHERRY PROFITT
DIANE ROHN	WAVIE RUDOLPH	BASIL SFREDDO
DIANNE SKINNER	MICHELE SMITH	MARSHA SORRELL
SUSAN VALENTINE	ALONZO WALKER principal	BECKY WERTZ
FAITH WILHITE	BETH WILKES	DEWEY WILLIAMS
VIRGINIA WILKINSON	JOHN WILLIAMS	LOWELL WILSON
ROBERT ZETZL	DAVID ZOELLE	KAREN OLIVER

J. COOPER	C. HALL	T. MORNING
K. OLIVER	A. FRIAS	N. BRUYN
L. DAILY	J. McMILLIN	K. FREEMAN
R. HAVENS	S. KING	JOE PEARSON
J. BAUMAN	J. CHANDLER	J. FUGUA
J. SCHREPFERMAN	MIKE SPRINGER	ALAN HAMILTON
E. OWENS	R. SLABACH	M. TOMLINSON
J. BURROUGHS	ROBERT WHITMORE	JASON BOWERS
GAIL OVERPECK	KENNY LONG	S. BELMER
D. JOHNSON	S. LIGGETT	P. SOVINSKI
J. DAVIS	LEONARD CANNON	D. LANANE
S. SHAW	F. PERVINE (ROTC)	J. SEIBERT (ROTC)
B. BOREL	A. DAVIS	A. MOSER
B. RICHARDSON	S. TOLIN	JOHNSON (ROTC)
K. BROWNING	C. ROBERTSON	STEVE SIRMIN
J. GAYNOR	D. PINNER	A. GLENN
H. STEINBERG	M. BLOOM	K. SUTHERLIN
J. PETERSON	NANCY EHRET	M. DUFF
R. BAKER	A. PERRIN	D. KEMP
A. FOX	S. WILLINGHAM	L. LOY
N. ROBINSON	S. SCHMIDT M. KARR	MONTGOMERY

No teaching descriptions or positions listed with the exception of the principal.
Very few pictures in the entire annual.

XI.

EPILOGUE

When I began my project of gathering as much information about Indianapolis Washington High School in 2001, I had specific pre-conceptions. Many of them have been proven false or, at least, not so obvious. I was biased toward the 1960's in athletics since that was when the 1965 basketball team announced Washington High's arrival as a somewhat consistent State Championship contender in basketball then football and track for the next thirty years. I overlooked the many shoulders upon which we stood.

My discovery of the great student-athletes of the 1930's, beginning with 1930 graduate Emerson Carter, changed my bias. The 1940's, starting with All-American Babe Dimancheff, proved to be a great generation of Continentals. And the 1950's was the decade during which I first began to hero-worship many teens from my Aunt Anita to the Purichias and Dave Sanders to basketball star Eddie Williams. The '70's and '80's had a number of top athletes and teams in football, basketball, and boys and girls track as the school fought through the adversity of social upheaval. And the 1990's also had high profile student-athletes from future boxing Champ Lamon Brewster to basketball great Jack Owens. It's too bad that the social atmosphere of the last part of the 20th century created perhaps an insurmountable uncommon culture that led to the 1995 closing.

The semi-autonomy that Mr. Gingery had begun, and Mr. Julian last practiced, could no longer exist in the era of the "hired gun" downtown superintendents beginning as early as 1969 when a man from the east coast addressed the pre-school gathering of teachers at Tech High School with the admonition that "I'm very pleased to be here in the Minneapolis School district." I experienced first-hand the unlikely collaboration of the Downtown administrators with the IEA teachers' union as they both seemed to dismantle the stable process of the developing of student-athletes in a community setting. But the lack of a Common Culture within inner-city communities also had an effect on IPS as the social fabric of our nation was tested. Too many bits and pieces of the social network of the Washington community had vanished, most by the mid-1970's. The Mothers' Club, Businessmen's Club, Intramural Fund, class Athletes of the Year, fund raising events (specifically the Continental Capers), PTA, school plays and musicals, Homecoming floats and dances and even the in-school publishing of newspapers and yearbooks had vanished by the 1980's. But high priced administrators flourished. Mr. Julian's highest salary his final year, in 1976-77, was only $30,000. Money can't really buy everything.

As TV and newspaper advertisements often highlight a national chain school "Providence Cristo Rey High School" (which is only two blocks from GWHS in the old School 50 building), "Andrew J. Brown Academy" managed by National Heritage Academies, Monument Lighthouse Charter School, and Herron School as schools to have as one's "choice," it became clear that it's a different world. The athletic-transfer scandal between Herron School and Manual High in 2009 was a prime example of student-athletes being used as pawns in the continuing episodes of "As the Schools Change" soap opera that had first been manifested by private school recruitment of athletes, which enticed many teen leaders from our struggling public schools in the 1970's. While neighborhoods crumbled, public schools inside the old city limits seemed to collapse.

At the November 2008 re-dedication of GWHS, after 97-year-old Jim Carter and almost-98-year-old ex-principal Cloyd Julian had both given inspiring talks, the IPS Superintendent gestured toward those two men sitting behind him flanking Sen. Lugar. Mr. White stated, "no disrespect to the gentlemen who've just spoken but we have a more demanding set of educational problems today." They had merely reminisced their Continental history. But he grew up in Alabama so the educational foundation in the 20th century within the Indianapolis Public Schools are rather insignificant to him, it seems. In September '08 he had announced in news reports that he was going to "transform" IPS athletics. In '09 it was rumored that he allowed a salary of $109,000 for a retired coach to become a Coordinator of Junior High Athletics, with few traditional responsibilities, while transforming one of his chosen high school basketball teams. And, in November 2009 after the Superintendent had announced that football at Washington, Marshall and Manual would be terminated for 2010, he spoke on a brief television report noting that, "it's a new day," in defense of his decision without School Board approval, or even allowing a vote. It sounded like a change that most of us cannot believe in. The August 2009 donation of almost $10,000 by Tom Chastain and the 1959 football team, to be used for the revived football program, became irrelevant. But, at least, the forward-looking superintendent was attempting to compete with the large-school, money-driven "programs" of a few of the suburban super-districts. Consequently, he seems to be headed toward a super-school football program, most likely at Tech. He's at least making an effort. The teachers' union and the School Board are not going to thwart his athletic vision, to his credit. I know that I took a considerable pay cut within IPS in 1976 when I was promoted to head coach in football, as compared with being an assistant in two sports. So I've seen the anti-sports (which became unintentionally demoralizing within IPS, especially for aggressive kids) mentality of the teachers' union. But that's past history. At least I hope I've clarified our school's 20th century history, based on my personal experiences but including other's views also.

And I was reminded of the first-year principal at an area high school in 1982 when he announced at a basketball banquet that he had helped in the transformation of athletic success "in matching tenures at (an Illinois school district) as well as in Washington Township which has led to State Championships in football, basketball, baseball, track, wrestling and other venues at both districts." He must have been confused about Washington Township's North Central High School and our Washington High. North Central finally won a basketball State in 1999 after class basketball emerged and have still never won in football, baseball or wrestling as of 2010. And he had only been a junior high principal in that suburban township. But he was a "Ph'D with a three-piece suit and $100 tie," as one of our other IPS superintendents in the 1980's described himself in a news story, so evidently he could boast to promote himself while using inaccurate information. But he did lead a surge of athletic prominence at his new school.

Continental-land was unique in many ways. Mr. Julian's often repeated admonition that "the best teacher is a good coach" reflected his philosophy. Unfortunately, one coach also often expressed that "people only remember your coaching record, not whether you were a good teacher or not." The proper balance between extra-curriculars and academics seemed to have been best served during the Julian years.

Consequently, I can only hope that this "new day" that the IPS head man touts will bring at least a modicum of success to the poor kids on the Westside. I know that our school, closed in 1995, gave many young people the social and educational foundation from which to succeed in life, "old school" or not.

XII.

Quiz Answers

1. Lamon Brewster
2. Larry Highbaugh
3. Cheryl Cook
4. George Avery
5. Justin Marshall
6. Flack's Field
7. circus
8. Wayne Whiffing
9. W.G. Gingery, 1927-1951
10. Barbara Jean Sullivan Hine
11. Cindy Fendley
12. Bill Niemann
13. Rick Thompson & Patty Medley
14. Don Leppert
15. Dick Lipscomb, 1947
16. Steve Downing
17. Leon Griffith
18. Mike King
19. Billy Keller
20. George McGinnis
21. Horace Mitchell
22. Boris "Babe" Dimancheff
23. Ray Knight
24. Marvin Winkler
25. Jim Emerson Carter
26. Grace & Jim Arvin
27. Bryan Hudson
28. Carl Ragland
29. (Jerry Lawlis, Darren Fitzgerald, Ricky Johnson, Jim Rhodes,
    Wayne Pack, Ralph "Buckshot" O'Brien, John Dowdell)
30. Johnny Williams
31. Gary Gunther
32. George Starkey
33. Don Phillips
34. 95
35. James Emerson Carter
36. George Theofanis
37. Dave Hine
38. Ruth Baird
39. Debbie Quarles
40. Norman Joe Shires
41. Sandy Spuzich
42. Joe Dezelan
43. Louie Leerkamp
44. Jerry Lawlis
45. Eddie Love
46. Elmo Carver
47. Harold Negley
48. Strother Martin
49. Rick Blake
50. Lamont Williams
51. Guy Fish
52. Bob Dietz
53. Harry Cherry
54. Dennis Grider
55. Frank, Carl, Reggie & Gary Opp
56. Hester Baker Bock Erwin
57. Danny Butler
58. Eddie & Reggie Williams
59. Jim Otto
60. Audie Watkins
61. Paul Hayes
62. Vi Sanders
63. Bill Purichia
64. Tony Allen
65. Lloyd Mann
66. Fred Medenwald
67. Jack Owens
68. 33
69. Bob Tillery
70. Bob Springer
71. Louie Day
72. Charles Bradshaw
73. Frank Luzar
74. Cloyd "Curly" Julian
75. Ibn Rasheed

76.	Jerry Oliver	121.	Thelma Bloomenstock
77.	Carl Roberts	122.	John Sipe
78.	Al Hamilton	123.	Boyd family
79.	Gene Robertson	124.	Henry Bogue
80.	Tony Burchett	125.	Rowland Jones
81.	Mark Gladson	126.	Monterrio Holder
82.	Ray Funk	127.	29
83.	Donald Barrett	128.	John Sherman Williams
84.	Phil Peterson	129.	Mike Furimsky & Steve Midkiff
85.	Bob Leeper	130.	Harry Northern
86.	Basil Sfreddo	131.	Tom Taft
87.	John Bradley	132.	Jerry England
88.	Cliff Baumbach	133.	E.B. Hargrave
89.	Leon Hunt	134.	Bob Komlanc
90.	Sue Wilson	135.	Walt Stahlhut
	Betty Voegel	136.	Leonard Cannon & Gary Baker
	Patty Whitmore	137.	Ronnie Hayes
91.	Attucks closed in '86 and all of their athletes came to GWHS; tribute to Attucks colors: green & yellow	138.	Virginia Garrabrandt Russell
92.	Rick Hightower	139.	Ricky Sylvester
93.	Ralph Taylor	140.	Don Mallory
94.	Tom Rosenberger & Joe Tofil	141.	Ivan Smith
95.	Stamatkin family	142.	Nick Purichia
96.	Wayne Pack	143.	Chuck Dulla & Jim Clevenger
97.	Porten family	144.	Nikki Sanders
98.	Senator Dick Lugar	145.	Committee of Correspondence
99.	Eddie Boswell & Bill Ott	146.	Rhyman Rhodes, #2
100.	Vicki Lynch	147.	Bobby Canady
101.	Darren Fitzgerald	148.	Slavie Lalioff
102.	Diane Kenley Arnold	149.	Fred VanAbeele
103.	Rick Thompson	150.	Bill Deem
104.	Eddie Bopp	151.	Ronnie Dillon
105.	Myron Newland	152.	Don Martin & Don Carter
106.	Joe Pearson	153.	Carter Byfield
107.	Bob Kersey	154.	Lafayette (Lafe) Hooser
108.	Hank Easter	155.	Dick Lahr
109.	George Malcolm Marlow	156.	Adrian Crenshaw
110.	Marion Carter	157.	Bill Springer
111.	Dave Sanders	158.	Don & Donna Pope
112.	Phil Bayt	159.	Steve Officer, Wayne Grace Ruben Timmons, George Russell
113.	Calvin Schaffer		
114.	Roy Jacobs, Frank Hines, Norman Dunn, John Jacobs	160.	Ron Heinrich
115.	Dick Boarman	161.	Nancy Fletcher Ehret
116.	Charlie Prince	162.	Rollie Schroder
117.	Charlie Leamon	163.	Larry Austin
118.	Jim Overstreet	164.	Mike Barrett
119.	Connie Higgins	165.	Pyatt brothers
120.	Bruce Hamman	166.	Principal Gingery

167. Ross T. Campbell
168. Henry Bogue (but it may have been Bess Wright, English teacher)
169. Kelly Faris, Heritage Christian All-Star; UConn basketball champion
170. Coliseum disaster and President Kennedy assassination
171. John Bradley
172. Larry Compton
173. Jim Rhodes (younger brother, Jeff)
174. Al Case
175. Nellie Carter
176. Marvin Homer Hawkins
177. Ken Corey
178. Glenn Carpenter, 174 points
179. Bonita Harrington
180. Don Baldwin
181. Evan Fine
182. Harvey Holmes
183. Jumpin' Johnny Wilson
184. Lou Moneymaker
185. The Trist
186. Ralph Chambers
187. Deakin family
188. Tommy Gregg
189. Waller & Walter O'Brien
190. Tom "Tiny" Taylor
191. Bonnie Harrington
192. Otto Ferguson
193. Dannie Johnson
194. Ann Miller-Oliver
195. Mabel Loehr—1963—Phys. Ed. & Science
    Mary Laatz—1965—Business
    Rowland Jones—1966—Math, Basketball coach, A.D.
196. Russell McConnell
197. Randy White
198. Wayne Grace
199. Jim Knobel
200. Indianapolis Washington High School

Index

Roberson, Tre 96
Roberts, Carl 11, 212, 233, 272
Roberts, Cheryl xiv, 17, 130, 134, 170, 174
Robertson, Bailey 67, 225
Robertson, Gene xiv, 23, 205, 234, 272
Robertson, Oscar 13, 14, 47, 48, 72, 74, 97, 111, 224, 225, 228, 239
Robinson, Cliff 84, 243
Robinson, Jackie 29, 42, 47, 236
Rockne, Knute 30
Rogal, William W. 63
Rogers, Ronnie xiv
Rogers, William 16, 111, 119, 138, 234
Rollings family 3
Romer-Purichia, Elaine 55
Romney, Mitt 106
Rosasco, Leo 9, 115, 143, 205, 211, 264, 265
Rose, Lee 79
Rosenberger, Tom 21, 22, 81, 103, 205, 267, 272
Ross, Don 13, 49
Rosser-Hayes, Ruth 146, 234, 240, 266
Rowland, Charlie 77
Royster, Charles H. 165
Rupp, Adolph 29
Russell, George 20, 81, 215, 272
Russell, Marsha 105
Rus-Sipe, Louise 156

S

Saipan 11, 62, 63, 143, 144, 145, 154, 244
Sanders, Dave 14, 131, 206, 220, 234, 269, 272
Sanders, Jerry xiv, 17, 107, 113, 140, 157, 206, 220, 221, 234
Sanders, Nikki 272
Sanders-Wesseler, Debbie 38
Satterfield, Betty Lou 151
Satterfield, Clarence 151
Satterfield-Golay, Mary 151
Satterfield, Lena 151
Satterfield, Lenora 151
Satterfield, Steve xiv, 151
Satterfield, William 151
Saunders, Pete 14, 52
Savage, Janet 54
Schaffer, Calvin 16, 71, 84, 113, 114, 175, 272
Schieb, Dave 193
Schott, Tom xiv
Schroeder, Rollie 13, 229
Schussler, John 12
Schwomeyer, Herb 116, 226
Scotten, Leonard 98
Scott, Miss 172, 173, 174
Searcy, Edgar 231

Seargent, Brian 22, 140
Sears, Ronnie 129
Sears, Ronnie Joe 183
Sears, Steve 129, 171, 172, 175
Sellers family 77
Serling, Rod 39
Sexson, Joe 23, 33, 67, 225, 228
Sfreddo, Basil xiv, 9, 21, 38, 117, 118, 139, 211, 212, 248, 267, 268, 272
Sfreddo, Bob 118
Sfreddo, Carolyn 117, 118
Sfreddo, David 117
Sfreddo, Susan 117, 118
Sharrette, Dennis (Bookie) 104
Shaus, Fred 37
Shearer-Sands, Samuella 9, 143
Shelton, Greg 75
Shepard, Alan 176
Shepard, Jerry 75
Sheppard AFB 108
Shiffman (Pauley), Mrs. 171, 172, 176
Shires, Bric 99
Shires, Charley 97
Shires, Chuck 97
Shires, Gloria 97
Shires, Greg 97
Shires, Joe 13, 20, 57, 67, 81, 97, 106, 140, 169, 205, 236, 248, 271
Shires, Sherry 99
Shires, Susie 98, 99
Shirkey, Gerald 26
Short, Carl 48, 205, 211
Shouse, Steve 17
Showalter, Cindy 59
Simon, Sam 91
Sims, John 81
Sipe, Bill 125, 156
Sipe, George 17, 101, 113
Sipe, John 10, 125, 272
Slaton, Amos 66, 97, 109, 122, 211, 265
Slinker, Ernie 55, 57, 213
Smeltzer-Lugar, Charlene 188
Smith, Alva 130, 174
Smith, Bob 176
Smith, Bruce 51, 206, 214
Smith, Clyde 33
Smith, Ernest (Chico) xiii, 23
Smith, Gail 176
Smith, Ivan 18, 236, 272
Smith, Jim 130, 133
Smith, Moose 170, 173
Smith, Phil 134
Smith, Ricky 21, 206, 213, 214, 220, 234
Smith, Robbie 173

Wright, Vicki 107
Wycoff, Sharon 129

Y

Yavonovich, Alex 32, 206
Yerich, Steve 13, 267
Young, Bill 18
Young, Steve 106

Z

Zenor, Carl 16, 117, 266
Zoitos-Baldwin, Chryssanthy (Connie) 100
Zoitos, Constantine (Dino) 100
Zoitos, Crist 100
Zook, Miss Marie 132, 143, 171, 176